D0492978

House of Commons Library
54056001067385

EAST-WEST-SOUTH

Economic Interactions between Three Worlds

In both the Western industrial countries and in the Soviet Union and Eastern Europe those concerned with economic inequalities in the world are giving increasing attention to new approaches to world development; meanwhile, the United Nations Third Development Decade opens in a political atmosphere of frustration and distrust. What opportunities are there for the countries of the West and of the socialist world to concert their activities and strategies for a New International Economic Order? The question deserves more attention than it usually gets. In the book, well-informed authors from fourteen countries and six international organisations present their opinions, based on both research and experience, about the theory and practice of development, about the policies that should be followed, and about the prospects for wider cooperation between the countries concerned. Differing views are frankly expressed and vigorously argued.

The book results from one of a series of Workshops, organised by the Vienna Institute for Comparative Economic Studies, devoted to various aspects of East-West economic interaction and bringing together a group of experts from market and socialist economies as well as from developing countries. The subjects covered comprise: argued statements of the concepts and objectives of development and analysis of the interests involved; ways of financing development and future needs for investment and aid, including assessments of the operations of transnational corporations; methods and purposes of the transfer of technology; the need for restructuring both advanced economies in East and West and the less developed countries for an improved international division of labour; and an assessment of experience in tripartite cooperation between enterprises from each of the three 'worlds'.

This book, presenting some urgently-needed new approaches to development problems, will interest people in business, in universities, in official organisations, in the media dealing with the developing world, and all concerned with the prospects for better international cooperation between East and West.

East-West European Economic Interaction

The Vienna Institute for Comparative Economic Studies organises a series of international workshops concerned with problems of East-West European economic interaction, guided by an International Steering Committee consisting of

Workshop Papers so far published are:

Series Editor: Franz Nemschak

Vol. 1* World Economy and East-West Trade (1976)
Vol. 2* East-West Cooperation in Business: Inter-firm Studies (1977)
Vol. 3* Industrial Policies and Technology Transfers between East and West (1977)

Series Editor: Philipp Rieger

Vol. 4* Money and Finance in East and West (1978)
Vol. 5 East and West in the Energy Squeeze (1980)
Vol. 6 East-West-South: Economic Interaction between Three Worlds (1981)

* These volumes were originally published by Springer-Verlag Vienna–New York and copies are now available from the Vienna Institute for Comparative Economic Studies, P.O. Box 87, A-1103 Vienna, Austria.

The present volume is based on Workshop session VI held in Dubrovnik in May 1980. The Workshop was funded by generous contributions from:

The German Marshall Fund of the United States
The Fritz Thyssen Stiftung
The Ford Foundation
Zentralsparkasse und Kommerzialbank · Wien

EAST-WEST-SOUTH

Economic Interactions between Three Worlds

Edited by Christopher T. Saunders

First published 1981 by
THE MACMILLAN PRESS LTD
London and Basingstoke
Companies and representatives throughout the world

ISBN 0 333 31870 6

Printed in Great Britain

Foreword

The sixth 'Workshop on East-West European Economic Interaction' organised by the Vienna Institute for Comparative Economic Studies was held in May 1980 at the Inter-University Centre, Dubrovnik. The genius loci of this enchanting Dalmatian city provided a most congenial setting for exploring the complex theme of this session — 'European Economic Relations and the Developing Countries'.

The relaxed atmosphere of a scholarly search for mutual understanding and feasible solutions, which has characterised our Workshop meetings, again prevailed, against a background of growing international tensions and a deadlock in the North-South-Dialogue. Nearly 50 economists with experience of development problems from East and West Europe, North America and the developing countries, and from international organisations, participated. This volume is based upon the papers presented to the Workshop and on selected contributions to the discussions. The participants are listed in the appendix.

We especially thank Professor Rikard Lang for his kind invitation to use the facilities of the Inter-University-Centre; and its President, Prof. Siegfried Korninger, and Mrs. Berta Dragičević, for hosting the session and kindly assisting in all arrangements.

The realisation of this project was facilitated by generous financial contributions from the German Marshall Fund of the United States, the Fritz Thyssen Stiftung, FRG, the Ford Foundation, New York, and the Zentralsparkasse und Kommerzialbank, Vienna.

The arduous task of editing the papers has again been skilfully executed by Professor C.T. Saunders. He wishes to thank the authors of the papers and discussants for their cooperation in preparing their contributions for publication. Special credit is due to the competent staff of the Vienna Institute for Comparative Economic Studies under the able directorship of Professor DDr. Friedrich Levcik, and to Mrs. Ingrid Gazzari who was largely responsible for the Workshop arrangements. To Mr. F. Prager we are particularly indebted for his painstaking editorial help, as well as to Mrs. R. Garbacz and Mr. M. Esterházy for typesetting difficult material so efficiently in an unfamiliar language. The index was prepared with great care by Mrs. Audrey Bamber. We are grateful to the Macmillan Press for their valuable cooperation in the publication.

Philipp Rieger
Chairman of the Workshop

TABLE OF CONTENTS

PART III – THE TRANSFER OF TECHNOLOGY

PART IV – IMPROVING THE INTERNATIONAL DIVISION OF LABOUR

ABBREVIATIONS

CIEC	Conference on International Economic Cooperation
CMEA	Council for Mutual Economic Assistance ('Comecon'), Moscow
DAC	Development Assistance Committee of OECD, Paris
DMEC s	Developed market economy countries
UN / ECE	Economic Commission for Europe, Geneva
EEC	European Economic Communities, Brussels
ECLA or CEPAL	Economic Commission for Latin America, Santiago
LDC s	Less Developed Countries
NAC s	Non-aligned Countries
NIC s	Newly Industrialising Countries
NIEO	New International Economic Order
ODA	Official Development Aid
OECD	Organisation for Economic Cooperation & Development, Paris
SITC	UN Standard Industrial Classification (of trade statistics)
TIC	Tripartite Industrial Cooperation
TNC	Transnational (or multinational) corporations
UNCTAD	United Nations Conference for Trade & Development, Geneva
UNIDO	United Nations Industrial Development Organisation, Vienna

Symbols

— nil or negligible
not available
Billion (or milliard): 1000 million (10^9)
Ton (or tonne): metric ton

EDITOR'S INTRODUCTION*
JOINT STRATEGIES FOR WORLD DEVELOPMENT

Christopher T. Saunders

The first purpose of this book is to assses the prospects for cooperation in world development among the three groups of nation states – loosely but conveniently described as 'East' (the Soviet Union and Eastern Europe), 'West' (essentially the OECD countries) and 'South', (basically the developing countries or the 'Third World'). Thus a special feature of the book is that it brings to the forefront a subject which is relatively little discussed (outside official documents) in the vast literature on development – the extent to which the market and socialist economies can combine forces in the raising of standards and the eradication of poverty in the world. The second purpose is to identify the extent of agreement, and the nature of the disagreements, among concerned scholars coming from the three different 'worlds'. The book contains, too, many illuminating insights into the general problems of development, of which increasing experience is being gained by informed people in all countries.

To stress this threefold division of the earth's economic and social geography can, of course, mislead. Each of the three 'worlds' encompasses a variety of societies at differing levels of economic and social development and with significant differences in their policies and international interests. Lack of homogeneity is most marked in the developing world; the old title of the 'Third World' is becoming a gross misnomer for a group of around 100 countries, containing at one extreme the rich members of OPEC and the successful New Industrial Countries (the 'NICs'), and, at the other, the poorest societies on earth. Nevertheless, members of each of the three groups have enough in common to justify certain cautious generalisations about each group's interests, attitudes and possible approaches to international policy.

* This Introduction is based in part on summary evaluations of the papers and comments, contributed by Friedrich Levcik, Deepak Nayyar, Marie Lavigne, István Dobozi and Norman Scott.

In Part I, the contributors expound their ideas of the philosophy of development and their views of the interests and objectives of the different groups of nations. The rest of the book is concerned chiefly with more specific analyses, policies and instruments of policy: Part II deals with the functions and forms of international financing of Third World development, whether through official aid programmes or through transnational companies and other forms of direct foreign investment; Part III takes up problems arising in the transfer of technology; Part IV is concerned with the central issue of improving the structural balance of production and trade between the different parts of the world economy — the international division of labour — and particularly with the much discussed question of the possible meanings of the 'New International Economic Order'; Part V reviews actual experience of cooperation between enterprises from each of the three groups — known as Tripartite Industrial Cooperation. Inevitably, because it is difficult to draw clear lines of demarcation between these closely connected topics, there is much overlapping between them. Each Part contains chapters discussed at the Workshop (subsequently revised when thought necessary) followed by a selection of comments made by participants. Only a few points are chosen in this Introduction to illustrate, rather than to summarise, the variety of opinions expressed — often, it must be admitted, leaving many questions open.

1. The objectives and nature of development

Although there is full agreement on the ultimate aim of promoting economic and social progress in the poorer nations, it is to be expected that differences of opinion should emerge about how to express this general objective and about the ways in which it could best be brought about. Such differences of opinion arise not only between East and West, but also among people within each group. Since the industrial West has hitherto played the major role in economic and political relations with the South — relations bound up in history — it is natural that Western governments and enterprises should bear the brunt of the vigorous criticism of the ways in which these relations have been conducted. To some extent, the differences can be regarded as differences of emphasis of priorities among the many issues involved, and some may be more verbal than substantial. But there is no virtue in concealing differences under a mask of consensus on a highly generalised and unexceptionable objective.

One issue does indeed arise about the objective of development, stressed particularly by contributors from Eastern Europe. It is put in antithetical terms by the suggestion that Western policies appear to conceive the aim of development as simply a redistribution of the world's income and wealth between the nations; the aim should be, rather, the establishment of a 'new order' in a much more fundamental sense — a major transformation of the social and economic structures of the poor societies (1). What does this latter concept imply in practice?

Development, it is asserted, must be conceived as an integrated and complex process, bringing together investment, infrastructure, social welfare, a more equitable income distribution, technological advance, agricultural reform, industrialisation and — emphasised by contributors from all sides — the creation of an educational system designed for the needs of the future. Only in this way, it is suggested, can the aim of independent, or self-reliant, development be achieved. There could be no dissent in principle. The question is how far current efforts, whether initiated within developing countries themselves or by foreigners, assist this progress towards autonomy (note that 'autonomy' and 'independence' are not taken to mean complete economic autarky). Thus critisism is directed towards forms of development concentrated on the implantation of modern methods of production which remain isolated 'enclaves', with only limited feed-backs into the economic progress of the whole society. Such enclaves tend to create dual economies split between modern and traditional sectors. They can also foster — or intensify — rupture between an élite and the masses, in terms both of inequalities of income and of ways of life, and can break down any sense of social cohesion already existing. Particular criticism is directed, in this regard, towards the transnational corporations — criticisms not restricted to authors from the socialist countries. This underlying theme — the need for integrated and self-reliant development — runs through much of the discussion of both national and international policies and performance.

A more philosophical contrast is observed between two ways of justifying the demand that the rich should take part in raising economic and social standards in the poor countries (2). One — the main thrust of much economic discussion in developed countries — is that global development will result in mutual advantage to both rich and poor; cooperation in world development is a positive-sum game. The other, said to be exemplified by the Brandt Report (3), is based on equity, and on the need of the South for a redistribution which would involve sacrifices by the rich — even if that means a zero-sum game. Both self-interest and a moral appeal to equity may inspire action, althouth it is suggested that the motive of self-interest is likely to carry the greater political weight.

2. International financing of the South

The transfer of resources to the South through loans, direct investment and grants is the main focus of public attention in development policy. Some take the view that it receives excessive attention, at the expense of the measures needed within developing countries to promote indigenous development from indigenous human and material resources. All would agree that money alone cannot ensure satisfying economic and social progress. However, international financing is bound to remain a major element in world development, and a number of questions arise about the forms which it takes, and should take in future.

(a) There is criticism of what is felt by some to be an undesirable change in the form which international financing has taken during the 1970s: the shift from official (national or international) grants and loans towards direct private investment by enterprise and borrowing through the international banking system at commercial rates of interest (4). In the late 1970s the greater part of the large current deficits of many non-oil developing countries was met by bank loans; thus to some considerable extent, these countries were financing the rising price of oil, a big element in their deficits - plus high interest charges - through the recycling of the OPEC surpluses. The first result is the swallowing-up by debt service of large proportions of export revenue. The second result is that since such loans are subject to commercial criteria of credit-worthiness, it is the middle-income rather than the poor countries which tend to be favoured. It is of course fortunate that during these years the banks were able to fill a potentially very dangerous gap left by the inadequacy of official funding (5). The question is whether this precarious and expensive form of international financing can be expected to continue.

(b) Foreign investors — and here the transnational corporations (TNCs) are a special target — inevitably seek profit where it is to be found. It is suggested that TNCs are unlikely to implant their production capacities in accordance with the long-term needs of the host country. Shorter-term interests — the earning of profits from cheap labour, in 'easy' industries with few linkages with the rest of the economy — are thought likely to dominate the TNCs' investment pattern. Thus foreign investment may not promote, and may even obstruct, the opportunities for more spontaneous national development.

(c) Further, some contributors call in question the extent of net transfer of resources to the South through foreign investment (6). Remittances of interest, profits, royalties and licence fees to the TNCs' home country can go far to offset, and in some cases exceed, the inflow of new funds (7). It is also claimed that TNC activities often have higher import coefficients, and lower export coefficients, than the average for manufacturing in the host country, and can thus have negative effects on the host country's current balance of payments.

(d) Despite these criticisms, it is generally recognized that international financing of the South must continue and, indeed, increase substantially. The use of East European credits by some developing countries is one sign of the need to diversify the sources of funds. Scenarios to illustrate orders of magnitude, based on satisfactory growth rates and on a clear relationship between growth, savings and investment, indicate the need for the net inflow of funds to reach a multiple of current amounts — possibly accelerating for a number of years but then falling off as developing countries achieve higher levels of efficiency and self-reliance (8). The scenarios proposed do not escape criticism (9).

The problem is then addressed of finding ways by which the flows of capital may be managed, and greatly expanded, to meet most effectively the major long-term needs of the South. Several proposals are offered.

(a) New forms of financing may be needed to bring a larger proportion of the Southward flow of funds under international management (10). The risks of continued reliance on recycling of OPEC surpluses through the banking system reinforce this need. If the existing international agencies are inadequate for the purpose, it may be that new international institutions for raising funds – either from governments or from joint operations with the capital market – and for allocating them may be required (reference may be made to the proposals under study in UNIDO for an international fund to finance industrialisation). Even if such loans were to be guaranteed by the international institution or by national governments, an element of subsidy would probably be needed to reconcile the remaining difference between commercial interest rates and what many developing countries could reasonably be expected to pay.

(b) Does international management imply multilateral funding? Some suggest that neither developed nor developing countries would necessarily welcome an extension of multilateral funding (grants or loans) on the scale required. Developed countries, East or West, particularly those having special links with individual developing countries, may be reluctant to accept further loss of control over their own contributions; developing countries may feel that better terms can be got by bilateral dealings. Bilateral dealings may of course imply 'tied aid' or tied loans, to which there are certainly objections; however it remains true that one incentive to industrial countries to promote Third World development is the search for markets in a period of unemployment and strong competition.

(c) One kind of compromise solution is suggested: a system of bilateral 'covenants' under which a developed and a developing country would commit themselves to joint responsibility for realising an agreed development programme. Such covenants would have to conform with an internationally agreed code and be supervised by an international body.

(d) It is also suggested that the agreements made in principle, but by no means fully observed in practice, that industrial countries should provide in official aid a specified percentage of their GNPs might be strengthened and given more automaticity by a form of progressive international tax, based for example on the level of GNP per head. A more enduring commitment might thereby be achieved (11). There are objections from the socialist countries to such proposals on the ground that these countries bear no responsibility for past exploitation of the Third World.

(e) Several contributors stress the familiar fact that far more resources could be found for development, in both rich and poor countries, by reducing the 5–6 percent of GNP (over $ 400 billions in 1977) spent for military purposes in each of the three groups of countries (12).

(f) Finally, the question is raised of how direct foreign investment in the South can be better assimilated to national development needs. Realistic solutions must be found for reconciling the need for foreign investment with the requirements of national sovereignty. Some Third World governments, it is pointed out, are learning to negotiate effectively the conditions under which TNCs can operate to serve better the interests of the host country (13).

Contributors from socialist countries not opposed in principle to foreign investment, and having in mind experience in CMEA, strongly advocate an extension of industrial cooperation and co-production arrangements between domestic and foreign enterprises (14). And a number of contributors support effective efforts to lay down codes of conduct to regulate TNC operations.

3. The transfer of technology (15)

Questions raised by transfers of technology, from the West or the East to the South, have many similarities with the questions raised by financial flows. Under both headings, there are problems of integrating imported facilities and production methods with the building up of national economic resources and with promoting rather than replacing independent progress. Technological advances have important social and political implications. They should not be regarded exclusively as ways of increasing technical efficiency in production.

In general terms, the issues revolve around the meaning of what is described as 'the much criticised slogan' of 'appropriate technology'.

(a) 'Appropriate' technologies should not be regarded simply as those appropriate to current or traditional values. This could perpetuate backwardness. True, the introduction of new techniques must be considered in the light of the specific conditions in each society, but always with the aim of progressively overcoming technological and economic backwardness.

(b) There is no one 'appropriate' technology. For example, it is not likely to be effective to concentrate in all circumstances on labour-intensive techniques. In some industries, capital-intensive methods and automated processes are justified even in a developing labour-surplus economy; direct employment may be small, but the indirect effects on employment in other branches of the economy – by providing cheaper products for use in other industries or for consumers, or by replacing more expensive imports – may well be very substantial. Moreover a labour-intensive process which is advantageous at one time may soon cease to be so when wages rise and techniques improve. Moreover, even though the developing world is 'a world of smallness' and should in many respects remain so, yet there are important industries in which the cost advantages of large-scale production – and their feed-back into the economy as a whole – should be accepted. In short, it is not *the* appropriate technology which should be sought, but the appropriate *mix* of technologies. Neither 'small is beautiful' nor 'big is wonderful' is a principle of general application in any sort of society.

(c) The aim of integrated and self-reliant development can be achieved only if the introduction of new technologies is associated with the building up of a national research and technological capacity. This may be among the most important conditions for avoiding the creation of a dual economy. It requires not only the establishment of R and D centres but also big changes in the educational system – a time-consuming process.

(d) Further, all-round adaptability of a society to absorb the fruits of technical progress depends not only on government policies or even on a suitable educational system; it depends also on creating a spirit of innovative enterprise throughout the production system – and particularly at the level of management. The transfer of technology cannot be a substitute for economic reform – as recent experience in some socialist countries has clearly shown. Introduction of improved technologies must go hand-in-hand with improved systems of economic organisation that afford both incentives and flexibility in business decision-making. This is one aspect of the distinction drawn between 'active' and 'passive' absorption of technical change. 'Active' absorption implies that the introduction of new techniques at one point is followed by multiplier effects elsewhere in the system.

(e) The enclaves of relatively advanced technical methods established by transnationals come in for criticism. But so does the opposite extreme – restricting the introduction of techniques to the obsolete and least sophisticated ('soft') technologies. Once again, the solution should be cooperation between foreign companies and national enterprises or governments. But that implies a clear understanding by national governments of the process of integrated development.

(f) Finally, the question arises of how the developed societies, containing over 90 per cent of the world's present stock of scientists and engineers, could better shape the pattern of their exports of technological goods and services to the South. It is pointed out that 'very little of the world's research budget is at present spent on the needs of the poor majority': for example on the improvement of small peasant farming, or on treatment, and prevention, of the diseases specific to the poor nations, or on adaptation of industrial or marketing techniques to the present, and likely future, circumstances of the economically backward.

4. Improving the international division of labour

It can be generally agreed that a 'better' international division of labour – a relocation of productive activities more in accordance with the comparative advantages (however that ambiguous term may be defined) of different societies – would increase the *global sum* of world output and, maybe, of welfare (however *that* term is defined). The problems of achieving this happy optimisation arise in part because what appears to be a positive-sum game with many players may imply losses for some individual players; in part because the present pattern of comparative advantage is not necessarily that which will hold in future — even in the near future; and in part because the costs of relocation, or adjustment, even if only temporary, are nevertheless substantial and painful for those individuals or societies which have to bear them. Such problems lead to conflicts of interest between, and within, nations, to uncertainties about what future pattern of production and trade will be regarded as optimal, and to the practical issues of determining just how the existing structures of activity can in practice be modified. These problems underlie any discussion — academic or political — of achieving a 'better' international division of labour.

It is obvious enough that reshaping of the patterns of world trade and of world production must go hand in hand. 'Trade is not an end in itself but a means to a more efficient allocation of resources and to greater consumers' satisfaction' (16); trade, it is said, enables a country to 'decouple' production from consumption and thereby increase the options for development policy. The complaint is made (17), that the proposals for a New International Economic Order have concentrated too much on the 'reshaping of relations in the sphere of distribution, while relegating . . . a restructuring of production to the background'. This may be because governments in all types of economic system have ways of influencing quite directly the flows of international trade (at least on the import side) and institutions have long existed for reaching international agreement on the 'rules of the game' of trade. The transformation of production structures is a much more difficult proposition.

The restructuring of world trade

At first sight, the three 'worlds' seem to offer great opportunities for the expansion of mutual trade based on their complementary patterns of comparative advantage: 'West with its high technology and surplus of capital, East with intermediate technology and much cheaper labour, while South should offer the cheapest labour of all and a wealth of resources'. There is some discussion, based on statistical analyses, of how far the actual trade flows in fact diverge from what might be expected on theoretical grounds (18). Reasons of a 'structural' kind are suggested for the current pattern and lead into proposals for changes in economic strategies.

(a) One suggestion (following Kornai, Kalecki and others) is that an important difference exists in concepts of the economic function of foreign trade between the 'demand-market economies of the West and the 'supply-led', or 'supply-constrained', economies of the East (19): in a demand-led economy, foreign trade arises (in part) from a tendency towards the emergence of excess capacity and a consequent drive for exports to support output and employment; in a socialist economy, planning avoids such surplus capacity and foreign trade takes a 'residual' character, the function of exports being that of financing imports not available domestically. Thus in a supply-constrained economy, an export surplus is a direct sacrifice of resources that might have been used at home; in a capitalist economy the export surplus generates additional income. In this respect, the foreign trade of developing countries, being also largely supply-constrained, has many affinities with that of the East. It is recognised that this contrast can be overdrawn (20), and that the trend in socialist countries, both in theory and practice, is increasingly to assign a much more positive function to foreign trade as an instrument of growth and efficiency (21). In much the same way, import-substitution policies in the industrialising South have given way to export-led growth strategies.

(b) Complementarity of economic structures is important; but the relationships between the three 'worlds' are also becoming highly competitive. In the markets for the less technologically advanced manufactures, in particular, East and South compete in the West, and West and East in the South. In trade with the South, both East and West are principally exporters of manufactures and importers of primary products. In trade with the West, both East and South export chiefly primary products and import manufactures. Further, the East's export surplus with the South offsets, in part, its hard currency deficit with the West (22).

(c) The question then arises of how far the interests of the three groups coincide in the efforts to intensify trade along all three sides of the East-West-South triangle. It is recognized that to speak of a 'triangle' is to use an over-simplified image of a much more complex and unbalanced system of trade flows. Thus the East–South flow, although increasing fast, has so far been relatively small; among the CMEA countries, only the Soviet Union and Romania are much involved (23). Even so, it is suggested that the forces inherent in the complementary pattern are approaching exhaustion (24). Adjustment to a much more competitive world is one way of expressing the conditions necessary for continued expansion of trade between the three groups.

(d) For the South, it is held, there is a strong interest in the development of more intensive economic relations between East and West, as well as in the political aspects of détente, because of perception that a *global* approach encompassing East–West relations is needed (25). Among other considerations, the development of Eastern industry, which could be helped by smoother East–West relations, would afford the South more opportunities for diversifying its sources of supply (26). At the same time, it can be maintained that the rivalry between East and West has brought advantages to at least some developing countries, and the growth of Eastern industrial exports to the West may prejudice the competitive power of some developing countries exporting manufactures to the same markets. So the balance of mutual and conflicting interests – apart from the interest of all in the preservation of world peace and the de-escalation of the arms race – is more complex than it might seem. Some take the view that mutual economic advantage – prizes for all in the positive-sum game – is unlikely by itself to override conflicting national and group interests in the search for greater world prosperity. While mutual interests must be stressed so far as possible, a radical reform of the 'world order' needs also a base in moral principle (27).

(e) A particular application of the complex of mutual and conflicting, short-term and long-term, interests is the anxiety, especially in the industrial West at a time of slow growth and heavy unemployment, about the increasingly competitive imports of manufactures from the new industrial countries (the 'NICs'). The defensive reactions of the West may be regarded as misguided by those who take a long-term view (28). It is noted that studies (by OECD, Balassa and others) have shown that the net effects on *total* employment and output in the Western importing countries have been either negligible or even favourable; this is because the additional imports from the Southern countries are bound to lead to increased exports to them (especially since the West has, and is likely to maintain, an export surplus with the non-oil South). This reflects the characterisation of Western economies as 'demand-led.' Moreover, the West's exports to the South are, in general, products of higher added value employing more qualified labour, than the imports. It is also pointed out that Western imports from the South play only a small part in the loss of employment in the industries affected when compared with increases in labour productivity and shifts in demand patterns (29). Thus greater liberalisation of imports from the South should produce mutual economic benefits. Why does the argument not prevail? The reasons are clear enough. There is no guarantee that any individual importing country will itself benefit from the exchange. And the social costs of disturbance and adjustment are very substantial. Overall, and in the long-term, it is rational to expect a net gain – but a loss to many of those directly concerned. Solutions, at least partial solutions, may be found in various kinds of adjustment assistance, but what may be termed adjustment resistance remains strong and will not easily be dispersed.

(f) Passing to a different topic, the authors of Chapter 3 venture a tentative projection of the volume of trade at the end of the 1980s between the European CMEA countries and the Third World (together with an analysis of recent trends in this trade) (30). The projections envisage a very substantial growth in East-South trade, especially a rapidly growing share of the South in Eastern imports (from 8 per cent in 1978 to 15 - 17 per cent in 1990 – implying a growth rate in the volume of imports by 14 - 15.5 per cent a year). A striking feature is that between one-third and one-half of this increase is expected to consist of oil and oil products; other Eastern imports from the South – meaning imports from the non-oil South – are expected to increase, but much more slowly (not enough, perhaps, to impart a real dynamism to trade between the East and the non-oil South). To pay for these imports, it is assumed that it will be possible for the East to increase exports to the South as a whole by around 10 per cent a year, embodying a substantial shift in the composition of exports towards engineering products (including complete plants); this shift, as the authors agree, assumes a rapid modernisation of Eastern engineering industries and a strongly export-oriented strategy – the major question-mark against hopes of a fast and balanced growth of East-South trade. (It is noted by one participant that there is only one way to this kind of objective in socialist economies – 'a happy marriage between market forces and central planning' (31). Even then, the implication of the projected increase in imports, especially of oil, is that the traditional Eastern surplus in trade with the South will disappear, and will no longer contribute towards covering the Eastern deficit with the West – which will be very difficult to eliminate in view of the burden of interest payments on debt to the West. Thus the projected pattern of trade depends either upon much greater competitiveness of the East in Western markets or that the problem of servicing Eastern debts to the West will be resolved in some other way. The assumptions are regarded by the authors as 'fairly optimistic'.

(g) The expectation of substantial increases in Eastern imports of energy and materials from the South is confirmed, although not in statistical terms, by another authoritative contributor from the East, associating the expansion of trade with a rapid expansion of various forms of East-South cooperation in the development of the natural resources, the industry and the infrastructure of the South (32). At least for energy, it should be noted, these expectations depend on the evolution of the international supply pattern and particularly upon the extent to which energy supplies from the Soviet Union can be increased, or even maintained (33).

Shaping production patterns

To reshape the pattern of production, as well as to enlarge it, can be regarded as the central aim of development strategy. Seen in the perspective of a more effective international division of labour, this aim calls for restructuring of economies in each of the three 'worlds'.

(a) Differences of opinion are expressed about the appropriate principles of structural strategy in developing countries. Some, particularly from the East, take the view that the achievement of economic independence demands a consistent policy of comprehensive *industrialisation* – naturally with regard to the specific conditions in each country: only industrial development can ensure the integration of a national economy into an organic whole based on a modern foundation, elimination of archaic practices hindering social progress, and unfolding the creative potential of the broad masses of the working people (34). The example of the formerly less industrialised East European countries is cited. This approach seems to underlie the Lima Declaration and Plan of Action of 1975 and proposals put forward by the group of 77 at UNIDO in 1980. Other contributors feel that in some quarters excessive attention is given to the promotion of small enterprises, labour-intensive technologies and the manufacture of simple goods, which, although meeting immediate needs, may perpetuate technical backwardness. Some contributors warn against a straightforward imitation of the paths followed by the present industrial economies; the example of Iran, and the growth of Islamic fundamentalism, in particular, are signs of increasing resistance to what is felt to be the flawed pattern of social, economic and cultural trends in the industrial societies (35). This is illustrated by the familiar scepticism about the use of GNP levels as the major measure of the level of development. It is suggested that much more attention should be paid to measures of 'physical quality of life' such as infant mortality, life expectancy, illiteracy . . . These could include, too, indicators of income distribution, of the extent of poverty and malnutrition, of access to water, provision of medical and educational services (36). It is encouraging to note that the international organs of the United Nations and the World Bank are now giving far more prominence than in the past to the analysis of such social indicators and are making considerable efforts to promote the compilation and policy use of these measures.

(b) The question is: what instruments exist for promoting a coherent strategy of development — whatever priorities are chosen? For the South, contributors from the socialist countries, in particular, insist on the leading role of the State, on medium and long-term planning, and on the use of the public sector for mobilising resources, for directing development in the interests of the society as a whole, and for strengthening the ability to use and control foreign capital.

(c) The need for restructuring, or adjustment, in industrial countries, East and West, is accepted but not here debated in detail. However there is some discussion of the old conflict between the relative effectiveness of market forces and of interventionist industrial policies. Contributors from the West generally favour a greater liberalisation of international trade, and particularly of imports from the South, as a way of bringing about the restructuring of production. The increasing use of protection and subsidies as defences against the shocks of competition is strongly condemned by some, partly because of the loss of economic efficiency and partly because such measures only delay inevitable change (37). Even if intervention is aimed at directly promoting new and hopeful industries, a more controversial issue, it is suggested that in general private investors and entrepreneurs, whose money is at risk, will do better than government officials at penetrating the uncertainties of the future. Thus government intervention should be limited to the most obvious failures of private enterprise to engage in forward-looking investment, and to 'adjustment assistance'. Other contributors from the West take a more pragmatic view of the effectiveness of industrial policies and a sceptical view of expectations that market forces can be relied upon to restructure world industries towards a rational international division of labour. Contributors from the East naturally go further, stressing that even if governments and planners are not all-wise, yet they are in a position to take a wider view than individual enterprises; the problem — again a pragmatic one — is to find the right areas for centralised decisions and decentralised reactions to the market (38).

(d) The question is discussed of how far a better international division of labour could be promoted by *international* coordination of structural change — a process inevitably implying a substantial degree of government intervention in the national structures. Some institutionalised coordination of industrial, and agricultural, strategies — if only exchange of information about plans, policies and expectations – between all three groups of countries, is thought desirable by some contributors, especially in view of the growing similarities of production structures and of the threat that competitive investments will lead to surplus capacities at one point and general shortages at others, intensifying the structural crisis already felt (39). On the Eastern side, it is held that negotiated coordination of economic plans between Eastern and Southern countries – bilateral or multilateral – could result in a much 'smoother and less arduous road' to adjustment and specialisation than the 'longer, hazardous and more painful' road of letting loose market forces (40). Such proposals are particularly, but not exclusively, relevant to the massive investments, often with lags of many years between initiation and operation needed in some sectors – notably for exploiting new sources of energy and of some raw materials. The example of plan coordination and the growth of specialisation within the CMEA is cited (41). Other contributors, however, are sceptical of the feasibility of effective international harmonisation of development plans on a 'three world' basis, having in mind the problems actually experienced in carrying out even national industrial policies, and, *a fortiori*, development coordination within regional groupings of nations.

(e) One issue to be faced is that restructuring is not just a matter of industrial countries withdrawing from such industries as textiles, clothing, light electronics, leaving demand to be met by imports from the South, while moving into the well-publicised industries of high technology. The industries for which prospects of fast-growth are obviously bright are few, and are unlikely to offset fully the losses in employment and output from the industries in retreat. Nor is it probable that the often advocated shift into service sectors – the process of 'deindustrialisation' – will prove an effective substitute. It is more convincing to suggest that restructuring should take the form of the up-grading of the whole range of industries in the advanced industrial countries – up-grading in quality, in technological content, in design and marketing and in the use of highly qualified manpower. This up-grading can go hand-in-hand with the extension of intra-industry trade and specialisation. Such a complex process can be encouraged by liberalisation of trade, as is indeed already happening. But if the process is to be accelerated, it needs more than top-level intergovernmental conferences or statements of high principle. It requires much detailed discussion and negotiation at a down-to-earth level involving not only official experts but also the enterprises – whether public or private, and including the transnationals. It is performance at the micro-level which has to change more rapidly.

(f) Moving back to the macro-level, contributors discuss the question whether the long drawn-out inter-governmental negotiations in the United Nations agencies will give the hoped-for new impetus to the establishment of a New International Economic Order. It is suggested that 'we have the framework for inter-government action, but it is largely unused '(42) and that after years of almost permanent negotiation 'a dominating sense of lassitude' prevails (43). Nevertheless, there have been achievements, if limited ones, in financing methods, in commodity agreements, in trading rules. The year 1981 sees the opening of the Third Development Decade and, it is hoped, should see also, in the 'global round' of negotiations within the UN system, the formulation of a new international strategy for world development. The negotiations should cover, within a specified time-frame, the whole field of international economic relations relevant to such a strategy – trade, energy, finance and the transfer of resources, commodity stabilisation, technology transfers, food aid, agricultural and industrial adjustment. The background – as seen late in 1980 – is described and the problems assessed (*Chapter 12*), but the outcome remains in the melting-pot (44). The preliminary negotiations have not been encouraging and have once again brought into prominence the considerable divergences of interest and approaches between, and within, the three groups of national governments: the South pressing, but with differences of attitude among its members so that its negotiating platform reflects a 'precarious balance of interests and compromises' (45), the West ready to maintain dialogue but reluctant to accept specific commitments especially at a time of general recession; the East in broad, but not uncritical, alignment with the South, objecting particularly to suggestions from the South that the socialist countries should bear the same kind of responsibilities as the West. The special positions of the OPEC countries and of the new industrial countries in relation to the low-income nations of the Third World are a particular source of complication. Will existing proposals for a New International Economic Order really serve the aims of meeting basic human needs and alleviating poverty *within* the societies of the Third World? To what extent can the monitoring by donor countries and international agencies of the distribution of assistance be reconciled with national sovereignty of the recipients? What should be the balance of power among nations in the formulation and execution of international development policies? How can new 'rules of the game' (e.g. for trade or other preferences) be framed so as to give fair chances for all (it is pointed out that 'equal treatment of unequals is not a principle of justice' (46))?

(g) The disappointing experience within the existing international organisations, and the wide range of issues that should be, but have not been, successfuly resolved – such as the speeding-up of structural adjustment – lead one author to consider the desirability of a new international institution which would embrace some functions covered by the present organisations such as GATT and UNCTAD and others not covered at all (47). The new organ could be described as an International Trade and Production Organisation (in some ways resembling the original post-war proposal for an International Trade Organisation which was never carried out); it would lay down principles and rules not only for tariff and non-tariff barriers to international trade but also for management of intra-firm trade, State trading, restrictive business practices, trade in agricultural products and raw materials, international transactions in services, and also for international investment. (This proposal may be aligned with the proposals mentioned above for improved institutions for the international flows of capital.) Conceivably the functions could be extended to the promotion of industrial cooperation arrangements between enterprises, which contributors from the East, in particular, regard as the effective method of cooperation.

5. New forms of East-West-South cooperation

Finally, returning to the micro-level, schemes of tripartite industrial cooperation (TIC) between enterprises of the three worlds are reviewed and assessed (48). In such schemes, firms from the West and from Eastern Europe join in the construction of industrial projects in a developing country with a greater or lesser degree of active assistance from local enterprises. In the 15 years ending in 1979, it is reported, 230 such projects have been completed in 56 developing countries – half of them, it is noted, in the oil-producing countries of the Middle East and Maghreb. A list and analysis of the known cases is provided (*Chapter 17*).

Such tripartite arrangements should, it appears, be a practical way of making use of the comparative advantages – in costs, financial resources, technical and administrative expertise – of each of the three partners. The question is raised, however, of how far the existing schemes exhibit a balanced division of responsibility and benefits between the three partners: it seems that most often the Southern partner plays only a small role – e.g. providing local labour for civil engineering and, sometimes, assembly work. Thus it is suggested that the practice generally represents cooperation *in* rather than *with* developing countries. Moreover many of such arrangements are only temporary, ceasing after a particular project has been completed. But a trend is observed towards longer term schemes. Thus it is suggested that the most interesting cases – of which there are only a few – are those involving consortia or joint ventures between Eastern and Western firms with a general purpose of executing projects in the South.

Even if TIC is at present, as is suggested, no more than a 'distinctly marginal phenomenon' (49), yet it makes a valuable base for joint action at ground level in promoting economic and technical progress in the developing world. It deserves more attention from governments and international organisations and deeper study of the opportunities which it offers.

References

(1) For example, Zevin (Chapter 15), Szentes (Chapter 16), Faulwetter (Comments Part IV)

(2) Hardt (Comments Part I p. 75)

(3) Willy Brandt (Chairman), *North-South; A Program for Survival;* MIT Press Cambridge Mass. 1980.

(4) Bhaduri (Chapter 5 p. 93)

(5) Nussbaumer and Rieger (Comments Part II)

(6) Calcagno/Kñakal (Chapter 6) and Faulwetter (Comments Part IV)

(7) See also UNIDO, *World Industry since 1960,* 1979, p. 301 for estimates of gross and net transfers

(8) Seton (Chapter 7)

(9) Laski and Ognev (Comments Part II)

(10) Streeten (Chapter 10) and Bakó (Comments Part II)

(11) Seton (Chapter 7 p. 139) and Streeten (Chapter 10 p. 242)

(12) For the figures, see World Bank, *World Development Report 1980* p. 29

(13) Calcagno/Kñakal (Chapter 6 p. 103)

(14) For example, Dobozi/Inotai (Chapter 3), Bogomolov (Chapter 11) Szentes (Chapter 16), Faulwetter and Kohlmey (Comments Part IV)

(15) These notes are based on Haustein/Maier (Chapter 8), Haselbach (Chapter 9) together with comments on Part III by Szentes and Lukaszewicz.

(16) Streeten (Chapter 10 p. 233)

(17) Zevin (Chapter 15 p. 298)

(18) Ohlin (Chapter 13 p. 275) and Nagy (Comments Part IV)

(19) Paszyński (Chapter 2 p. 38)

(20) Nayyar (Comments Part I)

(21) Dobozi/Inotai (Capter 3)

(22) Paszyński (Chapter 2), Fabinc (Chapter 4), Donges (Chapter 14), Lavigne (Comments Part IV)

(23) Paszyński (Chapter 2)

(24) Nayyar (Comments Part. I)

(25) Fabinc (Chapter 4)

(26) Nayyar (Comments Part I)

(27) Streeten (Chapter 10)

(28) Berthelot (Chapter 1)

(29) Donges (Chapter 14)

(30) Dobozi/Inotai (Chapter 3)

(31) Nagy (Comments Part IV p. 318)

(32) Bogomolov (Chapter 11)

(33) For a review of energy prospects, see C.T. Saunders (ed.) *East and West in the Energy Squeeze,* London, Macmillan, 1980 (reporting the Fifth Workshop in the present series).

(34) Zevin (Chapter 15 p. 297)

(35) Hardt (Comments Part I p. 78)

(36) Sołdaczuk (Comments Part II)

(37) Donges (Chapter 14 p. 289)

(38) Nagy (Comments Part IV p. 320)

(39) Dobozi/Inotai (Chapter 3), Szentes (Chapter 16)

(40) Paszyński (Chapter 2 pp. 42, 43)

(41) Kohlmey (Comments Part IV)

(42) Streeten (Chapter 10 p. 221)

(43) Berthelot (Chapter 1 p. 29)

(44) Jankowitsch (Chapter 12) and Macesich (Comments Part IV)

(45) Paszyński and Shalamanov/Sivov (Comments Part IV)

(46) Streeten (Chapter 10 p. 223)

(47) Streeten (Chapter 10 p. 237); reference is made to Miriam Camps, *The Case for a Global Trade Organization,* New York, Council on Foreign Relations, 1980

(48) Gutman (Chapter 17) and comments on Part V by McMillan and Basak.

(49) McMillan p. 366

PART I – THE BACKGROUND: INTERESTS AND PROSPECTS

Chapter 1

THE INTERESTS OF THE INDUSTRIAL WEST IN RELATIONS WITH DEVELOPING COUNTRIES

Yves Berthelot*

The 1930s obliged what is known as the West to become aware of its growing interdependence, but it took the Second World War to transform the resulting interdependence into an assumed solidarity: the European construction is the most elaborate manifestation; concertation within OECD shows the need, to manage this solidarity, of a permanent structure for dialogue.

In the quarter century that followed the War, an unprecedented economic expansion, both in the industrial Western countries and in many developing countries, has been accompanied, or rather been sustained, by a growing interlinking of the economies. However, until the last few years, the North-South interdependence was only vaguely perceived in the industrial countries; although sometimes felt as dependence by the developing countries, it was accepted because it seemed to provide the 'motor' needed for their growth.

The upheavals of the 1970s have also revealed the strength of the ties that have been forged between the countries. One may briefly recall the collapse of the Bretton Woods monetary arrangements in 1971 and 1973, the brutal rise in raw material and energy

* Head of Research, OECD Development Centre, Paris

prices between 1973 and 1974, the world food crisis in the same two years, the surge of inflation accompanied, in a novel association, by a stagnation which, in 1975, had dominated practically all countries in the world. Since then, the interdependence has increased still further. The financial surpluses of the petroleum producing countries have, to a considerable extent, been placed, through the Western banking system, in the developing countries. Today, one may wonder about their capacity to undertake new loans to support their development and to reimburse their debts, all the more so because the deceleration in the industrialised countries' growth limits the development of their exports.

These various manifestations of interdependence have not led to a durable desire for rupture: on the contrary, they have led towards dialogue and negotiation to construct rules and management instruments adapted to the reality of the world dimensions of economics. The progress achieved in this direction has so far been modest, but it exists, and what is essential is the will to persist in dialogue based on an awareness of the transformations which are underway and on a vision of the world society that one seeks to construct.

The term 'interdependence' was used above, and will be used below, in a sense that takes account of the recognised fact that the economies of the South are dependent on the development of the economies of the North and on the decisions that are taken by the actors in these economies, and on the fact, more recent but more and more important, that the development of the industrialised economies of the West is dependent on the development of certain economies in the South and on the decisions taken by their actors. This does not mean that the forces in play are of equal strength, and there remain many forms of dependence, if only through the mastery of technologies; however, if, in North–South relations, the relative powers are not symmetrical, they are not unilateral.

We seek in what follows to identify the interests of the industrialised West in its relations with the developing countries at the macro-economic level, in the international division of labour, in certain key sectors and in financial equilibrium.

1.1 The development of North-South relations: a factor for growth

OECD's 'Interfutures' team, in its report *Facing the Future,* proposes several scenarios for the development of the world economy up to the year 2000. In Scenario B, the industrialised countries experience a relatively slow growth, but no barriers are placed on trade with the Third World. Scenario C allows an exploration of the consequences of a rupture between OECD and developing countries. Finally, Scenario D shows the effects of an extension of protectionism in the context of slow growth in the industrialised countries with an intensification of preferential links between certain zones in the North and the South.

Two major conclusions emerge from *Table 1.1*, which shows the movement of income per head over the period 1975 to 2000 according to the different scenarios. An intensification of relations between industrialised and developing countries allows a stronger growth in both groups. Western Europe and Japan are much more in need of these relations than the US or the Eastern European countries.

Table 1.1

Gross domestic product per head in 1975 and 2000 by region on various hypotheses for North-South relations
(1970 US $)

	1975	2000		
		No trade obstacles	North-South rupture	Preferential links between zones
United States	5132	8130	7780	8450
Japan	2371	8230	3590	7560
EEC	2752	6110	4450	5680
OECD	3044	6470	4880	6270
Eastern Europe	1700	5080	4730	5080
Developing countries	290	790	656	750

Source: OECD, *Facing the Future,* 1979.

The scenarios confirm the intuition of those who, over the past four years, have proposed that financial and technical resources should be massively transferred to Third World countries, in order to contribute to their development and to facilitate the expansion of their relations with the industrial West.

1.2 Employment effects of changes in the international division of labour

The current dynamics of the international division of labour stem from two sets of forces each having its own logic and orientation. On the one hand, there is the logic of the existing industrial structure of the advanced countries; for them, recourse to trade with the rest of the world, going much beyond a simple search for raw materials, encompasses all the elements in the costs of production (access to raw materials, availability of cheap labour or capital, characteristics of the physical or legal environment); it also expands, to the dimensions of the planet, the outlets for a production which is becoming more and more massive and diversified: this transformation operates essentially through the 'multinationalisation' of the large firms of the industrialised countries. On the other hand, the developing countries themselves aspire to construct an industry which would be an engine of growth for their economies and an instrument to promote their autonomy of decision.

These two sets of forces have led to a considerable expansion of world industrial production, to a modification in its geographical distribution, and thus to profound changes in the structure of international trade. But beyond this obvious conclusion, the objectives and interests of the various parties involved in the emerging division of labour do not necessarily coincide. There is no guarantee, in particular, that the preoccupation of profitability reflected in the structural shifts promoted by the large industrial firms corresponds to the development objectives of the countries which receive them. There is no guarantee either that the industrialisation of certain Third World countries, whatever its origin, will not appear primarily as undesirable competition for the advanced industrial countries, especially while the latter are experiencing a particularly profound economic crisis. The outcome of these two dynamic trends is that the forms of industrialisation are necessarily multiple, and this raises the question of which forms should be promoted.

Faced with limited domestic markets, countries turn more and more towards world markets, which implies a progressive redistribution of market shares and profound readjustments in the industrialised countries. In a period when these countries are experiencing slower growth, this industrialisation process, based on exports, comes up against limits, while the production which would correspond to the needs of the large mass of populations in Third World countries is neglected.

How can we give greater dynamism to domestic markets so that they can support a more balanced industrialisation? This is a major challenge which calls for both an effort to promote rural development and a more willing industrial and financial cooperation on the part of the industrialised countries.

This readjustment of the equilibrium will not prevent trade with Third World countries from developing. The development of trade, necessary to the satisfactory functioning of industrial economies' production structures, provokes considerable resistance in the industrialised countries on the part of firms threatened by new competition, of unions which seek to protect jobs and of politicians.

It is rather curious that we are worried about imports from the Third World and the jobs lost as a result, but that we do not wonder about the exports to these countries and the jobs that they create. This defective vision of the problem leads to false analyses and inappropriate conclusions.

Estimates have been made of the net effect on industrial employment in the industrial Western countries of trade with Third World countries, using various methods: use of a general equilibrium model, estimation of the direct effects of imports and of exports, estimation of direct and indirect effects of imports and exports, techniques which decompose the results according to various factors which affect employment. Some estimates have aimed at analysing past developments, others at testing the effects of liberalisation policies, others at forecasting future developments.

Whatever the methods employed, the result remains the same: because of the very large industrial trade surplus, trade with Third World countries is beneficial in terms of employment to the industrialised Western countries. The development between 1970 and 1978, (that is the effects of the growth of exports and the growth of imports) is, according to the case, slightly unfavourable or slightly favourable.

For the future, the impact on employment clearly depends on hypotheses about the development of exports and imports. The available projections are all based on an extrapolation of trends for the last seven or eight years with inflections designed to take account of various hypotheses whose quantification is fairly arbitrary. For example, to what extent will the debt situation of certain countries lead to a deceleration in investment and thus in imports of equipment goods? How far will technological progress lead to a return, in the industrialised countries, to lines of production which were transferred to the Third World to benefit from low labour costs? There are, in fact, numerous examples of 'relocation' in the industrialised countries as a result of technical progress. However, whatever the hypotheses retained, the results converge: the effects (gains, losses, relocations) for employment in industrial countries of trade with the Third World will be relatively weak in the future and much less important than those due to the restructuring of trade within OECD and the gains in productivity.

The qualitative effect is clearly in favour of the industrialised countries, as is shown by Balassa, in a very significant table showing differences in the qualification of labour incorporated in exports to, and imports from, the Third World (see *Table 1.2*).

The conclusion to be drawn from the considerations above is that trade in manufactures with the Third World does not affect the balance of employment at the national level; if one adds that this trade yields a very favourable balance for the OECD countries ($ 109 billion in 1977), it appears clearly that policies aimed at disturbing this trade are both inappropriate to employment problems and unfortunate for the balance of payments.

These general conclusions, however, mask some regional and sectoral disparities. The generally accepted idea that the impact of trade with the Third World varies very much between regions of the same country is confirmed by the facts. For example, in West Germany comparative advantage in relation to developing countries is negatively correlated with the structure of employment of the poorest regions; moreover, one notices that certain sensitive industries are more concentrated regionally than the average (footwear, leather), although the contrary is the case for textiles (1). In France, an analysis has been made of establishments with more than 50 employees in 'sensitive'

Table 1.2

Labour inputs, by qualification, in trade of industrial countries with developing countries

(per cent)

	OECD		USA		EEC		JAPAN	
	Exports	Imports	Exports	Imports	Exports	Imports	Exports	Imports
Engineers and technicians	11.2	6.0	13.3	6.8	11.0	5.5	10.0	6.5
Highly skilled workers	23.2	13.5	20.8	13.4	22.1	13.0	27.3	15.0
Administration and salaried staff	19.6	16.9	20.7	17.4	20.1	16.6	17.4	17.1
Semi-skilled and unskilled workers	46.0	63.6	45.2	62.4	46.8	64.9	45.3	61.4
Total	100.0	100.0	100.0	100.0	100.0	100.0	100.0	100.0

Source: based on Bela Balassa, *The Changing International Division of Labour in Manufactured Goods,* World Bank Staff Working Papers No. 329, May 1979, Table 5. The estimates are based on United States labour input coefficients by occupational groups.

activities (2). 'The regional specialisation of French industry aggravates the problem of Third World competition, or more generally that of the decline of traditional activities, particularly in consumption goods' (3).

A conflict thus appears between interests at the national level, which point to the intensification of trade, and interests felt at the regional level, where public opinion is formed and elections take place. The OECD report *Facing the Future* condemns the oligopolisation of social structures in the OECD countries, which leads each group to organise itself in such a way as to defend its immediate interests, as an element of social rigidity. This makes the necessary social adaptations difficult, even when these countries possess, also, capabilities for scientific research and the technological innovations which would allow them to overcome the technical obstacles to their growth.

1.3 A rapid overview of interests in particular sectors

a) Energy

Energy is the sector where interdependence between nations is the most strongly felt. In 1976, the industrialised countries of OECD had a total production of primary energy (expressed in equivalent barrels per day of petroleum) of 46.5 million: by contrast, their consumption was as much as 69.8 million (4).

On the other hand, the oil exporting developing countries produced the equivalent of 36.1 million barrels a day and consumed only 5 million. The oil importing developing countries produced only 6.5 million equivalent barrels, and their consumption was almost double (12.6 million). This critical situation was aggravated by the fact that these countries were increasing their energy consumption very fast, faster than the industrialised countries.

At the level of groups of countries, the interests involved are the following:

— As a whole, the industrialised Western countries depend on external supplies for almost one-third of their energy consumption; this dependence is clearly most pronounced for Western Europe and Japan. These countries have now become aware of the excessively energy consuming nature of their model of development, and they are accepting the consequences by economising in energy and by searching for substitutes for petroleum. The energy saving programmes have already yielded results and the research underway holds out hope for considerable progress. Security of petroleum supply remains nevertheless one of their principal preoccupations in the coming years of transition.

— The petroleum producing countries have also become aware, on their side, of the strength of their position on the consuming market, and thus of the increased funds that they can extract from their resources to finance their own development and to develop African and Asian policies. But they also know that they have no interest in turning a real resource into a financial asset in a system of rapid inflation.

— Finally, the oil importing developing countries are torn between their satisfaction at seeing the increased negotiating power of the Third World, and their unease in the face of the profound aggravation of the cost of their development.

This situation indicates the directions to be followed to avoid profound disturbances which would benefit nobody:

— acceptance by the industrialised countries of a progressive increase in the price of petroleum;
— additional effort (economies, research on new energies) by the same countries, and by the non-producing countries, to reduce their dependence on petroleum;
— guarantees, by the producers, of supplies corresponding to irreducible needs during the transition period;
— recycling of petrodollars into productive activities in order to limit the risks of depression in the world economy.

b) Raw materials

Interdependence in the field of *raw materials* cannot be reduced to an opposition between the industrialised countries of the West and developing countries. For the 20 most important minerals, for example, 44 per cent of reserves are located in the industrialised market economy countries, 23 per cent in the socialist countries and 33 per cent in the developing countries. However, four countries (United States, Canada, Australia and South Africa) hold 80 per cent of the reserves of the industrialised market economy countries; the USSR holds 80 per cent of the reserves of the socialist countries; and a small number of developing countries (Brazil, Chile, Indonesia, Zaire, Papua New Guinea) hold the majority of the reserves of Third World countries.

Certainly, the dependence of the industrialised West on raw materials from the Third World is less acute than is generally believed; nevertheless, the insufficiency of mining exploration in these latter countries carries a long term risk of shortages at the world level. Loosening this constraint requires that the mining operators and the governments of the industrialised countries make available the necessary finance, but also that the developing countries which hold mineral ores find in the development of their resources a source of finance for their development. Two questions currently under discussion are essential from this point of view: the negotiations on stabilisation of raw material prices and the stability of export revenues on the one hand; on the other hand, the increased development of mineral processing at the point of extraction, which not only increases the value added accruing to the producing country, but can also constitute for some countries a source of funds for industrialisation.

c) Food

The response to *food requirements* — a basic need if any exists — constitutes one of the most worrying aspects in the present situation.

The world as a whole is in the process of settling into a situation of dependence vis-à-vis a small number of exporting countries (United States, Canada, Australia, and Argentina) for its cereal needs. This dependence has become worse in a most disquieting way for the Third World countries, which were in aggregate self-sufficient at the start of the 1950s, but whose imports have continuously increased since then, reaching 71 million tonnes in 1978. More recently, the USSR seems also to be slipping into an analogous situation, sacrificing its autonomy in order to import growing amounts of cereals, thus reducing the reserves available for developing countries. So far as the agriculture of the Western countries is concerned, it depends on petroleum (fertilisers, mechanisation).

These situations of mutual dependence open the way to the most dangerous international tensions. Reducing these tensions is a necessary objective which, while not implying a search at all costs for national self-sufficiency, implies an effort to increase the capability for regional self-sufficiency. The intensification of production can require a certain amount of protection, following the example of the European Common Market.

Since these capabilities cannot everywhere be assured, it is important, secondly, to organise the production of food surpluses in the countries which are capable of them, by reference to the needs which remain unsatisfied. It is scarcely necessary to underline the need for long term forecasts and above all for agreement at the international level required for the solution of this most basic problem.

d) Financing of development and the world financial equilibrium

Mobilisation of the resources necessary for development is primarily an internal task for each nation. But the inequalities in resource availabilities are today very profound; the result is that international financial flows are playing a more and more essential role in the Third World's development. For example, in 1975, one sixth of the gross investments of these countries was financed by foreign capital; for the low income African countries, this share is in fact much higher, above 50 per cent. The importance of private capital in these financial flows has increased significantly during the past decade: from 1970 to 1978, the net volume of resources made available on market terms to the developing countries has increased five-fold (from $ 11 mn. to $ 55 mn.), moving from 56 per cent to 70 per cent of their external resources. However, the poorest countries remain essentially dependent on official development aid which represents about 75 per cent of their net external resources.

Although the Western industrialised countries are still the most important source for these financial flows – for example, around three-quarters of the official aid – the resources coming from OPEC play a growing part in the constitution of world savings and in the financing of growth and industrialisation of many developing countries.

After 1974, the recycling of petrodollars was efficiently carried out and Third World demand contributed to sustaining the activity of the industrialised countries. For 1981 and the following years, most analyses agree: the developing countries, both the poorest and those already semi-industrialised, will have more difficulty in withstanding the latest rises in petroleum prices because of their indebtedness and because of the deceleration in growth in the industrialised countries which will not be able to absorb a sufficient share of Third World production; the annual debt service of the 'middle income' countries is expected (by the World Bank) to move on average from 12 per cent of their exports of goods and services in 1977 to 18 per cent in 1985 (5). These difficulties will have repercussions on their populations and on the world economy; fears of a financial collapse and a profound depression cannot be ruled out.

These analyses lead to a series of questions listed below. The purpose of these questions is to show the intertwining of the interests of the Western industrialised countries and the developing countries, even though they are grouped geographically.

Questions directly concerning OPEC's interests

How can the OPEC countries be encouraged to steer an increasing share of their financial surplus, whether directly or indirectly, towards productive investments in non-petroleum producing Third World countries? What guarantees can be given to avoid the surplus petroleum countries from preferring to keep their oil in the ground? How can one contribute to a real development of the OPEC zone?

Two questions about the interests of non-petroleum producing developing countries

How can the resources of the poorest countries which have no access to private finance be increased? For the others, how can the working of the system be assured and improved? This question can be divided into three: How to finance the existing debt which increases with rises in interest rates and the dollar exchange rate? How to direct new resources towards these countries? How to ensure that resources are used for development?

Questions concerning the interests of the industrialised West

How can adequate supplies of petroleum and raw materials be ensured? How can one ensure that the banks will have their loans to Third World countries repaid and will continue to contribute to recycling?

The questions listed above are linked; their solution requires a set of measures of which none is sufficient but each has a function and complements the others.

1.4 Conclusion: interdependence and negotiations

Conflict of interest, community of interest – the examples given above illustrate both at the same time. As against the short-term divergences, which reflect concerns to preserve advantages or the desire to shift an obstacle, it would be tempting to oppose a long-term convergence of interests based on a reasonable use of resources and an equitable distribution of products. In fact, there are already today convergences of interest, for example in developing alternative forms of energy, while conflicts of interest will always persist in the sharing of power and wealth. It is towards overcoming the conflicts and developing the points of common interest that current negotiations are striving.

After five years of almost permanent negotiation between the industrialised West and the developing countries, there is a dominating sense of lassitude, fed, on the one hand, by the feeling that no decisive progress has been made and, on the other hand, by a doubt as to the importance of Third World development in permanently overcoming the current crisis.

However, the achievements of the North-South dialogue are not negligible. The integrated programme on *raw materials* adopted at Nairobi in 1976 has made progress and agreement was reached in 1979 on the basic elements of a Common Fund and then on its implementation. Two new commodity agreements (olive oil, rubber) have been added since 1976 to the five that already existed (wheat, sugar, coffee, cocoa, tin). Preparatory work has begun on the other products in the integrated programme.

In *energy,* following a recommendation of the Conference on International Economic Cooperation, the World Bank has established a programme for the development of Third World energy resources and is shifting towards the financing of programme loans.

To meet the *monetary problems* of the developing countries, the IMF has created or adapted several facilities: enlarged facility, supplementary facility, compensatory financing facility, regulatory stock financing facility, petroleum facility, fiduciary fund, improvement in the conditions for loans, etc. Development financing has been the objective of many measures: increase in the capital of several regional banks, replenishment of the special funds at preferential rates as well as the International Development

Association, action by the International Fund for Agricultural Development, special action decided at the CIEC in favour of the poorest countries, relief of public debt for some of the poorest countries, etc.

In the field of *trade,* the Generalised Systems of Preference have been set up. The Multilateral Trade Negotiations have preserved, in a climate of crisis, a free-trade emphasis which can only benefit the developing countries: moreover, special provisions have been introduced for these countries in the non-tariff codes (anti-dumping codes, customs valuation codes, codes of standards, etc.).

For the future, if interdependence is a reality whose consequences will influence more and more the economies and populations of different industrialised and developing countries, the means must be provided for its management. The big meetings can provide the necessary guidelines, and lay down the frameworks, but economics is about day-to-day matters, conflicts to be resolved are daily matters, and so is progress.

Management implies both information and rules of the game. At the level of information, agreement on development strategies and major investments which in the long run will structure the world economy (petrochemicals, shipbuilding, iron and steel, information industries), will be seen to be more and more necessary. The partners involved (governments, firms, unions) will need to participate.

The rules of the game about trade, finance, movement of people, exploitation of common resources (water, ocean bed, space) are (or will be) the subject of negotiations. These rules, which are designed to structure the world economy and to give rights to everyone, even the weakest, imply the progressive establishment of authorities which will guarantee their application.

There are now many people in the industrialised countries who, basing themselves on the European example and the Marshall Plan, or on prospective studies such as that of the OECD Interfutures group, *Facing the Future,* accept that the development of the Third World countries is a condition for giving back to the economies of the industrialised West a new equilibrium and a new dynamism. But the passage from the analysis of a number of experts, however relevant, to implementation involving the different actors in the economy, is not easy, and governments can do no more than contribute to it. A profound recognition of interdependence on the part of public opinion is a necessary political condition for decisive change.

References

(1) Frank Wolter, "Adjusting to imports from developing countries", paper for symposium on the New International Economic Order, Kiel, December 1976.

(2) Sensitive products are considered to be those for which imports represented an important share of the domestic market or for which they were growing rapidly, and those for which exports represented an important share of production or whose growth was rapid in value terms.

(3) Dollé, Annexe 6 in Y. Berthelot et G. Tardy, *Le Défi Economique du Tiers-Monde,* Documentation Française, Paris, 1978. p. 185.

(4) World Bank, *World Development Report 1979,* Table 24.

(5) Ibid: Table 23.

ANNEXES TO CHAPTER 1

Annex Table I

Evolution of exports and imports of Western industrial countries by destination and origin
in billion $

	1963	1973	1978
Exports to			
Other Western industrial countries	69.3	289.0	579.5
Australia, New Zealand, South Africa	3.7	10.4	18.8
OPEC	3.8	16.0	78.9
Other developing countries	18.1	52.8	120.6
Eastern trading area	3.5	18.1	41.7
Unspecified	0.6	5.0	7.3
Total	99.0	391.3	846.8
Imports from			
Other Western industrial countries	69.3	289.0	579.5
Australia, New Zealand, South Africa	3.6	11.0	17.6
OPEC	6.7	31.8	105.7
Other developing countries	15.5	47.2	107.4
Eastern trading area	3.5	15.4	33.9
Unspecified	–	–	0.1
Total	98.6	394.3	844.2

Source: GATT, *International Trade 1978/79,* and earlier issues

Trade of Western industrial countries with Developing countries

in billion $

	EXPORTS						IMPORTS					
	1963		1973		1978		1963		1973		1978	
	Total	Excl. OPEC	Total	Excl. OPEC	Total	Excl. OPEC	Total	Excl. OPEC	Total	Excl. OPEC	Total	Excl. OPEC
Food	3.11	.	9.21	7.49	19.75	13.45	7.96	.	15.89	.	30.00	.
Raw materials	0.64	.	1.95	1.67	4.05	3.30	3.13	.	4.74	.	7.00	.
Ores and minerals	0.12	.	0.52	0.47	1.15	0.95	1.41	.	3.41	.	5.40	.
Fuels	0.47	.	0.77	0.64	2.85	2.00	6.52	.	33.63	4.32	119.50	17.50
Non-ferrous metals	0.30	.	0.94	0.78	2.45	1.70	1.28	.	3.77	.	4.60	.
Total primary products	**4.64**	.	**13.40**	**11.05**	**30.25**	**21.40**	**20.30**	.	**64.10b)**	**32.15**	**170.50c)**	**64.50**
Iron and steel	1.38	.	5.12	3.62	12.35	7.10	0.07	.	0.49	.	1.20	.
Chemicals	2.25	.	8.04	6.59	19.75	14.70	0.20	.	0.81	.	2.40	.
Other semi-manufactures	a)	.	3.31	2.65	10.60	6.90	a)	.	2.49	.	5.50	.
Engineering products	8.91	.	31.28	23.08	105.80	58.80	0.09	.	3.61	.	11.80	.
Textiles	1.66	.	3.24	2.41	5.95	3.80	0.74	.	2.10	.	3.50	.
Clothing		.	0.54	0.45	1.45	0.90		.	3.23	.	8.70	.
Other consumer goods	2.47	.	1.90	1.40	7.10	3.60	0.70	.	2.39	.	7.20	.
Total manufactures	**16.67**	.	**53.40**	**40.15**	**163.00**	**95.80**	**1.80**	.	**15.75d)**	**15.10**	**41.50e)**	**40.30**
Statistical discrepancy	0.83	.	2.30	1.90	6.75	3.80	0.13	.	0.45	.	4.00	.
Total	**22.14**	**18.10**	**69.10**	**53.10**	**200.00**	**121.00**	**22.23**	**15.81**	**80.30**	**47.70**	**216.00**	**109.00**

a) Included with other comsumer goods. – b) Including 2.64 non-fuel from OPEC not specified by commodity. – c) Including 4.00 non-fuel from OPEC. – d) Including 0.65 from OPEC. – e) Including 1.20 from OPEC

Source: from OECD *Statistics of Foreign Trade*

Chapter 2

THE ECONOMIC INTEREST OF THE CMEA COUNTRIES IN RELATIONS WITH DEVELOPING COUNTRIES

Marian Paszyński*

We do not intend to deal in this paper with the overall picture of economic relations between the CMEA and developing countries. Its purpose is much more limited. It will be confined to an attempt at analysis of the interests of the CMEA countries underlying the economic relations between the two groups of countries. Notwithstanding the close interrelationship between political and economic factors influencing these relations, the analysis will be restricted to the economic interactions between the CMEA and LDCs.

We will be concerned primarily with the bilateral side of such interactions. Multilateral relations will be, however, briefly considered at the end of the paper. As far as possible a descriptive approach to the issues considered will be minimised in favour of an analytical one though some descriptive material is necessary to illustrate the propositions contained in the text.

While discussing the economic interest in expanding relations with developing countries we must keep in mind that this category of countries is extremely heterogeneous. However, in a brief paper one cannot take into account all the diversity of the Third World that may affect the issues under review. The same goes for certain simplification in the argumentation, unavoidable within the scope of a concise exposition of the author's thoughts on the matter under consideration. In view of the foregoing, the paper concentrates upon the most important aspects (in the author's view) of the problem, leaving aside other issues that might also have a certain significance.

2.1 The developing countries in CMEA trade

The place developing countries occupy in the CMEA trade (1) is illustrated by *Table 2.1* below.

Though the period 1955 through 1979 has witnessed a considerable increase in developing countries' share in CMEA trade, it still remains at a relatively low level, especially if we exclude the USSR from the total. For the other socialist countries, the share of

* Foreign Trade Research Institute, Warsaw

Table 2.1

Percentage share of developing countries in CMEA trade

	1955		1970		1978		1979	
	Total	USSR	Total	USSR	Total	USSR	Total	USSR
CMEA Exports								
LDCs total	6.1	4.4	13.2	20.9	14.7	21.5	14.2	19.8
OPEC	..	..	2.2	2.9	3.7	3.9	3.5	3.7
Other LDCs	..	..	11.0	18.0	11.0	17.6	10.7	16.1
CMEA Imports								
LDCs total	5.7	5.5	9.6	14.8	10.0	14.1	11.0	16.8
OPEC	..	..	0.8	1.3	2.2	2.4	2.2	2.2
Other LDCs	..	..	8.6	13.5	7.8	11.7	8.8	14.4

Source: UNCTAD, *Handbook of International Trade and Development Statistics 1979,* New York; UN, *Monthly Bulletin of Statistics,* Nos. 6 and 12, 1979.

developing countries amounted in 1978 in exports to 9.0 per cent (3.5 per cent for OPEC and 5.4 per cent for other LDCs) and in imports to 7.1 per cent (2.1 per cent for OPEC and 5.0 per cent for other LDCs). The part developing countries play in the CMEA trade is less significant that their position in the trade of developed market economy countries (DMECs); in 1978, LDCs took 23.8 per cent of developed market economies' exports and supplied 25.0 per cent of their imports. However, that difference results to a considerable extent from the more important position of the OPEC countries in the overall trade of DMECs. If we take only non-OPEC developing countries, their share in DMECs exports in 1978 amounted to 14.7 per cent as against 11.0 per cent for the CMEA. In imports the respective shares were 12.2 and 7.8 per cent.

There are several factors that cause the position of developing countries in CMEA trade to be relatively small. Apart from historical reasons (the fact that trade relations with the majority of developing countries were initiated only after the decolonisation period), geographical factors play a considerable role (2). However, more important are factors connected with the function that foreign trade performs in the socialist economy, to be considered below.

As a result, the trade of the CMEA with developing countries seems to acquire, at least to some extent, a residual nature. (3) If that is the case, it should follow that the demand for CMEA exports from developing countries and from DMECs are alternatives, even substitutes, for each other and that the growth of the first may lead to a shift in trade flows to the advantage of the LDCs and vice versa. (4)

The role of developing countries in the trade of the CMEA should also be considered from the point of view of the commodity pattern of trade, which is presented in *Table 2.2.*

A glance at *Table 2.2* shows that in relations with developing countries the CMEA has a commodity-wise pattern of trade characteristic for developed economies, though its

Table 2.2

Commodity pattern of trade
(percentage shares)

	CMEA total exports		CMEA exports to LDCs		LDC total imports	
	1955	1976	1955	1976	1955	1976
Food	14.0	7.9	5.0	8.6	16.6	11.5
Agricultural raw materials	11.9	4.9	7.3	3.3	6.2	3.0
Ores and metals	13.2	10.9	6.7	4.8	7.1	6.8
Fuels	13.9	19.6	10.0	9.5	11.7	15.7
Manufactures	46.1	49.7	46.0	47.7	52.6	60.0
	CMEA total imports		**CMEA imports from LDCs**		**LDC total imports**	
	1955	1976	1955	1976	1955	1976
Food	21.9	14.6	41.7	49.9	36.7	15.0
Agricultural raw materials	16.4	3.8	51.1	8.8	20.5	4.5
Ores and metals	15.4	13.5	2.7	7.4	10.1	5.4
Fuels	9.4	9.9	0.5	22.5	24.9	58.9
Manufactures	37.3	55.0	3.6	11.4	7.6	15.8

Source: UNCTAD, *Handbook of International Trade and Development Statistics,* 1979, Note: Food, SITC 0+1+22+4. Agricultural raw materials, SITC 2-22-27-28. Ores and metals, SITC 27+28+67+68. Fuels, SITC 3. Manufactures, SITC 5+6+8-(67+68). SITC 9 (Unclassified items) omitted.

trade with DMECs resembles that of developing countries (5). However, the commodity pattern of trade shows also certain peculiarities, especially on the import side. Food plays a much more important role in CMEA imports from LDCs than in CMEA total imports or in LDC total exports. On the other hand, fuels occupy a much less important position in CMEA imports from LDCs than in LDC exports, though their share has been growing quickly. The share of other primary commodities in the CMEA imports has been gradually declining, which reflects the overall trend in CMEA imports (with the share of ores and metals increasing and that of agricultural raw materials rapidly diminishing). Generally, it could be maintained that, given the existing overall pattern of exports of the CMEA, socialist countries are in a position to satisfy their import requirements by exports of a more advantageous commodity-mix in their relations with LDCs than in their trade with DMECs.

Nevertheless, the role of developing countries as a source of imports and, in particular, as an outlet for exports, remains relatively small for most commodity groups (as shown in *Table 2.3*).

Table 2.3

LDCs as export outlets and sources of imports for the CMEA and for DMECs
(percentage shares of total exports or imports and of trade in individual SITC groups)

	For CMEA		For DMECs	
	1955	1976	1955	1976
Exports				
Total trade	6.1	12.9	27.7	22.9
Food	2.2	14.1	21.0	19.3
Agricultural raw materials	3.7	8.7	7.5	11.7
Ores and metals	3.1	5.7	19.1	18.4
Fuels	4.4	6.3	15.6	6.2
Manufactures	6.1	12.4	34.3	25.8
Imports				
Total trade	5.7	10.7	28.1	27.2
Food	10.8	36.4	46.3	29.9
Agricultural raw materials	17.7	24.4	39.2	23.0
Ores and metals	1.0	5.8	26.6	17.8
Fuels	0.3	24.3	56.6	74.9
Manufactures	0.6	2.2	4.0	7.8

Source: as *Table 2.2*

The figures in *Table 2.3* should be considered against the role of DMECs as sources of primary commodity imports of the CMEA. For example, in 1976 DMECs covered 37.5 per cent of the import requirements of the CMEA in food, 33.6 per cent in agricultural raw materials, 45.4 per cent in ores and metals. Only in the case of fuels was the DMECs' share less than that of LDCs (2.6 per cent). Therefore, even in the goods where developing countries, by the very nature of their export specialisation, should have played an important role in supplying the CMEA markets, their share in total imports in a given commodity class, though growing, was smaller than that of developed market economies.

It has been shown already that the USSR occupies a prominent place in the CMEA trade with developing countries. Its share in the CMEA exports to LDCs increased from 31.3 per cent in 1955 to 65.9 per cent in 1978 and in imports from 38.8 to 58.2 per cent respectively (6). The greater degree of involvement of the USSR in economic interaction with developing countries is also reflected in a higher share of LDCs in the Soviet Union's total trade in comparison with other CMEA countries (as shown in *Table 2.4*).

Table 2.4

Percentage share of developing countries in the trade of the CMEA countries, 1977

	Exports	Imports
Bulgaria	12.6	6.7
Czechoslovakia	11.9	9.5
GDR	7.4	8.1
Hungary	14.4	11.7
Poland	10.5	7.5
Romania	18.9	17.1
USSR	24.0	19.0

Source: UNCTAD V, *Statistical review of trade among countries having different economic and social systems,* TD/243/Suppl. 1, Manila, May 1979.

The differing importance of developing countries in the trade of individual CMEA countries depends to some extent upon their different degrees of trade dependence, the smaller ones tending to be more open to trade with other parts of the world (7). However, that does not apply to the USSR. First of all, the USSR as a global power naturally developed a wider network of trade links with the world outside the CMEA area (8). Moreover, geographical location allows it to expand trade with limitrophe or neighbouring countries (9). The difference in the commodity pattern of trade could also conduce to a greater trade expansion, the USSR for example being in a position to satisfy LDCs needs for food, fuels and other primary commodities to a much greater extent than other CMEA countries (10). Romania, on the other hand, belongs to the group of '77' and declared itself a developing country which induced it deliberately to increase, by preferential treatment, the LDC share in its trade .

The diversity of the CMEA countries will have an impact upon their interests in economic relations with developing countries in the future. Nevertheless, the common features that determined the historical development of their trade relations with LDCs will exert a predominant influence over the prospective expansion of these relations.

2.2 The function of foreign trade in socialist economies

The greater role of imports in trade between the CMEA and developing countries and the somewhat residual nature of socialist countries' exports to LDCs result from a similarity in the mode of operation of the socialist and developing economies by contrast with that of the developed market economy (11). The similarities and differences stem from the fact that while the developed capitalist economies operate under conditions of structural excess of industrial capacities, both socialist and, to a great extent, also developing economies face productive capacities lagging behind the expanding domestic demand (12). For this reason, socialist countries were described by Kalecki as 'supply-led' or 'supply-constrained' economies, while DMECs were labelled 'demand-led' economies (13). The idea that supply-side economics are typical for the development process was stressed by L. R. Klein, who rightly applied it also to the socialist countries.

> 'The centrally planned economies are for the most part industrial economies and have the same needs for supply-side analysis. In their case, the supply side has perhaps been excessively developed with inadequate attention paid to the demand side, not from the viewpoint of deficient demand but from the viewpoint of chronic excess of demand, with latent inflationary pressures.' (14)

The same idea was also expressed by J. Kornai (15), and G. R. Feiwel coined a term 'high pressure economy' to describe the realities of economic development in socialist countries. (16)

Different reasons are advanced to explain why there exists such a difference between the mode of operation of the socialist and of the developed capitalist economy. I would be inclined to give credit primarily to two of them. First, adherence to the basic law of socialism — namely to satisfy the ever-growing needs of the society and to secure the universal progress and prosperity of its members — implies that the growth of productive capacities should be directed towards meeting the real needs of the population. In such circumstances, structural excess capacities – characteristic of the wasteful mass-consumption society – are unlikely to emerge. Moreover, the effects of the operation of the law are greatly intensified by the time-lag in entering the path of accelerated economic growth vis-à-vis the developed capitalist countries; this causes the well-known demonstration effect, enhancing consumer expectations and bringing about the unending race between growing demand and the possibilities of its satisfaction (17). Secondly, implementation of the principle of the planned and proportional development of the economy – a basic tenet of socialist economic thought – causes the central planner to abhor installation of surplus capacities or the growth of capacities outpacing the growth of demand. Surplus capacity has been always taboo in the socialist economy (18).

In these circumstances, the functions of foreign trade in the socialist economy differ from those in the developed market economy. In the latter, exports play the more prominent role, supplementing insufficient domestic demand, and imports are treated as deflationary because they compete with domestic supply. In the socialist economies imports perform an important function of catering to the needs of the national economy and are beneficial as they complement insufficient domestic supply. Exports, on the other hand, compete with domestic demand for the indigenous production under conditions of supply lagging behind the growth of demand (19). Therefore, at present the main function of exports in a socialist economy is not to provide for the most effective resource allocation and to optimise capacity utilisation but to secure revenue to cover indispensable import requirements. Unlike the developed market economy, in the socialist economy imports are more important than exports.

The same goes, naturally, for an export surplus over imports. In the 'demand-led' economies a positive trade balance acts – like investment – as a stimulus to growth of demand, through the multiplier effect, and to fuller capacity utilisation. In view of the growing openness of the developed market economies, its role is even more significant. For the 'supply-constrained' economies a trade surplus cannot be considered as performing an analogous function of demand stimulation. In this case exports perform primarily a transformation function converting the available domestic supply pattern into a more desirable one and, by the same token, assist in the restructuring of the economy. For a growing socialist economy a trade deficit is, therefore, more advantageous (20). This is the reason why, apart from other considerations, a socialist country cannot treat resource transfers in the same way as a 'demand-led' economy. Kalecki and Sachs expressed this idea in the following way:

> 'Turning now to the definition of aid from the point of view of the donor country, we should make a clear distinction between two positions: a) The donor country has no free productive capacities (as e.g. usually happens in socialist countries); b) The donor country does not fully use its productive capacities, because of lack of effective demand (a frequent situation in developed capitalist countries).

In the former case giving foreign aid, embodied in export surplus, means a sacrifice because the aggregate internal expenditure (i.e. national income less exports plus imports) will be less than the income generated, which cannot be stepped up above the maximum level warranted by the productive capacities. Would there have been no export surplus, the aggregate internal expenditure would be equal to the income generated at a maximum level.

In the latter case the picture changes entirely: the export surplus, similarly to investment, has a "multiplier" effect, so that the aggregate domestic expenditure after deduction of the export surplus from the income thus generated is higher than the income which would be generated without the export surplus. We may say, therefore, that by giving economic aid to other countries a developed country with free productive capacities assists its own economy in obtaining a higher level of economic activity.' (21)

A question might arise why, in such circumstances, socialist countries provide economic assistance to developing countries by delivering to the latter capital goods on credit terms. There seem to be two answers to this question. First, socialist countries do try to assist LDCs in expanding their economies, though they extend this assistance within the limits of their economic means and taking into account other priorities calling for the allocation of scarce resources (22). Second, socialist countries are inclined to accept deferred payment conditions for that part of their exports which consists of goods that are usually traded internationally on credit terms. An export surplus in this case serves also to finance imports, but at a later stage (23).

A similar situation exists in the case of joint ventures with capital participation of the socialist countries, where the aim is not to export capital as an instrument of profit maximisation or of realisation of any other entrepreneurial advantages, but simply to facilitate export of equipment. Therefore, socialist countries' participation in joint productive ventures takes, as a rule, the form of a counterpart to the value of the capital equipment installed in the venture and lasts usually so long as is needed for repayment of deliveries of such equipment (24). Industrial cooperation with developing countries is also considered an alternative to domestic investment (25).

2.3 Medium and long term prospects

The specific role that external economic relations play in the socialist economy determines the interest of the CMEA countries in their trade and economic relations with developing ones. This problem must be, however, considered in the medium and long-term perspective as the nature of the interest may depend upon the time factor.

In the medium-term there exists no possibility for a radical change in the situation and, in particular, in the volume and structure of productive capacities. The foreign trade of socialist countries has already been determined for the few years ahead by the investment made or in course of execution.

Therefore, the 'catering' function of foreign trade will prevail in the medium-term and it will also fashion trade and economic relations of the CMEA with developing countries. These relations will be determined by the import requirements of the CMEA countries, exports serving primarily as means of procuring foreign exchange to finance purchases abroad. The CMEA countries will not be eager to maintain an export surplus in trade with developing countries, with the exception of crediting deliveries of capital equipment (26). With the growing imports of oil the presently existing surplus may have a tendency to dwindle or may disappear altogether and a switch to a deficit position could emerge in the majority of the CMEA countries with the notable exception of the USSR.

The other probable area for a considerable increase in import requirements of the CMEA countries is not so much raw materials but food (especially tropical products and fodder) and possibly other consumer items (27), as the present trade indicates (see *Table 2.3*). There might occur certain shifts in the directions of procurement of primary commodities from the USSR to developing countries, but that will not alter to any great extent the existing pattern of raw-materials self-sufficiency within the CMEA (28). It should also be borne in mind that a good part of commodity requirements of the CMEA is covered by supplies from DMECs, as mentioned earlier.

The present slow-down in growth rates of the CMEA countries, aggravated by the decline in demand in the world economy and by severe perturbations in the international markets (29), will affect to some extent trade and economic relations between the CMEA and developing nations – not so much, perhaps, in respect of the value of imports as by limiting possibilities for a continuing change in import diversification.

In the long run the situation might be different. When we consider a period exceeding that of an investment cycle, i.e. a time-span within which there exists a possibility for a considerable change in the strategy of economic relations with abroad, the CMEA interest in expanding economic relations with developing countries might be viewed from another angle. Three main factors will influence the shaping of such a strategy.

First, come the changes in economic structure and policies in the CMEA countries. The change in economic structure, substitution and technical progress will obviously lead to reduced dependence of the CMEA economies upon raw-material imports, a phenomenon which is already taking place, and which in all probability will be accentuated in the future (30). On the other hand, a shift from the extensive to an intensive type of economic growth, with a greater role accorded to foreign trade in the allocative process (31), would lead to a greater specialisation in production and trade. Secondly, the structural change in developing countries, resulting in a modification of their import requirements and export supply and in their increased competitiveness in international markets, must affect the perception by the CMEA countries of their interest in expanding economic relations with the LDCs. Thirdly, such a perception must, likewise, be influenced by a change in the nature of the international division of labour from complementary to competitive (32).

It seems that in the long run exports will begin to play an independent and more important role in the foreign trade of the CMEA countries, their previous function of securing means for financing indispensable imports receding to the background. However, without overcoming the obstacles connected with the creation of reserve productive capacities that could be utilised exclusively to cater to the external demand, the change in the function of exports could not be fully achieved.

The foregoing should not mean that imports of primary commodities would diminish. They would grow, but at a rate that could not be regarded as dynamising the overall trade with developing countries (33). On the other hand, greater production-cum-export specialisation of the CMEA countries should bring about a growing demand for industrial products of which the output will not be undertaken or which will be gradually phased out as a result of such specialisation.

All this would in the long-term lead to a situation where the CMEA interest in maintaining and expanding relations with developing countries might concentrate upon exports rather than imports; this would constitute a reversal of the historic and prospective medium-term patterns of economic relations of the two groups of countries. While historically, under the influence of the existing structure of international trade, commercial relations between the CMEA and LDCs were fashioned along the complementary (not competitive) model of international division of labour, in the new situation the structures of economic interaction might be otherwise moulded. Changes in development patterns and strategies of the CMEA and developing countries might eventually lead — within a longer time-span — to a change in the division of labour from complementary (inter-sectoral) to inter-branch trade and, subsequently, to intra-branch and intra-product specialisation in production and trade.

2.4 Institutionalising CMEA-LDC cooperation

Greater interest in export based upon specialised production capacities needs, however, to be somewhat institutionalised. First of all, the process of adjustment should be not unilateral but reciprocal. In view of the previously indicated similarities in the operation of the economic mechanism (both socialist and developing countries are predominantly supply-led economies) the adjustment process has to be undertaken simultaneously at both ends. It might also be spontaneous but this kind of adaptation of economic structures would be at the same time much longer, more hazardous and more painful to both developing and socialist countries. A far smoother and, in every way less arduous road to adjustment would be a programmed process based upon negotiated commitments on both sides. This, by the way, makes the specialisation process less tricky as it might allow for the avoidance of the 'discontinuation of access to market' trap. The CMEA countries, being centrally planned economies, would obviously prefer a programmed and anticipatory approach to the shifts in trade patterns (34) which will anyway occur.

If the change in the division of labour between the CMEA and developing countries is both desirable and inevitable, it is preferable to effect such a change by a programmed, negotiating process, and institutional arrangements should be sought to assist in bringing about the change. It is understandable that a planned economy with a state monopoly of foreign trade and a centrally steered allocative process could hardly lend itself to multilateral solutions of specialisation problems based upon the free play of market forces. The same applies to those developing countries that effectively programme their economic development. Neither group can afford to expose itself to an unrestricted elemental influence of the external environment that might seriously affect the implementation of development objectives. That is why the centrally planned economy lends itself rather to a bilateral regulation of international specialisation and investment (35) that corresponds better to the planned nature of the allocative process.

Therefore, institutional arrangements that would bring about a planned change in international specialisation should take the form of long-term bilateral agreements. It is difficult at this stage to dwell more extensively upon the proper patterns of such agreements. They should, nevertheless, be sufficiently elastic to respond to shifts in the intersectoral division of labour, through intermediary stages, up to intra-product specialisation in the pattern of production of components. In line with this sequence, specific institutional arrangements might evolve. Some of them would entail government-to-government cooperation like the coordination of long-term plans or investment programmes or agreements on specialisation in specific industrial branches. Others might be built at an operational level and include industrial cooperation, subcontracting, cooperation in third markets, etc. The specific form of institutional arrangements would reflect not only the pattern of expected international specialisation but also the degree of governmental intervention in the economic process in the cooperating countries (36).

Such forms of specialisation arrangements could also constitute a viable alternative to straightforward resource transfers. If we can agree that the foreign exchange gap represents a more obvious barrier to economic development than the savings gap, the former being to a greater extent beyond the influence and control of domestic policies in LDCs, we come to the conclusion that the establishment of a mechanism allowing for an expansion of non-traditional exports from developing countries (and thus narrowing the foreign exchange gap) can perform to some extent a similar function to a pure transfer.

At the same time, programmed adjustment would assist in resolving the contradiction between the reluctance to create surplus capacities and the need for specialisation in production and trade. It would, however, necessitate the overcoming of several objective and subjective difficulties that stand in the way of a long-term programming of mutual adjustments in export specialisation – difficulties both for CMEA and the LDCs (37). Not the least important among them are systemic ones, including the inward-looking mentality of the economic administrations, shaped by the historical process of the development of socialist economies, and reflecting the practice of structuring the economy in conformity with internal needs only (38).

The programmed adjustment arrangements would not immediately apply to all developing countries. For a number of them, the old pattern of trade will prevail for a longer period. In relations with the more advanced developing countries, that represent a bigger economic potential and are principal trade partners of the CMEA countries (39), such an adjustment is, however, in the offing. Since these countries represent the bulk of the present-day CMEA trade with the Third World this will determine the overall picture.

The interest of the CMEA in economic links with developing countries goes beyond bilateral trade relations and extends to multilateral efforts aiming at a change in the structure of international economic relations. European socialist countries, that did not take part in establishing the rules of the game governing the old economic order and have not acquired the place in international exchanges commensurate with the change in their economic potential and structures, are – naturally – in favour of restructuring the world economy so as to take into account their legitimate interests. They consider that these interests coincide in principle with those of developing countries in the North-South dialogue (40). It is, therefore, imperative for them to convince developing countries that the restructuring of international economic relations, if it is to be successful, must encompass international economic interaction in all its aspects, and that both developing and CMEA countries are in the same boat in this exercise (41).

The CMEA countries perceive their interest in strengthening links with LDCs not only in the context of the drive for a New International Economic Order but also in the development of multilateral interaction in other spheres, including trade and industrial cooperation (42). It would be beneficial for them, and, obviously, for the international economy as a whole, if trade and economic relations between East, West and South were not compartmentalised but should emerge as a system of communicating vessels with each side contributing, within its possibilities, to the expansion of these relations.

References

(1) For convenience, UN data for the Socialist Countries of Eastern Europe are taken to represent the CMEA trade, which seems to be a reasonable approximation.

(2) Distance and transport costs, dispersion of markets, knowledge of markets and business practices, jurisdiction, languages etc. Cf., Adam Broner, "The degree of autarchy in centrally planned economies," *Kyklos,* Vol. 29, Fasc. 3, 1976, p. 481. This seems to be confirmed by the part played by developing countries in trade of European DMECs in a similar position (historically and geographically), e.g. Scandinavian countries, Austria, etc.

(3) Cf., Richard Portes, "Est, Ouest, et Sud: le rôle des économies centralement planifées dans l'économie internationale," *Revue d'études comparatives Est-Ouest,* Vol. 10, No. 3, 1979, p. 62.

(4) Cf., Zbigniew M. Fallenbuchl, "Les changements récents dans la structure industrielle et leur impact sur le potentiel d'exportation des pays du CAEM dans le commerce Est-Ouest", *Revue d'études comparatives Est-Ouest,* Vol. 10, No. 4, 1979, p. 98.

(5) Cf., R. Portes, op. cit., pp. 39-40. Portes points to the fact that while in the intra-CMEA trade there exists a competitive trade pattern, typical for the modern international division of labour, the extra-CMEA trade reflects a complementary type of international specialisation.

(6) The USSR share in the overall trade of the European CMEA countries in 1978 amounted to 43.8 per cent in exports and 40.4 per cent in imports and was considerably lower than its share in trade with developing countries. (Based on data from: SEV, *Statisticheski Yezhegodnik Stran-Chlenov Sovieta Ekonomicheskoy Vzaimopomoshchi,* 1979, Moscow, p. 371.)

(7) Cf., A. Köves, "Socialist economy and world economy", *Acta Oeconomica*, Budapest, Vol. 21, No.4, 1978, p. 300.

(8) Cf., A. Broner, op. cit., pp. 488-489.

(9) Cf., Leon Zevin and Grigoriy Prokhorov, "Ekonomicheskoye sotrudnichestvo socialisticheskikh i razvivaiushchikhsia stran: problemy i perspektivy", *Obshchestviennye Nauki*, No. 4, 1977, p. 77; and G. Prokhorov, "Proizvodstviennaya kooperaciya stran SEV s razvivaiushchimisia gosudarstvami", *Voprosy Ekonomiki*, No. 11, 1979, p. 85.

(10) Cf., O. Bogomolov, "Strany SEV i razvivaiushchiyesia gosudarstva", *Miezhdunarodnaya Zhizn*, No. 6, 1979, p. 29.

(11) M. Kalecki first turned attention to this difference in "Theories of growth in different social systems", *Scientia,* Milano, Vol. VC, No. DCXCVII-DCXCVIII, V-VI-1970, esp. pp. 315-316.

(12) It does not follow that excess capacities do not appear in the socialist or developing countries. The surplus capacity is caused, however, in this case not so much by the lack of effective demand but, as a rule, by bottlenecks in the supply of production inputs, transportation, or deficiencies in the organisation of production. Even when there occurs a lack of effective demand as a cause of the underutilisation of capacities, it is a temporary rather than a structural phenomenon. It stems from disproportions emerging in the course of economic expansion and usually disappears with the further growth of the economy and of the welfare of the society.

(13) On the wave of contemporary criticism of the Keynesian economics some economists question nowadays the validity of the concept of demand-led economies (Cf., e.g., Victoria Curzon, "Price, Surplus Capacity and What the Tokyo Round Failed to Settle", *The World Economy*, Vol. 2, No. 3, September 1979, p. 314). While not neglecting the emergence of certain supply constraints in the economic development of Western capitalist countries, the demand-constrained pattern of the economy is far from being supplanted by the supply-constrained model, the two rather complementing than substituting for each other. (Cf., Lawrence R. Klein, "The Supply Side", *American Economic Review*, Vol. 68, No. 1, March 1978).

(14) L. R. Klein, op. cit., p. 6. Similar concepts were presented in: Lloyd G. Reynolds, "Capitalism: Myths and Misunderstandings", *Economic Impact*, No. 1/25/, 1979, pp. 57-58.

(15) J. Kornai, "Resource-constrained versus demand-constrained systems", *Econometrica*, Vol. 47, No. 4, July 1979.

(16) G. R. Feiwel, "On the economic realities of socialism: high pressure economy and reform", *Economia Internazionale*, Genoa, Vol. XXXII, No. 1, Febbraio 1979.

(17) The same process as perceived by developing countries was highlighted in Jahangir Amuzegar, "International growth, equity, and efficiency", *Finance and Development*, Vol. 15, No. 1, March 1978.

(18) J. Kornai, e.g., points to the two-sided nature of the shortage situation — beneficial (no unutilised capital, full employment) and detrimental. He also analyses certain properties of the economic mechanism at a micro level that constantly reproduces shortages (op. cit., p. 802 passim). Cf. also M. Fallenbuchl, op. cit., p. 95.

(19) This resembles the "siphoning-off" effect described by Kornai (op. cit., pp. 815-816) with respect to various domestic demand pressures, but in this case growth of domestic demand might limit the exportable surplus.

(20) O. Bogomolov pointed to the inflow of foreign credit as an important manifestation of the role economic links with abroad play in the Soviet economy (Cf., O. Bogomolov, "O vnieshnie-ekonomicheskikh sviaziakh SSSR", *Kommunist*, No. 5, 1974, p. 91).

(21) Michal Kalecki and Ignacy Sachs, "Forms of foreign aid: an economic analysis", *Social Sciences Information*, International Social Science Council, Paris, Vol. V — 1, March 1966, p. 3. Similar views on foreign aid can be found in: Georgiy Skorov, "Kryzys gospodarczy a kraje rozwijające się", *'Problemy Pokoju i Socjalizmu*, Warsaw, No. 11, 1978, pp. 114-115.

(22) Cf. the declaration of the USSR Government in the United Nations: "O pierestroykie miezh-dunarodnikh ekonomicheskikh otnoshenii", *Vneshnaya Torgovla* No. 1, 1977, p. 6.

(23) O. Bogomolov stresses that function of economic assistance (Cf., Strany SEV, op. cit., p. 32).

(24) Cf., Elisabeth Kriedl Valkenier, "The USSR, the Third World, and the Global Economy", *Problems of Communism*, July-August 1979, p. 32 and Sandor Uvardi, "Vklad VNR v razvitiye ekonomicheskikh otnoshenii stran-chlenov SEV s razvivaiushchimisia stranami", *Ekonomicheskoye Sotrudnichestvo Stran-Chlenov SEV*, Moscow, No. 5, 1978, p. 76. That might in part explain why joint ventures of socialist and developing countries are predominantly located in industry (Cf., Carl H. McMillan, "Growth of External Investment by the Comecon Countries", *The World Economy*, Vol. 2, No. 3, September 1979, p. 369).

(25) G. Prokhorov, op. cit., p. 84.

(26) At present this is the main reason for the existence of the positive balance in trade of the CMEA with developing nations (Cf., O. Bogomolov, Strany SEV, op. cit., p. 29).

(27) V.E. Gankovskiy turns attention to the role of food and other consumer goods in the CMEA imports from developing countries in his article: "SEV i razvivaiushchiyesia strany: problemy torgovo-ekonomicheskogo sotrudnichestva", *'Viestnik Moskovskogo Universiteta*, Ser. G., *Ekonomika,* No. 3, 1979, p. 40.

(28) Cf., István Dobozi, 'Problems of Raw-material Supply in Eastern Europe', *The World Economy*, Vol. 1, No. 2, January 1978, p. 219.

(29) Cf., Richard Portes, "Effets de la crise sur les pays de l'Est", *Revue Economique*, Vol. 30, No. 6, novembre 1979. J. Bognar stresses the vulnerability of some socialist countries to the abrupt changes in the external environment (Cf., "A new era in the world economy and Hungarian foreign economic strategy", *Acta Oeconomica*, Vol. 17, Nos. 3-4, 1976, p. 229).

(30) Cf., M. Paszynski, "Developing countries in the international division of labour", *Oeconomica Polona*, Vol. VI, No. 4, 1979, pp. 504-506.

(31) Cf., V.E. Gankovskiy, op. cit., p. 43.

(32) Cf., Henri Francois Henner, "Les tendences profondes du commerce international", *Problèmes Economiques*, No. 1503, 29. XII. 1976.

(33) The more dynamic growth of oil imports cannot be taken to represent trade with developing countries as a group but with a handful of them and should not, because of this and other reasons, be identified with imports of other primary commodities. In this respect I cannot share the views presented by I. Dobozi, op. cit., pp. 209-210. Cf. also E.K. Valkenier, op. cit., p. 17.

(34) G. Prokhorov stresses the emergence of a new tendency — that of concluding long-term economic cooperation agreements as means of securing stability in socialist countries' relations with developing ones (Cf., Grigoriy Prokhorov, "Sotrudnichestvo stran SEV s razvivayushchimisia stranami", *Obshchestviennye Nauki*, No. 2, 1979, p. 51).

(35) It should be once more stressed that such a bilateral approach refers to the adjustment process and does not prevent the CMEA countries from practising multilateralism in settlements in their trade with developing countries (where multilateral forms of settlement are rapidly expanding). Therefore, I could not agree with Kostecki's contention that central planning necessarily entails bilateralism in commercial policy (Cf., Maciej Kostecki, "L'U.R.S.S. face au système de commerce multilatéral", *Revue d'études comparatives Est-Ouest*, Vol. 10, No. 3, Sep. 1979, p. 80).

(36) I have presented my views on this issue in "Economic relations between socialist and developing countries in the changing world" published in: I. Dobozi (ed.), Economic Cooperation Between Socialist and Developing Countries, *Trends in World Economy*, Budapest, No. 25, 1978. Cf. also, T. Szentes, "A few thoughts on the problem of Hungarian cooperation with developing countries", *Acta Oeconomica*, Vol. 17, No. 2, 1976, pp. 151-152.

(37) For a more detailed exposition see: M. Paszynski, "Economic Relations ...", op. cit.

(38) Cf., J. Bognár, op. cit., p 232.

(39) Cf., O. Bogomolov, Strany SEV, op. cit., p. 34.

(40) Cf., O pierestroykie, op. cit., pp. 3-4.

(41) Cf., A. Manzhulo and G. Krasnov, "Miezhdunarodniy forum po torgovo-ekonomicheskim problemam (K itogam V sessii UNKTAD)", *Vneshnaya Torgovla*, No. 9, 1979.

(42) Cf., E.K. Valkenier, op. cit., p. 26. But note opposite view of M. Fallenbuchl, op. cit., p. 98.

Chapter 3

PROSPECTS OF ECONOMIC COOPERATION BETWEEN CMEA COUNTRIES AND DEVELOPING COUNTRIES (1)

István Dobozi*
András Inotai*

This paper provides an overview of the present state and anticipated future trends of economic cooperation between the European CMEA countries (2) and the developing countries. Starting with an analysis of the international political and economic environment influencing the economic interaction of the two groups of countries, the paper reviews the major general, sectoral and institutional issues of economic cooperation. The conclusion is a forecast of trade for the 1980s, a quantified summary of tendencies disclosed in the foregoing.

International politics and international economic relations

The prospects of economic cooperation outlined in this study are based on the expectation that the atmosphere of international politics in the 1980s will be milder than in early 1980. Détente (which is not incompatible with competition between East and West) is indispensable for creating the confidence necessary for a long-term international division of labour, for the taking of reasonable risks, for the avoidance of autarkic measures in the economies. An atmosphere of cold war would hamper not only the relations between the developing and the CMEA countries, but also the overall interests of Third World development: it would hardly be possible to implement the plans for the 1980s in a world embarking on an extremely costly and escalating arms race.

In the interplay of most developing countries with the European CMEA countries, political relations were apt in the 1970s to further economic relations. We expect developments in this sphere to remain propitious also in the 1980s. If international détente were to contribute a favourable background, this would be advantageous for trade, for economic cooperation, and especially for the joint realisation of great projects embodying important mutual interests. In turn, an intensification of the international division of labour between the two groups of countries, in the awareness that the other party will also gain in support and expansion by a feedback mechanism acting upon mutual relations, would tend to strengthen the political ties between the two groups of countries.

* Institute for World Economics of the Hungarian Academy of Sciences, Budapest

In addition to development and structural transformations taking place in developing and CMEA countries, the economic interaction between the two groups of countries is influenced strongly by the international economic environment. The world economic activity of the European CMEA countries, including their relations with the developing countries, will be influenced strongly by the tempo and trends of further development of CMEA integration. An acceleration of production specialisation and a further progress in the institutions for economic cooperation may favourably affect cooperation with the developing countries. Having outgrown the extensive model of development (meaning the exhaustion of the driving forces behind that model and the necessity of replacing them by others), most of the CMEA countries have entered upon a phase of growth where foreign economic relations have acquired a momentous importance for them, their merging into the international division of labour being an essential precondition for the improvement of their economies' efficiency and viability.

The economic situation and policies of the developed market-economy countries may affect the economic relations between the developing and the European CMEA countries in a variety of ways. The two groups of developed countries tend to meet as competitors on the markets of the developing countries but, in quite a few instances, they have participated as cooperating partners with complementary deliveries to given projects. On the other hand, the developing countries and the European CMEA countries meet on an increasing scale as competing suppliers of manufactures on the markets of the developed market economies. To foresee such situations of interdependence and the indirect effects on the relations of the developing countries with the European CMEA countries may help to mitigate or, indeed, to eliminate possible conflicts of interests. Two approaches present themselves. The first and more important is the modification of production patterns in the European CMEA countries towards higher-technology goods satisfying a more sophisticated demand, with a view to letting the two groups of countries offer different ranges of export goods on the world market. The second is the reinforcement of cooperation and coordination in production and marketing between the two groups of countries.

The pioneering grand conception of the New International Economic Order envisages no less than the transformation of international interdependence. It includes principles and conclusions affecting also the relations between the Third World and the European CMEA countries.

The economic relations between the developing and the CMEA countries are determined by the pattern of their interests, in the broader sense of the term. This interpretation does not confine the concept of 'interest' to immediate economic interests; it regards economic aims as a part of societal aims, and embodies the relations between the two groups of countries in the context of world-wide issues.

Both for the European CMEA countries and the developing countries, the intensification of the international division of labour is an important growth-promoting factor. This is the basic common interest on which is predicated the importance of expanding the relations between the two groups of countries. The radical transformations in the world economy in the 1970s, and their internal economic development trends, modified the interest pattern of the two groups of countries so that each has found the economic relations with the other more important than before.

Trade relations between the European CMEA countries and the developing countries in the 1970s

Trade between the two groups in the 1970s increased at a faster rate than either world trade as a whole or the European CMEA countries' trade overall. The developing countries' share of the European CMEA countries' exports was 13.2 per cent in 1970 and 14.7 per cent in 1978, with a fourfold increase in value; their share in the European CMEA countries' imports increased from 9.7 to 10.0 per cent over the same period, corresponding to a fourfold increase in value (see *Table 3.1*).

Trade between the two groups of countries was characterised by a persistent and comparatively high surplus of the European CMEA countries, which further increased somewhat between 1970 and 1978.

Changes in the geography of trade were determined by the differing possibilities of increasing the exports of the European CMEA countries, on the one hand, and by the European CMEA countries' purchases of raw materials, food and tropical produce and animal feed, on the other. The most important novel element is an increase in the importance of the Middle East and of North Africa, for the time being, in the exports of the European CMEA countries above all, but in the last few years also in their imports, as a result of increasing purchases of petroleum. Trade with the developing world is concentrated in most of the European CMEA countries on a few key countries, among which only India and Brazil rank high in addition to the countries of the Middle East and North Africa.

As a result of a commodity pattern evolved over the last 15 years or so, the main exports by the European CMEA countries are engineering goods, making up more than 40 per cent of total exports to the developing countries. (See *Table 3.2*) Their value doubled between 1973 and 1977, yet could not keep abreast of the worldwide expansion of trade in engineering products. Within engineering imports by the developing countries overall, the share of the European CMEA countries actually declined, owing in part to changes in some key markets and partly to the fact that the engineering exporters of the European CMEA were not sufficiently successful in penetrating the most dynamically growing import markets of the developing world, Latin America and Southeast Asia. In exports as a whole, industrial consumer goods amounted to some

20 per cent, agricultural goods to about 11 per cent and fuels – boosted by the explosion of prices – to about 12 per cent. Around half of the imports by the European CMEA countries from the developing countries were made up of food, feed and raw materials of agricultural origin, and about 20 per cent each of minerals and fuels. Partly as a result of the price shifts, the share of manufactures declined from 16.8 per cent in 1973 to 11.3 per cent in 1977.

Table 3.1

Trade between the developing countries and the European CMEA countries (a)

	1970	1973	1975	1976	1977	1978
Exports by the European CMEA, $ million						
total	30523	52253	77358	84110	98883	114160
to the developing world	4028	6713	10231	10859	14652	16780
developing-world percentage	13.2	12.8	13.2	12.9	14.8	14.7
Imports by the European CMEA, $ million (b)						
total	28614	50554	82588	87048	95845	111870
from the developing world	2783	4185	9117	9494	10221	11140
developing-world percentage	9.7	8.3	11.0	10.9	10.7	10.0
The European CMEA countries' percentage share of						
– world exports	10.0	9.3	8.9	8.5	8.8	8.7
– world imports	9.7	9.6	9.5	8.8	8.5	8.7
The developing countries' percentage share of						
– world exports	17.7	19.2	24.2	25.8	25.7	23.4
– world imports	17.3	16.9	23.0	22.1	23.0	23.1
World trade percentage share of trade between the developing and the European CMEA countries (c)						
– world exports	1.3	1.2	1.2	1.1	1.3	1.3
– world imports	0.9	0.9	1.0	1.0	0.9	0.9

(a) In keeping with the statistical breakdown used by the UN, the aggregate figures for the developing countries include Turkey and Cuba. Leaving out Cuba, the European CMEA's exports to the developing world are reduced by 15 to 20 per cent, their imports from the developing world by some 25 per cent, which accordingly reduces the aggregate indices presented by 2 to 2.5 percentage points.

(b) Calculated from exports to CMEA.

(c) Derived from the European CMEA countries' exports to and imports from the developing world.

Source: United Nations, *Monthly Bulletin of Statistics,* June 1979 and United Nations, *Yearbook of International Trade Statistics* (data for 1970 and 1973).

Experiences and trends of cooperation in manufacturing

In the evolution so far, it was in manufacturing that the closest ties came to exist between the European CMEA countries and the developing countries. Profiting by their experience in industrialisation and by the industrial structures developed historically, the individual European CMEA countries took an active part in the industrialisation of many a developing country (particularly in power generation and heavy industry, in the development, extraction and processing of raw materials, in engineering, electrical engineering and several branches of light industry).

The specific features of industrial cooperation in the 1980s will be determined by certain processes in the world economy which have emerged in no uncertain fashion in the last decade. Among these are the accelerated structural transformation of the world economy, the increased developmental role of technology, the changing domestic economic environment of CMEA countries (growing shortage of labour, hardening conditions for satisfying incremental demand in raw materials), a significant progress in industrialisation in the developing countries, etc.

In future, just as in the past, the European CMEA countries will regard accelerated modernisation, rather than the redeployment of declining branches of industry, in the developing countries as the principal area of industrial cooperation. The demand of the developing countries for complex, system-oriented industrial cooperation is expected to increase. Besides that, however, increased attention will have to be paid to cooperation with viable small- and medium-scale industries. All this will affect the fields and forms, the choice of the most appropriate technology, etc. The areas of industrial development achieved in the past will persist, but the focus of cooperation will be displaced towards industrial activities connected with agricultural development, geological prospecting and mining development, power generation, and the industrial division of labour connected with the development of education, health, communications and infrastructure.

In today's changing world economy, the importance of relations between industries will grow for the European CMEA countries on the import as well as on the export side. These countries, now in the process of modernising their industrial structures, will offer markets of greater absorptive capacities than today to the developing countries implementing programmes of export-oriented industrial development. At the same time, opportunities will arise in certain fields for the coordination of industrial development and occasionally for joint action on markets where the developing and European CMEA countries, with their similar supply of industrial goods, are liable to affect adversely each other's positions if they act without prior coordination.

A structural development essentially complementary between the two groups of countries can be ensured also in the 1980s by maintaining a desirable rate of structural

Table 3.2

Commodity group breakdown of the European CMEA countries' exports to and imports from the developing world

	1973	1974	1975	1976	1977
Exports			million dollars		
SITC 0 + 1	576	1247	1049	888	1106
SITC 2 + 4	279	515	484	461	593
SITC 3	299	737	963	1031	1344
SITC 5	240	480	658	542	681
SITC 7	2045	2421	3167	3502	4125
SITC 6 + 8	935	1528	1558	1599	1934
Total (a)	4374	6928	7879	8023	9783
	(6844)	(8912)	(10231)	(10859)	(14652)
			percentage shares (b)		
SITC 0 + 1	13.2	18.0	13.3	11.1	11.3
SITC 2 + 4	6.4	7.4	6.1	5.7	6.1
SITC 3	5.8	10.6	12.2	12.9	13.7
SITC 5	5.5	6.9	8.4	6.8	7.0
SITC 7	46.8	34.9	40.2	43.6	42.2
SITC 6 + 8	21.4	22.1	19.8	19.9	19.8
Imports			million dollars		
SITC 0 + 1	1885	2969	4342	4311	5037
SITC 2 + 4	1207	1859	1792	1859	1927
SITC 3	654	1131	1763	2244	2095
SITC 5	60	98	139	115	127
SITC 7	27	24	51	48	34
SITC 6 + 8	673	851	993	915	997
Total (a)	4506	6932	9080	9492	10217
	(4509)	(6930)	(9117)	(9494)	(10221)
			percentage shares (b)		
SITC 0 + 1	41.8	42.8	47.6	45.4	49.3
SITC 2 + 4	26.8	26.8	19.7	19.6	18.9
SITC 3	14.5	16.3	19.3	23.6	20.5
SITC 5	1.3	1.4	1.5	1.2	1.2
SITC 7	0.6	0.3	0.6	0.5	0.3
SITC 6 + 8	14.9	12.3	10.9	9.6	9.8
Manufactures (SITC 5–8)	16.8	14.0	13.0	11.3	11.8

SITC 0 + 1 Food etc.
SITC 2 + 4 Materials
SITC 3 Fuels
SITC 5 Chemicals
SITC 7 Machinery & vehicles
SITC 6 + 8 Other manufactures

(Footnotes: see next page)

change in the European CMEA countries' economies. It is through this complementarity that direct bilateral industrial cooperation is to expand. Within it, a process already appearing in the late 1970s, by which some of the European CMEA countries will phase out the production of certain goods and satisfy their demand by imports from developing countries, will acquire a certain importance. The sphere of industries to be redeployed will, however, not be confined solely to light unskilled labour-intensive manufactures, but will include some branches of engineering and of fine chemicals with a high skilled-labour content, as well as some raw material-intensive branches.

Cooperation in raw materials supply

Although the CMEA is essentially self-sufficient in fuels and minerals, its imports from the developing countries have become fairly important. In money terms, 20 per cent of total mineral and fuel imports of the European CMEA countries came from the developing countries in 1977. The European CMEA countries have been providing significant assistance to the developing countries in the creation and/or development of their domestic mining and mineral processing.

Up to 1990, the CMEA will continue to be essentially self-sufficient in fuels and minerals. In the 1980s, however, under the influence of a number of factors (inadequacy of domestic resources, the extremely high cost of domestic resource development, the relatively high rate of growth of minerals and fuels demand, the increasing difficulties and rising costs of imports from socialist sources and the anticipated slowdown in the rate of growth of socialist imports over the long term), most of the CMEA countries are expected to push more strongly towards increasing the share of the developing countries in their total imports of fuels and minerals. According to our estimates, the European CMEA countries' import demand from the developing countries may by 1990 attain 80 to 100 million tons of petroleum, 30 to 40 thousand million cu.m of natural gas, 30 to 40 million tons of iron ore, 13 to 15 million tons of rock phosphate, bauxite and alumina equivalent to 1 to 1.5 million tons of primary aluminium, and 100,000 tons of copper.

The relative extroversion that will become necessary in the fuels and minerals procurement of the CMEA group will render indispensable the extension of cooperation in raw

(Footnotes to Table 3.2)

(a) The differences between the two rows of sums are due to the fact that no commodity-group breakdown is stated for a substantial share of Soviet exports.

(b) Percentages invariably refer to the upper row of sums (the de facto sums of the figures listed) rather than to the sums in parentheses. Percentages may not add up to 100.0 owing to rounding errors.

Sources: UN *Monthly Bulletin of Statistics.* Special Table D. May 1979.

materials and the modernisation of its mechanisms. It will be necessary to rely, to a greater extent than heretofore, on such closer and more direct forms of cooperation in production as compensation agreements, joint companies, international consortia and service agreements. Cooperation in mining demands multilateral arrangements more than in any other field. It will be necessary to establish in the European CMEA countries the conditions of motivation, organisation and crediting that are the prerequisites of wide-ranging multilateral cooperation. In developing cooperation in raw materials between the two groups of countries, the striving of the developing countries to export increasing percentages of the minerals and fuels extracted on their territory in processed form must be satisfied to the greatest possible extent. This requires the setting up of a complex vertically integrated system of cooperation which can contribute to the satisfaction of the European CMEA countries' demand for raw materials and semis in such a way as to promote at the same time also the sphere of raw materials processing in the developing countries. Complex programmes of cooperation covering the entire chain from mining to processing and manufacturing can be built on a safe marketing basis if part of the output is earmarked for satisfying the demand of CMEA countries. Under such programmes it would be possible to organize trilateral cooperation arrangements based on participation by one or more economic organisations of developing, advanced market-economy and CMEA countries. Experience has shown that the scope of optimisation inherent in the most reasonable combination of the inputs (labour, technology, capital, management, marketing, etc.) of cooperating partners can be exploited to the best advantage in complex and large-scale projects.

The future expansion of cooperation in raw materials between the two groups of countries presupposes a substantial expansion and modernisation of transportation infrastructure in both the developing and the European CMEA countries.

Facts and prospects of cooperation in agriculture

Cooperation so far between the two groups of countries in agriculture and the food industry has been fairly restricted and has not come anywhere near to exploiting the opportunities objectively existing on the side of both country groups.

In the 1970s, the most important form of relations was straight commerce, characterised by increasingly significant deliveries and involving a growing surplus of agricultural exports from the developing countries, primarily as a result of fast-expanding imports of tropical goods and animal feed by the European CMEA countries.

We expect the importance of the problems connected with agriculture and food supply to increase in the 1980s. In part because of their climatic and soil conditions, the European CMEA countries regard as the main area for strengthening agricultural cooperation many-sided contributions to the advancement of agriculture in the developing countries (by supplies of agricultural machinery and of high-yield seed grain, by the creation of food processing plants, the establishing of the required cold and conventional storage capacities, by specialised training, contributions to water resource management, etc.) rather than direct trade in agricultural goods, even though the prospects of direct trade are also highly valued by those European CMEA countries that are in favourable positions for such trade (e.g. Hungary, Bulgaria). At the same time, the markets of the European CMEA countries will demand increasing amounts of agricultural products, raw and processed, from the developing countries.

On the import side, the principal trade partners of the European CMEA countries have been the same countries for some time, and are expected to remain so in the 1980s. For reasons of geographic proximity, buying power and a substantial import-absorbing capacity, a concentration on the Middle East and North Africa is to be expected in the export of agricultural products by the European CMEA countries. Some developing countries are in turn expected to emerge as exporters on some of the markets where the European CMEA countries are holding strong positions. This may require the strengthening of agricultural cooperation in the field of marketing also.

One viable opportunity would be a wide-ranging multilateral cooperation in the exchange of feed for meat, an undertaking that would fit the existing conditions on both sides: the substantial surplus of animal feed in certain developing countries, the large-scale animal husbandry programmes embarked on by some of the European CMEA countries and the growing demand for animal products in a number of developing countries.

An evolution toward a complex type of cooperation (that is, the extension of cooperation to spheres and branches that are not directly agricultural but connected with agrarian development, such as processing, regional planning, rural development, storage capacities, joint marketing, specialised training, etc.) is bound to gain in importance. The European CMEA countries are expected to expand their cooperation in the 1980s especially with those developing countries whose climatic conditions do not differ too much from their own (temperate-zone, Mediterranean and subtropical cultures).

Issues of technology transfer

Over the past 15 years or so, technology transfer was one of the elements of outstanding dynamism in cooperation between the two groups of countries. The complementarity of economic conditions in this respect was one of the prime movers of technology transfer. Increasingly purposeful efforts are being made by the European CMEA countries towards an integrated, system-oriented type of technology transfer. This envisages the creation of national development centres able to generate integrative intersectoral linkages and to promote a higher degree of technological and economic integration within the developing economy.

It is suggested that scientific-technological cooperation between the two groups of countries should be further developed in the following principal directions. (a) A faster increase than in the past decade of exports of high-technology goods from the European CMEA countries to the developing countries. (b) On the basis of favourable past experience, the mechanisms of the integrated transfer of technology should be relied on more extensively and intensively than heretofore. (c) The elimination of the 'information gap' which especially hampers technology transfer. (d) The flow of technology into the developing countries would be greatly accelerated by a substantial increase in the number, comparatively restricted today, of tripartite cooperation agreements. (e) Within technology transfer to the developing countries, the share of intangible items should be increased (at present, project and engineering designs, consulting engineering and the transfer of licences and know-how are rather restricted). (f) In scientific-technological cooperation, the elimination of the technological bottlenecks connected with specific problems and requirements of economic growth in the developing countries is to be given more emphasis. The development priorities of a majority of developing countries indicate the need to perform R & D adapted to the specific conditions of those countries in the following areas above all: food production in agriculture and fishing, the search for energy sources and research into energy, technology for handicrafts and small-scale trades, control of environmental pollution, water supply and regulation, reclaiming of arid and semi-arid regions, control of illnesses and epidemics, meteorology, protective measures and emergency warning systems. (g) It is a mutual interest to increase the number of specialists sent from the European CMEA countries to the developing countries. In an international comparison, the two groups of countries have so far exploited only to a limited extent the opportunities of technical assistance inherent in the sending of specialists. (h) In education and training, significant structural-qualitative changes will be needed in the future, in addition to a quantitative expansion. The developing countries will increasingly strive for cooperation in education to involve special training rather than general education. In university education, the enhancement of postgraduate studies and of the practice-oriented disciplines is desirable.

Trade policy instruments and the institutions of economic cooperation

The set of trade policy instruments of the European CMEA countries underwent some significant changes in the 1970s. Early in that period, most of the CMEA countries introduced tariff systems granting preferential treatment to the developing countries. Most of the products purchased in the developing countries enjoy substantial non-reciprocal tariff preferences; indeed, in several countries, a number of products or product groups purchased in the developing countries are tariff-free.

An important institutional feature of economic cooperation between the two groups of countries is the direct, active participation of the respective governments in defining the sphere of cooperation and in regulating and controlling the implementation of programmes. This is embodied above all in intergovernmental economic, trade, industrial and scientific-technological agreements and in the creation and operation of joint intergovernmental commissions. Joint intergovernmental commissions play a decisive role in the preparation of medium and long-term intergovernmental economic and scientific-technological agreements that are gaining increasing importance nowadays between the developing and the European CMEA countries and are helpful in identifying the long-term scope, contents and trends of economic relations between them and in regulating their implementation. On the basis of experience collected so far, the operation of the joint intergovernmental commissions is favourably looked on by both groups of countries. In the sphere of institutional ties at the non-governmental level, chambers of commerce play a prominent role in promoting cooperation. Agreements on multilateral cooperation between the CMEA as such and certain developing countries (Iraq, Mexico) are novel among the institutional mechanisms of economic cooperation between the two groups of countries.

Modernising the institutional mechanisms of economic cooperation between the two groups of countries is an indispensable prerequisite to elevating economic cooperation to a higher level. In a situation of growing world economic instability, comprehensive long-term agreements must be relied on increasingly as elements of stability in the international division of labour. The conclusion of such agreements is to be sought in those areas where none exists as yet. The scope of the agreements is to be expanded to include such essential areas as planning and policy coordination and long-term division of labour at the branch and intra-branch level. It is desirable to extend the time horizon of the agreements to 10, 15 and even 20 years in those relations where agreements of much shorter range are the rule today. It is necessary to strengthen the role of the joint intergovernmental commissions, and to increase the efficiency of their operation. In the commissions, more emphasis than is usual nowadays is to be placed on the practical implementation of the agreements.

The contributions by the various non-governmental organisations must be relied on more than today in the furthering of economic relations between the two groups of countries. It is desirable to make efforts in future towards a broader application of multilateral institutional mechanisms. An issue to be given some thought for the longer term is the conclusion of treaties of association between the CMEA and certain interested developing countries.

Relying on the above-mentioned institutional mechanisms, it is important to strive for the elimination of the presently existing 'information gap' between the developing and the European CMEA countries.

Cooperation in planning

Cooperation in planning is an essential and distinctive feature of economic cooperation between the two groups of countries. It is realised in two basic forms: (a) a variety of forms of assistance by the European CMEA countries in the creation of national planning systems in the developing countries and in the elaboration of macro-level plans; (b) coordination of the national-economy plans and development programmes of the developing and the European CMEA countries with a view to a structural adaptation to each other's long-term needs. Today, the form of cooperation under (a) is still predominant in planning cooperation between the two groups of countries. Such cooperation has unfolded in the following main directions: the creation or improvement of bases of information and methodology for national planning, participation in the elaboration of the developing countries' national-economy plans, the secondment and/or training of planning specialists.

Plan coordination, as the second form of cooperation, is encountered only occasionally as yet in economic cooperation between the two groups of countries. There are, however, numerous essential arguments for the partial or full-scope coordination of plans and developments strategies, which may acquire an important role in the future long-term shaping of the division of labour between the CMEA countries and the developing countries maintaining extensive economic relations with them and also possessing appropriate development plans. The arguments in question include the growing malfunctions of the world economy, the need to prevent the coming into existence of large-scale parallel export-oriented productive capacities harmful to the interests of both groups of countries, the necessity to exploit more purposefully the opportunities of cooperation inherent in the economic complementarity of the two groups of countries. The conditions are maturing both in the European CMEA countries and in the developing countries maintaining extensive economic relations with them for the establishing of a coordinated division of labour, permitting the mutual realisation of the comparative advantages of both by deliberate efforts on both sides to adapt to each other's long-term needs.

Plan coordination can most expediently be concentrated on those branches or product groups where familiarity with the other party's long-term demand and supply orientation and investment ambitions is most likely to promote the long-term division of labour. Cooperation in planning is presently being hampered by differences in the time horizons of planning in different countries, so that it seems reasonable to strive for their harmonisation. A harmonisation of planning time horizons would, in all probability, result in a more direct incorporation into the development plans of the agreed tasks of cooperation. The spreading practice of long-term comprehensive economic, scientific and technological cooperation agreements creates favourable conditions for establishing partial coordination in production and investment.

A rational division of labour, based on a partial form of plan coordination, would substantially contribute to the strengthening of the world economic positions of both groups, to the injection of a greater stability into their mutual economic ties, to the avoidance of undesirable economic competition between them, to a more advantageous exploitation of their existing economic complementarity and, in the final reckoning, to a more rational allocation of the economic resources of both groups of countries.

Problems of inter-firm cooperation

The CMEA countries have so far participated in some 2700 projects, industrial and other, in 78 developing countries, largely under bilateral agreements. Individual large-scale investment projects play key roles in cooperation. A large number of assembly plants has also been constructed. In many cases, part of the output of the plant created in the developing country is purchased by the European CMEA partner under a buy-back deal. More developed forms of cooperation such as production sharing and production combined with technology transfer also came into being.

In recent years, changes in the world economy and the processes unfolding in the European CMEA countries have modified the outlook concerning joint companies of developing and CMEA countries. While taking care to guard the fundamental interests of the developing partners, the requirements concerning profitability and efficiency of production and marketing have been enhanced. Joint ventures and the establishment of companies in the developing countries with equity participation by the European CMEA countries are fairly small-scale as yet. The individual European CMEA countries have different attitudes to this form of cooperation, which is expected to gain ground in the 1980s.

The 1970s saw the emergence of the first instances of tripartite cooperation, in step with the increasing development demand of the developing countries and, not least, as a result of East-West cooperation. More recently, some of the more industrialised developing countries have also emerged as partners to the European CMEA countries' enterprises in third, mostly developing, countries. The existing information suggests that tripartite industrial cooperation will continue to enjoy popularity among the various forms of cooperation.

A forecast of trade between the European CMEA countries and the developing countries up to 1990

Our forecast — which, of course, is fraught with all the incertitudes of any long-term forecast — has for its anchor points the expected growth trends of the two groups of countries and the information available — unsatisfactory both as to quality and quantity — on the future of trade between them.

We started from the assumption that the factors promoting trade between the two country groups will gain the upper hand, and that it will be possible over the years to come to eliminate or at least substantially mitigate the obstacles that do exist. For lack of comprehensive data (plans, official forecasts), we had to make up our forecast out of an incomplete set of building blocks (information published in the special literature of the individual European CMEA countries or acquired in the course of consultations). The indicator which could be secured most often was the share that the developing countries are expected to have of the European CMEA countries' exports and imports in the late 1980s. It is from these, and from the annual average growth rates of the European CMEA countries' foreign trade, that we calculated our volume forecasts stated in *Table 3.3.* We took the basic stance that the European CMEA countries will by 1990 either have managed to eliminate their current trade account deficits or that those deficits will not increase (their aggregate debt will either 'get frozen' at the 1978 level or increase but slightly). Of course, this view presupposes, firstly, that the changes necessary to prompt a significant expansion of their export potential will in fact take place and, secondly, that the world economic (world trade) situation will get better rather than worse.

The figures reflect the expected tendency that, up to 1990, the European CMEA countries' trade with the developing countries will increase faster than their foreign trade overall. The difference will be more significant in the European CMEA countries' imports than in their exports. For the European CMEA as a whole, the share of the developing countries in their exports may increase up to 1990 by 2 to 4 points (to 14.5 - 16.5 per cent) from the 12.2 per cent in 1978. Over the same period, the developing-country share of their imports, only 7.6 per cent in 1978, may well double (to 15 per cent) under the impact of enhanced imports of both raw materials and manufactures.

One of the essential changes in trade between the two groups of countries will be that, by 1990, the surplus of the European CMEA countries will disappear. This shift in trade balance is bound to modify the view, widespread enough in the European CMEA in the 1970s, that the surplus of trade with the developing countries is to be used to reduce the trade deficit with the developed market-economy countries.

The expected commodity structure of trade, which in its turn has a bearing on trade volume, merits a more detailed analysis. (*Table 3.4*). The extra-CMEA petroleum imports of the European CMEA group will probably reach $ 21.2 to $ 26.5 billion in 1990 (in 1977 dollars). Even assuming that part of this total will come through West European middlemen (Rotterdam), the value of petroleum bought direct from the developing countries is hardly likely to be less than some $ 15 to 20 billion, implying that, of the total imports worth $ 41 to 49 billion forecast for 1990, petroleum will make up one-third at best, one-half at worst (as against 20 per cent of $ 2 billion in 1977). In other words, of an import increment of $ 32 - 40 billion, $ 13 - 18 billion is to be taken up by petroleum, which rather restricts the prospects for other imports. If

Table 3.3

Forecast of trade between the developing countries and the European CMEA countries up to 1990

	Value, $ thousand million				Average growth, per cent per year		Share of developing countries per cent	
	total		developing		total	developing		
EXPORTS	1978	1990	1978	1990	1978-90		1978	1990
Bulgaria	7.4	16.8	0.71	2.0	7	9	9.5	12
Czechoslovakia	11.7	29.5–36.8	0.93	3.0–3.7	8.0–10	10–13	7.9	10
GDR	13.3	30.0–33.4	0.64	2.1–3.3	7–8	10.5–14.5	4.8	7–10
Hungary	6.3	20.0–22.2	0.55	2.4–2.9	10–11	13–15	8.7	12–13
Poland	13.5	37.9–42.2	1.12	4.7–6.1	9–10	12–13	8.3	12–14
Romania	8.0	22.5–25.1	1.58	5.6–7.5	9–10	11–14	20.0	25–30
Soviet Union	52.2	118.2	8.24	20.4–23.2	7	8–9	15.8	17–20
European CMEA	112.4	274.9–294.7	13.77	40.2–48.7	8–8.5	9.5–11	12.2	14.5–16.5
IMPORTS								
Bulgaria	7.6	17	0.31	2.1	7	17	4.3	12.5
Czechoslovakia	12.6	29–35	0.58	2.8–3.5	7–9	14–16	4.6	9.5–10
GDR	14.6	31–35	0.73	2.5–3.5	6.5–7.5	11–14	5.0	8–10
Hungary	7.9	20–25	0.76	2.5–3.0	8–10	10.5–12	9.6	12–13
Poland	15.3	40–45	0.90	5.5–6.5	8.5–9.5	16–18	5.9	14–15
Romania	8.0	20–25	1.44	6–7.5	8–10	12.5–15	18.0	30
Soviet Union	50.5	118–109	4.04	20–23	7.5–6.5	14–15.5	8.0	18–20
European CMEA	116.5	275–291	8.76	41.4–49.1	7.5–8	14–15.5	7.6	15–17

Source: Author's estimates based on various issues of the UN *Monthly Bulletin of Statistics,* on national statistics, oral information and consultations.

Table 3.4

Forecast of the commodity structure of trade between the developing countries and the European CMEA countries in 1990

(in per cent)

<table>
<tr><th></th><th colspan="2">Exports</th><th colspan="2">Imports</th></tr>
<tr><th></th><th colspan="4">by the European CMEA countries</th></tr>
<tr><th></th><th>1977</th><th>1990</th><th>1977</th><th>1990</th></tr>
<tr><td>SITC 0+1 Food etc.</td><td>11.3</td><td>10</td><td>49.3</td><td>20 – 25</td></tr>
<tr><td>SITC 2+4 Materials</td><td>6.1</td><td rowspan="2">10</td><td>18.9</td><td>10 – 12</td></tr>
<tr><td>SITC 3 Fuels</td><td>13.7</td><td>20.5</td><td>35 – 45</td></tr>
<tr><td>SITC 5+6+8 Other manufactures</td><td>26.8</td><td>25</td><td>11.0</td><td rowspan="2">20 – 25</td></tr>
<tr><td>SITC 7 Machinery & vehicles</td><td>42.2</td><td>55</td><td>0.3</td></tr>
</table>

Sources: For 1977: UN *Monthly Bulletin of Statistics,* Special Table D. May 1979. For 1990: Author's estimates

we make the likely assumption that the share of manufactures will also increase, we must infer a substantial reduction in the share of other products (other raw materials and products of agricultural origin).

What countervalue can be offered in payment for the imports? The European CMEA countries envisage – in keeping with their practice so far, only more so – that their exports of machinery and equipment and, more specifically, the exports of complex plants within that group will be the main vehicles of their exports. This fits the evolution of demand in the developing countries, and parallels the strivings of the developed market-economy countries in the late 1970s (one-third of whose deliveries to the developing countries consisted of complete plants).

In view of the above, we have forecast a growing share of engineering exports in the total exports of the European CMEA countries, at the expense, almost in full, of raw materials exports.

All this boils down to the finding that the European CMEA countries' engineering exports are to be increased from $ 4 billions' worth in 1977 to $ 22 - 27 billions' worth in 1990. We see the satisfaction or otherwise of this criterion as the greatest question mark against both the dynamic growth and the balance of trade with the developing countries.

Engineering exports in the 1970s chalked up a dynamic growth but, at the same time, also suffered a loss of position in international competition. Achieving the required export volumes is contingent, among other things, on the following:

- Rapid modernisation of the European CMEA countries' economies.
- An export-oriented development policy which regards the creation of the required exportable goods base as a high-priority task.
- Establishment of an adequate organisation (mechanism) in the domestic economies, clearly setting out the roles of prime suppliers and subcontractors.
- A permanent presence on external markets; a rapid elimination of the problems bedevilling the after-sales servicing of, and spares supplies to, products sold abroad.
- An enhanced exploitation of chances of multilateral cooperation (of the advantages both of intra-CMEA specialisation and of cooperation with companies of the developed market-economy countries and with partners in the developing countries).
- Adaptation to the needs of (the right choice of partners in) the developing countries.
- Preference for the forms of cooperation most likely to generate exports.

Based on fairly optimistic assumptions, our forecast supposes that it is not inconceivable for the European CMEA countries to pay for their petroleum imports by their engineering exports. Instances of such and similar forms of compensation were frequent and manifold in past practice and will presumably remain so in future.

To sum up, the following major conclusions can be drawn:

(a) Trade between the European CMEA countries and the developing countries will grow about twice as fast up to 1990 as world trade overall, and significantly faster even than the overall trade of the European CMEA countries.

(b) The trade balance surplus of the European CMEA countries vis-à-vis the developing countries, well-nigh traditional by now, will disappear. The account will be balanced at best.

(c) Balancing the trade requires two things:

- raw materials purchases, petroleum purchases above all, should remain near the lower limit of the forecast range, or possibly below it;
- engineering exports by the European CMEA countries should increase at the forecast rates.

(d) The dynamic evolution of relations towards a balanced or near-balanced trade will require fundamental changes which must have an essential bearing on the European CMEA countries' development policies in the 1980s (the moderation, within the bounds of the possible, of growth in raw materials imports, the 'convertibilisation' of engineering exports, the establishing of a legal-institutional-economic background for the deliveries of complex systems, an improvement in intra-CMEA cooperation, etc.).

These same requirements, in part at least, must play a significant role also in determining the future of trade and economic relations with the developed market-economy countries. If they are successfully implemented, the world economic importance of the European CMEA countries is bound to increase over the decade before us, contributing greatly to the creation of a more favourable environment also for the developing countries in their unfolding struggle for economic independence.

References

(1) This paper is based on the monograph 'Economic Relations between the European CMEA Countries and the Developing Countries and their Role in Development', UNITAR Research Project directed by Professor József Bognár, Budapest, 1980.

(2) The European CMEA countries are as follows: Bulgaria, Czechoslovakia, GDR, Hungary, Poland, Romania, Soviet Union.

Chapter 4

THE DEVELOPING COUNTRIES' INTEREST IN EAST-WEST RELATIONS

Ivo Fabinc*

We live at a time when an individual — having ample information at his disposal — is in an ever easier position to consider and discuss global problems; yet his possibilities of expressing the views of the groups he is talking about are ever diminishing. In the same way, it is difficult for him to rise — even if he wishes — above conflicting interests and to look for a synthesis if such a synthesis is even possible. Such limitations are felt even more by the author when the objects of his consideration are the developing countries, with their difficult problems of liberation and development on the one hand, and the complicated East-West relations (frequently 'non-relations'), on the other hand.

4.1 Southern attitudes

When the developing countries from the South view the North, they could be influenced by historical associations reaching far back into the period of real colonialism and similar forms of domination. Those are not, as we all know, pleasant reminiscences. The parts played therein by either side are so clear that it is unnecessary to call for evidence. The North, it suddenly appears, is no more a grey, amorphous unit and even the division into East and West is not satisfactory for a substantial disentaglement of past events. The places of countries in history have been inexorably marked.

Having said this, I would like to express my opinion that the reality of the developing countries is such a coarse one that they have no possibility, and no desire either, to be too much concerned in their practical behaviour with their past. Perhaps the expression is not a good one, but I still think that we should not attribute an almost inevitable revengefulness to the developing countries. Exceptions prove the rules. The present intense interest on the part of almost all developing countries in their own past should be understood, first of all, as an element of self-assertion of their national or state identity, and also as a way of helping them to seek roads to a better future.

For these reasons, an image of the countries of the East and of the West is essential for the developing countries, being exhibited in their present attitude and in the persuasiveness of the promises of such an attitude in the future. This does not mean that the developing countries fail to understand, or do not want to understand, the long-term tendencies (or even some laws) changing the world. They are aware that this image is

* Ekonomska faculteta Borisa Kidriča, Edvard Kardelj University, Ljubljana

not perfectly objective, and that it is formed in part by subjective influences. It is, perhaps, most important that the developing countries have endeavoured to consider, examine and assess the countries of the East and of the West, and seek to understand their behaviour.

Being aware of the simplification dictated by the theme, I would argue the thesis that the relations between East and West, (their mutual behaviour and interlinking) have been mainly a source of serious anxiety. Now and then there might appear some brighter spots, but not enough to modify the fundamental impressions.

It would be good to remove this anxiety by repeating once again how troubled we are about the bloc polarisation and how much better people would feel in the world if there were no blocs. And we would feel easier if we could discover and fix to the cross of truth those who are guilty of these and of other difficulties in the world.

The world cannot be changed by mere desire. The developing countries have been aware of this for a long time. The political blocs were created in the extraordinarily complicated circumstances of the post-war period. Certainly, they are not eternal. It is not our task to enquire into ways of transforming these circumstances. It is sufficient to repeat that the genesis of the links between East and West was, nevertheless, an essentially different one and a reflection of the peculiarities of the development of their socio-economic environments and political systems. What was common to both groups was their initial convictions – above all, their illusions – about a rapid disintegration of the opposite socio-economic system. We would not want to test the readiness of either side genuinely to endorse the expected process.

More encouraging were the times when the developing countries observed changes in behaviour that could be regarded, in a conciliatory spirit, as realistic – and necessarily so – rather than revolutionary. We would not, of course, be serious if we suggested that the changes resulted from scientific findings about world situations and processes. It is more convincing to suggest that experience – as always – prevailed over dogmas of all kinds. The changes in the world have revealed alternatives to that extreme 'optimum' solution where the opposite side simply disappears, or is removed, from the surface of the earth. Subsequently it has been possible to adopt processes of détente in the strategic tensions by using a relatively neutral, or technical approach which has encouraged hopes, in particular in the less developed countries of this world.

These countries, weak in economic power, have for a long time voiced their view that there should exist alternative solutions for the world, other than extreme ones. A series of significant figures emerged from the developing countries – Nasser, Nehru, Tito and a number of others who talked of peace. Such an atmosphere generated Bandung and also a gathering-together of the non-aligned countries. In the developing countries the conviction also prevailed that any war or collision between the blocs could push the whole world into the abyss, including the new countries that had just started on the road of a free life, and were far from prepared to commit collective suicide.

I do not want to generalise: but for Yugoslavia we can say that she resisted, making the same efforts, the views formerly held by the largest developing country conceiving a destructive war of world dimensions as a road to world revolution. And that is why we in Yugoslavia were pleased to find that that country, too, has discovered an alternative way of improving living conditions on our planet. But we were ready to understand the reasons engendering cynicism on the soil of poverty and reflecting the big difficulties met in overcoming underdevelopment.

Northing that has been said should be understood to imply that in the final analysis it would make no difference to the developing countries if the destructive conflict were limited to the countries of East and West. This is certainly not so. The developing countries have always been well aware of the fact that the world represents a structured community where, in addition to the East-West relations, there exist historical and other links between the Eastern and Western countries and the developing nations. These links have never been final. The influences exercised by the big centres of economic and political power have been mutually competitive and have in a special manner, and within the limits of their powers of attraction, divided (or tried to divide) the underdeveloped world. The changes in the atmosphere of the East-West line have always spread rapidly to every quarter of the world. Already, preparations for a possible conflict, and the policies of deterrence, have changed life on the earth into life on a volcano. History – when the time comes – will even more convincingly explain the background of tensions and conflicts among the developing countries (and even among the non-aligned countries).

Hence the conviction held by the developing countries, and by the non-aligned, of the necessity for a global détente (to include the world as a whole), not excluding, but reinforcing an active coexistence, and thus détente between East and West. However, every step in the right direction, even the most modest, has always been well accepted and supported if support was necessary and sought.

4.2 Interdependence and the need for adaptation

Hence the developing countries have looked more and more frequently towards that part of the world accumulation of wealth which has melted away in large expenditure on armaments and in strengthening the military-industrial complexes. We know, however, that not even the minimum promises to transfer resources to the developing countries (1 per cent of GNP) have been carried out. Various projects for their development have failed. It has been alleged that the problem was not lack of accumulation, but a collective irrationality. The term is not a scientifically suitable one, but well reflects relations to the problems of peace and war, and to the planetary problems of the existence and of the development of us all.

These are also the reasons why the developing countries have followed with great attention the ups and downs causing anxiety in the relations between East and West, expecting and hoping that the trends would finally turn upwards. Although trade, in history, has not always been an engine of growth, it has still brought its participants together, leading them towards mutual interdependence, even when the relationship was that of master and servant, as suggested by Hegel's work. And if such a role was played by trade, it applies even more to the other dimensions, richer in content, of international economic relations.

That the countries in the world have become highly interdependent is an increasingly familiar statement, already established in textbooks. Nevertheless, within the international organisations it has still to be understood that this statement is indeed true; adequate evidence has to be furnished. Let us leave aside the slightly malicious comparisons with the interdependence between the horse and the rider. The fact is that it would be rather difficult to understand the notion of interdependence in the world if the significant relationships between East and West were eliminated from it. It would be difficult to carry out any programme which tried to link interdependence with the practical efforts made for change in the principles and practice of international economic relations.

Practice has convincingly enough confirmed that the differences between the national or broader socio-economic groupings and systems are not *per se* a cause for non-cooperation between the countries (and between the economic agents in these countries). Practice confirms basic interest in cooperation. If this is taken as a starting-point, we cannot deny the (potentially) broad platform for economic cooperation between the countries of East and West. In view of the high level of economic development and organisation in most countries of East and West, we should not expect that the *economic* relations should become a serious mechanism for transferring unwanted impacts of one kind or another. Nor should there be uncontrolled relations of domination and exploitation. These are, it is true, the problems which the developing countries face. If, however, the tendency towards normalisation prevails in relations between East and West, then these problems cannot play a decisive part: indeed the economic relations strengthen the positive tendency. Of course, if there is no such tendency, these considerations make no sense.

Some difficulties probably originate from differing theoretical and practical interpretation of the targets, contents and mechanisms of international economic relations. In the world of today, these differences are taken for granted. We should, therefore, expect a readiness for mutual adaptation among the participants in these relations.

This need for adaptation is well known to the developing countries, since their economic and political power does not allow them too frequent an assertion of their own interests. For the developed countries of East and West such adaptation is somewhat more difficult; they have been living for many years in the firm conviction of the optimality of their chosen (national or regional) systems of international relations. There is also the question of the instruments for strong protection of one's own interest with a weakened sense of the partners' interests (actual or potential). For a long time the belief persisted in the possibility of a lasting universalisation of one's own concepts and practice in international economic relations.

Developments in the world economy are, of course, leading towards a stricter appraisal of existing concepts and systems of international economic relations, and towards a more relative view of imaginary optima. This is universally confirmed by the recent history of the prevailing system of international economic relations, developed under the strong influence exerted by the USA. We could say that the problems of the world economy have become too wide and too difficult for concepts of international economic relations accepted until recently.

For our theme, the essential point is that the developing countries are interested in diminishing the conviction of the validity of the existing systems of international economic relations. Pragmatic assessment of the system now practised should lead to their improvement — or else into looking for new roads. It is not sufficient to find out that the system is not efficient or that it intensifies the difficulties instead of removing them. It is necessary that the supporters of these systems should themselves perceive how perseverance in the old ways begins to do harm to them, too. Only then will the benevolent criticism from outside attain its true goal.

The developing countries do not talk too much about what economic relations between East and West ought to be; this is certainly a matter primarily concerning those countries. The developing countries do not like giving advice, and even less do they want to interfere in East-West relations, for, as is well known, they do not want others to meddle with their own mutual relations; they want to solve, above all, their own problems, even when they offer global solutions. Yet in doing so they do not follow the impulses of blind egotism not unknown in world affairs.

In this sense, the mutual adaptations observed in East-West relations present a good omen for the developing countries. These adaptations support a more global transformation of the system of international economic relations. And this is — as we know — one of the conditions for solving the current, medium-term and long-term problems of developing countries.

The developing countries see in these processes the abandonment of the idea of isolationism: we observe this abandonment also in the history of developing countries, where isolationism was, at best, an expression of distrust in the future of their relations with developed countries. Sooner or later, however, isolationism proves to be the expression of a real, or apparent, weakness. And in practice it does not exclude the possibility of aggressive reactions.

On the other hand, the process of international adaptation originates from a conscious understanding of both national and foreign interests and from a capacity to approach their coordination. Where interests conflict, this means the search for a synthesis. It is here that the problem arises of how to move forward on the world level.

This transformation, however, proceeds by changing both practice and principles. If, in relations between East and West, adaptation becomes an established practice, confirming the need for the countries concerned to show their understanding of the balance of payments difficulties of their partners, this is the first step towards reducing these difficulties. In this way grows conviction of the potential mutual benefit of economic relations. In this way, too, the partners become increasingly aware that their own systems of economic relations with foreign countries – mechanisms characteristic of monopoly of foreign trade, or of the highly organised systems of business operations established by transnational corporations – must take into account the limitations on contacts with other countries. Thus discussions with foreign countries about policies for economic relations become simplified – not to say more frank. An area is opened for a realistic exploitation of the possibilities of forms of production cooperation or joint ventures.

Since the developing countries, too, in their relations with the developed countries face these or similar problems, positive and practical moves towards closer economic relations between East and West could also exercise a favourable influence upon the relations of the East or the West with the developing countries.

4.3 Prospects and hopes for a new order

The scenario is somewhat complicated if we take into consideration that the East and West are not – as we have already stated looking back on history – homogeneous units, but have their own internal structures displaying differences and similarities among the constituent countries.

Many changes have occurred during the post-war period. In the West, there has not only been the long road from Bretton Woods up to the present situation, but also a different array of forces and changes in organisation of the economic potential in North America, Western Europe and a part of the Asian-Australian area of the Pacific. Different strategies for a possible integrating of narrower groups of interests within the world economy are operating in parallel. But some common interests, and possibilities for common actions, have appeared. In the East, we can see, without resorting to deep analysis, the heavy weight of the vast economic potential of the Soviet Union, and the significance of the differences in the rates of development and in production structures among the other CMEA member countries.

This paper cannot aim at ascertaining the direct consequences for their mutual economic relations of these characteristic features and changes in the countries of the East and West. We can, however, draw from the facts already known the conclusion that the countries of East and West cannot all assess in the same way the significance, contents and mechanisms of East-West relations; this leads us to stress the bilateral structure of these relationships (with unequal weights attached to different elements).

Because of the different economic situations, of the extent of economic recession and various oscillations in the political relations between East and West, the interests of the Western countries in relation to the Eastern group – to say it in a simplified way – have been competitive. The coincidence of the economic recession and of the political détente have enhanced this competition. The differences among the Eastern countries have appeared in another manner, in particular in an unequal and changing intensity of the need for links with the individual countries (or with groups of countries) in the West; the differences depend also upon how far Western countries are able and willing to take account of these needs and to satisfy them. The motives stimulating East-West relations have thus become increasingly differentiated on both sides, even more so as, in general, the economic element has carried increasing weight. Thus, in my opinion, the détente (and its opposite) have been losing their global character.

These processes are basically a reflection of deeper changes in the world, laying more and more stress on the need for all the developed countries to look for solutions of the problems of their stability (and of their development as well) in the world area, through an elastic, active strategy in international economic relations. For well-known reasons, this need is not felt equally by all countries, nor are the contents, forms and methods of optimal strategies equally conceived. It is understandable that this engenders the struggle for influence precisely in the developing countries – not a completely new development. It would be a new development if the competition for a greater participation in the economic relations with the developing countries were not associated with the relatively narrow issues arising in the East-West relations; but in fact it originates from a correct interpretation of the national long-term economic (and thus also political) interests in this area.

Such an approach has, of course, to take into account that the Third World has changed, too, and that we have to deal with an increasingly differentiated scenario, embracing the different interests of the old and of the new developing countries. Because of prolonged hesitations and inadequate operations some unsoundly mature situations have developed. It would be good if the conviction were to prevail that strategies of domination – where there are such — must be replaced by coordinated strategies; these, too, represent a special sort of adaptation. And, let me say, we rightly expect most just from the strongest states.

This leads us into the theme of a new international economic order. We may conceive it broadly as an expression of the conviction that many things in the existing system are out of order, and as a reflection of the efforts being made to change the situation.

The United Nations was the forum where some years ago this idea of a new order began to display the emerging outlines for an international economic community; but it was clear that the idea would have lasting success only if it began to be realised. Reports from the UNCTAD meeting in Manila and more recently from the UNIDO in New Dehli could not animate anybody with enthusiasm; yet they demonstrate moves in conscience, if not yet in action. We are entering the stage of global negotiations, perhaps full of scepticism; yet we are all aware that scarcely ten years ago the word 'negotiations' was itself unacceptable for a lot of people in the developed world. In the same way, we can have doubts, for instance, about the capability of the Western countries to implement an efficient strategy of really universal significance and thus take seriously a scenario 'D' of the OECD Interfutures team, with its strongly polarised structure of economic relations between North and South. The more distrusting will move even to scenario 'C' showing the consequences of rupture between North and South (1). However, anyone who has begun to grasp the deeper meaning of interdependence in the world will retain that dosage of self-confidence and of confidence in others which is necessary for a humane life.

Such confidence should include, perhaps, some characteristic features in a vision of the future. But such a vision, incorporating the different relations between countries and peoples, should react on the atmosphere of East-West relations. The picture is becoming increasingly clear: in addition to an undoubted influence exercised by East-West relations on the destiny of the developing countries, it contains also an influence spreading from the South.

In this context, the European picture, with its changed and improved content, is also gaining a new significance. The European countries belong both to the East and to the West. Europe was a symbol and basis for the Helsinki Conference on Security and Cooperation, and now for the subsequent meeting in Madrid. The Havana summit of the non-aligned countries confirmed that there is a European component to the non-aligned group. The South of Europe still feels the consequences of non-development or is still in that state. In spite of being small and not too young, Southern Europe, and the develop-

(1) OECD 'Interfutures', *Facing the Future,* 1979 (see also Chapter 1, Section 1.1, in this volume).

ments there, exerted and will exert a strong influence upon relationships within the triangle (which is not a true triangle): the East, the West and the developing countries.

To secure a better content for our lives, in Europe and in the world, means many things: but must always include the overcoming of an open, or concealed, egotism. And it is a true satisfaction to accept Arthur Schopenhauer's aphorism on egotism – that the one who relies upon it does not need evidence, but curing.

COMMENTS ON PART I – THE BACKGROUND: INTERESTS AND PROSPECTS

John P. Hardt*

My comments are primarily on the major thrust of Chapter 1, by *Berthelot,* contrasting it with the Report of the Brandt Commission.

(a) Mutual benefit through global growth and mutual advantages in increased production and employment are possible (Berthelot). Preferential policy to South, requiring redistribution of Northern, especially Western, income and capital, to the South, is necessary and should be based primarily on need and opportunity. (Brandt Report) (1)

The OECD research cited by Berthelot projects significantly larger GNP per capita for OECD countries, especially in Europe and Japan, if North-South trade increases. Moreover it is argued that the employment effect, especially for skilled workers, would be positive. The Berthelot conclusions are based on a larger OECD study, *Facing the Future.* Thus the argument for greater Northern economic involvement in the South is based on the interests of both sides, and, inideed, is presented as critical to the economic well-being of each. In contrast, the Brandt Commission argues, in the main, for redistribution of resources from North to South on the basis of need. An expanded Northern foreign assistance programme based on need is prescribed by the Brandt Commission precisely at a time when the nations of the North, especially the United Kingdom, Sweden and the United States, are reducing their domestic welfare programmes. Likewise

* Associate Director, Senior Specialist Office, Congressional Research Service, The Library of Congress, Washington, DC

the Soviet Union and the other Eastern nations in the North face a decade of sharply reduced economic growth and attendant limits of resources available for foreign programmes. If the merits of both the material benefit and need approaches may be accepted, the former would seem to be far more politically attractive in both North and South.

(b) Interdependence will be increased through negotiations by the policy makers of the North and South using their power to defend their national interests (Berthelot); whereas the Brandt Commission, the Group of 77, and other nations of the South, argue for new economic relations based on meeting Southern needs at the expense of Northern economic interests on the basis of equity, not necessarily by power marshalled in negotiation.

Characteristically, changes in foreign relations occur more often from negotiation than from demonstration of need. The Berthelot approach, implying negotiation, would seem to be more realistic than the Brandt Commission approach, apparently based on demonstrable need. The negotiations of economic powers in the North and South would logically need to start at least from a position of Pareto optimality, i.e. no gain by one side at the expense of the other. This negotiating posture would be especially appropriate as the North, the side likely to be affected, happens to have power and control. Put another way, why would the Western industrial nations of the North voluntarily accept sacrifices that they have the power to avoid?

The assumption of the utility, indeed the necessity, for negotiated change focusses attention on the need for the South to marshall its bargaining power. Power in the South may be enhanced by unity and control of scarce resources, e.g. OPEC control of petroleum sales. Even without the effective oil weapon, non-petroleum exporting nations of the South may increase their bargaining positions by reducing regional disunity, or by increasing international or regional unity on specific issues related to North-South negotiations, e.g. commodity negotiations. By encouraging regional disunity through political-military competition, developing nations of the South reduce their scarce marketable resource, i.e. hard currency goods, by using hard currency income for arms rather than for high technology goods; they thereby weaken the basis for regional unity on economic issues of importance in dealing with the Northern countries. The South may also reinforce its bargaining power by a demonstrated ability to control and ensure dependable supplies of products to the North, e.g. petroleum, raw materials. This ability to assure supplies would not only enhance bargaining power in Northern markets for goods but ensure more favourable terms for financing development and repayment of debts.

Thus political and military rivalry in Southern regions, accentuated by the purchase of arms from East and West, reduces the economic bargaining position of the South and creates not only instability but violence endangering human lives and resources. The cost in economic benefits to the South arising from a unified Southern position in negotiations might be viewed in the North as more than offset by the benefits of Southern political stability and economic vitality.

(c) Shrinking supplies of critical economic resources available in North and South to meet development needs: a problem for both the Berthelot and Brandt approaches.

In the Northern countries slower growth of GNP and government revenues, with rising domestic claims on resources, reduces resources disposable for aid or redistribution to the South. This process is likely to continue in the 1980s.

In the South, non-petroleum producers will have limited ability to generate net hard currency income while sustaining their debt service burdens. This reduced financial capability to import will make it increasingly difficult to afford increased imports from the developed countries of the North. Dissipation of these limited hard currency supplies on imports of arms, luxury goods, and other non growth-generating goods and services, exacerbates difficult internal problems and constrains economic growth.

The increasingly limited supplies of resources disposable for foreign economic programmes, for both North and South, restrain an effective dialogue. These are the very resources needed to foster international development in order to make possible the OECD's growth projections of global GNP based on expanded North-South trade, and cited by Berthelot. As growth in the East may be even less than in the Western industrial nations, the narrowing of disposable Northern resources for North-South expansion is an East-West phenomenon.

(d) Internationalisation of output and marketing may facilitate East-West cooperation in Southern economic development.

Tripartite agreements involving nations of the West, East and South may be unique and interesting, but are likely to remain modest. In the future, significant developments in the internationalisation of production and marketing may come from the advantages of the international division of labour – expanding the supply systems of transnational enterprises to a global basis to reduce the costs of labour, natural resources, and processing, while maintaining competitive market advantages. Internationalisation of hydrocarbon and automotive output and supply may be two early examples of this development. Such complicated global competition does not preclude some offsetting of North-South trade by increasing East-West trade, or other changes in shares of the global market, ever if global trade turnover grows slowly. In this triangular development, the West has superior output and marketing technology, the East selected resource, output, and market access advantages, and the South expanding resource production, labour supply and market base. If the Western transnationals can be viewed as more apolitical and effective than other mechanisms, they may take the lead in creating an institutional framework for expanding economic regional trilateralism.

(e) While reform may not be a substitute for technology transfer from West to East or South (2), institutional change is not easy to attain. The European CMEA nations may wish to increase significantly their oil imports from non-CMEA sources to a level of 80 – 100 million tons by 1990 as suggested by Dobozi (Chapter 3), because they can neither reform their economic structure to conserve energy nor accept slower development. However, as *Dobozi* suggests, exports of Eastern manufactured goods to finance oil imports from OPEC will be difficult in a competitive world market in which East European nations must compete with advanced Western economies in areas of traditional Western superiority. Also reforms, new machinery, and institutional change may be more costly and less beneficial than expected. The often-quoted notion of old wine in new bottles might be cited; its caution that new forms would not be able to perform the tasks of the older vessels should be recalled (3).

(f) Eastern nations may become more competitive with the West by adopting some demand-oriented programmes, such as those that derive from sales of advanced industrial products to the West (autos, computers, agricultural equipment). They may also become more complementary to Southern production and trade.

The supply directed development of both East and South may be a barrier in increasing East-South trade, as *Paszyński* (Chapter 2) suggests. However, the more important problem of South and East alike is lack of competitiveness with the West rather than complementarity. This may be addressed by East-West-South cooperative arrangements, compensation agreements, counter-trade or other mechanisms to offset competitive disadvantages. However the more constructive approach is Eastern modernisation to enhance competitiveness.

(g) A lesson and challenge for the petroleum exporting countries, which is highlighted by Iran's disruptions, is that financing unlimited imports from technologically advanced countries of the West and East may contribute to political instability rather than economic development.

Both Berthelot (Chapter 1) and the Brandt Report imply that the transfer of resources alone will improve economic performance in the South. The experience of politically unstable and economically chaotic nations, such as Iran, suggests that development must be conducted on a broader basis of social, political, and economic change. Even effective transfer of Western systems of technology, although facilitating absorption, diffusion, and effective economic utilisation of technology, may have unintended political, social, even religious consequences. These consequences may not be limited to the Islamic nations that are now facing a tide of rising fundamentalism and the sentiment that Western-style development is flawed. Although the contrasts in the impact on the oil-rich developing nations are dramatic, the appearance of political, social and religious forces antagonistic to economic development seems at present to be the rule rather than the exception. The Southern inability to use Northern resources effectively, when they are available – because of forces external to the economic development process – needs to be given more consideration in the North-South dialogue.

References

(1) Willi Brandt (Chairman), *North-South, A Program for Survival,* MIT Press, Cambridge, Mass. 1980, p. 304.

(2) As pointed out by Dobozi and Inotai in Chapter 3 of this book.

(3) New Testament, St. Matthew 9:14, And no one puts a piece of unshrunk cloth on an old garment, for the patch tears away from the garment, and a worse tear is made. Neither is new wine put into old wineskins; if it is, the skins burst, and the wine is spilled, and the skins are destroyed; but new wine is put into fresh wineskins, and so both are preserved.

Deepak Nayyar*

The literature on international economics abounds with studies of the interaction between rich and poor countries in the world economy. More often than not, however, these studies focus attention on the western capitalist countries and their economic relations with the less developed nations of the world. Surprisingly enough, economists have paid scant attention to the relationship between the rich socialist countries and the poor nations. This book should, to some extent, redress the balance.

For the analyst interested in examining the prospects for LDCs in the contemporary world economy, it is clearly important to distinguish between East and West in the industrialised world. I therefore focus attention on the economic interaction between the industrialised CMEA countries and the developing countries, which is the subject of Chapters 2, 3 and 4. It need hardly be stressed that for both the East and the South, interaction with the West is an overwhelmingly important part of the same picture.

* School of African and Asian Studies, University of Sussex, UK; now Professor of Economics, Indian Institute of Management, Calcutta.

Two themes emerge from these chapters: (i) an ever-increasing interdependence in the world economy; and (ii) a potential for harmony which must be mobilised to realise mutual interests. The discernible conflict of economic interests between nation states is noted but not quite incorporated into the analysis. Obviously, it is important, as well as constructive, to discuss possible mechanisms for extending East-South economic co-operation. In my view, however, it would be a mistake to ignore the potential sources of conflict for, at present, the interests of nation states in the world economy are characterised as much by contradiction as by harmony.

Chapter 4, by *Fabinc* is divided into three sections. The first provides an overview of East-West-South relations in the world political system. The second shifts the focus to economic relations, particularly trade: the author argues that a stable growth in East-West economic interaction would have a favourable impact on the South's ties with both East and West. It is not entirely obvious why. There is a presumption that the cold war era was detrimental to the interests of LDCs, and that international cooperation would benefit all nations insofar as it promotes economic growth. The third section, interestingly enough, suggests that East, West and South are perhaps inappropriate categories which do not represent homogeneous entities but are constituted by countries whose interests might diverge significantly from one another. Unfortunately, the implications of this proposition are not examined further.

Chapter 2, by *Paszyński,* on the economic interest of the CMEA countries in relations with LDCs, is interesting in content and perceptive in analysis. His theoretical basis stresses (i) structural similarities between the socialist countries and the developing countries insofar as productive capacities lag behind domestic demand in both sets of economies; (ii) structural differences between the socialist economies and the developing countries on the one hand, and the developed market economy countries on the other, insofar as the latter economies are characterised by a structural excess of production capacities. The distinction between supply-constrained and demand-led economies implies that the role of foreign trade is significantly different: in developed market economies, the author suggests, external markets support capitalist development, whereas in the economies of the East and the South Imports are fundamental to the growth process and exports simply finance imports. It is worth noting that the analogy between the socialist economies and the developing countries, though interesting, is clearly overstated: external markets and export-led growth are an important element of development strategy in many underdeveloped economies, particularly where the size of the domestic market is small. All the same, it is argued by the author that, given the structural characteristics of socialist economies, there is no prospect for radical change in East-South economic interaction in the medium term because the structure and volume of productive capacities is already determined by the planners, so that foreign trade must remain a residual category in the CMEA. In the long run, however, Pasyński believes that the situation could be transformed, as part of the process of structural change in the world economy brought about by the changing international division of labour. The role performed by imports of primary commodities in socialist economies is bound to diminish and must be replaced by a more positive role for exports in particular and for foreign trade in general, which, in turn, must adjust to structural change in the economies of LDCs where import requirements and export prospects are changing rapidly. The future of East-South economic interaction therefore depends on a successful transition from the complementary to a competitive pattern of trade; in other words, inter-sectoral trade must be replaced by intra-sectoral or intra-industry trade and specialisation. This transition, in my view, is likely to pose significant problems both in principle and in practice. I shall come to my reasons shortly. The author recognises that the mechanism for such adjustment must be reciprocal and simultaneous: a programmed, negotiated process which can emerge from planned changes in international specialisation through long-term bilateral agreements. In this context the following problems are worth noting: (i) is it possible, even in principle, to plan the integration of production capacities between centrally planned economies on the one hand and developing market economies on the other? (ii) the experience of socialist countries at different levels of development – say in the CMEA – attempting planned economic integration through trade and specialisation, highlights the problems which are likely to arise. The process would be all the more difficult in relations with developing market economies.

Chapter 3, by *Dobozi* and *Inotai*, deals with the prospects of economic cooperation between the East and the South. The crux of the chapter explores the possibilities of cooperation between the industrialised CMEA countries and the developing countries, in the spheres of manufacturing, raw materials, agriculture and technology transfer. The authors are positive in their approach and set out plans for cooperation in production/trade/specialisation, but without according due recognition to the problems and lessons to emerge from the past experience of economic interaction between East and South. In considering the institutional mechanisms of economic cooperation, the authors write of cooperation in planning but admit that this has so far been confined to assistance in the setting-up of national planning systems in LDCs. The next step, planned integration in production through trade and specialisation, is an aspiration rather than a realistic objective. I would stress, once again, the difficulties experienced in this process within the CMEA, particularly between economies at different levels of development. The last section of the paper provides projections of East-South trade for the period 1980 – 1990. It assumes that the industrialised CMEA countries will increase their trade with the developing economies faster than their total trade: an unrealistic assumption which leads to overoptimistic forecasts. The composition of this trade at the end of the projected period is, nevertheless, revealing. Manufactures would account for an even larger proportion of CMEA exports to the South (at 80 per cent), while diversification in the exports of LDCs to the East would not be very significant, except that primary agricultural commodities would be replaced by minerals and fuels. That is clearly not the basis for a new international division of labour.

In my view, the impact of East-West relations on the development process in poor countries can be understood and analysed only if it is placed in historical perspective. Such a view would not only highlight the economic interests of the industrialised CMEA countries in the developing world but would also shed some light on the prospects of economic interaction between the East and the South. Of course, it would not suffice to focus on economic factors alone; political forces are rather important determinants of the relationship.

Consider, first, the past experience, which, in my perception, reflects the mutual interests insofar as the interests of the rich socialist countries appear to coincide with the needs of Third World development. From the late 1950s to the early 1970s, there was a remarkable expansion of trade and economic relations between the USSR and Eastern Europe on the one hand, and the non-socialist LDCs on the other. From 1955 to 1970, East-South trade was the most dynamic component of world trade. The growth rate exceeded that of both intra-CMEA trade and East-West trade, though in the 1970s East-West trade increased faster than East-South trade. Two basic factors underlie this remarkable trade expansion.

First, in a situation where scarcities of foreign exchange were a constraint on international trade, bilateralism made possible a much higher turnover of trade. Multilateral trade might have been superior in principle, but during the period 1955 – 1970 it was not an option available to the socialist economies nor was it a feasible option for many developing countries. Although one cannot be certain, it is extremely unlikely that socialist countries would have increased their trade with the developing world to the extent that they did in the absence of special payment arrangements which eliminated the use of convertible currencies in trade. For the South too, without bilateralism the East might not have emerged as an alternative source of imports and as an alternative outlet for its traditional exports.

Second, complementarities of demand between the two sets of countries were fundamental to the expansion in trade. In the East the relative isolation from the world economy, and the prevalent level of consumption, meant that the income elasticities of demand for primary commodities exported by the South were high: a sharp contrast with the near-saturated markets in the West. At the same time, in the Third World, the needs of industrialisation meant high income elasticities of demand for intermediate and capital goods exported by the socialist economies of Eastern Europe. During the 1960s, therefore, trade expansion was indeed remarkable; the growth began to taper off in the mid-1970s and a threshold was reached when the existing complementarities were exhausted.

These two factors were also the principal sources of mutual benefit, for the scarcity of foreign exchange and the constraints on exports in both sets of countries meant that gains from trade were ensured. The principle of bilateralism, which governed a substantial proportion of such trade flows, had several virtues in this phase. Most important, given the extreme shortage of foreign exchange, it enabled both the socialist countries and the Third World to avail themselves of international trade opportunities which might not have been possible otherwise. For the industrialised socialist countries, the South was a useful source of imports and an obvious market outlet for exports; the USSR and Eastern Europe sold machinery and other manufactured goods which were probably difficult to sell in Western markets, in exchange for primary products which would otherwise have involved an expenditure of hard currencies. For the LDCs, the East provided welcome new markets for a large number of traditional commodity exports which faced near-saturated markets and rather low income elasticities of demand in the West. At the same time, imports from the socialist bloc were constituted by capital goods and intermediate products which were essential to the industrialisation programmes in LDCs.

It is worth noting that both factors ran out of steam by the mid-1970s. The *modus operandi* of East-South trade shifted markedly from bilateral payments arrangements to transactions in convertible currencies. Between 1970 and 1975 the share of trade conducted through clearing agreements declined from 73 per cent to 67 per cent in the USSR, and dropped rather sharply from 75 per cent to 42 per cent in the rest of Eastern Europe. There was, of course, a corresponding increase in the share of convertible currency transactions. As a result, perhaps, the industrialised CMEA countries derived a special benefit from their trade with the South: their trade surplus with developing countries, insofar as it was in convertible currencies, financed 14 per cent of their deficit in trade with the West in the mid-1970s; the proportion was significantly greater for some countries in certain years (1). By the mid-1970s, the growth potential of the complementary trade patterns was also nearly exhausted. The import requirements, and the export prospects, of both sets of economies changed rapidly in the late 1970s, and are likely to change even further in the future. The past pattern of trade, which remains prevalent to this day, is, however, worth noting. The composition of East-South trade, at least as far as the non-socialist LDCs are concerned, is not significantly different from that of West-South trade; the Third World exports primary commodities and raw materials to the rich countries, both capitalist and socialist, in exchange for manufactured goods. Indeed, it has been observed, as Paszyński also hints, that in terms of trade patterns, LDCs are to the rich socialist countries what the latter are to the advanced capitalist economies (2). Such traditional patterns of trade, however, can neither transform the structure of production in the South nor make for a new international division of labour. Admittedly, patterns of production and trade that have evolved in the poor countries over a long period of time could not have been changed overnight and during the 1960s there was a discernible increase in the share of manufactures in Third World exports to the East, but notably less than the diversification in trade with the West (3).

All the same, the East and the South had some interests in common, political as well as economic, which are visible from past experience of the relationship between the two sets of countries. I have already referred to the mutual economic gains during the period from the late 1950s to the early 1970s. As for the political sphere, interests were mutual in the context of international relations. To begin with, the process of decolonisation in the Third World matched the anti-imperialist posture of the socialist countries. Thus, in the early stages of the post-colonial era, several Third World countries sought to exploit cold war rivalries and to use relations with the socialist bloc to accelerate the process of decolonisation and assert their national economic independence. Later, for countries in the South, it became a method of improving their bargaining position vis-à-vis the West. In fact, the existence of the socialist countries on the international scene did add to the bargaining strength of LDCs. This may have been because the industrialised socialist economies were an alternative source of armaments, technology, imports or finance, and an alternative outlet for the traditional exports of LDCs. Close ties with the East were also valuable for internal political reasons; they enhanced the 'socialist' image of governments which made no effort to alleviate poverty but made a great deal of political capital out of the relationship.

Mutual interests were probably rather important in the first phase of the relationship between the East and the South. However, the potential sources of conflict, some of which have existed all the time, are beginning to surface and might indeed become significant in the near future.

The conflict of economic interests between the industrialised socialist countries on the one hand and the developing world on the other, might stem from issues relating to trade, joint ventures or international factors. First, in the area of trade, the likely points of contention are the distribution of gains, the need for a diversification in the pattern of trade, and market access for manufactured exports from LDCs. Internal factors in the socialist economies, such as the nature and pace of technical progress, are bound to push in the direction of more East-West trade in the 1980s, rather than East-South trade, as there is a growing need in the industrialised CMEA countries to import Western technology and thereby increase productivity. In the circumstances, the difficulties faced by attempts to diversify the composition of trade with the South are likely to be compounded. At the same time, the European socialist countries might compete with the more industrialised LDCs in Western markets for manufactured goods. Second, joint ventures in the Third World are a possible source of conflict. While the USSR government does not share in equity or profits, some East European countries do, and in any case, the distribution of benefits might introduce contradictions between partners. This problem might be even more acute where the USSR, or Eastern Europe, in collaboration with more industrialised LDCs, establish joint ventures in other underdeveloped economies, on account of conflict with the host countries; economic disparities between countries in the South are, after all, a sensitive issue. Third, on international matters, the self-interest of the socialist countries might create problems; for instance, in several international negotiations at UNCTAD, UNIDO or at the Law of the Sea Conference, the industrialised CMEA countries have, in effect, opposed the Third World position. Moreover, the political compulsions of international relations might also bring conflict to the surface. In particular, the objective of détente, and the desire not merely to preserve but to develop the East-West relationship, might supersede the prospects of East-South cooperation.

As an aside, it is perhaps worth noting that there might be a conflict of political interest for the rich socialist nations in Third World development because, apart from the developing market economies, there now exists a small group of poor countries in transition to socialism. It is possible that the interests of the Soviet Union and Eastern Europe in the development of the latter might be rather different from their interests in the non-socialist Third World. In principle, there is meant to be a preference for socialist LDCs and it is said that Soviet economic ties with them are specially close and effective. But it is made equally clear that the internal political system in LDCs is not an obstacle to the development of a close economic relationship with the USSR (4). What is more, in practice, the geo-political interests in the non-socialist countries of the South might sometimes take precedence over the ideological preference for socialist LDCs.

References

(1) The figures cited in this paragraph are taken from D. Nayyar, "The Interests of Rich Socialist Countries and Third World Development", paper for a conference on *Rich Country Interests and Third World Development* at the Institute of Development Studies, University of Sussex, October 1979.

(2) This view has been put forward by, among, others; A.G. Frank, "Socialist Economies in the Capitalist International Division of Labour", *Economic and Political Weekly,* Annual Number February 1977; and R. Portes, "East, West and South: the Role of Centrally Planned Economies in the International Economy", Harvard Institute of Economic Research, Discussion Paper No. 630, Cambridge, Mass. June 1978.

(3) For evidence on this point, see Nayyar (reference 1 above). It is also worth noting that, in 1976, there were only five developing countries where manufactures constituted more than 25 per cent of total exports to the USSR: India, Pakistan, Bangladesh, Syria and Egypt. See UNCTAD *Review of Trends and Policies in Trade Among Countries having different Economic and Social Systems* (TD/B/708 Add. 1), Geneva, July 1978.

(4) For a brief discussion of this issue, see I. Kulev, "The Soviet Union and the Developing Counries", *International Affairs,* Moscow, November 1976.

Marie Lavigne*

In commenting on chapters 2 (*Paszyński*) and 3 (*Dobozi/Inotai*), I want to raise two points: the similarities between socialist and developing countries, differently seen by the authors; and the question of hard currencies surpluses in trade between the two groups of countries.

Paszyński considers that developing and socialist countries are similar from the point of view of the mode of operation (both are 'supply-led' or 'supply-constrained'). Dobozi and Inotai see a similarity from the point of view of the industrialisation pattern. This leads Paszyński to emphasise the trade problems, with a much more restrictive view than Dobozi and Inotai on the possible prospects for the expansion of trade; the latter focus on problems of cooperation and specialisation.

The authors disagree about the role of foreign trade. It is a growth-promoting factor for industrial development, both in LDCs and CMEA countries; for Paszyński, the exports of CMEA countries toward the industrial West are bound to remain of a residual nature; but without solving the contradiction connected with the creation of reserve productive capacities 'the change in the export function could not be fully achieved'. On CMEA imports, whereas Paszyński foresees a stabilisation of imports of primary commodities, Dobozi and Inotai expect these imports to retain fundamental importance in the coming years. If CMEA trade with LDCs is going to develop as the most dynamic component of CMEA foreign trade, on what side will be the reduction in relative shares (in intra-CMEA trade or in East-West trade)?

Dobozi and Inotai seem to see the improvement of intra-CMEA cooperation as a prerequisite for the improvement of LDC-CMEA cooperation. This needs some elaboration. A related point concerns the cooperation agreements signed between the CMEA as such and some developing countries – in fact, only two: Iraq and Mexico – in 1975. These agreements do not seem to have influenced strongly the development of trade and cooperation between the partners. This leads me to a broader question: if cooperation and specialisation do not develop to such an extent that the parallel structure of industrialisation patterns is really changed, then what about the risk of competition of LDC and CMEA countries on third markets, especially in manufactures?

Both chapters evoked the problems of the trade surpluses of the European CMEA countries with LDCs; so do the comments (above) of D. *Nayyar*, who focuses mainly on the convertible currency surplus. This question is very puzzling. First of all, we do not have precise statistical data in this field, and this is why I feel very puzzled by Nayyar's

* Director, Centre d'économie internationale des pays socialistes, University of Paris I. Panthéon-Sorbonne.

statement that 14 per cent of the CMEA's trade deficit with the West in the mid-1970s, was financed by the hard currencies surpluses with the LDCs. This is hardly consistent with the fact that in most cases it is the developing partner who asked for the suppression of the clearing arrangement and the introduction of settlements in convertible currencies. What makes things even more obscure is that between two countries, two different types of settlements may exist: in convertible currencies for trade; in clearing schemes for cooperation arrangement; the statistics do not make a distinction between these two flows.

Adolf Nussbaumer*

There can be no doubt that the industrialised West has a keen interest in a favourable development of North-South relations. Economic interdependence and mutuality of interest are not just handy catchwords; they are generally accepted facts, especially since the world has gone through another international oil crisis and since a new round of Global Negotiations to introduce a New International Economic Order is under discussion. *Berthelot* (Chapter 1) is certainly right in saying that an intensification of relations between industrialised and developing countries allows for a stronger growth in both groups of countries. As is well known, Austria and especially Chancellor Kreisky was among the first protagonists to call for a massive transfer of resources to developing countries so as to provide for a more rapid development of infrastructure and thereby faster growth in these countries and at the same time make full use of Western industrial capacity. Mutuality of interest is stressed again by Berthelot when saying that a high industrial trade surplus – made possible by extensive industrial credit – in trade with Third World countries is beneficial in terms of employment for the industrialised Western countries.

It goes without saying that the evolving distribution of labour between North and South can only be developed and safeguarded within the framework of an open international trading system, which also provides for unilateral benefits for developing countries to the extent that these are necessary in order to compensate for relative underdevelopment.

* Secretary of State in the Federal Chancellery of Austria, Vienna

Especially, small industrialised countries such as Austria must have a specific interest in preserving free international trade, since they usually sell a much larger part of their product abroad and in doing so are able to benefit from economies of scale. It must be noted, however, that in turn they are much more exposed to international business fluctuations and might see their exports crippled by a reduction of international demand while their imports are still going strong due to continuing full employment at home. Small industrialised countries are therefore likely to show stronger fluctuations in their balance of trade, and especially greater deficits in times of international recession, than big countries. This view is supported by recent figures on international trade for the whole group as well as for Austria in particular.

Finally a word on the net effect of increased North-South trade on industrial employment in the West. Recent studies by the OECD suggest that negative employment effects in industrial countries due to an increased division of labour with the South should not be overestimated – in some instances the effects might even be positive. But much depends on the sectoral composition of production and industrial employment in each country. Furthermore, weak and newly exposed industries might be concentrated in regions lagging behind in their development in relation to the rest of the country. Further detailed investigations would therefore be desirable so as to make available as accurate an analysis as possible, which might help us to reduce scepticism about the advantages of enhanced international economic cooperation.

Marian Paszyński

I would like to respond to some of the issues raised by comments on Chapter 2.

(a) The first concerns the balance of the chapter. It was suggested (i) that more attention should be given to the areas of mutual benefit in relations between socialist and developing countries; (ii) that the areas of conflict between them should not be bypassed. It would certainly be improper to overlook the need for discussion of the mutuality in benefits from expansion of economic relations between the two groups. It seems to me impossible to develop such relations in the absence of the mutuality of benefits. In fact, I consider our debate a bit one-sided in that it approached the East-West-South relations predominantly from the point of view of the interest of the South. Unless there is a correspondence of interests of all partners the beneficial growth of economic links will not materialise. I refer to this aspect of economic relations in my chapter when discussing the question of structural adjustment facilitating expansion of future trade and economic ties between the CMEA and developing countries. Likewise, I certainly do not lose sight of the potential or actual conflicts that may emerge in the course of expansion of relations between the two groups of countries. However, the topic of my chapter is the interest of the CMEA countries in these relations and I could not dwell upon the issues of the mutuality of benefit or potential conflict areas without deviating from my main theme.

(b) It is suggested by Nayyar that the analogy between socialist and developing countries in respect of supply versus demand constraints to economic development is somewhat overstated. I have never questioned the possibility of demand constraints on economic expansion in both socialist and developing countries. But I do suggest that, in contrast to developed capitalist countries, this is not a typical situation for the two other groups, ever for those with a small domestic market. The overall demand pressure hinders the generation of an export surplus in most developing countries, especially for non-traditional exports. I would be inclined, however, to agree that there are specific features of the operation of the socialist economy that might accentuate this process.

(c) The possibility of a programmed adjustment has been put in doubt in view of the systemic differences between centrally planned socialist countries and market-oriented developing countries, Three comments are called for.

(i) Developing countries are predominantly mixed economies with a considerable public sector and a good deal of economic planning or programming at a governmental level. In such cases, a programmed adjustment at a higher level (government, or branch of industry) is not out the question. (ii) I do not exclude the possibility of programming an adjustment process at an operational (enterprise) level through contractual obligations. (iii) What I do, in fact, rule out is a change in the system of operation of the socialist economy that would allow for market-based adjustment through private investment. It would be unreasonable to expect or assume that expansion of trade and economic relations between the two groups of countries could be conditional upon a change in either economic system. If the institutional solutions just mentioned for the adjustment process prove inadequate – and I agree that there exist several obstacles to such an adjustment, both in developing and in socialist countries (another potential area for conflict) – some new mechanisms must be devised. Otherwise, the structural adjustment will be a more hazardous and painful process for both socialist and developing nations.

(d) It follows from the previous considerations that the socialist system does not lend itself to multilateralism in the adjustment process. With a centrally determined allocative process, neither socialist countries, nor those developing countries that plan their economic development, could allow a free flow of international investment to shape the structure of their economies. But socialist countries are quite willing to multilateralise settlements of trading accounts and in fact are making steady progress in switching from bilateral (clearing, barter) to free currency settlements. To take the example of Poland, it is the developing countries (India, Brazil) that — for various reasons — have expressed interest in continuation of bilateral forms of payments.

(e) On the future prospects for economic relations, I would be inclined to agree that in the 1950s and 1960s (and in some cases also in the first half of the 1970s), trade and economic relations between socialist and developing nations could have been expanded rapidly by use of reserves, or extensive sources of development of trade links (including bilateral payments agreements) that did not require deeper changes in economic structures and in the mechanisms of economic interaction. These possibilities may have been exhausted by now. However, the danger that further development of these relations will run out of steam seems to me to lie not so much in the expansion of East-West relations as in the obstacles to structural transformation in the socialist countries (into export surplus generating economies) and to the mutual structural adjustment in their relations with developing nations. I am not preoccupied excessively by the question of making socialist countries more demand-oriented. The potential demand for increase in imports, including import purchases from developing countries, is already there. If this potential demand cannot be made effective, it is because of the insufficiency of export proceeds to finance imports; and that, in turn, results primarily from the inadequate capability of the socialist economies to generate export surpluses. Therefore the future prospects of economic relations depend mainly upon structural changes within the socialist economies, and upon finding the way to secure mutual, anticipatory and programmed structural adjustment in relations between centrally planned and developing countries. In their absence not only East-South but, likewise, East-West relations could be adversely affected.

PART II – INTERNATIONAL FINANCING

Chapter 5

CREDITS TO THE SOUTH AND INTERNATIONAL FINANCIAL RELATIONS

Amit Bhaduri*

5.1 The international financial setting

Recurring financial problems are usually a surface phenomenon reflecting deeper malaise in the underlying economic structure. International financial problems are no exception to this general rule. The recurring payments difficulties in international transactions faced by the non-oil developing countries of the South cannot therefore be understood in isolation from the pattern of international trade and capital movements in which they have been caught.

From the point of view of the non-oil developing countries, at least four distinguishing features characterise the present international financial setting. *First,* their trade relations are highly asymmetrical. The external economic relationships of the countries in the third world are overwhelmingly with industrialised countries of the West, rather than with socialist countries or with one another – a pattern which has shown very little sign of change in recent years. About 75 % of their external trade is with OECD countries, 15–20 % among themselves and only about 5 % with the centrally planned economies of the CMEA bloc (1). Such a pattern of international trade makes the third world countries highly sensitive to prosperity and depression in the rich industrialised West, but the reverse is not equally true. OECD countries do much more trade among themselves than with the rest of the world, including third world countries (2), and this insulates them considerably from the economic fluctuations or retarded growth of the

* Professor of Economics, Jawaharlal Nehru University, New Delhi, India.

third world. Thus, what goes under the slogan of 'international interdependence' is, in fact, a highly asymmetrical pattern characterised more by one-sided dependence of the non-oil third world on OECD.

There is another aspect to the present pattern of international trade which must be briefly mentioned. Roughly a quarter of world trade is 'invisible' – made up of services like transport, banking, insurance and transfer of investment income. The entire sphere of trade in invisibles is completely dominated by rich industrial countries and they regularly run a large surplus on their invisible account – it was of the order of 8 billion U.S. dollars in 1968, and almost doubled by 1977 (3). A virtual monopoly of the so-called 'Trade and transport margin' in international trade gives a kind of strategic advantage to the rich industrialised countries of the 'North'; indeed, much of their favourable terms of trade effect arises precisely from this source, in addition to the generally recognized price advantage of manufactured over primary commodities. In brief, the existing pattern of international trade makes the non-oil 'South' highly vulnerable to the economic performance of the 'North', without the reverse being true to any significant extent.

The *second* characteristic feature of the present pattern of international trade follows precisely from this highly asymmetrical relationship. This has been highlighted by recent experiences in international balance of payments adjustments on current account since the series of dramatic oil price rises by OPEC from 1973 onwards. The changing pattern of international payments following the oil price rise since 1973 has resulted in current account surpluses for both OECD and OPEC countries (4). Rising oil prices from OPEC are countered by rising prices of OECD exports (including a very sharp rise in the prices of invisible exports of 'services'), and the non-oil South had to pay both for higher oil prices and for rising prices of their imports. Thus, international inflation results in massive deficits on their current trade account (5), which is simply the other side of the corresponding surplus for OPEC and OECD. *Table 5.1* provides a rough picture of these trends in international payments (6).

Inspite of the very gross statistical nature of the above table, it unambiguously indicates a high degree of resiliency of the industrial North to balance its international payments and even produce a surplus, inspite of rises in oil prices. This resiliency is lacking for all primary producing countries in general and for the non-oil developing countries in particular, who are left holding almost the entire deficit in international payments.

The *third* major feature of the present international financial situation follows from this pattern of surplus and deficit in the international payments situation, where the global current account surplus is almost exclusively shared between industrialised OECD and OPEC (7). An inevitable outcome of such a mechanism of international payments has been to force the non-oil producing developing nations of the South to finance their

Table 5.1

Payments balances on current account of market economies
(excluding official transfers)
(in billions of US dollars)

	1973	1974	1975	1976	1977	1978	1979
Industrial countries	19	– 4	25	7	4	33	10
Developed primary producing countries	1	– 14	– 15	– 14	– 13	– 6	– 10
Major oil exporting countries	6	68	35	40	32	6	43
Non-oil developing countries	– 11	– 30	– 38	– 26	– 21	– 31	– 43
Total of groups above (a)	15	20	7	8	2	2	–

(a) If all countries were included, then the algebraic sum of the world total should be zero. The non-zero totals thus reflect inconsistencies in the recording of the balance of payments total as well as inadequate coverage for centrally planned economies.

current account deficit through rapidly mounting external debt. Here, in essence, lies the problem of so-called 'recycling' in international finance – how is the current account surplus of the OECD and OPEC to be continuously lent out to the deficit South, without creating major problems in the working of the international financial system?

But in one sense, some sort of 'recycling' has already been in operation for quite some time, since well before the dramatic rises in the price of oil took place. Thus, the total external debt of non-oil developing countries was of the order of 36 billion U.S. dollars in 1967, about 56 billion in 1973 and about 169 billion in 1976 (8). Thus, during the first three years after 1967, total debt grew by about 56 %, in the next three years (over the 1970 base) it grew by about 71 %, and in the next three years (over 1973 base) it grew by another 76 %, marking a steady acceleration in the growth rate of external debt of the non-oil South over time. But these figures are inadequate to bring out two other important tendencies which have been in operation in the international financial scene with respect to the financing of payments deficits on current account by non-oil developing nations. Both these tendencies relate to the composition of overall external debt by sources of credit. First, a more detailed analysis of the composition of debt shows how the private creditors, primarily transnational banks, have increasingly come to dominate as lenders to the non-oil developing nations. Indeed, this tendency is strikingly demonstrated by the fact that non-guaranteed private credit has grown approximately ten times between 1967 and 1976 (from 2.7 billion to 27 billion U.S. dollars), while debt to public creditors during the same period has grown only about 3.5 times (from 23.8 billion to 80.8 billion) and all publicly guaranteed debt has grown by about 4.3 times (from 33 billion to 141.8 billion). One could generalise the overall pattern by broadly saying that the degree of 'publicness' of negotiated debt has moved almost in inverse relation to the accelerated growth of total external debt. This brings us to the second tendency which is closely related to the first: debt from all private sources (whether publicly guaranteed or not) as a percentage of total outstanding external debt has steadily increased over time; from about 33.3 per cent in 1967, it rose to 37.7 per cent in 1970, 45.4 per cent in 1973 and 52.1 per cent in 1976. What is really remarkable in the second tendency is not only the increasing importance of the private sources of credit, but the more or less *steady* rate at which their importance has increased throughout this entire period. This tends to falsify the widely held impression that the dominance of private creditors in the external debt of developing countries is exclusively or even primarily due to the rise in oil prices since 1973. This tendency towards domination by private creditors of international lending has systematically been in operation at least since 1967, with no dramatic break in the 'statistical trend line' around 1973–74. Thus, it seems valid to point out that the increasing dominance of private creditors in the international capital market has been an almost inherent tendency of that market, rather than the outcome of some 'special event' like the rise in oil price. This tendency has now almost reached its climax. In 1978 net new borrowing (minus repayments) by the non-oil-producing developing countries from private banks equalled 81 % of that year's current account deficit. The net loans totalled 26 billion US dollars, which is more than double the level in 1977 (9). In brief, the 'recycling' of international finance to cover deficits and surpluses on current account in international payments has become more and more of a private affair, depending on business calculations of transnational banks, rather than being settled through intergovernmental negotiations. This could hardly be called a model of international cooperation and interdependence.

The *fourth* and final aspect of the present international financial setting that we wish to deal with in this paper is very much related to the third aspect discussed above, namely the growing tendency of transnational banks to dominate the international capital market. This tendency must have, on the one hand, further accentuated imbalances in international payments. Given the near-monopoly position of OECD countries in the international trade in invisibles (including banking and insurance) mentioned earlier, such a tendency can be expected to strengthen further their current account position at the cost of a corresponding weakening of the payments position of the non-oil South. On the other hand, the dominance of private banking in the 'recycling' of international finance has resulted in a highly discriminatory credit policy towards developing countries of the South. It is important to realise that the poorest countries in the South have very little bank debt, simply because no bank would lend to them. Thus, Brazil and Mexico together represent about 50 per cent of all the outstanding private external debt of the South, while nine countries (Brazil, Mexico, South Korea, Taiwan, the Philippines, Argentina, Peru, Colombia and Israel) account for more than 80 per cent of such debt (10). These are some of the decidedly better-off countries in the South in terms of per capita income. They are also countries with stronger political and economic ties to the rich, industrial West. They have managed to have wide access to the private credit market, while the poorer countries have had to rely more on official development assistance.

The situation would have looked more tolerable, had official development assistance (ODA) from the OECD been forthcoming on a generous enough scale. But the performance of the donors has been dismal. Concessional flows from OECD countries have not been increasing in real terms. The total ODA as a percentage of gross national product of OECD countries has fallen from 0.42 in 1966 to 0.33 in 1976 and 0.31 in 1977, figures which are less than half of the 0.70 per cent goal accepted by the United Nations General Assembly in 1970. It is still more revealing to know that the three largest ODA contributors – the United States, the Federal Republic of Germany and Japan – have typically been the least generous. In 1977, the ODA to GNP percentage was 0.22 for the United States (down from 0.25 in 1976), 0.27 for FRG (down from 0.31 in 1976) and almost stationary at about 0.20 for Japan, while Sweden, Netherlands and Norway actually exceeded the target of 0.70 (11). For comparison, it should also be reported that the total concessional assistance from OPEC has been only slightly less than 3 per cent of GNP during the same period.

Let these figures on concessional assistance speak for themselves – about how much international cooperation actually exists. From the overall perspective of the South however, the whole 'recycling operation' in international finance cannot but look a vicious cycle: almost the entire deficit in international payments is held by the non-oil developing countries. Instead of this leading to larger development assistance, the payments deficits are used as a potential market for private banking operations from the rich North. This results in further imbalance in the international trade of invisibles in favour of the North on the one hand, and heavily discriminates against the credit needs of the poorest countries in the South on the other hand. From this chain of reasoning, it could almost follow that the low ODA assistance has almost been a conscious policy to facilitate transnational banking operations in the South. This may not in reality be a matter of conscious policy, but nevertheless remains an objective fact. And, it is such objective facts rather than subjective perception which have, in the long run, been important in shaping international economic relations.

5.2 Problems and prospects of credit to the South

Against this background of marked asymmetry in international trade and financial relations, it is hardly surprising that the question of credit to the non-oil developing countries looks very different from different angles. From the point of view of the industrial North, it is essentially a question of *manageability of debt* within the existing pattern of recycling of international finance. Indeed, the question has become increasingly important for them on two counts. First, the very rapid and accelerated growth of external debt of the non-oil South (12) forces them to recognize the long-term unviability of the present pattern of international payments, which results in cumulative surpluses and deficits, without any visible self-correcting mechanism. The financial strains generated by such a system cannot easily be accommodated by the present international monetary arrangements. Second, and more important perhaps from the point of view of the industrial North, is the increasing involvement of their transnational banks and financial institutions in the growing external debt of the non-oil South. This is fast reaching the point of a liquidity crisis as debt servicing problems assume higher proportions and the maturity structure gets shortened. Because of the increasing share of private debt – which carries shorter maturities (usually only up to 5 years) than official debt – the maturity structures of the external debt of developing countries have steadily worsened over time. Maturities are not only shorter but they are bunched together, with the result that 70 per cent of the outstanding debt in 1977 to private creditors needs to be repaid before 1982. In contrast, only 24 per cent of the public debt owed to such multilateral agencies as the World Bank needs to be repaid by 1982. *Table 5.2* indicates how the repayment burden in terms of the 'time-profile index of debt' (13) hardened for developing countries between 1969 and 1974.

Table 5.2

Time profile index of debt burden

86 developing Countries

	1969		1974	
	5-year ratio of Profile	10-year ratio of Profile	5-year ratio of Profile	10-year ratio of Profile
Loans from governments	39	71	38	71
Loans from international organisations	38	75	31	69
Loans from private sources	75	106	79	124
Total Loan	48	84	52	90

Source: World Bank, *World Debt Tables* Vol. 1, October 1976, p. 18

While *Table 5.2* gives an unambiguous picture of the shortening maturity structure of overall debt — the five-year-ratio rising from 48 to 52 and the ten-year-ratio rising from 84 to 90 within a short period of 5 to 6 years; the table also indicates how this is almost entirely accounted for by a shift in favour of private sources of credit. Consolidated data for later periods are not available, but the World Bank estimates that by 1985, developing countries will have to repay principal and interest at a rate of U.S. $ 115 billion, an almost sixfold increase since 1976 (14).

The shortening maturity due to private sources of finance is further accentuated by the problem of what bankers call 'maturity matching'. Since petro-dollars are mostly held in short-maturity deposits (of an average maturity of about 93 days in 1977) while lending is, on an average, for a maturity of 4 to 5 years for developing countries, the maturity structures on the deposit and on the lending side are grossly unmatched, heightening further the fear of a liquidity crisis.

In such circumstances, it is almost inevitable that debt will either have to be rescheduled or refinanced by new loans to be used for repayment, the so-called 'roll-over' of debt. But these are clearly stop-gap arrangements, which leave the whole question of longer-term manageability of debt completely unanswered.

There has been a vast and somewhat technical literature on the subject of long-term debt manageability, useful for identifying the essential problem. Without going into the details of assumption or the mathematical modelling involved (15), it appears that outstanding debt, resulting from the cumulative gap between domestic investment and savings plus interest obligations, would reach a steady proportion of national income only if the steady annual growth rate of income exceeds the interest rate on loans advanced (16). Since an overwhelmingly large volume of private lending has in fact been to middle-income developing countries which had a fairly high growth rate during the 1970's, the problem of managing external debt by these middle income developing countries would not seem altogether insoluble. But a few practical points arising from the present international scene make this a dubious proposition. First, the longer term recessionary trends in OECD countries make it quite difficult for those middle-income developing countries to maintain their past growth performance, as their export markets begin to dwindle. Many of them (to whom the transnational banks have lent heavily in the past) experienced a sort of export-led growth whose pace is becoming increasingly difficult to maintain in face of recession in OECD areas. Secondly, rolling-over of debt through ever increasing borrowing reduces the availability of net funds for investment and thus reduces the growth rate from the supply side. And finally, the various protectionist measures that are being increasingly followed by the industrial North make both debt servicing and export-led growth an increasingly difficult task, even for developing countries who can break into the market of OECD. Thus, in the face of recession in OECD countries coupled with their increasing protectionism in international trade, even the middle income developing countries may not be able to maintain a satisfactory enough growth rate to avoid the problem of recurrent rescheduling and rolling over of external debt. For transnational banks with heavy international 'exposure' this has the concomitant danger of getting into a liquidity crisis which may ultimately engulf the OECD countries themselves. On the other hand, if the banks decide not to 'over-expose' themselves through international lending, the question of their finding a market for financial lending operations will immediately become most pressing; for, it is precisely the recession and sluggish investment demand in OECD which makes them look outward for lending operations.

Debt manageability is however only one aspect of the larger question of credit to the South. This aspect is of primary concern to the industrial North and its transnational banking system. But from the point of view of the non-oil South, the question of credit is linked to their pace and pattern of economic development. It is essentially a question of their being able to maintain a sufficiently high pace of economic development, relying on foreign credit when necessary, although in practice, foreign aid and financial flows have often become a 'soft option' replacing efforts at mobilising domestic savings (17). But, whatever may have been the theory and practice of accepting international credit by countries of the South in the past, three distinct and recent developments in the field of international finance have overtaken past events. Indeed, there has almost been a coincidence of these three factors in recent years, which has begun to create a significantly different climate for negotiations of future credit to the South.

First, the highly vulnerable external debt position of the South seems to have led to a wrong type of reaction in OECD financial circles. Instead of trying to reduce the probability of a sudden liquidity crisis through a gradual reduction in the proportion of private to total debt, their reaction has been to induce international agencies like the World Bank and the IMF to do the policing job for transnational banks. Thus, public lending and official development assistance (ODA) are kept at low levels, transnational banks are allowed to operate in search of their profits at dangerously high levels of international exposure, while international agencies are expected to support and salvage these operations in case of difficulty. From the point of view of the South, this has the danger that international agencies will soon begin to act in unison with the transnational banking interests of the North. It also creates the added problem that large scale involvement of private banks in the economic affairs of developing countries will begin to influence wider political relations among governments (18). These have dangerous implications for the sovereignty of the borrowing country; there is a pressing need for countries in the South to be as self reliant as possible and at the same time, to diversify their sources of credit.

Diversification of credit has two components, namely composition in terms of public to private sources of credit and geographical diversification among donor countries. As we have already pointed out, given exceptionally low flows of official development assistance from OECD in recent years, there is not much likelihood of changing the composition of debt in favour of public sources of credit. Hence, geographical diversification in the sources of credit becomes an extremely important avenue to explore from the point of view of the South. And this assigns a special significance to the availability of credit from the CMEA to the non-oil South. According to US government estimates, from 1955 to 1976 the USSR extended credit of the order of US 11.8 billion dollars, over 95 per cent of which was loans. East European countries together extended another 6.5 billion (19). Compared to the current account payments deficits of the non-oil South (see *Table 5.1*), these are small orders of magnitude and cannot be expected to cover more than 4 to 5 per cent of their current account deficits annually.

But just as private credit from the North has almost exclusively favoured a few middle-income developing countries, financial flows from the Soviet Union have also been country-specific and highly selective. Thus, almost 28 per cent of the Soviet aid has gone to only two countries during this period, Egypt and India, while another 43 per cent has gone to only six countries of the Middle East (20), so that eight countries of the South together account for more than 70 per cent of Soviet aid during the period 1955-1976. By and large, Soviet aid has been characterised by lower interest rates, but a shorter maturity structure, compared to ODA from OECD countries. But its worst feature has usually been its 'double-tied' nature – it is tied to particular projects as well as to the origin of the goods. As a matter of fact, even the existing low volume of trade between the South and the centrally planned economies (about only 5 per cent of total trade of the South) is quite significantly dependent upon tied aid and credit flows from CMEA.

But in spite of the rather low volume and problematic nature of credit from CMEA in many instances, geographical and political diversification of credit flows on a larger scale is absolutely essential for the non-oil South. It is here that a second development in international relations has coincided with the economic compulsions for diversifying sources of credit. The non-aligned movement is having a widening circle of membership among countries of the South over the years and, undoubtedly, a strong case can be made for providing a clear economic dimension to the non-aligned movement by attempts to develop a more diversified trade and credit structure for its members.

The third, and in some ways the most important development that has taken place in the sphere of international finance is the large volume of the OPEC surplus. There are various alternative estimates of its size. These collated in the following *Table 5.3*, (21) while *Table 5.4* gives the pattern of investment of this OPEC surplus by the broad regional pattern over time (22).

In spite of the very rough and tentative character of the two tables above, at least three broad facts seem to stand out: (a) a definite tendency towards lower rater of annual

Table 5.3

Various estimates of the surplus of OPEC (a)
(US dollars billion)

Source:	1973	1974	1975	1976	1977	1978	1979
Bank of England (b)	–	–	31	37.2	33.3	11.9	–
Chase Manhattan Bank (c)	6	64	30.7	35.4	29.7	10.7(d)	11.2(d)
Morgan Guaranty Trust Company (e)	–	68	36	38	29	9	10(d)
OECD (f)	9	62	27.3	37	31.5	11	7.5

(a) These figures are netted for official transfers and represent the resources available for commercial investment. – (b) *Quarterly Bulletin,* March, 1979, p. 29 and June, 1979, p. 132. – (c) Economics Group Publications, *International Finance,* 11 December, 1978, pp. 6-7. – (d) Projected figures. – (e) *World Financial Markets,* December, 1978, p. 8. – (f) *Economic Outlook,* December, 1978 and December 1977, p. 49 and p. 64 respectively.

Table 5.4

Pattern of deployment of OPEC surplus, by broad regions: 1974–78
(in percentage)

	1974	1975	1976	1977	1978	1974-78
United States	21.3	24.3	30.2	22.9	7.4	22.8
Rest of OECD	22.9	20.5	17.1	21.6	32.9	21.9
Eurobanking market	38.3	20.5	26.9	29.6	9.1	28.0
International financial institutions	6.4	10.9	4.3	1.2	0.6	5.3
Developing countries & Socialist bloc	11.1	23.7	21.4	24.7	50.0	22.0

Source: see Reference 22

OPEC surplus from its 1976 peak; (b) more or less complete failure of international financial institutions to attract OPEC funds and finally, (c) the growing importance of the developing countries and the socialist bloc as an avenue for deployment of the OPEC surplus. This last point – the growing importance of the non-oil South for deployment of surplus originating in the oil-producing countries of the South – is easily explicable, not so much in terms of a policy of collective self-reliance of the South, but by rapid inflation in the OECD area, the depreciating dollar and the vulnerability of the

OPEC to economic and political pressures from OECD in general and from the United States in particular. Whatever may have been the reasons behind the increasing deployment of OPEC surplus towards the South, this tendency merges with the other two broad developments in the international scene mentioned earlier, namely unwillingness of the North to extend enough public credit and an economic compulsion on the non-aligned countries to diversify their sources of credit. The financial power of the OPEC, represented by its existing large surplus, could really play a catalytic role in uniting these three broad tendencies and creating a new mechanism of credit to the South in a changed pattern of cycling of international finance. At least one important aspect of this changed pattern will be a less rentier-like dependence of the low-absorber OPEC countries on the OECD capital market and a direct or 'primary cycling' of a major part of OPEC surplus through their own financial institutions, not controlled by the North. Only then would be created preconditions for a new mechanism of credit to the South – a mechanism which could begin to counter, at least partly, the built-in asymmetries in the present pattern of international trade and finance.

References

(1) M. Abdel-Fadil, F. Cripps and J. Wills, 'A new international economic order p', *Cambridge Journal of Economics,* Vol. 1, no. 2, June 1977, p. 207.

(2) Approximately, OECD accounted for about 64 per cent of world exports in 1977, and of that total, nearly 70 per cent is accounted for by trade among the member countries. *The Economist,* February 10, 1979.

(3) This is matched by corresponding deficits on invisible current account of *both* the oil and the non oil producing countries. It is interesting to note that although rich countries as a rule have surplus invisible trade, the two otherwise major surplus countries, West Germany and Japan, had large deficits in invisible trade in 1976-77. *The Economist, op. cit.*

(4) There is a sharp and increasing difference among members of the OPEC in terms of their balance of payments positions. A few 'low absorber' countries – Saudi Arabia, Kuwait, Qatar and United Arab Emirates – accounted for $ 33.6 billion, out of a total OPEC surplus of $ 34.1 billion in 1977. See, Morgan Guaranty Trust, *World Financial Markets,* September 1976 and June 1977.

(5) This is the visible trade account. For some countries of South Asia, there has recently been some relief through net positive remittances from abroad, mainly from migrant workers to the Middle East.

(6) *Far Eastern Economic Review,* October 19, 1979, p. 56, based upon IMF, *Annual Report, 1979* and World Bank, *World Development Report, 1979.*

(7) Or, more exactly the 'low-absorber' countries in OPEC (see Reference 4).

(8) These figures (among many floating alternative estimates) are based upon, World Bank, *World Debt Tables,* 1976, vol. 1, pp. 31-33 and vol. 2 (relevant country pages).

(9) See Ho Kwon Ping, 'Caught in the oil-debt trap', *Far Eastern Economic Review,* 19 October 1979.

(10) See, D. O. Beim, 'Rescuing the LDCs' in *Foreign Affairs,* July 1977.

(11) Based upon various published OECD reports, especially the 1978 report of the DAC Chairman, Maurice J. Williams.

(12) Approximately, external debt grew at an annual compound rate of 21 per cent between 1967 and 1977, at current prices. More detailed statistical analysis shows definite acceleration of the rate of growth of external debt from slightly less than 15 per cent per annum to almost 31 per cent per annum during this period, so that an average (constant compound) growth rate seems misleading.

(13) This is the percentage of debt service (interest and principal), summed over a given number of years — usually 5 or 10 years in accordance with banking convention — to the total outstanding debt at a given point of time. Thus, the time profile index is a ratio of two stock items (while the debt service ratio is a flow to flow ratio) at a given point, primarily used to emphasise the maturity structure and bunching problem of debt.

(14) World Bank, *World Development Report, 1979,* Table 6.

(15) D. Avramovic and others, *Economic growth and external debt,* Johns Hopkins Press, Baltimore 1964; G. Ohlin, *Aid and indebtedness: the relation between aid requirements, terms of assistance and indebtedness of developing countries,* OECD, Paris, 1966 and R. Solomon, 'A perspective on the debt of developing countries' in *Brookings Papers on Economic Activity,* No. 2, 1977.

(16) This result was first observed by Domar and has since reappeared in various forms in the literature on external debt (see previous reference).

(17) See, G. Papnek, 'The effect of aid and other resource transfers on savings and growth in less developed countries', *Economic Journal,* September 1972 and a particularly illuminating mathematical model along this line in B. Wasow, 'Dependent growth in a capital-importing economy: the case of Puerto Rico', *Oxford Economic Papers,* March, 1978.

(18) For a brief account of how it happened in three countries — Argentina, Peru and Zaire — during 1976, see D. O. Beim, 'Rescuing the LDCs', in *Foreign Affairs,* July 1977.

(19) Quoted in S.K. Mehrotra and P. Clawson, 'Soviet economic relations with India and other Third World countries', *Economic and Political Weekly* (Bombay) Special Number, August 1979, p. 1368.

(20) *ibid.,* p. 1369.

(21) Compiled by R. Sobhan, 'The pattern of OPEC investments: the logic of redeployment' (unpublished, to appear in *Economic and Political Weekly* (Bombay).

(22) Based upon information contained in 'The international deployment of OPEC's gross investent with emphasis on the US', *Economics Group, Chase Manhattan,* February and March 1979 and Bank of England Quarterly Bulletin, June 1979 (as quoted in Rehman Sobjan *ibid.*) and recomputed for our present purpose.

Chapter 6

TRANSNATIONAL COMPANIES AND DIRECT PRIVATE INVESTMENT IN DEVELOPING COUNTRIES

Alfredo Eric Calcagno*
Jan Kñakal*

There is no need to stress the importance of the role played by the transnational companies in world economic development from the standpoint both of the industrialised and of the developing countries. Few subjects have received more attention in recent years, as is shown by the voluminous bibliography and by the growing number of institutions engaged in analysing this phenomenon; these include the United Nations Centre on Transnational Corporations (CTC) and the Joint CEPAL/CTC Unit. In recent years CEPAL has published several papers dealing with the Latin American experience in this field (1).

6.1 Some basic data

The direct private investment accumulated in developing countries at the end of 1977, by regions and main countries of destination, is shown in *Table 6.1*, from which we see that 55 per cent is located in Latin America, 13 per cent in Africa, 4 per cent in the Middle East, 25 per cent in South and South-East Asia and the remaining 3 per cent in other developing countries. Ten of the recipient countries account for more than half the total (Brazil, Indonesia, Mexico, Bermuda, Venezuela, India, Malaysia, Panama, Argentina and Peru). As regards the countries from which the investments originated, 51 per cent comes from the United States, which, together with the United Kingdom, the Federal Republic of Germany, France and Japan account for 85.5 per cent (see *Table 6.2*).

A bird's eye view of the sectors shows that direct private investment is concentrated in the manufacturing sector (see *Table 6.3*), and that in the most dynamic industrial branches, such as chemicals, rubber, steel and mechanical engineering, foreign capital is dominant (see *Table 6.4*). By contrast, investment in the extractive sectors has decreased substantially, mainly because of the nationalisation policies adopted by several developing countries. The share of mining, smelting and petroleum in the United States foreign investment in developing countries went down from 42.5 per cent in 1967, to 35.4 per cent in 1971 and 17.9 per cent in 1978.

* Director of the International Trade and Development Division of the Economic Commission for Latin America (CEPAL in Spanish, ECLA in English) and Regional Adviser of the Joint CEPAL/ CTC Unit, respectively. The opinions expressed in this chapter are those of the authors and do not necessarily reflect the views of the United Nations Economic Commission for Latin America.

Table 6.1

Developing countries: cumulative amount of foreign direct investment at 31 December 1977
(Millions of US dollars)

Argentina	2 850	Iran	1 000
Brazil	10 700	Turkey	500
Chile	1 215	**Total Middle East**	**2 830**
Colombia	1 410		
Mexico	5 070	Hong Kong	1 730
Panama	2 750	India	2 450
Peru	1 930	Indonesia	5 160
Venezuela	3 300	Korea	1 280
Total Latin America a)	**31 790**	Malaysia	2 700
		Philippines	1 620
Trinidad and Tobago	1 260	Singapore	1 500
Jamaica	900	Taiwan	1 720
Total Caribbean b)	**2 980**	**Total South and South-East Asia**	**19 825**
Bermuda	4 065	**Other developing countries**	**2 045**
Total other colonial areas c)	7 620		
Total developing America	**42 390**	**Total developing countries d)**	**77 291**
Liberia	1 035		
Nigeria	1 040		
Zaire	1 100		
Gabon	740		
Total Africa	**10 201**		

a) Excluding Cuba. — b) Including Barbados, Belize, Guyana, Jamaica, Surinam and Trinidad and Tobago. — c) Including European countries' territories. — d) Excluding Gibraltar, Greece, Israel, Malta, Portugal, Spain and Yugoslavia.

Source: OECD, *Development co-operation, 1979 Review,* Paris, 1979.

The predominance of United States enterprises is linked, *inter alia,* to the post-war expansion of the US economy and to the role of the dollar in the international monetary system, as well as to the technological advances made by United States enterprises with major government support; as a result these firms hold a leading position in very dynamic sectors of international manufacturing. It should also be stressed that the 228 subsidiary companies of continental European enterprises operating in the United States, and the 905 subsidiaries of United States companies operating in continental Europe, at the beginning of the 1970s, deal predominantly with the same branches of industry: the majority of the enterprises in both cases are in the electrical, machinery and chemicals sectors. Meanwhile, the share of German and Japanese foreign investment in developing countries more than doubled in the last two decades (from 9 to 19 per cent: see again *Table 6.2*).

Table 6.2

Net foreign direct investment flows from DAC countries to developing countries

(Millions of US dollars)

	1961/1965a)	1966/1970a)	1971/1975a)	1976	1977	1961/1977a)	% (1961/ 1977)a)
Canada	146.4	244.2	870.0	430.0	390.0	2 080.6	2
United States	4 092.0	7 022.0	17 399.0	3 119.0	4 866.0	36 498.0	50
France	1 553.0	1 523.9	2 239.3	245.5	264.7	5 826.4	8
Fed. Rep. of Germany	472.1	1 068.1	3 263.1	765.4	846.0	6 414.7	8
Italy	398.5	474.5	989.4	212.9	162.2	2 237.5	3
Netherlands	269.4	651.8	1 010.2	244.7	485.7	2 661.8	3
Switzerland	197.1	...	555.5	226.1	211.3	...	..
Sweden	112.9	172.3	235.1	125.0	126.3	771.6	1
United Kingdom	1 041.0	1 339.1	2 604.4	953.9	1 223.3	7 161.7	10
Belgium	210.0	152.9	252.8	235.8	69.5	921.0	1
Japan	370.2	669.1	2 666.1	1 084.2	724.4	5 514.0	7
Total DAC countries	8 917.1	13 917.1	31 640.9	7 823.9	9 498.9	71 797.9	100

a) Total accumulated in the period.

Source: OECD, *Flow of Financial Resources to Less-Developed Countries,* Paris, 1973;
OECD, *Development Co-operation, 1975 Review,* Paris, 1975, and *1979 Review,* Paris, 1979.

Table 6.3

Stock of direct investment in selected developing countries and territories, by major industrial sectors, selected years

		Total stock of foreign direct investment (Millions of US dollars)	Percentage breakdown			
			Extractive sector	Manufacturing sector	Service sector	Other
Latin America:						
Argentina	1973	2 275.2	5.6	65.0	24.5	4.5
Brazil	1971	2 911.0	0.9	81.8	14.9	1.4
	1976	9 005.0	2.5	76.5	18.6	2.0
Colombia	1971	962.0	27.3	50.0	19.0	3.7
	1975	965.0	36.0	44.2	18.3	1.5
Mexico	1971	2 297.4	5.9	75.2	16.4	2.5
	1975	4 735.8	4.1	77.5	18.1	0.2
Panama	1969	214.1	21.1	27.0	51.7	–
	1974	353.5	16.1	37.4	46.4	–
Asia:						
Hong Kong	1971	759.5	–	100.0	–	–
	1976	1 952.4	–	100.0	–	–
India	1974	1 682.8	4.2	92.0	3.7	–
Indonesia	1970	1 581.4	74.9	19.2	5.5	–
	1976	7 077.0	37.5	57.0	10.3	–
Philippines	1973	146.0	5.7	39.2	52.5	2.6
	1976	513.0	12.6	48.7	34.0	4.7
Korea	1973	582.2	1.3	76.9	21.8	–
Republic of	1975	926.9	1.4	80.1	18.5	–
Singapore	1971	1 575.0	47.7	52.2	–	–
	1976	3 739.0	40.6	59.3	–	–
Thailand	1969	70.2	0.1	97.3	2.5	–
	1975	174.7	–	93.1	6.8	–
Africa:						
Nigeria	1968	999.2	53.7	24.5	18.8	2.0
	1973	1 998.6	63.3	25.2	10.3	1.2

Source: United Nations Centre on Transnational Corporations, *Transnational corporations in world development: a re-examination,* (E/C. 10/38), March 1978, p. 259.

Table 6.4

Indicators of foreign participation in selected industries in certain developing countries, selected years

		Estimated percentage foreign share of:					
		Chemicals	Rubber products	Iron and steel	Non-electrical machinery	Electrical machinery	Motor vehicles
ISIC Group		(351-352)	(355)	(371)	(382)	(383)	(3843)
Country and year							
Argentina	1969	37	75	...	82	33	84
Brazil	1976	51	44	61	55	33	100
India	1973	27	52	41	25	33	10
Korea, Republic of	1970	22	...	37	19	...	...
Mexico	1973	67	84	37	31	63	...
Peru	1969	67	88	...	25	62	...
Philippines	1973	...	73	...	...	...	43
Singapore	1968	46	76	21	...	...	...

Source: United Nations Centre on Transnational Corporations, *Transnational corporations in world development: a re-examination, op. cit.*

6.2 Main orientations of foreign direct investments

Direct foreign investments are mainly oriented towards the exploitation of the natural resources, internal markets and cheap labour of developing countries. In the following paragraphs, the main features of these activities will be outlined.

(a) *Natural resources*

Two opposed positions confront each other: on the one hand, the developed countries demand free access to raw materials and security of supply, at the lowest possible prices; on the other hand, the developing countries claim the sovereign right to exploit their natural resources according to their own development needs (rather than in keeping with any hypothetical duty to meet the requirements of developed countries) and to sell exportable surpluses at the highest possible prices.

Mining and petroleum extraction are old targets for foreign investment in developing countries. In 1967 these two activities accounted for more than one-third of the stock of foreign investments, although during the 1970s they have decreased substantially as a result of the nationalisation policies of developing countries. Traditionally, this pattern of investment was esentially extractive, and was linked to the productive system of the developed investor country; it usually resulted in enclaves, located in developing countries but generating little value added, since commodities are generally taken out of developing countries to be processed in developed countries. Out of a fairly exhaustive list of 27 commodities (2), the OECD countries in 1975 imported 58 per cent of them without processing, 20 per cent semi-processed and 22 per cent in processed form. These commodities amount to two-thirds of the OECD countries' total imports – excluding petroleum – from developing countries. In particular, the share of non-processed imports by OECD countries was 80 per cent for fruit, coffee, tobacco, manganese, rubber, wool, fish, phosphates, and iron ore. At the other extreme, more than half the exports of cotton, leather, palm kernel and copra are imported in processed form.

For the developing countries, this situation means both a hindrance to the industrialisation processes and a loss of export earnings. Inasmuch as the investments constitute an enclave economy, their multiplier effects are very weak. Further processing would not only generate a greater value added but would also favour the industrialisation process (by improving labour training, infrastructure, local subcontracting and external economies in general). As regards the loss of earnings, the UNCTAD secretariat has estimated that local semi-processing before export of 10 commodities (3) could provide the developing countries concerned with gross additional export earnings of about US $ 27 billion (on the basis of 1975 trade figures).

From a different point of view, comparisons have been made between the prices received by the producer countries and the consumer prices paid by users in developed countries. The results show that exporting countries receive less than 10 per cent of the final price for iron ore and bauxite; between 20 and 30 per cent for tea, coffee, cocoa, citrus juices, bananas and jute; and between 40 and 55 per cent for sugar (4).

In many cases, internal taxes levied by developed countries are similar to, or higher than, the share received by developing countries for their natural resources. The most important example is the petroleum produced by the OPEC countries and consumed in European markets. In 1972, the total price was US $ 12.60 per barrel of the final product, of which US $ 1.70 was attributable to taxes in the producing countries; US $ 4.10 to distribution costs and profits of enterprises; US $ 5.40 to taxes in developed consumer countries, and the remainder to production, transport and refining costs. Thus, the taxes received by the consumer country were three times as high as those received by the producer country. In 1974, however, with the new price of petroleum, these shares changed. In the first quarter, out of a total price of US $ 21, the shares were: US $ 7.85 for taxes in producer countries; US $ 5.30 for distribution and profits of enterprises, and US $ 6.00 for taxes in consumer countries (5).

The economic policies followed by the developed countries – mainly through the barriers raised by their governments – have had a great influence on the lack of local processing. Tariff protection tends to increase with the degree of processing undergone by the product concerned, and this discrimination is further aggravated by escalations of freight rates and by customs valuation procedures; in the case of non-tariff barriers, the average frequency of restrictions tends to rise in accordance with the stage of processing (6).

To counteract these policies, the developing countries have made use of several instruments aimed at increasing the level of local processing: export prohibitions, quotas or taxes on the export of non-processed goods. Incentives to industrialisation and the export of manufactures also have an important indirect effect. These policies have had some success in the leather and wood industries, while in the mining sector several public enterprises have been established to enter into joint ventures, and other types of agreements, with transnational corporations to increase the forward linkage of the industries concerned.

Other obstacles to a higher level of local processing include a new kind of protectionism in the form of 'negotiated restrictions', 'voluntary export restraints' or 'orderly marketing arrangements'; there are also barriers raised by private firms and stemming from market structures, such as cartel practices and the control by the transnational companies over factors of production, marketing and access to markets. Other restrictions are related to the capital intensity of the industry: this problem is particularly important in mineral processing (7).

(b) *Protected internal markets*

In the post-war period many developing countries undertook import substitution policies. One response by developed countries to this challenge was to develop an 'export substitution' policy by which transnational enterprises oriented towards the internal market were established in developing countries. This kind of enterprise eventually led to 'indirect exports' of the greatest importance. Total sales of foreign affiliates (excluding intra-firm sales) of US and Swiss enterprises, in developed and developing countries, are calculated to have been equivalent to 4.6 times the total exports of the home countries (1976 data); for the UK, the corresponding ratio was 2.6 and for Japan, Canada, the Netherlands, France and the FRG, the ratios lay between 0.7 and 1.1. (These are estimates, calculated by assuming total annual sales of the foreign affiliates to be equal to 3.8 times the book value of the cumulated foreign direct investment at the beginning of the year) (8). These investments, oriented towards the internal market of host countries, are concentrated in manufacturing activities. Of 1,664 foreign affiliates of companies from Europe, Canada and Japan, in 1971, 97 per cent had the internal market as the main outlet for their production (9). The foreign affiliates of US companies, in 1977, sold 94 per cent of their manufacturing output in the internal market of the host country (10).

The market for manufactures in developing countries, it is pointed out in a CEPAL study (11), can be divided in three main cases:

(i) goods requiring simple and practically changeless technology: generally non-durable consumer goods; (ii) consumer goods requiring medium or high-level technology: mainly consumer durables; (iii) basic capital and intermediate goods: mainly chemicals.

For the goods in the first group, a large proportion of the demand in developing countries is covered by domestic production. The domestic market in such countries is already considerable, and will grow a great deal more as the large percentage of the population which is at present marginal is incorporated into the labour and consumer markets. Foreign investment and transnational corporations, generally speaking, have little direct involvement in the production of these sectors in the Latin American countries (although tobacco products would be an important exception).

Consumer goods of intermediate or high-level technology, generally consumer durables (motor vehicles, domestic appliances, etc.), and some non-durables, are in demand among the intermediate and high-level income strata. To increase the real demand for these goods, a large share of national savings is mobilised to provide credits for their acquisition. Advertising, the demonstration effect of consumption in more developed countries, and the action of the transnational corporations themselves, are also important elements in expanding demand in these sectors. The participation of transnational corporations in the developing countries' production in these sectors will possibly continue to be substantial; naturally, the modes of participation at present differ from one case to another and may evolve, in the future, from direct production in the hands of the transnational corporations to the participation of these enterprises in specific aspects of the production, marketing and distribution cycle, such as the supply of technology.

The increase in the domestic output of the two groups of consumer goods mentioned, and of others not explicitly considered here, generates the market for the goods of the third group, i.e., capital goods and chemicals, expanding, particularly, in relatively more developed countries.

(c) *Cheap labour*

An important share of foreign investment originating in developed countries is aimed at taking advantage of cheap labour costs in developing countries. Behind this policy there is the double purpose of reducing costs, and of diverting the labour force of developed countries to more productive and sophisticated activities.

The first outstanding fact is the huge difference between wages in developed and developing countries (*Table 6.5*).

Table 6.5

Relative nominal and productivity-weighted wages 1973 (USA = 100) (a)

	Nominal wage per capita (1)	Wage costs per unit of output (b) (2)	Wages % of value added (3)	Wage weighted by productivity (d) (4)	Wage weighted by productivity (e) (5)
Developing (13 countries)	8.0	45 (c)	47.3	17.3	39.3
Developed (5 countries)	79.0	.	94.5	.	73.6
Japan	47.0	.	77.3	44.3	64.3
Fed. Rep. of Germany	79.0	.	.	99.8	.
USA	100.0	100.0	100.0	100.0	100.0

(a) Wages plus salaries. — (b) Steel only. — (c) Brazil. — (d) $WEij = \frac{Wij \times Pj}{Oij}$

where WEij = weighted wages
Wij = total nominal wage bill of branch i, in country j
Pj = unit price
Oij = total output of the branch (in value)

(e) $WEij = \frac{Wij}{Nij} e^{(Lg\, 1 - \alpha i\, Lg\, GDPHj - \beta i)}$

where WEij = weighted wages, branch i, country j
Wij = total nominal wage bill
Nij = number of employees
GDPHj = gross domestic product per capita

Source: United Nations, *Yearbook of Industrial Statistics,* 1975, volume I and (for column 2) Commodities Research United Ltd., *Study on the degree and scope for increased processing of primary commodities in developing countries,* prepared for UNCTAD, New York, 1975.

However, it has been argued that the low wages in LDCs must be viewed in the light of low productivity: low wages are justified, it is claimed, because more manpower is required for producing the same amount of goods in developing countries than in developed ones. To assess the real meaning of this reasoning nominal wages should be weighted by productivity. In *Table 6.5*, column 1 shows the wages per head in the manufacturing sector of different countries (in 1973), expressed in US dollars at the international exchange rate. This would reflect actual labour costs per unit of output only if labour productivity were the same in every country. Two factors might support such an assumption: (i) transnational enterprises usually use the same technology in all countries: (ii) this technology is in most cases very standardised and automatised, especially in industries like iron and steel and non-ferrous metals, so that the difference in manpower skill between countries should not have a significant impact on labour productivity.

The figures demonstrate the enormous gap in average wages per employee between developed and developing countries (USA = 100 and developing countries = 8).

Columns 2 to 5 show the results of different methods of adjusting for productivity. Column 2 takes into account the output per worker for relatively homogeneous products of the steel industry. While the production of 1,000 tons requires 3.5 man/years in the USA, it requires 9.2 man/years in the UK and 15.7 man/years in Brazil, the nominal ratios being 100, 38 and 10, respectively. Column 3 considers the ratio of nominal wages to value added per employee. Column 4 shows wages weighted by an accounting price system (12) using a price system determined from a basket of goods. The last method used (column 5) is based on productivity estimates from the level of development (measured by GDP per capita).

In short, the great difference between wages in developed and developing countries is *not* substantially justified by differences in labour productivity. From several points of view, and using different methods of analysis, the results are essentially the same: for a transnational enterprise, the level of wages — weighted by productivity — in the same industrial branch is substantially lower in developing countries. *Table 6.5* gives the results of different hypotheses, showing how the gap can range from 50 to 80 per cent, according to the branch and method of calculation.

International subcontracting, as practised by several transnational enterprises in developing countries, has very low capital requirements. The average fixed capital needed for each labour unit in Kaohsiung (Taiwan) export factories is around US $ 1,500, while in Mexico the average in subcontracting factories in 1974 was US $ 840 per worker. To appreciate fully the extremely low level of these investments, it is worth comparing them with the US $ 31,000 invested per worker in average manufacturing industries in the USA.

The differences in labour costs connected with the different levels of per capita income has also led to labour migration from countries with lower income levels towards more developed countries. This explains, for example, migration from Mediterranean countries to more developed countries in Northern Europe and from Latin America to the United States.

6.3 Balance of the contribution made by foreign direct investment

It is argued that three of the main benefits of foreign investment to developing countries are their financial contribution to development, the improvement of the balance of payments situation, and the raising of the technological level. In the following paragraphs we will see what actually occurs under these heads.

(a) *Financing*

For the financing of their foreign direct investments, transnational enterprises make use of several sources. From a recent study on the sources and uses of funds of foreign affiliates of US enterprises in developing countries, we see that in 1966 – 1972, 55 per cent of the funds came from internal sources (of which, two-thirds were depreciation and similar charges) 42 per cent from sources external to the affiliate, and 3 per cent from other sources (*Table 6.6*). Only 9 per cent of the total funds originated in the US (9 per cent for petroleum, 21 per cent for manufacturing and minus 5 per cent for 'others'). Simultaneously – as we shall see below – these transnational affiliates were transferring to the developed countries, in the form of profits, interest, royalties and the provision of technical assistance, an amount several times greater than they were receiving as investment funds.

The fact that only 20 per cent of the funds available to the manufacturing affiliates in developing countries comes from the parent country has been presented as evidence of the catalytic action of foreign investment, which is thus claimed to have the effect of mobilising internal savings (13). If this thesis were correct, it would imply that without foreign investment the national resources would remain unemployed; but the real situation seems to be the opposite – foreign enterprises compete with national enterprises for local credit in developing countries. Between December 1977 and December 1978, for example, seven countries, accounting for 82 per cent of Latin America's total GNP, saw their consumer prices increase by more than 30 per cent. Consequently, anti-inflationary policies have been applied, including credit restrictions. Moreover, this inflation has sometimes led to very low or even negative interest rates. As a result, competition for internal credit is strong. Furthermore, in the phase following the maturity of investments – which include a high component of internal savings – profits sent back to developed countries are calculated on the basis of the total investment, including the local savings utilised.

Table 6.6

Sources of funds for a sample of majority-owned foreign affiliates of US companies in developing countries (1966 – 1972) (a)

	Million US $				Percentages of total funds			
	Total	Petroleum	Manufacturing	Others	Total	Petroleum	Manufacturing	Other
Total sources of funds	16 221	8 339	4 277	3 605	100	100	100	100
Unidstributed profits	2 854	1 498	608	748	17.6	18.0	14.2	20.7
Depreciation and similar charges	6 020	4 060	1 157	803	37.1	48.7	27.1	22.3
External funds (external to the affiliate)	6 830	2 512	2 463	1 855	42.1	30.1	57.6	51.5
of which:								
Net funds from US	1 422	713	884	– 175	8.8	8.6	20.7	– 4.8
Net funds other than from US	5 408	1 799	1 579	2 030	33.3	21.5	36.9	56.3
Other sources	517	269	49	199	3.2	3.2	1.1	5.5
In addition to the above items –								
Distributed profits	17 715	15 505	741	1 469	109.2	188.0	17.3	40.7

(a) Figures represent the total accumulated in the period 1966 – 1972.

Source: Ida May Mantel, "Sources and uses of funds for a sample of majority-owned foreign affiliates of US companies, 1966 – 1972", US Department of Commerce, *Survey of Current Business,* Vol. 55, July 1975, pp. 30-52.

(b) *The balance of payments*

The transnational corporations engaged in manufacturing activities in developing countries often have a negative effect on the balance of payments. For these enterprises, the import coefficient is higher than for national enterprises, while the export coefficient is only about the same. Moreover, their import coefficients are higher than their export coefficients. Transnational corporations generally operate in sectors of industry where the import coefficients are higher than the manufacturing average. Their presence promotes the development of these sectors and in many cases encourages an increase in the consumption of goods with a high import content, thus aggravating the tendency towards a trade deficit in the recipient countries. On the other hand, their export coefficient is very low. As a general rule, the transnational corporations have been reluctant to export, except where permission for their investment has been conditional on the export of part of the production.

In this connection we may also note the effects of intra-company trade and the problem of transfer prices, which may adversely influence the balance of payments – although it is difficult to evaluate this factor exactly. *Table 6.7* shows that 43 per cent of US imports from developing countries in 1977 were intra-company trade (49 per cent for raw materials, 17 per cent for semi-manufactures and 37 per cent for manufactures).

Payments of profits, interest and royalties are also relevant. For the impact of these types of payments (see *Tables 6.8* and *6.9*). *Table 6.8* shows that in the period 1970 – 1977 the flow of direct investments to developing countries was about US $ 35 billion, while the earnings of the developed countries from these investments came to US $ 83 billion. *Table 6.9*, for its part, shows that the stock of US direct investments in developing countries in 1979 was US $ 34 billion, and over the period 1955 – 1977 the outflow from the US was over US $ 8 billion; meanwhile the earnings credited to the US balance of payments came to US $ 43 billion. Finally, *Table 6.10* shows the balance of payments of eleven transnational companies in Brazil over the period 1965 – 1975. These companies, with an initial investment of US $ 299 million, have reinvested US $ 693 million and repatriated US $ 774 million.

The information quoted provides clear evidence that the process of foreign direct investment implies a net transfer of resources from the developing to the developed countries. This is in keeping with the logic of the capitalist system: the investor company intends to take out greater profits than the initial investment.

(c) *Technology*

Transfer of technology is one of the main contributions that could be expected from transnational enterprises. Among the problems that this issue raises, however, are those of the kind of technology and of its cost.

Table 6.7

Intra-company trade in US imports, 1977

Area of origin	Degree of processing	Total US imports (millions of dollars)	Percentage of intra-company trade
Developed countries	Raw materials	10 781	41.3
	Semi-manufactures	19 830	43.4
	Manufactures	45 937	61.1
	Total	76 548	53.8
Socialist countries	Raw materials	216	2.8
	Semi-manufactures	345	8.9
	Manufactures	871	8.1
	Total	1 432	7.5
Developing countries	Raw materials	42 158	49.1
	Semi-manufactures	5 103	17.0
	Manufactures	18 165	37.0
	Total	65 876	43.2
Total World	Raw materials	53 155	47.3
	Semi-manufactures	25 278	37.6
	Manufactures	65 423	53.6
	Total	143 857	

Source: UNCTAD, on the basis of information from G.K. Helleiner and R. Lavergne of Toronto University, supplemented with figures from the Foreign Trade Division of the US Census Bureau.

Table 6.8

Flows of foreign direct investments to developing countries and flows of income to investor countries: accumulated amounts, 1970 – 1977 (millions of US dollars)

	Direct foreign investment in developing countries	Investor countries' income from direct investment
Total developing countries	34 915	82 919
Latin America	18 756	22 052
Africa	3 780	13 327
Middle East	– 411	33 090
South and South-East Asia	12 167	13 862
Oceania	623	587

Source: UNCTAD, *Handbook of International Trade and Development Statistics,* New York, 1979, p. 364.

Table 6.9

US investment in developing countries, 1966 – 1977
(millions of US dollars)

	Total	Petroleum	Manufacturing	Others
Stock of direct investment (1979)	33 706	3 014	12 239	18 454
New outflow from US (1966 – 1977)	8 158	– 3 960	3 648	8 470
Reinvestments (1966 – 1977)	13 559	2 584	5 651	5 324
Income in US balance of payments from direct investments (1966 – 1977)	42 600	26 887	3 864	11 849

Source: US Department of Commerce, *Survey of current business,* August 1978.

On the kind of technology, a double question arises: that of the technology effectively demanded by the developing countries, and the ability of the developed countries to satisfy these demands. First, the nature of the technology demanded depends to a large extent on the consumption patterns of dominant social groups and on the massive advertising that promotes them. This demand is conditioned by the distribution of income and by the 'demonstration effect' promoted by the dominant foreign advertising companies (in 1975, foreign and mixed companies were responsible for between 62 per cent and 72 per cent of advertising in Brazil, Argentina, Mexico and India). This effect is not confined to the high income groups: it also pushes the medium-income groups into debt and influences the aspirations of the low-income groups.

The second question concerns the supply of technology from the developed countries. These countries transfer their own technologies, worked out to meet their own needs. Of course, the developing countries are of only marginal interest to enterprises engaged in technological research in developed countries, so the latter offer technologies that are generally labour-saving and aimed at social groups with an average income comparable to that of the developed countries. Consequently, these technologies are often adequate neither to the needs of the developing countries nor to the requirements of the majority of the population (since only a minority has the living standards of the population of developed countries). Moreover, this technology overlooks important problems of developing countries (for instance, it does not take into account tropical agriculture or tropical diseases).

Figures for payments of royalties and fees by seven developing countries in recent years ranged between one and three per cent of the total value of their exports, and in Mexico

Table 6.10

Brazil: Remittances of profits and technology costs to the home country 1965 – 1975: eleven transnational corporations
(millions of US dollars)

Company	1 Total investment in Brazil including years before 1965	2 Reinvestment	3 Profits and dividends remitted	4 Remittances on purchase of technology	5 Total remittances	6 Profits made in Brazil	7 Ratio of profits in Brazil to initial investment (6/1)
Volkswagen	119.5	72.8	70.6	208.5	279.1	351.9	2.94
Rhodia	14.3	108.7	39.9	20.7	60.6	169.3	11.84
Exxon	1.8	67.7	44.5	–	44.5	112.2	62.33
Pirelli	28.7	37.8	45.1	19.8	64.9	102.7	3.58
Philips	9.9	51.2	5.0	9.4	14.4	65.6	6.63
Firestone	4.1	44.5	48.1	2.1	50.2	94.7	23.1
General Electric	13.9	32.2	19.4	4.3	23.7	55.9	4.02
Souza Cruz	2.5	129.5	81.3	1.0	82.3	211.8	84.7
Johnson & Johnson	0.7	34.0	17.0	5.7	22.7	56.7	81.0
Anderson Clayton	1.4	28.2	16.8	–	16.8	45.0	32.14
Brazilian Light	102.0	86.4	114.7	0.6	115.3	201.7	1.98
Total	*298.8*	*693.0*	*502.4*	*272.1*	*774.5*	*1.467.5*	*4.91*

Source: Banco Central do Brasil.

they reached 11 per cent. These are mainly payments among affiliates and parent companies (75 per cent in 1972), and could hide profit remittances.

6.4 Bargaining power and new modalities in links with transnational enterprises: recent experiences of Latin America (14)

As noted above, the expansion of the transnational enterprises in developing countries gives rise to a variety of reactions, but in most cases two basic considerations prevail: firstly, the contribution which these firms can make in providing technology, capital, access to external markets and business and plant management; and secondly, the desire to avoid any interference by foreign investors in domestic policy matters, to ensure that investment is in keeping with each country's development strategy and policy guidelines, and to see to it that the *modus operandi* of these investors is the most suitable for local needs and circumstances.

These fundamental concerns are reflected in the common principles upheld by the developing countries in connection with the preparation of an international code of conduct for transnational corporations. They were also confirmed in the Latin American *Guatemala Appraisal,* which held that transnational enterprises must comply with the laws and regulations, and submit to the exclusive jurisdiction, of the host country; refrain from any interference in domestic matters, international relations and external policy; respect national sovereignty over natural and economic resources; comply with national policies, objectives and priorities; report on the enterprises' activities; make net contributions of financial resources; contribute to local scientific and technological capacity; and, finally, refrain from restrictive trade practices (15).

Obviously, the preparation and international acceptance of a code of conduct for transnational corporations is a complex and difficult process, related to the establishment of the New International Economic Order and to the objectives pursued by the developing countries in the North-South dialogue. Without neglecting the prime importance of intergovernmental negotiations on this subject, it should be borne in mind that the bargaining capacity and courses of action of developing countries *vis-à-vis* the transnational enterprises are related to the real conditions and experience of the different countries — to the links between the two sides and to bargaining powers and government policies.

Latin America has become one of the most attractive regions of the developing world for the operations of transnational corporations. This is due to (i) the increasing size of Latin American domestic markets, (ii) the availability, cost and skills of its labour force, and (iii) the existence of some comparative advantages, including the difference in the costs and level of priority attached to the solution of environmental problems in Latin American countries by comparison with the industrialised countries. In any case, it has been shown that Latin America is absorbing a very large proportion of total foreign investment in the developing world, and that the transnational corporations are interested in the opportunities of producing within the Latin American markets. More important, because of its dynamic impact on the economies of the region, manufacturing has apparently become the most attractive sector for foreign investment as a result of the above-mentioned long-term evolution and extension of the 'import substitution' phase in Latin America; during that phase, the sectors preferred by foreign investors have changed substantially, with a sharp decline in mining, oil and services, and a proportionally large increase in manufacturing (and recently also in financial services).

Another important element of the negotiating capacity of Latin American governments is the growing competition among transnational corporations of different developed countries for access to various markets. Over the last decade, the share of the United States in world foreign investment dropped from 54 to 48 per cent and that of the former colonial powers (the United Kingdom, France, Italy and Belgium) from 26 to 17 per cent; meanwhile the share of Germany and Japan increased from 4 to 14 per cent, and that of a group of smaller market economies (Canada, the Netherlands, Switzerland and others) from 14 to 19 per cent. This has meant that the developing countries, particularly in Latin America, have been able to diversify their sources of supply of technology, and their access to international markets and entrepreneurial capacity, and have consequently been able to increase their bargaining power *vis-à-vis* the transnational corporations.

The Latin American countries are now tending to play a more active role in dealing with the transnational corporations, with the object of influencing their relations with the national economy in the following ways: (i) inducing the corporations to enter into some degree of partnership with national capital, whether public or private, thus enabling national interests to become increasingly acquainted with, and involved in, decision-making on aspects of production, marketing and financing of the activities in question; (ii) strengthening the role of the public sector in some strategic areas (such as minerals, steel and petrochemicals) in which the transnational corporations are interested or active, with a view to reducing the possible weakness of the national private sector in these areas and giving more leverage to the government in the implementation of its economic policies; (iii) stimulating the creation of multinational enterprises among several countries of the region, with the same object of increasing the negotiating capacity of Latin American enterprises. Government bargaining power has also been increased by the competition in some markets of State firms from the socialist countries, as well as of medium-sized and small firms from the industrialised market economy countries.

Naturally, the use made of these new tendencies depends on the firmness with which each government defines and applies clear policies taking advantage of the new opportunities. Recent experience in Latin America and other areas of the world indicates that when circumstances demand it, the transnational corporations can display a significant degree of flexibility and adaptation of their operations to local conditions. When their interest in the market of a given country or group of countries is very great, and when they face a government exercising its bargaining power reasonably and firmly, they tend to alter significantly their traditional forms of operation and to accept conditions more favourable to the host countries in order to gain entry. Symptoms of this are the recent agreements between transnational corporations and socialist countries, and the appearance of a new *modus operandi* of the transnational corporations. The partial information available seems to indicate that corporations wishing to enter or expand in the market of a country or region tend to adopt a more flexible attitude and offer more favourable conditions in order to be able to penetrate oligopolistic markets, and in so doing usually push the already established corporations into similarly improving their operating practices to face the new competition.

New forms of cooperation have arisen from the negotiations between transnational corporations and developing countries, the major forms being:

(a) co-production and specialisation agreements;
(b) sub-contracting;
(c) cooperation arrangements limited to technology and marketing; and
(d) joint ventures between foreign and national firms.

(a) *Co-production and specialisation agreements*

These are undertaken between plants located in developed countries and plants situated in developing countries. Under co-production agreements, a plant of a foreign enterprise located abroad and a public or private national or regional enterprise, or a subsidiary of the foreign enterprise located in a developing country, share out the components or types and models of a specific product, each producing part and marketing it in such a way that exports are made by both the developed and the developing country. In specialisation, which is similar to the above arrangements, the developing country becomes responsible for distributing at the world level the finished product rather than parts or components.

These arrangements are different from what usually occurred in Latin America during the import-substitution process, when the enterprise or subsidiary of the developing country produced only for the domestic market. In co-production and specialisation, the developing country exports some of the goods produced while at the same time importing others.

Arrangements like these have recently been made by Fiat and Volkswagen with Brazil, by Nissan with Mexico and by Peugeot with Argentina. Fiat had to agree to undertake exports of parts and components as a condition of producing in Brazil; Nissan produces parts and components in Mexico which are sent to Japan; while the Volkswagen 'beetle' and Peugeot '404' are still being produced for export in Brazil and Argentina, respectively, because although they have ceased to be produced in the countries of origin, there is still world demand for them. These arrangements are positive; although they do not eliminate the countries' dependence on the transnational corporations in technology and marketing and are not a substitute for the creation of greater local capacity in those fields or for strategies for the export of advanced manufactures, they do represent a step in that direction.

(b) *Sub-contracting*

Under a sub-contracting agreement, a developing country firm undertakes on behalf of a developed country some stages of the production of a product, which is transferred from the developed to the developing country at a certain stage of production to incorporate the stage in question and is then re-exported. The stages located in the developing country usually make intensive use of unskilled labour. The technical specifications are fixed by the foreign enterprise, which also supplies technical assistance and equipment. The most important examples in Latin America of such arrangements are the *'maquila'* industries in Mexico, involving clothing, electronics and other types of industry, with a value added in the country of US $ 468 million in 1975 and gross exports of US $ 1021 million in the same year. These operations have been facilitated by United States tariff items 806-30 and 807-00, where the basis for the customs tariff evaluation is the value added abroad rather than the total value of the import, thus making it possible to transfer parts of some production processes and make use of cheap labour.

Sub-contracting bears some resemblance to co-production and specialisation, but is limited to isolated processes and does not involve the complete production of final products or parts and components. The advantages for countries with surplus labour are clear, since it generates employment and foreign exchange. However, such activities located in developing countries remain very vulnerable from the standpoint of the foreign corporation, which may at any moment decide to transfer them to another country. In addition, the investment in the developing countries is generally minimal, and in the great majority of cases only relatively unskilled labour is employed, at low wages. The effects in terms of the diffusion of technology and the promotion of other industries – i.e., external economies – are practically non-existent, since the semi-processed goods employed are totally imported from a developed country for the sole purpose of building into them a labour-intensive process and then re-exporting them. These limitations have meant that in Mexico an attempt is being made to ensure that these industries acquire other inputs in the country, and are located not only on the border where they were initially set up (as twins of the parent companies located on the other side of the border) but in other regions of the country as well, so as to integrate them more successfully with the rest of local manufacturing industry.

(c) *Cooperation agreements limited to technology and marketing*

These arrangements are used to break down the direct investment 'package' so that the developing country can acquire only the elements it does not possess, thus supporting efforts to create greater local capacity for decision and action in industry and technology. Technology itself can be broken down into its various parts or components (design, construction and operation of the plant, improvement of products and production processes, development of new products, research, etc.), and an effort is made to acquire each of these from the source of supply which is cheapest and best suited to local conditions; the object is to make better use of local production resources, to narrow the technological gap, and to produce goods better adapted to the specific use which will be made of them in the markets for which they are destined. The relatively less developed countries perhaps lean towards agreements under which the foreign firm sells the plant on a turnkey basis to the local public or private enterprise, initially trains technical personnel and a certain proportion of skilled workers, and provides advisory services during the first years of operation of the plant until the latter can gradually do without foreign support. To diversify its sources of supply, the developing country must have a sound knowledge of the alternative sources of the desired elements and have the ability both to analyse the different options in the light of its own needs and to absorb, handle and disseminate the different types of technology.

Marketing agreements are less frequent; they are used in some cases – for example, between transnational enterprises and socialist countries – and are beginning to appear in Latin America. This cooperation, limited to specific activities, also helps to avoid or reduce certain drawbacks – observed in the intra-firm transactions common in Latin America and throughout the world – whereby the exports of the transnational enterprises are carried out between affiliates of the same enterprise or between them and the parent company. When the same company is both purchaser and seller, it is hard to verify that the prices established truly correspond to the market value of the product, and that the developing country is really obtaining the income corresponding to the value added by the activities of the enterprises in its territory and is paying proper prices for the inputs imported by the enterprise.

Some recent cases illustrate new forms of transfer of technology and marketing of goods. In Brazil, there are examples in petrochemicals, computers and aircraft manufacture. In the design and manufacture of civil aircraft, for example, the foreign enterprise provides technical assistance for the production of parts, assembly, quality control, etc., and has the right to export, while the Brazilian State enterprise can export in its turn, possibly using the foreign firm's distribution network. In synthetic fibres, Mexico encouraged competition among foreign enterprises of different origins and in choosing among them took into account not only the provision of technical assistance during the initial and future stages, but also the possibility of reserving the right to acquire the different technological components separately. In 1978, Ecuador and Venezuela imposed the following conditions on the transnationals competing for markets allocated under the motor-vehicle sectoral programme: the vehicles and their components must comply with United States standards on pollution, fuel consumption and quality control; no payment shall be made for patents and licences, but only for technical assistance and material costs; and training will be undertaken so that production can begin with a minimum of 50 per cent of local technical and administrative staff, to reach 90 per cent after five years of operation. These conditions will affect not only exports within the Andean Pact but also exports to third markets, and targets have been fixed for the future.

(d) *Agreements between foreign and local enterprises for joint ventures*

These agreements usually cover capital, technology and managerial capacity provided by one or more foreign enterprises (which may even come from different developed countries), combined with local elements from the developing country. Agreements to establish joint companies are frequent between transnational corporations and governments, between transnationals and State enterprises, and between transnationals and national or regional private enterprises. For example, the Brazilian State enterprise Petroquisa set up Copene (Petroquimica Nordeste), a firm combining local public and private capital with capital from a number of transnational enterprises from different industrial countries, which also contributed contracts for licensing, management, etc. The advantages for the countries of the region are clear, since they have a real share in the firm's ownership, technology, administration and marketing; the training of local managerial staff is promoted; and the State has influence over basic areas of development. The agreements also suit the transnational enterprises, since they are able to share risks with the State, can use relatively cheaper resources, and overcome administrative obstacles because of their direct cooperation with the public sector.

6.5 Some conclusions

From this review of the expansion and effects of foreign private investment and of the activities of transnational corporations in the economies of developing countries, we can draw some brief conclusions:

(a) Foreign private investment in developing countries implies only a minimal flow of capital from the country in which the investment originates. It consists principally of the procurement of external financial resources by foreign enterprises (local funds of the host developing country and international funds), and of the sale of technology and know-how, rather than the flow of real resources. In particular, the difference between the inflow of foreign investments into the host country, on the one side, and its payments of interest, profits and royalties to the foreign firms, on the other, is strongly negative for developing countries and has a negative effect on their balances of payments;

(b) The bulk of foreign investment in developing countries is oriented towards their internal markets. Nationalisation processes have considerably diminished the proportion invested in petroleum and mining. The cheap labour available in developing countries is an additional element, but not decisive (except in special cases like South-East Asia);

(c) The technology introduced into developing countries originates in industrialised countries with higher income levels and in many cases is designed to save labour, so that it is often unsuited to the needs of developing countries;

(d) In Latin America, new forms of links with transnationals have arisen as a result of the region's increasing negotiating capacity vis-à-vis transnational corporations. These new forms include co-production and specialisation agreements, sub-contracting, co-operation arrangements limited to aspects of technology and marketing, and agreements for the carrying out of joint ventures.

References

(1) See the select bibliography below. In this chapter, the authors draw particularly on items *3, 5* and *7* of this bibliography.

(2) Coffee, cocoa, sugar, natural rubber, cotton, jute, sisal and henequen, copper, tin, meat, peanuts, copra, palm kernel, wood, iron ore, phosphates, manganese, aluminium, fish, fruits, vegetables, tobacco, leather, pulp and paper, wool, lead and zinc. See UNCTAD, *The processing before export of primary commodities: areas for further international cooperation,* Geneva, December 1978.

(3) Copper, bauxite, phosphates, natural rubber, cotton, jute, hides and skins, non-coniferous timber, cocoa and coffee. See UNCTAD, *The processing ... op.cit.*

(4) See UNCTAD, *Proportion between export prices and consumer prices of selected commodities exported by developing countries,* Nairobi, May 1976.

(5) See UNCTAD, *Mobilisation des ressources intérieures. Pays membres de l'Organization des pays exportateurs de pétrole (OPEP) et développement* (paper by consultant Abdelkader Sid-Ahmed, October 1978).

(6) See UNCTAD, *The processing ... op. cit.*

(7) The range of average investment costs in minerals and metals activities was estimated as follows (at 1975 costs): for the setting up of an aluminium plant of 500,000 tons/annual capacity, $ 1,200 million; a copper plant of 100,000 tons/years, $ 600 million; an iron-ore pellets plant of 10,000,000 tons/year (66 per cent Fe content), $ 800 million; a nickel plant of 25-30,000 tons/year, $ 480 million; a lead plant of 100,000 tons/year, $ 140 million; a zinc smelting plant of 50,000 tons/year, $ 80 million; (see UN Economic and Social Council, Committee on Natural Resources, Geneva, document E/C. 7/68, 29 March 1977).

(8) UN Centre on Transnational Corporations, *Transnational Corporations in World development: a re-examination* (E/C. 10/38) March 1978 pp. 35 and 236; UN, *Statistical Yearbook 1978.*

(9) See Lawrence G. Franke, *The European Multinationals,* London, Harper and Row, 1976, p. 126.

(10) See US Department of Commerce, *Survey of Current Business,* Vol. 57, No. 2.

(11) See CEPAL, *The economic relations of Latin America with Europe,* Santiago, Chile, May 1979.

(12) The accounting price system is described in H. F. Lydall, *International Trade and Employment,* ILO, Geneva, 1978.

(13) See Raymond Vernon, *Sovereignty at bay,* London, Longman, 1971, p. 171 and the refutation of this thesis in Daniel Chudnovsky, *Empresas multinacionales y ganancias monopólicas en una economía latinoamericana,* Buenos Aires, Siglo XXI Editores, 1974.

(14) This discussion is based on studies *2* and *3* of the select bibliography.

(15) See the *Guatemala Appraisal,* adopted in ECLA resolution 362 (XVII), in the series Cuadernos de la CEPAL, No. 17, 1977, paragraphs 169 to 173.

Select Bibliography

1 United Nations Economic Commission for Latin America (CEPAL), "Trends and changes in the investment of transnational corporations in the developing countries and particularly in Latin America", in *Economic Survey of Latin America,* 1977 (Sales No. E. 79.II.G.1), pp. 520-536.

2 CEPAL, "Transnational corporations in the present stage of Latin American development", in *The Economic and Social Development and External Economic Relations of Latin America,* (E/CEPAL/1061), February 1979, Volume II, pp. 168-189.

3 CEPAL, "Direct private investment", Section III of *The Economic Relations of Latin America with Europe,* (E/CEPAL/L.192), May 1979, pp. 1-52.

4 United Nations Centre on Transnational Corporations (CTC), *Transnational corporations in world development: a re-examination,* (E/C.10/38), March 1978.

5 A.E. Calcagno, "Informe sobre las inversiones directas extranjeras en América Latina", *Cuadernos de la CEPAL,* (E/CEPAL/G.1108), February 1980.

6 E.V. Iglesias, "Transnational Corporations in Latin America", *The CTC Reporter,* United Nations, New York, No. 6, April 1979.

7 J. Kñakal, "Las empresas transnacionales en el desarrollo contemporáneo de América Latina", *Estudios Internacionales,* Universidad de Chile, No. 47, July-September 1979.

Chapter 7

THE ROLE OF DEVELOPMENT AID FACILITIES

Francis Seton*

To evaluate the 'role' of anything in any context one needs to measure it against the background or canvas on which it appears. The role of an actor, be he hero or villain, is the greater, the larger the portion of the stage he fills, and the longer his allotment of the play's time. But what actor, and what play? Indeed, what *are* development aid facilities?

The term itself is redolent of *Ideengeschichte.* How did 'aid to developing countries' almost imperceptibly turn itself into 'development aid' with its connotation of a direct spur to economic development rather than succour to the poor, the hungry, and the naked? For close on three decades now the whole paraphernalia of economic theory has been harnessed to the task of justifying the kind of aid which would in as short a time as possible create the conditions for its own redundancy, by 'helping the poor to help themselves', bringing about the 'take-off into self-sustained growth', or 'breaking the vicious circle of underdevelopment'. The good Samaritan was urged to keep his coat as undivided as possible and send the naked poor shivering into evening classes in dress-making, to speed the day when they would importune him no longer. What other 'role' for Development Aid could there be? It was a 'stop-gap' to tide the poor over for the time being, until the gap – or gaps – had been eliminated. But what gaps?

7.1 'Gap theory' and development aid – statics

The highly influential theory of development gaps, also known as 'two-gap theory', is a simple extension of elementary Keynesian statics: the fertile notion that, provided only our accounting concepts are properly formulated, we can use them to uncover causal links between the economic variables of the real world as they strain to fit themselves into this inevitable framework. Desired or intended investment, unless it exactly matches the saving we are prepared to do, will bring about involuntary stock movements sufficient to force investment desires into the straitjacket of our accounting identities, simultaneously furnishing a proximate cause for readjustments in demand, incomes, and other macroeconomic variables. If our intended behaviour offends against the logic of

* Nuffied College, Oxford

Note: the abbreviations and symbols used in this chapter are defined at the end of the Mathematical Annex, pp. 158 - 159 accounting, then some hidden hand must alter the incentives or resources on which these intentions are based until they are revised into mutual consistency. This is the thinking behind a famous geometric device known to generations of first-year economics students as the 'Keynesian' or 'Samuelson' cross, in which desired or *ex ante* investment and saving are plotted against national income and their intersection is unveiled as the equilibrium position which the logic of events will enforce. On the simplifying assumption that 'savers always get their way' it can moreover be shown that in *all* positions, whether in or out of equilibrium, *ex post* investment will equal saving, once involuntary stock movements are duly taken into account.

I apologise for travelling over this *pons asinorum* at such length, but a good deal of confusion over the 'two-gap theory' has been caused by failure to absorb the true nature of this conceptual apparatus into everyday consciousness. It was discovered somewhat triumphantly, for instance, that the two gaps — let me call them the 'users' gap' between investment and saving (U) and the 'traders' gap' between imports and exports (T) — were in fact necessarily of the same size, being only two sides of the single accounting identity

$$Y \equiv C + I + E - M \text{ (income} \equiv \text{consumption + investment + exports – imports),}$$

whence of course

$$I - (Y\text{-}C) \equiv M - E, \text{ or } U \equiv T$$

Some economists had even forgotten the nursery school distinction between *ex ante* and *ex post* to the extent of denying the separate identity of the two gaps altogether. It was felt necessary to add a special appendix to an authoritative OECD report (1) to put the practitioners right on this. But there is still the ghost of a suspicion in many people's minds that those who differentiate between U and T may be 'seeing double', and no demonstration so far seems to have carried the sort of conviction that is only born in economists' breasts when matters are spelt out and understood in fully diagrammatic form. As it seems important that this ghost should be finally laid, let me attempt to do this here and now.

The diagram below (2) analyses the basic GNP-identity ($Y = C + I + E - M$), converted into *ex ante* form by interpreting the two expressions equated as supply- and demand-side respectively, to be denoted by Z and V to make this explicit. The total supply of resources from domestic production is the GNP, Y (reproduced vertically and re-labelled Z), contrasted with the total demand facing domestic producers (V) composed of consumption (C), investment (I), and exports (E), the latter being assumed independent of income while investment is shown as weakly dependent on it. The two domestic demand components (C and I) are combined into a single function 'Domestic absorption' (D), with foreign demand (E) superimposed to show the total demand function Q.

To emphasize the *ex ante* nature of all these components we might have written them with the prefix $\underline{x}$, e.g. ^{x}C, ^{x}I, ^{x}M, etc., thus distinguishing them clearly from the corresponding *ex post* variables C^{x}, I^{x}, M^{x}, etc. We shall have occasion to do this later in the argument, but have omitted it so far in true text-book fashion in order not to overburden the diagram.

Diagram 7.1

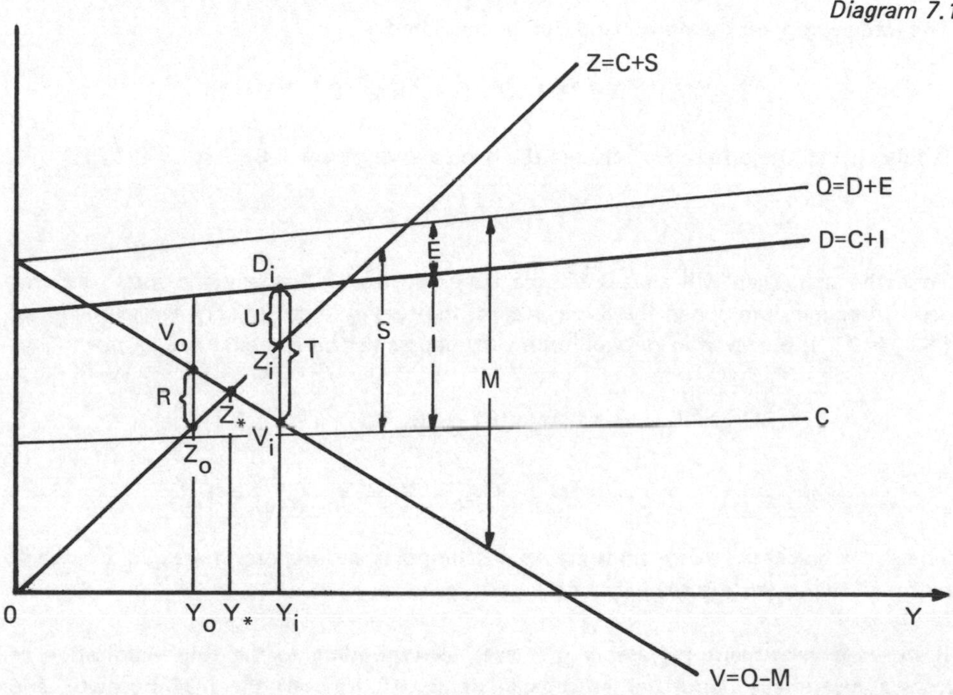

Clearly, any excess of total supply over demand, such as $Y_1Z_1 - Y_1V_1$, must betoken an accumulation of unwanted (=undemanded) stocks V_1Z_1, while the opposite discrepancy, e.g. Z_oV_o, implies a 'resource gap' $\underline{R}$, which must be 'filled' in some way. In a closed economy this could only be done by drawing on initial domestic stocks, i.e. by allowing unplanned (= undesired) stock depeletion of the kind which creates increased demand for re-stocking. In an open economy, however, the gap may also be filled by 'drawing on the outside world', possibly by sucking in more imports than anticipated or by using domestic resources destined for exports, i.e. by opening up or widening what we have called the 'traders' gap' $\underline{T}$. This second option must be the one chosen by less developed countries (LDCs) which are presumed to have no depletable stocks inherited from the past. In the opposite situation of glut (e.g. V_1Z_1), however, an LDC might experience the same unwanted stock accumulation as a more developed country (MDC) or a closed economy, with the same Keynesian tendency to reduce demand and income, and saving and investment in its train.

We can now use the diagram to make the two gaps explicit: without any particular assumption on the level of income (i.e. the numerical suffix of our symbols), the *ex ante* users' gap is evidently

$$^{x}U \equiv {}^{x}I - {}^{x}S = {}^{x}I + C - C - {}^{x}S = YD - YZ = ZD$$

The traders' gap, on the other hand, can be measured as

$$^{x}T \equiv {}^{x}M - {}^{x}E = {}^{x}M - Q + Q - {}^{x}E = YD - YV = VD$$

It follows that the difference between the two *ex ante* gaps will be:

$$^{x}U - {}^{x}T = ZD - VD = ZV \equiv R$$

Thus the users' gap will always diverge from the traders' gap by the total 'resource gap'. In equilibrium, when the latter is zero, the two *ex ante* gaps are necessarily equal ($^{x}U_{*} = {}^{x}T_{*}$); but even in disequilibrium the gaps must be of equal size *ex post.* Thus

$$^{x}U_{o} = {}^{x}T_{o} + R = ({}^{x}M_{o} + R) - {}^{x}E_{o} \equiv M_{o}{}^{x} - E_{o} \equiv T_{o}{}^{x}$$

or $$= {}^{x}M_{o} - ({}^{x}E_{o} - R) \equiv M_{o} - E_{o}{}^{x} \equiv T_{o}{}^{x}$$

where the bracketed expressions are *ex post* imports and exports measured after their enforced adjustments in the light of the users' gap.

If *ex ante* investment represents the level corresponding to the full exploitation of known investment opportunities capable of contributing to the LDC's growth, and *ex ante* saving the flow consistent with consumption standards that cannot, or should not, be reduced, it must be the function of 'development aid' to allow the *ex ante* users' gap to be 'realised', i.e. to ensure that $\underline{U^{x} = {}^{x}U}$, so that I^{x} and S^{x} can be equal to ^{x}I and ^{x}S respectively. This has immediate implications for the amount of aid (and/or capital inflow) required:

In the case where $\underline{^{x}U > {}^{x}T}$, foreign aid must fill the (larger) users' gap; for only this will enable the *actual (ex post)* traders' gap to widen and the additional resources imported (or withheld from exports) to be devoted to making up investment- or consumption-deficiencies. Thus:

$$A = {}^{x}U \equiv {}^{x}T + R \equiv T^{x} \equiv U^{x}$$

In the opposite case where $^{x}U < {}^{x}T$, on the other hand, the filling of the users' gap by foreign aid or capital inflows would be insufficient; it would only allow a *portion* of the traders' gap to be filled, and enforce the rest to be closed by diverting resources from investment or consumption which, by hypothesis, should be left unimpaired. In terms of our diagram, it must now be the role of aid not merely to close the (smaller) users' gap, but also to inject sufficient extra resources into the economy to replace the consumption- and investment-losses which result from the enforced income deflation from Y_1 to $Y_*(V_1Z_1)$, in symbols:

$$A = {}^{x}T \equiv {}^{x}U - R \equiv U^{x} \equiv T^{x}$$

In summary, any 'gap-filling' development aid, to be fully effective, must always fill the larger of the two gaps. The two-gap theory in this form can thus be exonerated of double vision in the sense that it never requires the *sum* of the two gaps to be filled. At the same time it is not redundant, as it requires the two gaps to be distinguished from each other and to be compared in their *ex ante* size.

7.2 Gap theory – dynamics

Much of the longstanding popularity of gap theory is due to the ease with which it can be made to 'move through time'. Indeed, the Harrodian concept of an equilibrium or 'warranted' growth rate is directly related to what we have called the users' gap (U), and may be defined as that growth rate which will annihilate the gap at any stage of the growth process by generating a flow of domestic saving exactly matching the investment induced by it. This is the only growth rate which users can 'tolerate', and we shall take the liberty of re-naming it the 'users' growth-tolerance' or 'internal growth-tolerance' $\underline{\omega}$ defined as $\underline{s/\kappa}$, i.e. the ratio of the average savings rate to the *ex ante* capital-output ratio. The analogous 'traders' or 'external growth-tolerance' $\underline{\tau}$ can then be defined as $\underline{e/\mu}$, i.e. the ratio of the average export propensity to the 'import accelerator' $\underline{\mu}$, which will ensure the vanishing of the traders' gap (T) at any stage of the process. Both gaps may be expressed as a simple function of the shortfall of the 'growth-tolerance' below the actual growth-rate $\underline{y}$ at any period $\underline{t}$, i.e.

$$U_t \equiv I_t - S_t = \kappa \Delta Y_t - s_t Y_t = \kappa Y_t (y_t - \omega_t)$$

$$T_t \equiv M_y - E_t = \mu \Delta Y_t - e_t Y_t = \mu Y_t (y_t - \tau_t)$$

The assumption of a constant ratio $M/\Delta Y$ (the 'import-accelerator') may cause some raising of eyebrows but gains in plausibility when it is recalled that development imports are largely capital goods contributing to a stock of imported installations or technology $\underline{J}$ with its own 'capital-output' ratio $\underline{J/Y}$, whose *ex ante* incremental value $\underline{\mu}$ $(= \Delta J/\Delta Y = M/\Delta Y)$ may be assumed constant with the same degree of justification as that attaching to $\underline{\kappa}$.

It is clear from the equations above that the assumption of rigid growth-tolerances $\underline{\omega}$ and $\underline{\tau}$ (as implicit in the original Harrod model) would lead to the indefinite perpetuation and limitless growth of the two development gaps. Those who wish to persuade us that development aid can be instrumental in 'phasing itself out' will therefore have to cast about for models which allow the 'growth-tolerances' to increase towards equality with some desirable actual growth-rate y as time goes on.

Probably one of the earliest systematic and fully exploited efforts in this direction is Professor Rosenstein-Rodan's one-gap model (3) which allows the average savings ratio to grow as autonomous consumption (C_o) falls relatively to rising incomes, thus continuously raising the internal growth-tolerance ω (warranted rate of growth), given a constant *ex ante* capital-output ratio:

$$\omega_t = s_t/\kappa \equiv S_t/Y_t\kappa = \frac{\sigma Y_t - C_o}{\kappa Y_t} = \frac{\sigma}{\kappa} - \frac{C_o}{\kappa Y_o \tilde{y}^t}$$

where $\tilde{y} \equiv 1 + y$. Assuming a constant growth-rate for income y, it is then possible to compute the time-span t after which ω_t will equal y, and aid can stop. Professor Rosenstein-Rodan does such calculations for no less than 85 LDCs and presents estimates for their total aid-requirements on this basis during three successive quinquennia spanning the years 1961 - 1976. Drastic simplifications were needed to stretch the meagre ration of available statistics, including a rule of thumb equating marginal savings-rates to twice the average rates observed and the assumption of a uniform and stable capital-output ratio of 3 : 1 throughout the developing world in all the periods considered. The author is well aware of these shortcomings and of his own heroism, but does at least offer orders of magnitudes on which further analysis could be based. According to him India required a total capital inflow of 13,980 $ mil. in the decade following 1961, after which no more inflows would be needed. The only other graduates to self-reliant growth in the seventies would be Mexico, Jamaica, Yugoslavia and Israel. Trinidad, the Belgian Congo, and Malaya were expected to graduate as early as the preceding quinquennium (late sixties), while Rhodesia and Mauritius were rated to have passed the post already by 1961. Much as this pioneering effort deserves admiration, its results have by now been hopelessly overtaken by events, and cannot be up-dated without repeating the whole operation *ab initio.*

A more elaborate model, this time of the two-gap variety, was constructed by Chenery and Strout, some five years later. (4) This widens the range of structural parameters by adding a growth-target for GNP, a limit to investment growth set by 'absorptive capacity', an exogenous growth-rate for exports and a constant marginal propensity to import. Investment, even if proceeding at the maximal rate, is assumed to yield a proportional income-increment ($\Delta Y = \frac{1}{\kappa} I$), so that the growth-rate of income becomes a fixed proportion of the investment rate i ($\equiv I/Y$):

$$y \equiv \frac{\Delta Y}{Y} = \frac{1}{\kappa} I/Y = \frac{1}{\kappa} i$$

It is further assumed that the initial growth-rate of income (y_o) is lower than that of potential investment (β) – the latter being assumed constant throughout the growth progress. It follows that the investment-rate $\underline{i}$ must steadily increase with time, thus causing the growth of income to accelerate from $\underline{y_o}$ until it reaches a target rate ($\bar{r}$) thought to be the upper limit of what is maintainable on other (capacity) grounds. Once this is achieved, the growth-rate of investment can moderate from $\underline{\beta}$ to $\underline{\bar{r}}$ and we enter a 'golden age' – phase II – in which all domestic variables grow at the steady rate $\underline{\bar{r}}$. As this process unfolds the traders' gap might at various stages come to exceed the users' gap, only to give pride of place to the latter again at some later stage; and the 'gap-filling' capital-inflow requirement can be computed for each stage as one or the other gap predominates, until the process results in a 'gap-less' constellation of variables and foreign inflows can cease. The authors followed this procedure in the case of Pakistan, and in somewhat less detail for some 50 other LDCs, deriving their parameters from past performance and national economic plans.

In this paper we propose to draw freely on the features of both models in order to derive a 'development scenario' yielding rough estimates of inflow-requirements against which actual aid performance and 'the role of aid facilities' can be evaluated.

7.3 A possible development scenario

After a good deal of experimenting with statistical data the author has come to believe that an ambitious programme of bringing the totality of Less Developed Market Economies (LDMs) to the present level of per capita GNP ($\underline{Z}$) enjoyed by the average Developed Market Economy (MDM) could be completed within little more than a generation (say 55 years), given certain optimistic, but not implausible assumptions. Apart from the intrinsic, and possibly practical, interest of such a Scenario, its rationale in the present context is to derive orders of magnitude for various LDM's external finance requirements, against which the adequacy of present development cooperation can be measured and the role of development aid assessed in concrete, quantitative terms.

We shall confine attention to *market* economies, both in the developed and the underdeveloped world, in order to side-step the difficulties arising from conceptual or statistical incompatibilities (GNP vs 'Material Product', etc.) and to utilise the fund of data systematically documented in United Nations and similar international publications. We shall also take the liberty of widening our concept of 'development aid' to include all external finance representing net resource flows into LDMs, including private aid, portfolio investment, bank lending, and direct investment (incl. reinvestment), regardless of its main objectives or 'concessionality', although some attempt to measure the latter will be made as a spin-off of our exercise. The detailed country calculations are presented and explained in *Tables 7.1 - 7.4* and footnotes below and in the Mathematical Annex. In the body of the paper we merely aim to illustrate the general procedure in rough outline, taking as our example the fictional country of 'Eldemia', an artificial amalgam of all Less Developed Market Economies (LDMs) separately documented in international statistics (5).

The Scenario is a one-gap model which traces the time-profile of the 'user gap' (Investment – Saving) through two successive development phases (either of which may be skipped by particular LDMs) until it is closed, or more than closed (allowing debt-repayment or external lending) by the time Eldemia's GNP per head has reached the average level of MDMs.

To fix ideas, we define the 'development lag' at time t as the ratio of per capita income of the average MDM (at present $ 6590 p.a.) to that of the LDM under consideration. For Eldemia the initial lag in this sense is the ratio 11.36, i.e. the average per capita income of LDMs was just over one twelfth the average level of MDMs at the turn of the present decade (6). It is the aim of the Development Scenario (DS) to eliminate this gap in the n years of the Development Period, on the assumption that the growth of population can be kept down to 2 1/4 % p.a. on average (it is already down to 2.35 % at present). If the present GNP-growth-rate of 5.5 % were to stay constant, i.e. the growth-rate of *per capita* GNP was no greater than 3.2 % p.a., it would take nearly 80 years to achieve this – an unacceptably long delay before the ideal of 'one world' is achieved. The process can however be speeded up by promoting an initial 'acceleration phase' (APh) of say k years, during which the growth-rate of GNP rises from year to year from its initial level of 5.5 % p.a. (y_o) to some higher level (g) which is still deemed to be sustainable for prolonged periods (7). In the case of Eldemia the latter is set at 6.7 % p.a., as attested by the 8-year period 1967 - 75 (8). This acceleration may be achieved by promoting a steady growth rate in investment, again as high as is deemed to be sustainable for k years in the light of past or analogous experience (9). Once GNP growth has been jacked up to its maximal level, it is easy to ascertain what residual lag in per capita income still remains, and how many years of steady growth at that level would be needed to eliminate it. This constitutes the 'Steady-Growth Phase' (SGPh) of m years, which completes the total Development Period (DP) of n (= k+m) years. For Eldemia and each of the 30 LDMs considered we ran a series of computer programs, letting k increase from 0 to anything up to 80 and ascertaining the steady growth-rate (g) and duration of SGPh (m) which would result in each case. From among these we chose the alternative which seemed most plausible (in view of g) and most acceptable (in view of m) and fastened on the corresponding (k, m, n)-combination as the most suitable Development Scenario for the LDM in question. For Eldemia this was an Acceleration Phase of 7 years, bringing GNP growth from 5.5 to 6.7 % p.a. by means of an annual investment growth of 9 %, followed by a Steady Growth Phase of 51 years, during which GNP growth would be maintained at 6.7 % p.a. and investment growth could gradually moderate from 9 % towards 6.7 % p.a. as time wore on (10). This implies a total Development Period of 58 years – probably the shortest achievable without overstepping the bounds of plausibility. The procedure was then repeated for each of the 30 LDMs listed in the Tables, and Development Periods within sight of a human life-span found for all of them, with the exception of Burma, Kenya, Nigeria, Sri Lanka, Tanzania, and Zaire.

Aid requirements

Our next step was to trace the time-profile of the 'user-gap' between investment and saving both in APh and SGPh, and to cumulate them throughout the years of both phases during which they remained positive (the 'aid stages').The results were averaged for each of the two phases by simple division by the number of years involved, to give the figures in col. 9 of *Table 7.2* and col. 5 of *Table 7.3* ($ 13.8 billion and 74 billion in the case of Eldemia for 6 and 17 years respectively). The figures were finally weighted for each country in proportion to the duration of the two aid stages, to yield the average annual aid requirement of col. 1 in *Table 7.4*. All figures were computed by formula as given in the Mathematical Annex and individually referred to in the footnotes to the Tables.

We can spell out the results for Eldemia as follows: Aid requirements appear as $ 58.2 billion p.a. for a total period of 23 years (last col. of *Table 7.4*), subdivided into an earlier phase of $ 13.84 billion p.a. for an initial 6 years (the APh of *Table 7.2*), and a later phase of some $ 74 billion p.a. for the SGPh of 17 years (*Table 7.3*), the two phases being separated by an interval of 1 year (col. 8 of *Table 7.2*) during which a fraction of the first dose could be repaid. On completion of the second phase, 34 more years remain to complete the catching up process (col. 4, *Table 7.3*) during which the aid receipts of the later phase (but not of the earlier one) could be repaid at an interest charge of anything up to 7.5 % p.a. (*Table 7.3*). It is clear from *Table 7.5*, however, that the *total* aid required in both phases could not be repaid within the development period of 58 years, and that consequently the aid scenario must make provision for a grant element and a 'free-loan' element within aid if Eldemia is to complete the development scenario free of all debt, which we take to be the final aim throughout.

Repayment capabilities

The completion of each 'aid stage' is by definition the point in time when the user gap reduces to zero. This must be followed by a succession of years in which it will be negative, thus implying an excess of domestic saving over investment needs out of which the previously incurred aid debt could be partially or completely repaid. We have cumulated these excesses (negative user gaps) during the 'repayment stages' of r and s years respectively (cols 10 and 6 of *Tables 7.2* and *7.3*) to arrive at the total repayments or new credit positions that could be shouldered. Where these are in excess of the original aid debt there is room for a service charge equivalent to the annual interest rate shown in the last columns of *Tables 7.2* and *7.3* (see also Mathematical Annex, Equations 25 and 32). These are crude calculations which take no account of the exact time-profile of debt- and repayment-flows and should not take precedence over the discounted cash-flow calculations of *Table 7.5* where, moreover, all stages are consolidated and repayment refers to the *total* aid-flows in both APh and SGPh. It is not of course suggested that donor countries should feel free to impose such charges on their aid in all cases; the calculations merely specify the maximal charge that could be borne while leaving the recipient just free of debt by the end of each phase. Where this turns out to be negative, some part of the aid-debt would still remain to be repaid at the end of the Development Period unless given in grant form. In these cases the figure measures the notional interest on past aid disbursements to which a waiver of the outstanding debt residual would be equivalent.

Unfortunately international aid statistics are not couched in terms of 'equivalent interest charges' as a measure of the 'concessionality' of aid, but use a special criterion known as the 'grant element' in aid. The latter is based on present-value calculations and deviations from a conventional market rate of interest of 10 %. In principle either measure should be convertible into the other, although the informational requirements would be heavy and the calculation would be complicated and hazardous. We have none the less attempted to go some way towards it in *Table 7.5* where the same development scenarios are used to derive aid requirements to cover the user gap as it develops through time by discounting the latter back to the 'present' for both APh and SGPh at the conventionally fixed market rate of 10 % p.a. (col. 2). We have then calculated the annuity to which this present value would be equivalent if paid out yearly throughout the total 'aid period', i.e. both of the aid stages in APh and SGPh during which the user gap is positive. The result, shown in col. 3, is probably a more 'scientific' way of stating annual aid requirements than the crude averaging of *Table 7.4*, although its meaning is not as immediately obvious to the normal intuition. We have dealt in the same way with negative user gaps representing repayment capability without however computing annuity-equivalents. In those cases where the repayment capability falls short of the required aid we have computed the 'grant element' in the aid (as a % of total) which would be needed if the LDM was to emerge from the total Development Period clear of debt. In the remaining cases where the repayment capability extends beyond the aid absorbed, there is room for a service charge equivalent to an annual interest rate shown in col. 6. Where this falls short of the conventional market rate of 10 %, we have computed the 'degree of concessionality' required in terms of the percentage of aid needed in the form of interest-free loans, on the assumption that the rest is loaned at 10 % p.a. (the 'free-loan element' of col. 7). The last two columns of the Table are merely added as a guide to intuition and convey no information additional to that of col. 6. It should be remembered, moreover, that the percentages stated apply to the *total* capital inflow requirements, including direct investments and reinvestments undertaken on commercial criteria, and not merely to official development aid as normally quoted in aid statistics.

Caveats

Our calculations are based on a number of highly questionable assumptions which ought to be spelled out in their full starkness — for simplicity with reference to Eldemia only, though of course they apply *mutatis mutandis* to all 30 LDMs listed in the Tables.

a) The volume of investment can be increased by 9 per cent p.a. throughout the acceleration phase (7 years). This may seem unrealistic and is indeed optimistic, but LDMs as a whole have already shown themselves capable of increasing investment by 9 per cent p.a. over the 8-year period 1966 - 74, and have indeed exceeded this at various times. Their 'absorption capacity' does not therefore seem to be in serious doubt.

b) Population growth in the Third World can be kept down to 2 1/4 per cent p.a. on average over the next half century. This again may seem optimistic, but rates as low as 2.3 -2.4 per cent p.a. have already been observed during the past two decades and it is generally accepted that population control methods are beginning to bite.

c) Marginal capital-output ratios will remain fairly constant nothwithstanding the massive increases in investment assumed. The author is fully aware of the hazards attaching to operations with this concept at the best of times, and resorts to it only with reluctance and for want of other time-saving alternatives. This constancy assumption is probably the most heroic of all; for, clearly, these ratios are simply the reciprocals of what might be called the 'income-yield' of investment. The assumption therefore appears to place reliance on a practically inexhaustible pool of investment opportunities of undiminishing profitability or on steadily increasing ingenuity on the part of planners, investors, or international agencies in ferretting out more and more such opportunities as time goes on. It is, however, an assumption usually made in this type of model building and is, moreover, compatible with quite conservative estimates of $\underleftarrow{\kappa}$ (exceeding the time-honoured average of 3) which might allow for some diminution in investment yields from higher initial values as time proceeds.

d) The initial income growth-rate is put at 5.5 per cent p.a. for Eldemia, and equal to growth-rates observed in various countries at the turn of the present decade (usually 1977 or 1978). This may seem an excessively optimistic starting point for a period of acceleration in some cases (e.g. Botswana, Morocco, or Turkey), but some downward adjustments have been made where this seemed warranted, and in no case does the final growth-rate of the acceleration period exceed performances which have already been observed for continuous periods in the past. In extreme cases, like Botswana, no acceleration is assumed at all.

e) Constant coefficients of any kind must be highly suspect to all experienced students of developing countries. They are, however, all but unavoidable in time-constrained exercises of this sort, and are likely to do more good than harm when the objective is confined to getting illustrative figures and orders of magnitude for purposes of comparison and rough 'targeting' rather than operative planning. It should again be stressed that our exercise does not aim at anything beyond this and that no 'forecasts' of any kind should be read into our figures. They are examples or illustrations on how it should be possible to construct 'development scenarios', and little more.

f) Above all it must be remembered that the aid needs dealt with here cover no more than the annual estimated user gap between saving and investment, and that no account is taken of balance of trade deficits where these exceed the latter, natural disasters, or any of the multifarious needs that arise in LDMs. In the 'New International Cooperation Order', to be discussed below, these additional needs fall to be covered by special facilities outside the framework of normal organised 'scenario aid'.

The last column of *Table 7.4* makes it clear that the degree to which recent aid performance matches up to our scenario requirements varies enormously as between one recipient country and another. Nigeria appears to be getting less than 7 per cent of scenario requirements while the Philippines get over ten times as much. It must be remembered, however, that the performance figures include direct investments and reinvestment of earnings by foreign companies made under the lure of profit and their own consolidation or growth without having directly in view the purposes of their hosts' development or local welfare. The comparison is therefore vitiated by extraneous factors like historical penetration by foreign companies, the interest of multinationals, enclave economies, or new profitable ventures perceived from abroad. It might be argued that a more appropriate comparison would fasten on official development aid (col 4) in which the showing against requirements is more uniformly inadequate.

The figures for Eldemia as a whole (last row) make actual inflows appear in a particularly favourable light, until it is realized that they include foreign investment and reinvestment in meteoric LDMs like Singapore, Taiwan, Hong Kong, and South Korea, as well as capital inflows into oil-rich countries like Iran and Venezuela. Short of a major research project there is at present no way of purging the published performance figures of this incubus and measuring them against what can properly be termed 'development needs'. It is hoped, however, that our tentative and admittedly shaky calculations will give a much needed impetus to the collection and elaboration of more appropriate statistics, besides promoting the search for meaningful 'aid targets' for future international action.

For completeness we have added a further table (*Table 7.6*) to show the more ambitious requirements which would need to be fulfilled if the LDMs were to complete the Development Period clear of *all* debt, whether incurred by virtue of our scenarios or prior to the aid effort envisaged here. The existence of the outstanding debt of 1977 is here assumed to leave the Acceleration and Steady-Growth phases unaltered, and to act merely as an addition to the total debt to be cleared, thus reducing the equivalent interest-rate at which repayments could be made and/or increasing the degree of concessionality required.

7.4 A new international cooperation order (NICO)

If development scenarios for individual LDMs can be worked out on the lines suggested here, or on broadly similar lines commanding a modicum of general assent, they should be acceptable as a basis for a system of international taxation and bilateral sponsorship which would offer a better guarantee for progress towards 'one world' than we have so far been able to devise. If countries earning more than 500 $ per head per annum could be persuaded to submit to international taxation or forced lending at rates rising with each major income bracket ($ 500-2000, –$ 5000, $ 5000 and above) from 1/2 to 1.5 per cent of their total GNPs, a development fund of some $ 90 billion would become available, greatly exceeding any 'scenario aid' likely to be required per year (11). Past experience unfortunately suggests that nothing resembling this is likely to be forthcoming in the near future unless the relevant recommendations of the Brandt Commission are taken to heart by all concerned. The best contribution that economists as such may be able to make towards this goal is to provide target figures or methodologies for finding them, however impeachable in detail, and to suggest international tax bases as little destructive of incentives , or as palatable on other grounds, as human ingenuity can make them, leaving it to politicians to devise efficient methods of persuasion or arm-twisting to secure the necessary consensus.

Beyond this, however, we must cast about for a system of basic aid allocations and supplements which takes the fullest possible account of the specific needs of each developing country. To this end there may be special merit in a system of 'bilateral sponsorship' which would encourage every donor country to enter into binding 'development covenants' with individual client countries in the Third World, with the object of making both parties mutually responsible for the realisation of a particular development scenario agreed between them and ratified by international action. The sponsor would then be responsible for the annual financing of the programme, either with his own funds (in return for international tax concessions) or via access to the international Tax Fund (acting rather like an Accepting House on behalf of his client), for technical cooperation, joint ventures, consultancy, etc. One might even visualise the formation of a Community for Organised Economic Development (COED) as an outgrowth or successor of the OECD, with its own network of institutions approximating those of the EEC and possessed of a modicum of 'teeth' to validate its decisions and code of behaviour in aid matters. COED might act as the initiator and agent of international taxation through an annual budget; it would scan and ratify development covenants conforming to its agreed code (absence of tied aid, 'neo-colonial' strings, restriction of local competition, etc.), grant the consequential tax exemptions, monitor the fulfilment of covenants on both sides together with side conditions on social indicators, and possibly allocate premia or bonuses for early completion of various stages or overfulfilment in selected aspects. It might also raise loans on its own behalf to create incentives for the proliferation of such covenants, stand in for unforeseen default, and possibly arrange for incentive allocations of SDRs by the International Monetary Fund, thus giving a new pragmatic content to the fertile idea of the 'link' in a less automatic and therefore more acceptable way. Above all, it would stand ready to supplement the covenant finance offered by sponsors 'on tender' by additional aid 'on tap' to prevent the disruption of ratified development scenarios by circumstances beyond the control of either sponsor or client. First and foremost among these would be the opening of trade gaps in excess of user gaps on the balance of payments of an LDM, particularly if caused by unforeseen rises in import prices (like the present oil facility), protection measures by third countries impeding an LDM's export programme, etc. It would also lend funds to sponsors where the time-profile of aid scenarios put excessive strain on them in particular peak years.

Some of these 'facilities' might be codified and come into operation automatically when certain conditions are met. Others, no doubt, would need to be *ad hoc*, and subject to COED's discretion. The role of 'aid facilities' in the accepted sense of sources available 'on tap' without special pleading can only be supplementary to a system of regular, organised development aid and can hardly be understood outside the context of the latter. The arrangements going under the name of 'facilities' to date are aimed merely at insulating developing countries from certain inclemencies of the world economic climate (compensatory financing, oil facility, etc.). We must seek to build them into the equipment of the hothouses which provide sustained nurture and promote successful growth. Without this they are at best aids to survival, not aids to development.

TABLES

The assumed initial

	GNP(b) ($ bil)	Dev't(b) Lag (ratio)	Growth rate p.a. GNP(a) (%)	Pop'n(a) (%)
1. Argentina	48.7	3.5	4.7	1.3
2. Bangladesh	6.5	82.4	4.8	4.8
3. Bolivia	2.5	3.5	4.7	1.3
4. Botswana	.4	12.2	18.6	1.9
5. Brazil	163.9	4.7	6.8	2.9
6. Burma	4.3	47.1	5.0	2.2
7. Cameroon	3.3	15.7	5.7	2.2
8. Chile	13.2	5.3	6.3	1.7
9. Colombia	18.8	8.7	4.7	2.1
10. Ecuador	6.0	8.0	8.1	3.0
11. Egypt	12.9	19.4	4.2	2.1
12. Ghana	3.9	17.8	5.1	3.0
13. India	100.2	41.2	4.9	2.1
14. Indonesia	42.7	20.6	7.2	1.8
15. Kenya	4.3	22.7	7.0	3.8
16. Mexico	73.7	5.7	3.0	3.3
17. Morocco	11.1	10.8	8.9	2.7
18. Nicaragua	2.1	12.9	4.2	3.3
19. Nigeria	40.5	12.9	4.2	2.6
20. Pakistan	15.1	32.9	4.9	3.1
21. Papua NG	1.5	12.9	5.5	2.4
22. Philippines	20.4	14.3	6.8	2.7
23. Sri Lanka	2.3	41.2	3.3	1.7
24. Sudan	5.6	20.0	6.5	2.6
25. Tanzania	3.4	31.4	5.3	3.0
26. Thailand	18.7	15.3	7.2	2.8
27. Tunisia	4.9	7.8	7.5	2.0
28. Turkey	46.6	5.9	8.5	2.5
29. Zaire	5.3	31.4	3.8	2.7
30. Zambia	2.4	14.3	3.5	3.0
Total above	685.2	15.3	5.7	2.5
ELDEMIA	1186.1	11.4	5.5	2.3

* 'Stylised' data are values reported for 1977, 1978 or 1975-7, with occasional amendments 'by hand', where the figures reported were felt to be freakish.
Bracketed references in the footnotes denote pages (p) or equations in the Mathematical Annex I (A) where definitions or explanations may be found.

(a) 1977 data from World Bank, 1979 *World Bank Atlas,* Washington D.C. Growth rates for 1970 – 1977.

(b) Computed as explained in (A 1), based on data from the source of footnote (a).

situation (stylised)*

Rate of Inv't(c) (%)	Rate of Saving(c) Av. (%)	Marginal(d) (%)	Marginal cap/ output(e) (ratio)	Pop'n(a) (mil)
20	8	60	3	26.0
10	8	30	3.5	81.2
17	7	45	3	5.2
20	10	45	2	.7
18	9	45	3	116.1
9	8	20	3	31.5
17	14	30	3	7.9
4	2	20	3	10.6
11	9	25	3	24.6
17	2	40	3	7.3
5	4	25	3	37.8
16	2	40	3	10.6
16	14	28	3.7	631.7
28	23	80	4	133.5
30	15	70	3	14.6
12	4	45	4	63.3
15	12	30	3	18.3
18	5	75	4	2.4
15	8	40	3	79.0
11	9	30	2	74.9
18	15	70	3	2.9
20	17	35	2.5	44.5
10	2	50	4	14.1
5	2	23	3	16.9
15	3	40	4	16.4
15	13	30	3	43.3
16	12	30	3	5.9
12	10	30	3	41.9
7	5	30	4	25.7
12	10	40	4	5.1
–	–	–	–	1594.8
12	10	25	3.25	2045.1

(c) Generally values of the late seventies, given in or computed from U.N. *Yearbook of National Accounts Statistics* 1978, Vol. II (International Tables). Radical alterations were however made, e.g. for Kenya, Mexico, Nigeria, Tanzania, and a few others, where the late seventies appeared to have been exceptional years.

(d) In most cases derived from curve-fitting to national accounts data (source of footnote c) by hand, but often radically adjusted to produce plausible rates of 'autonomous consumption' (difference between marginal and average saving rates) at low levels of development. The figures are little more than guesses.

(e) Curve-fitting as above, supplemented by guesses.

	Duration of total Dev't Period (Yrs) (1)	Of which: Accel'n Phase (Yrs) (2)	Steady Gr. Phase (Yrs) (3)	Acceleration Phase Growth rate of GNP Initial (%) (4)	Final (%) (5)	Growth rate o Inv't (%) (6)
1. Argentina	31	3	28	4.7	5.6	11.1
2. Bangladesh	75	7	68	4.8	8.7	18.0
3. Bolivia	27	6	21	4.7	6.4	11.1
4. Botswana	16	0	16	18.6	18.6	9.0*
5. Brazil	21	10	11	6.8	11.8	15.4
6. Burma	105	65	40	5.0	6.6	6.1
7. Cameroon	78	1	77	5.7	5.8	8.5
8. Chile	38	0	38	6.3	6.3	5.1
9. Colombia	51	12	39	4.7	6.8	8.9
10. Ecuador	31	3	28	8.1	10.3	18.2
11. Egypt	64	6	58	4.2	4.9	14.9
12. Ghana	79	11	68	5.1	7.0	9.0*
13. India	80	30	50	4.9	7.3	7.8
14. Indonesia	38	4	34	7.2	10.4	19.2
15. Kenya	89	1	88	7.0	7.3	15.0
16. Mexico	59	18	41	3.0	7.0	10.0*
17. Morocco	41	0	41	8.9	8.9	13.1
18. Nicaragua	45	9	36	4.2	10.4	17.5
19. Nigeria	98	6	92	4.2	5.4	9.0*
20. Pakistan	84	9	75	4.9	7.6	12.0
21. Papua NG	50	3	47	5.5	7.9	20.0
22. Philippines	68	0	68	6.8	6.8	6.8*
23. Sri Lanka	88	10	78	3.3	6.3	11.5
24. Sudan	80	0	80	6.5	6.5	8.4
25. Tanzania	98	15	83	5.3	6.5	7.3
26. Thailand	55	2	53	7.2	8.0	13.3
27. Tunisia	30	7	23	7.5	9.6	12.4
28. Turkey	31	0	31	8.5	8.5	11.3
29. Zaire	88	6	82	3.8	6.9	16.1
30. Zambia	78	20	58	3.5	7.0	9.0*
Total above	–	–	–	–	–	–
ELDEMIA	58	7	51	5.5	6.7	9.0

† Based on a steady growth-rate of investment (column 6), causing an annual rise in the GNP growth-rate from 'initial' to 'final' level (columns 4 and 5) during the period whose length is shown in column 2. Bracketed references in these footnotes refer to the Mathematical Annex (A).

(1) Sum of columns 2 and 3.

(2) See A/10.

(3) No. of years needed to reach 'final' growth-rate (column 5), see A/4 and A/5.

– acceleration phase[†]

Aid Stage (Yrs) (7)	Rep't Stage (Yrs) (8)	Acceleration Phase Aid Reqm't p.a. ($ bil) (9)	Rep't Capability p.a. ($ bil) (10)	Interest-equiv. of Rep't Capability (% p.a.) (11)
3	0	5.54	0	–
7	0	.11	0	–
6	0	.23	0	–
0	0	0	0	–
10	0	11.47	0	–
4	61	.061	.030	3.15
1	0	.10	0	–
0	0	0	0	–
9	3	.26	0	–
3	0	.93	0	–
4	2	.133	.013	– 2.48
11	0	.40	0	–
12	18	1.47	4.05	6.55
4	0	1.86	0	–
1	0	.64	0	–
18	0	4.77	0	–
0	0	0	0	–
9	0	.25	0	–
6	0	2.46	0	–
9	0	.25	0	–
3	0	.04	0	–
0	0	0	0	–
10	0	.11	0	–
0	0	0	0	–
9	6	.24	.18	– 1.78
2	0	.24	0	0
7	0	.19	0	0
0	0	0	0	0
6	0	.12	0	0
5	15	.03	.03	– 33.90
–	–	32.08	4.30	–
6	1	13.84	2.37	– 2.90

(4) *Table 7.1,* column 3.

(5) g ≡ Maximal growth-rate of GNP observed since 1960 over at least 4 years (U.N., *Yearbook of National Accounts Statistics* 1978, Vol. II), with some amendment to scale these down where they are not deemed sustainable for the long Steady Growth Phase which is to follow.

Footnotes continued on next page

Footnotes to Table 7.2

(6) $\beta \equiv$ Maximal growth-rate of investment (generally gross) reported since 1960 over at least 4 years (U.N., *ibid.*), with some scaling down where these are not deemed sustainable throughout the acceleration phase. Where reported figures cover insufficient periods, the average growth-rate of 9 or 10 % reported for LDMs as a whole is arbitrarily assumed (figures marked *).

(7) $a \equiv$ time taken for user gap (I–S) to disappear A/23.

(8) $r \equiv k\text{-}a$. Only repayment during APh is considered here. Later repayment during the SGPh is considered in *Table 7.3.*

(9) $u_A.Y_o$, see A/23, divided by $\underline{a}$ to convert to annual basis.

(10) $u_K.Y_o$, see A/24, divided by $\underline{r}$ to convert to annual basis.

(11) The cumulative user-gap at year $\underline{k}$ is given by u_K (A/24). If this is negative, the country has repaid the aid-debt u_A, and was additionally able to export capital to the tune of $-u_K$, i.e. to incur a service charge of u_K/u_A over $\underline{r}$ years. This was computed and converted to the annual base r_a (A/25). Negative figures denote incomplete repayment equivalent to additional aid at that interest-rate on the original debt p.a.

* See footnote 6.

The development scenario — steady growth phase*

	Duration of SGPh (Yrs) (1)	Growth rate of GNP (%) (2)	Duration of Aid Stage (Yrs) (3)	Duration of Repaym't Stage (Yrs) (4)	Aid Reqm't p.a. ($ bil) (5)	Repaym't Capability p.a. ($ bil) (6)	Interest-equiv. of Repaym't Capability (%) (7)
1. Argentina	28	5.6	1	27	.78	31.16	14.6
2. Bangladesh	68	8.7	36	32	1.88	– 10.27	– 5.4
3. Bolivia	21	6.4	1	20	.08	.81	12.3
4. Botswana	16	18.6	9	7	.07	.04	7.7
5. Brazil	11	11.8	4	– 7	14.3	20.74	5.4
6. Burma	40	6.6	2	38	.17	1.70	6.2
7. Cameroon	77	5.8	3	74	.07	7.56	6.5
8. Chile	38	6.3	38	0	1.93	–	–
9. Colombia	39	6.8	8	31	.79	6.21	6.9
10. Ecuador	28	10.3	12	16	1.03	2.05	4.4
11. Egypt	58	4.9	20	38	1.33	9.02	5.2
12. Ghana	68	7.0	1	67	.05	28.02	9.9
13. India	50	7.3	14	36	5.73	46.02	6.0
14. Indonesia	34	10.4	1	33	1.79	157.07	14.5
15. Kenya	88	7.3	1	87	1.93	191.23	5.4
16. Mexico	41	7.0	0	41	0	125.55	–
17. Morocco	41	8.9	20	21	1.07	2.18	3.4
18. Nicaragua	36	10.4	0	36	0	4.66	–
19. Nigeria	92	5.4	0	92	0	299.98	–
20. Pakistan	75	7.6	11	64	.95	63.77	4.7
21. Papua NG	47	7.9	2	45	.06	6.96	13.6
22. Philippines	68	6.8	1	67	.07	66.07	10.8
23. Sri Lanka	78	6.3	3	75	.15	20.99	6.8
24. Sudan	80	6.5	28	52	.66	7.21	4.3
25. Tanzania	83	6.5	2	81	.08	38.09	7.9
26. Thailand	53	8.0	12	41	1.14	19.51	7.1
27. Tunisia	23	9.6	15	8	.20	– .24	– 2.3
28. Turkey	31	8.5	7	24	1.01	7.34	11.7
29. Zaire	82	6.9	31	51	.80	8.90	4.8
30. Zambia	58	7.0	1	57	.10	9.15	8.2
Total above	–	–	–	–	38.22	1176.89	–
ELDEMIA	51	6.7	17	34	73.96	71.743	7.44

* Based on a steady growth-rate (column 3), equal to or just short of the maximal rate reported for at least 4 years since 1960, and thought to be attainable by acceleration from initial growth-rates (column 2 of *Table 7.2*) during the Acceleration Phase. Bracketed references in these footnotes refer to pages or equations in the Mathematical Annex (A).

(1) $\equiv m$ (A/10)

(2) $\equiv g$ (A/8) as for *Table 7.2*, footnote 5

(3) $\equiv e$ (A/30)

(4) $\equiv s = m - e$ (col. 1 – col. 3)

(5) $\equiv v_E$ if $e < m$ or v_M if $e \geqslant m$, see A/31

(6) $\equiv v_M$, (A/31) by substitution of $\underline{m}$ for $\underline{e}$

(7) $\equiv r_e$ (A/32)

Table 7.4

Aid requirements and resource flows*

	Average Scenario Reqm't Annual Sum ($ bil) (1)	Dura-tion (Yrs) (2)	Actual Net Inflow of Resources 1977 ($ bil) (3)	Of which: Bilateral ODA ($ bil) (4)	Coverage of Scenario Reqm't (%) (5)
1. Argentina	4.348	4	.37	.00	8.5
2. Bangladesh	1.577	8	.76	.16	48.2
3. Bolivia	.214	7	.17	.00	79.4
4. Botswana	.072	9	.04	.00	55.6
5. Brazil	12.278	14	2.25	.00	18.3
6. Burma	.097	6	.11	.00	113.4
7. Cameroon	.078	4	.33	.01	423.1
8. Chile	1.929	38	– .12	.00	– 6.2
9. Colombia	.509	17	.23	.00	45.2
10. Ecuador	1.008	15	.21	.00	21.0
11. Egypt	1.113	24	3.07	.88	271.0
12. Ghana	.362	12	.16	.00	44.2
13. India	3.762	26	1.07	.16	28.4
14. Indonesia	1.844	5	.90	.03	48.8
15. Kenya	1.285	2	.52	.00	40.5
16. Mexico	4.766	18	1.85	.00	38.8
17. Morocco	1.071	20	.54	.08	50.4
18. Nicaragua	2.457	10	.07	.00	2.8
19. Nigeria	2.457	6	.16	.00	6.5
20. Pakistan	.632	20	.62	.06	98.1
21. Papua NG	.054	5	.26	.00	481.5
22. Philippines	.070	1	.71	.00	1014.3
23. Sri Lanka	.122	13	.17	.01	139.3
24. Sudan	.656	28	.40	.10	61.0
25. Tanzania	.211	11	.42	.01	199.0
26. Thailand	1.038	14	.27	..	26.0
27. Tunisia	.194	22	.35	.02	180.4
28. Turkey	1.011	7	.91	..	90.0
29. Zaire	.692	37	.51	.00	73.7
30. Zambia	.043	6	.17	.00	395.3
Total above	43.758	–	17.48	1.52	39.9
ELDEMIA	58.253	23	54.49	3.89	93.5

* 'Actual resource flows' include grants from private agencies, export credits, bilateral portfolio investment (incl. bank lending) from DAC countries, direct investment (incl. reinvested earnings) and security purchases by international development organisations. It is thus a much more comprehensive concept than 'development aid' which is normally confined to 'official development assistance' (ODA) in the form of grants or loans with development and welfare as main objectives made at concessional financial terms (i.e. containing at least 25 % 'grant element' if a loan). The table thus compares needed and actual inflows of different degrees of 'concessionality' (cols. 1 and 3).

Footnotes to Table 7.4

(1) and (2) Average of APh and SGPh aid requirements as given in *Tables 7.3* and *7.4*, weighted in proportion to the duration of the two phases.

(3) OECD, 1979 *Development Cooperation Review,* Paris, Nov. 1979, pp. 250-1.

(4) *Ibid.,* pp. 274-5.

(5) col. 3 : col. 1 in %.

Table 7.5

Aid and 'concessionality' required — D.C. calculations*

	Requirements for Aid			Repayment Capability		Required Concessionality		
	Aid Period (Yrs) (1)	Present Value ($ bil) (2)	Annuity Equiv. ($ bil) (3)	Repaym't Period (Yrs) (4)	Present Value ($ bil) (5)	Equiv. annual int. (%) (6)	Grant element (%) (7)	'Free loan element' (%) (8)
1. Argentina	4	15.91	5.02	27	117.09	7.67	0	23.3
2. Bangladesh	43	9.47	.96	25	.86	−9.13	90.9	9.1
3. Bolivia	7	1.18	.24	20	2.61	4.00	0	60.0
4. Botswana	9	.50	.09	7	.64	3.76	0	62.4
5. Brazil	14	151.29	20.54	7	63.93	−11.58	57.7	42.3
6. Burma	6	.11	.02	99	3.15	3.49	0	65.1
7. Cameroon	4	.27	.09	74	5.10	4.04	0	59.6
8. Chile	38	22.29	2.29	0	0	–	100.0	–
9. Colombia	17	3.52	.44	34	8.63	2.68	0	73.2
10. Ecuador	15	9.06	1.19	16	11.02	1.23	0	87.7
11. Egypt	24	8.88	.99	40	8.33	−.16	6.2	93.8
12. Ghana	12	3.05	.45	67	5.68	.93	0	90.7
13. India	26	13.32	1.45	54	.53	−5.78	96.0	4.0
14. Indonesia	5	7.89	2.08	33	174.37	9.84	0	1.6
15. Kenya	2	.81	.47	87	23.48	3.94	0	60.6
16. Mexico	18	57.63	7.03	41	57.87	.01	0	99.9
17. Morocco	20	12.04	1.41	21	9.50	−1.12	21.1	78.9
18. Nicaragua	10	1.68	.27	35	6.57	3.98	0	60.2
19. Nigeria	6	11.99	2.75	92	80.46	2.09	0	79.1
20. Pakistan	20	5.83	.68	64	10.73	.96	0	90.4
21. Papua NG	5	.23	.06	45	7.53	8.10	0	19.0
22. Philippines	1	.10	.11	67	41.35	9.38	0	6.2
23. Sri Lanka	13	1.02	.14	75	4.52	2.01	0	79.9
24. Sudan	28	.92	.10	52	4.01	2.88	0	71.2
25. Tanzania	22	1.75	.27	87	2.92	.59	0	94.1
26. Thailand	14	8.93	1.21	41	20.59	2.06	0	79.4
27. Tunisia	22	2.01	.23	8	1.02	−8.16	49.2	50.8
28. Turkey	7	2.95	.61	24	35.92	10.97	0	–
29. Zaire	37	3.56	.37	51	5.15	.73	0	92.7
30. Zambia	6	.15	.03	72	.96	2.62	0	73.8
Total above	–	358.30	–	–	717.65	–	–	–
ELDEMIA	23	456.76	51.42	35	182.28	−2.59	60.1	39.9

* D.C. = Discounted Cash-Flow

(1) Addition of the aid stages within APh and SGPh to produce continuous, or almost continuous, total 'aid periods'.

(2) Flows of 'scenario-aid' during both APh and SGPh (as for *Tables 7.1, 7.2* and *7.3*) discounted to the present at the conventional market rate of 10 %.

Footnotes continued on next page

Footnotes to Table 7.5

(3) Annual value of an annuity payment over the aid period yielding the given present value at 10 % interest p.a.

(4) Addition of the repayment stages within both APh and SGPh (= Development Period – Aid Period) to produce a continuous, or almost continuous, Repayment Period.

(5) As column (2)

(6) Ratio of present values of Repayment Capability to Aid Requirement, reduced to an annual basis over the duration of the Repayment Period. Negative values denote incomplete repayment by the end of the Development Period equivalent to a supplementary annual grant during that Repayment Period.

(7) Shortfall of repayment capability below assumed aid disbursements as a percentage of the latter (in terms of present values).

(8) The percentage of total aid which must be loaned at zero interest to yield the given degree of 'concessionality', on the assumption that the remainder is loaned at the conventional market rate of 10 %. Where a grant element is required, the total remaining aid must be assumed to be on a free-loan basis. In other cases the free-loan element stated assumes that none of the aid is given in the form of grants.

Table 7.6

Aid and 'concessionality' required allowing for clearing of pre-existing debt*

	Outstanding Debt 1977 ($ bil)	Requirements for Aid-Present Value ($ bil)	Aid Period (Yrs)	Repayment Capability Repaym't Period (Yrs)	Repayment Capability Present Value ($ bil)	Required Concessionality Equiv. annual int. (%)	Required Concessionality Grant element (%)	Required Concessionality 'Free loan' element (%)
1. Argentina	6.16	22.07	4	27	117.09	6.37	0	36.3
2. Bangladesh	2.30	11.77	43	25	.86	– 10.06	92.7	7.3
3. Bolivia	1.45	2.63	7	20	2.61	– .38	.8	99.2
4. Botswana	.29	.79	9	7	.64	– 2.96	19.0	81.0
5. Brazil	32.10	183.39	14	7	63.93	– 13.98	65.1	34.9
6. Burma	.52	.63	6	99	3.15	1.64	0	83.6
7. Cameroon	.82	1.09	4	74	5.10	2.11	0	78.9
8. Chile	3.78	26.07	38	0	0	–	100.0	–
9. Colombia	2.96	6.48	17	34	8.63	.85	0	91.5
10. Ecuador	1.34	10.40	15	16	11.02	.36	0	96.4
11. Egypt	8.14	17.02	24	40	8.33	– 1.77	51.1	48.9
12. Ghana	.79	3.84	12	67	5.68	.59	0	94.1
13. India	14.93	28.25	26	54	.53	– 7.10	98.1	1.9
14. Indonesia	12.04	19.93	5	33	174.37	6.79	0	32.1
15. Kenya	1.14	1.95	2	87	23.48	2.90	0	71.0
16. Mexico	25.50	83.13	18	41	57.87	– 8.80	30.4	69.6
17. Morocco	3.61	15.65	20	21	9.50	– 2.35	39.3	60.7
18. Nicâragua	.87	2.55	10	35	6.57	2.86	0	71.4
19. Nigeria	1.76	13.75	6	92	80.46	1.02	0	89.8
20. Pakistan	6.85	12.68	20	64	10.73	– 2.61	15.4	84.6
21. Papua NG	.36	.59	5	45	7.53	5.82	0	41.8
22. Philippines	4.71	4.81	1	67	41.35	3.26	0	67.4
23. Sri Lanka	.80	1.82	13	75	4.52	1.22	0	87.8
24. Sudan	2.04	2.96	28	52	4.01	.59	0	94.1
25. Tanzania	1.17	1.94	22	87	2.92	.47	0	95.3
26. Thailand	1.82	10.75	14	41	20.59	1.60	0	84.0
27. Tunisia	2.00	4.01	22	8	1.02	– 15.73	74.6	25.4
28. Turkey	5.30	8.25	7	24	35.92	6.32	0	35.8
29. Zaire	2.76	6.32	37	51	5.15	– 1.61	18.5	81.5
30. Zambia	1.48	1.63	6	72	.96	– .73	41.1	58.9
Total above	149.79	508.09	–	–	717.65	–	–	–
ELDEMIA	264.42	721.18	23	35	182.28	– 3.85	74.7	25.3

* For explanation of headings see note to *Table 7.5*

Mathematical Annex

To fix ideas, we define the 'present' as the late seventies, i.e. mostly 1977 or 1978 or an average of the period 1975-1978, as later data are not yet available in sufficient range or detail. A typical 'less developed market economy' (LDM) can then be characterised, amongst many other things, by its 'present development lag' (λ_o), defined as the multiplicative factor by which its GNP per head (Z_o) is exceeded by the average GNP per head of the 'more developed market economies', or MDMs at 'present' (Z'_o), i.e. $\lambda_o \equiv Z'_o/Z_o$. (12) It is then assumed that our Development Scenario will aim to reduce this gap to zero in a 'development period' (DP) of n years, such that $\lambda_n \equiv Z'_o/Z_n = 0$. Note that this does not imply catching up with MDMs as they will *then* be, but merely catching up with their average per capita GPN *as it was in the late seventies;* but this in itself is no mean task.

With a present GNP of Y_o growing at y_o per annum (see p. 134), it would take the typical LDM between 120 and 200 years to reach Z'_o, – an unacceptably long period. Any acceptable scenario therefore must start off the development period of n years by an 'acceleration phase' (APh) of, say, k years, during which y_o accelerates to $y_k \equiv g$, where g is the maximal growth-rate of GNP which the LDM is deemed to be capable of (its 'potential growth rate'). This is achieved by promoting a rate of growth in capital investment (β), again as large as the country is thought to be able to absorb, which – given a constant marginal capital-output ratio κ – will cause the *increment* in GNP (ΔY) to grow at the same constant rate, thereby accelerating the growth-rate of the *level* of GNP ($y \equiv \Delta Y/Y$), provided only that it was initially below β (i.e. $y_o < \beta$), which we assume. Throughout the k years of the Acceleration Phase, we therefore have

(1) $$I_t = I_o\tilde{\beta}^t \text{ (where } \tilde{\beta} \equiv 1 + \beta) \text{ (13)}$$

(2) $$\Delta Y_t = \kappa I_t = \Delta Y_o \tilde{\beta}^t$$

(3) $$Y_t = Y_o + \sum_o^{t-1} \Delta Y_t = Y_o + \Delta Y_o B_T \text{ (where } B_T \equiv \frac{\tilde{\beta}^t - 1}{\beta})$$

$$= Y_o (1 + y_o B_T)$$

At the end of APh, we therefore have

(4) $$\tilde{y}_\kappa \equiv Y_k/Y_o = 1 + y_o B_\kappa$$

(5) $$g \equiv y_k \equiv \Delta Y_k/Y_k = \frac{\Delta Y_o \tilde{\beta}^k}{Y_o(1+y_o B_\kappa)} = \frac{\tilde{\beta}^k y_o}{1 + y_o B_\kappa}$$

This last expression measures the rate of growth in GNP to which $\underline{y_o}$ can be made to accelerate in k years. The period growth factor in *per capita* GNP over the APh will therefore be

(6) $\tilde{z}_\kappa = \tilde{y}_\kappa / \tilde{p}_\kappa = \tilde{y}_\kappa / \tilde{p}^k$,

where $\underline{p}$ is the assumed annual growth-rate of population.

After $\underline{k}$ years of acceleration the residual development lag behind our chosen target will therefore be

(7) $\lambda_k = \lambda_o / \tilde{z}_\kappa$

thus necessitating a further $\underline{m}$ years' growth in GNP of $\underline{g}$ ($\equiv y_k$) per annum – the 'steady-growth phase' (SGPh) – to eliminate the lag, where $\underline{m}$ is defined by

(8) $\tilde{g} = \tilde{p}\lambda^m{}_k$, i.e. $m = \ell g \lambda_k / \ell g(\tilde{y}_k / \tilde{p})$

This can be simplified by adding the obvious definition of the steady annual growth-factor in per capita GNP during SGPh:

(9) $\tilde{z}_k \equiv \tilde{y}_k / \tilde{p}$, reducing (8) to

(10) $m = \ell g \lambda_k / \ell g \tilde{z}_k$

The total length of the development period (APh + SGPh) is obviously

(11) $n = m + k$

Throughout APh the user gap in year $\underline{t}$ is defined by

(12) $U_t = I_t - S_t = I_o \tilde{\beta}^t - S_t$

Assuming a constant marginal propensity to save, the amount of saving in year $\underline{t}$ becomes

(13) $S_t = \sigma Y_t - C_*$

where $\underline{C_*}$ is 'autonomous consumption', i.e. the vertical intercept below the origin of the saving function, representing dissaving (i.e. consumption above income) which would take place regardless of income (i.e. even at zero income). By putting t = 0, $\underline{C_*}$ can be expressed in observable parameters:

(14) $$C_* = \sigma Y_o - S_o = Y_o(\sigma\text{-}s_o),$$

where s_o stands for the 'present' average saving ratio S_o/Y_o. Equation (13) therefore becomes by virtue of (14)

(15) $$S_t = \sigma Y_t - Y_o(\sigma\text{-}s_o),$$

or by virtue of (3)

(16) $$S_t = \sigma Y_o\ (1 + y_o B_t) - Y_o\ (\sigma\text{-}s_o)$$

(17) $$s_t \equiv S_t/Y_o = \sigma\ (1 + y_o B_t) - c_*,\ \text{where } c_* \equiv C_*/Y_o = \sigma\text{-}s_o$$

By virtue of (12) and (15) we can now express the user gap in APh as

(18) $$U_t = I_o\tilde{\beta}^t - \sigma Y_o\ (1 + y_o B_t) - Y_o c_*$$

or in terms of present GNP ($\underline{Y_o}$) taken as the unit (14)

(19) $$u_t = i_o\tilde{\beta}^t - \sigma\ (1 + y_o B_T) + c_*$$

Remembering the definition of B_T in (3), this can be written more explicitly for t = k as

(20) $$u_k = \left(\frac{\sigma y_o}{\beta} - s_o\right) - \left(\frac{\sigma y_o}{\beta} - i_o\right)\tilde{\beta}^k \equiv \sigma_* - \iota_*\tilde{\beta}^k$$

This formula shows that the user-gap will steadily decrease from $(i_o - s_o)$ as the APh wears on, and will disappear completely by <u>a</u> years (to be called the 'aid stage'), provided <u>a ≤ k</u>. The length of the aid stage may be computed from

(21) $$\sigma_* - \iota_*\tilde{\beta}^a = 0$$

or

(22) $$a = \frac{\ell g\ (\sigma_*/\iota_*)}{\ell g\tilde{\beta}},\ \text{where}\quad \sigma_* \equiv \frac{\sigma y_o}{\beta} - s_o,\quad \iota_* \equiv \frac{\sigma y_o}{\beta} - \iota_o$$

If <u>a ≤ k</u>, the total aid required during <u>APh</u> can be computed by cumulating (20) from 0 to a-1:

(23) $$u_A = \sum_{o}^{a\text{-}1} u_t = a\sigma_* - \iota_* B_A$$

In this case the user-gap will be negative during part of APh, i.e. the LDM will be able to repay part or all of the previous aid, or even accumulate external credits, from excess saving done during this residual 'debt clearing' stage, assuming the aid was given in the form of interest-free loans or its equivalent grant-loan mix. The extent of 'over-repayment' potential by the end of APh can be calculated by cumulating (20) from 0 to k-1:

(24) $$u_\kappa = \sum_{o}^{k-1} u_t = a\sigma_* - \iota_* B_\kappa$$

The LDM's 'debt-service capability' during APh after year a can be converted to a notional annual interest charge by computing

(25) $$r_a = \left(\frac{u_\kappa}{u_A}\right)^{\frac{1}{k-a}}$$

and this gives the notional 'average terms' on which loan aid could be given during APh

In general, however, and in particular if $a > k$, aid will need to be given during SGPh also, as a positive user gap will normally continue well into SGPh, where GNP grows at the steady rate g, and Investment needs only adapt itself to this as shown in (2). The size of the gap in year r of SGPh, i.e. r years after k is

(26) $$V_r = I_r - S_r = \kappa\Delta Y_r - S_r = \kappa g Y_r - S_r$$

$$= \kappa g Y_k \tilde{g}^r - S_r$$

or, by virtue of (4) and (15):

(27) $$V_r = \kappa g Y_o \tilde{y}_\kappa \tilde{g}^r - \sigma Y_o \tilde{y}_\kappa \tilde{g}^r + c_*$$

Again adopting Y_o as our unit, we can write this

(28) $$v_r = c_* - (\kappa g - \sigma)\tilde{y}_\kappa \tilde{g}^r \equiv c_* - K\tilde{y}_\kappa \tilde{g}^r, \text{ where } K \equiv \kappa g - \sigma$$

Given that $\kappa g - \sigma > 0$, this shows that the user gap will continue its downward path during SGPh and must eventually disappear, say e years after k, unless it has already done so in APh. Subject to this proviso, e can be computed from

(29) $$c_* - K\tilde{y}_\kappa \tilde{g}^e = 0,$$

and is therefore

(30) $$e = \ell g(c_*/K\tilde{y}_\kappa)/\ell_g \tilde{g}$$

The aid needed during SGPh can thus be computed by cumulating (28) from r = 0 to e-1:

(31) $$v_E = \sum_{o}^{e-1} v_r = c_* b - K\tilde{y}_K G_E, \text{ where } G_E \equiv \frac{\tilde{g}^e - 1}{g}$$

Normally this second aid-requirement must be added to APh-aid (24) to give the total aid requirement of the n-year Development Scenario. The 'debt-service capability' during SGPh can again be computed as a notional interest charge

(32) $$r_e = \left(\frac{v_M}{v_E}\right)^{\frac{1}{m-e}}$$

Moreover, whenever $a > k$, i.e. the user gap, does not disappear during APh, the total aid requirement will be

(33) $$u = u_A + v_E$$

with debt-servicing capability

(34) $$r = \left(\frac{u_K + v_M}{u_A + v_E}\right)^{\frac{1}{m-e}}$$

or, if in addition $e > m$,

(35) $$u = u_A + v_M$$

with no 'debt-servicing capability' within the development period.

Abbreviations and Symbols (reference to equations in brackets)

AGF	Annual growth factor
APh	Acceleration Phase
ARG	Annual rate of growth
Eldemia	The total less developed market economy
DP	Development Period
DS	Development Scenario
GNP	Gross National Product
LDM	Less developed market economy
MDM	More developed market economy
PGF	Period growth factor
PRG	Period rate of growth
SGPh	Steady-growth Phase
a	Duration of aid stage in APh (in years) (22)
β	Potential of investment growth p.a. $\tilde{\beta} = 1 + \beta$
B_T	PGF of investment for $\underline{t}$ years (3)
e	Duration of aid stage in SGPh (in years) (30)
$g\ (\equiv y_k)$	ARG of GNP in SGPh (5)
G_E	PGF of GNP for $\underline{e}$ years (31)
I_t	Investment in year t
i_t	Investment in present GNP units (footnote to 19)
ι_*	Auxiliary parameter (20) $\equiv \sigma y_o/\beta - i_o$
k	Duration of APh (in years)
κ	Marginal capital-output ratio (2)
λ_t	Development lag in year t (7)
m	Duration of SGPh (in years) (10)
n	Duration of DP (in years) (11)
p	ARG of population $\tilde{p} = 1 + p$
r_a	Debt-service capability in APh (interest-equivalent) (25)
r_e	Debt-service capability in SGPh (interest-equivalent) (32)
r	Debt-service capability in DP (34)
U_t	User Gap in year t of APh (18)
u_t	User Gap in terms of present GNP (19)
u_k	User Gap at end of APh (20)
u_A	Gap-aid requirement during APh (23)
u_κ	Cumulative user gap in APh

V_r User Gap in year r of SGPh (27)
v_r User Gap in terms of present GNP (28)
v_E Gap-aid requirement during SGPh (31)
v_M Cumulative user gap in SGPh (32)

References

(1) OECD, *Quantitative Models as an Aid to Development Assistance Policy,* Paris 1967.

(2) I am indebted to Professor K. Laski, of the Joh. Kepler University of Linz, Austria, for a valuable suggestion which resulted in a useful simplification of my original diagram.

(3) P.N. Rosenstein-Rodan, "International Aid for Underdeveloped Countries" *in The Review of Economics and Statistics,* May 1961, pp. 107-138.

(4) Hollis B. Chenery and Alan M. Strout, "Foreign Assistance and Economic Development", *American Economic Review,* September 1966, pp. 679-733.

(5) See particularly UN, *Yearbook of National Accounts Statistics,* 1978, Vol. II (International Tables), e.g. p. 3 *et seq.*

(6) *Ibid.,* p. 3.

(7) As attested by past experience or by analogy with similar countries if past experience is insufficiently documented or felt to be an inadequate guide.

(8) UN, *op. cit.,* p. 184.

(9) 9 % p.a. in the case of Eldemia, see *ibid.,* p. 185 (1969-74).

(10) See last row of *Table 7.2*, cols. 1-6.

(11) Alternatively taxation might be restricted to, say, .65 % of all incomes above the $ 500 per capita level, 1 % of those above $ 2000 per head, and 1.33 % for all beyond $ 5000. Such a regime would still yield about $ 50 bill. p.a. and entail no more than about .75 % of GNP for the average MDM earning above $ 500 per head p.a.

(12) Z'_o will be assumed equal to $ 6590 p.a., the 1977 per capita GNP of MDMs as given in U.N., *Yearbook of National Accounts* 1978, Vol. II., p. 3.

(13) Throughout this paper the *tilde* (~) over a symbol denotes the value of that symbol increased by unity, a simple device to save tedious algebraic brackets in complicated expressions. Thus $\tilde{g}$ ($\equiv$ 1+g) stands for the annual growth *factor* where g is the annual growth *rate.* The capital suffix, as in the growth factor y_K refers the symbol to the period as a whole, i.e. identifies *period* growth rates or factors in contrast to *annual* rates denoted by lower case suffixes.

(14) We shall from now express all user gaps and related variables in present GNP units, and use lower case letters to indicate this, e.g. $u_t \equiv U_t/Y_o$, $i_o \equiv I_o/Y_o$, $s_o \equiv S_o/Y_o$, etc. Absolute values can always be restored later by multiplying the results by the LDM's present GNP (Y_o).

COMMENTS ON PART II – INTERNATIONAL FINANCING

Ede Bakó*

I cannot disagree with *Bhaduri* (Chapter 5) who writes that recurring financial problems are usually surface phenomena reflecting a deeper malaise of the underlying economic structure. In commenting I will be pragmatic, because I do not want to run the manifold risks of theorising. Simultaneously, however, I must divide my heart among creditors and debtors, so that some kind of Janus-faced remarks seem to be justified, too. Hungary provides medium- and long-term credits, loans and aids of different forms to the developing countries, roughly to the extent of 0.6 – 0.7 per cent of GDP, although – and this is the opposite side of the coin – in recent years we have often appeared in the international capital markets as borrowers. Consequently, I should be less critical of the deficit countries and give proof of some understanding of the creditors as well.

I think that the long-lasting, enormous and enlarged needs of the developing countries, in terms of external financial resources, have been rooted in three groups of structural characteristics of the Third World:

(a) The heritage of history justified wide-ranging efforts towards a sounder economic order; these efforts, however, are handicapped by the existing international economic establishments, by the shortage of exchange reserves, by inadequate rates of domestic capital formation and savings, and by lack of experience in production and organisation.

(b) To make up for lost time, the developing countries are endeavouring to develop agricultural production, to improve public education and medical care and to enlarge industrial production for a more efficient use of their own natural resources and of the available labour force – while all the applicable development models run the risk of high-level vulnerability to external economic factors.

(c) Because of their structural weakness and intense vulnerability, the current account deficits of the developing countries have been swollen by the explosion of oil-prices, and, directily and indirectly, by the deteriorating general economic situation. Two aspects should be considered: the present size of current account imbalances and some problems of recycling surpluses to deficit countries.

I would like to underline the word *imbalance* because both the surplus positions of the oil exporting countries (now expected to reach $ 115 billion in 1980), and the combined deficit of the oil-importing developing countries (about $ 60 billion and to increase still further in 1981) are much larger than in any earlier year. This unprece-

* Chief Economic Adviser, National Bank of Hungary, Budapest

dented swing in financial flows (or in requirements for financing) could generate severe external financial difficulties for many developing countries as well as endangering the world economy as a whole. Both elements call for proper attention to be given to the recycling channels of the 1970s – namely to the fact that transfers of surpluses to the deficit countries have been largely, and spontaneously, administered through the commercial banking community of the industrially developed countries instead of through an international, and multilaterally supervised, mechanism established on an adequate scale by all interested countries. So long as common interests, based on profit motives, financing needs and risk-assessments, gave enough support to this spontaneous recycling within the carrying capacity of the commercial banks and international credit markets, the former mechanism could work; but it seems by now to have reached beyond its limits. Even developing countries with the most advanced manufacturing industry and general economic background found access to international financial markets worsening in recent months, both in terms of loan operations and in volume terms.

Thus, considering the very complex character of the basic reasons bringing about financing needs in the developing countries, *new forms of international financial and general economic cooperation* are urgently needed. Criticism and self-criticism are useful ways of diagnosing the causes, but much more should be done. The new forms require conscious planning and well-defined rules of specialisation, including joint enterprises not only on a bilateral, but also on a multilateral basis. Past experience shows that such ventures, with participation of corporations in East and West and in the developing regions themselves can be carried out efficiently. They need, however, efforts, initiatives, long-term agreements, financing facilities and, accordingly, a close cooperation among both governments and business sectors. The rich oil countries could also be helpful in supporting or even developing such initiatives on a larger scale.

Socialist countries have for a long time been interested in fostering their economic relations with the developing countries. They have tried to apply various trading practices, not neglecting the significant differences within this group of countries. They have offered technological transfers, exports of capital goods and adequate credits and have, in turn, accepted payment in goods, etc. It is, however, necessary to go further, and the socialist countries are prepared to participate in new forms of cooperation.

Nevertheless, there are certain factors imposing some limits on what the socialist countries are able to undertake in financing development needs of the Third World. To be frank, I see three kinds of limitation:

– a few of the socialist countries are themselves developing countries, making efforts to overcome all the structural shortcomings characteristic of the developing world as a whole;
– other socialist countries, like Hungary, are also trying to meet the challenge imposed by the price explosions – to restore their foreign trade balances by buying advanced

technology, equipment, know-how, and licences; and to transform their industrial structures to meet the requirements of the international markets, in conditions marked by generally lower domestic rates of growth than before;
— the relatively low percentage of trade turnover with the developing countries — together with similar economic policy priorities of restructuring the economies — also impose limits on transferring resources to those countries on a much larger scale.

On the other hand, developing countries must also take important measures to improve their economic systems and fundamentals. These efforts cannot be entirely replaced by the various forms of foreign aid or cooperation. A wider concentration and centralisation of financial resources for financing basic economic policy priorities, a better adaptation of the banking systems and legal rules to those requirements, some more careful hedging against losses caused by unjustifiable profits of the foreign investors etc., should also be considered. These changes, representing supplementary instruments and use of the hidden reserves of economic and financial managements, could also play some role in an efficient and integrated process of economic growth and deficit financing.

Kazimierz Laski*

Bhaduri (Chapter 5) draws attention to the fact that 'NOPECs' (non-oil developing countries) are the first to suffer from price increases as well as from world depression. In these conditions, we should try to diminish the vulnerability of those countries, first of all by increasing the official development assistance from the OECD countries. It is convincing, too, to require that OPEC countries should extend credits to developing countries directly, and not by the mediation of the industrialised North. It seems, however, that, while rightly criticising the North, Bhaduri forgets to mention the monopolistic price-setting of OPEC.

Bhaduri seems to overestimate, too, the ability of OECD countries to absorb the increases in oil prices. The deficit on their current foreign trade account was US $ 30.5 billion in 1979 and is expected to reach about $ 60 billion in 1980. It is typical of this situation that the FRG and Japan, formerly surplus countries, have gone into deficit since 1979.

* Johannes Kepler University, Linz; and Vienna Institute for Comparative Economic Studies

Bhaduri points to the importance of the availability of credits from the CMEA countries to the non-oil South and underlines their low level as well as their 'double-tied' nature. It is true that aid given by a socialist country, where no free productive capacities exist, means a true sacrifice (as we are reminded in Chapter 2 by *Paszyński*). This is not so in a capitalist, demand-constrained system, where aid can generate a higher level of economic activity in the donor country. Nevertheless this argument does not take into account the general responsibility of the more developed countries, capitalist and socialist, towards their less succesful neighbours.

Calcagno and *Kñakal* (Chapter 6) draw an impressive picture of the negative role played by direct private investment of the transnational companies in developing countries. This picture would, however, be more convincing if the authors were also to show the positive side of these activities. If those activities had negative consequences only, the best solution for the developing countries would be to forbid them completely. But, as Joan Robinson once said, the only thing that is worse than to be exploited is not to be exploited at all. She was referring to the workers but her saying can be applied to the developing countries as well.

On *Seton* (Chapter 7) I would like to comment on four points: (a) the role of demand constraint in the developing countries; (b) the problem of employment; (c) the problem of difficulties in foreign trade; (d) the problem of resource availability.

(a) Seton introduces a very useful distinction between the 'users' gap' (U = I–S) and the 'traders' gap' (T = M–E); the surplus of total supply over total demand, the 'resource gap', being the difference (both *ex ante*) between the latter and the former (R = T–U). Characteristic for the developing countries is $R < O$, i.e. an excess of total demand over total supply. The role of foreign aid consists exactly in filling this gap. When, however, $R > O$, i.e. in the case of a glut, a developing country might experience the same consequences as a developed country with a Keynesian tendency to reduce national income and employment. The economy of a developing country cannot then be characterised simply as a supply-constrained economy and identified with a socialist economy where planning takes care of total demand being at least equal to total supply. One can speak of a supply-constrained economy only in those developing countries where the government takes care directly of a great part of investment decisions, i.e. in the case of so-called 'mixed' economies.

(b) Seton's scenario might encounter labour shortages. Assume that the initial rate of growth of employment in Eldemia is 2.3 per cent p.a., which implies a constant rate of unemployment. In that case, the rate of growth of labour productivity is initially 3.2 per cent p.a. because the initial rate of growth of national income is 5.5 per cent p.a. It is safe to assume that with a constant capital-output ratio the rate of growth of labour productivity would also remain constant during the period of 'catching up'. The implied rate of growth of employment would then be about 3.5 per cent p.a. (6.7 – 3.2 per cent). Thus, in 57 years total employment would have to increase 7.1 times while the population is assumed to increase 3.5 times only (at 2.3 per cent a year). Assuming, further, a constant participation rate, labour shortage would arise unless the initial unemployment rate (measured as a percentage of population) is at least 50 per cent. Even for developing countries this is a rather high estimate.

(c) The scenario concentrates on the 'user gap' only, and derives from it the aid requirement. There is, however, another problem which can be as important as insufficient saving – bottlenecks which arise as a result of the acceleration of growth and which lead finally to the foreign trade difficulties. To reduce these difficulties would as a rule require an increase in the capital-output ratio as well as in the import-output ratio. Both factors would increase the foreign aid requirement, the former because the investment necessary for a given rate of growth would increase, the latter because the exports cannot accelerate pari passu with imports. Indeed, commodities which could be exported would as a rule be in short supply, and others, which can be supplied, would as a rule be non-exportable.

(d) The consequences of the 'catching up' process on demand for natural resources such as raw materials, energy and food derserve attention. The population of Eldemia has to increase from ca. 2 billions to ca. 7 billions. The global national income of Eldemia has thus to increase from ca. $ 1.1 to 46.1 thousand billions. Assuming that the global national income of developed market economies would increase at the same time by only 2 per cent p.a., with constant population of ca. 0.5 billion people, their global national income would increase from ca. $ 3.3 to ca. 10.2 thousand billions. This means an increase of the total national income of both groups from ca. $ 4.4 to ca. $ 56.3 thousand billions, i.e. by ca. 13 times, *not* taking into account the socialist countries with far more than 1 billion people now. The required increase in supply of natural resources is immense, even if due account is taken of technical progress. It is not just the possibility of an increase of production of raw materials and energy of this order that is questionable, but the possibility of such an expansion in the relatively short period of 'catching up'. Thus serious attempts to help the South would require an enormous increase in production. From this point of view, one can but wonder at the shortsightedness of the apostles of zero-growth.

Alexandre P. Ognev*

I should like to devote myself to *Seton* (Chapter 7) 'The role of development aid facilities'.

(a) As I understand this chapter, the main task in helping the poor countries to overcome economic backwardness is regarded as the assignment of the necessary means, mainly money. The scenarios and calculations presented by Seton show the amounts of financial help needed in given periods. Obviously, this may help the poorer countries to overcome a lot of the existing difficulties which they face for the time being. Nevertheless, in our view, providing financial assistance alone does not afford the possibility of a full solution of the problems of equalising levels of economic development. It is hardly possible to overcome existing economic differences except by the formation of a comprehensive industrial base linked with harmonious development of the main economic branches of the countries concerned. Moreover, many notorious examples exist of aid being used by developing countries only to satisfy current needs, without integrating it with perspective planning of their economic and social development. Thus the question arises how Seton's model can be used to calculate the costs and time needed for completing the main branches of the economy – without which it is impossible to achieve a comprehensive solution of the problems of equalising economic levels and catching up the backlog.

(b) My second question arises from the purely mathematical construction: how could the model be applied to any country whatsoever? It treats the developing countries as an uniform whole, while actually, as we know, there are deep differences between developing countries from the economic, political and social points of view, and in the orientation of their development path. Thus, the model, as a universal remedy, can hardly be applied to determine the efficiency of aid rendered, in the same measure for all countries, without taking into account such factors as differences in the level of economic potential, of raw material reserves, size of population, and so on. If one adds the differences in development orientation, the necessity of differing methods to overcome economic backwardness becomes self-evident. As regards different methods of equalising economic levels, the example of CMEA countries may be quoted: according to the economic potential of European socialist countries, of Mongolia and of Cuba, diverse concrete methods were of course used, and influenced the amount of capital investments needed. Thus I would suggest that Seton should specify more precisely how the factors making for differentiation between developing countries, and the dissimilarities in their development orientation, could be taken into account in the model.

* Principal Scientific Secretary, Institute of World Economy and International Relations, Moscow

(c) A third point: the model does not take fully into account the ranges of application, and the ultimate efficiency, of the aid received by developing countries.

Where can financial aid come from? In the present world economic situation, above all in inflationary conditions with increasing prices for energy and raw materials, for industrial finished products, and so on, developing countries need to get increasingly greater amounts of aid. So an essential question arises – the search for the necessary financial resources. Seton even presents a system of international taxes to get the necessary means. In fact, real resources do exist throughout the world. I think especially of armaments expenditures exceeding $ 400 billions a year. In this area, the USSR's proposals for reducing armaments expenditures, and using the proceeds to help developing countries, are well known.

I should like to call attention to a second circumstance – the armaments expenditures of developing countries, indirectly influencing the speed at which they can overcome their backwardness. The following example may serve – standing for the full solution of only one among the burning problems of the day – the food problem. According to calculations of FAO experts, about $ 20 billion a year are needed, for 1975 – 90, for agricultural investment in the developing countries, an amount which they cannot raise without external help; the expenditure of Asian, African and Latin American countries for armaments during the last twenty years comes to about $ 450 billions, including about $ 180 billions in the last five years.

Furthermore, the growth of armaments expenditures in the developing countries exceeds that in the developed (industrial) countries. In the light of unproductive expenditure on such a scale, no amount of assistance can exercise much positive impact on economic development and living standards. I give only the example of unproductive expenditure in the armaments race. But, as we know, the developing countries have large enough unproductive expenses also in other branches of economic and social life. In our view, the developing countries could go further and more quickly in overcoming economic backwardness only if they cut down their unproductive expenses. In that connection, the question may be raised of how the present model for determining the efficiency of aid, and the time necessary to overcome backwardness, takes into account the fact of the unproductive expenditures in developing countries.

I believe that it is hardly possible to calculate the development assistance needed by the developing countries without taking into account these few but important facts.

Józef Sołdaczuk*

Seton (Chapter 7) is both general and specific; he is theoretical and he presents a study in practical possibilities; he formulates general objectives and concrete ideas for dealing with the financing of economic growth of LDCs and for narrowing the income gap between the LDCs and the developed market economies.

(a) *The model*

Seton displays two gaps, *ex-ante* and *ex-post*, which he further identifies as 'user's gap' and the 'trader's gap'. This simple scheme serves as a useful starting point in any discussion of economic development, not only in LDCs but in any socio-economic system. From the 'real' point of view, the two gaps may be redefined as a resource gap. But we may still ask the question 'what are the gaps?'.

In developing countries we may first distinguish, as Kalecki has pointed out, the gap in the domestic supply of necessities, mainly staple foods which are the most essential for a non-inflationary growth, and further, capital equipment and technology gaps, gaps in the supply of fuel (in most developing countries except oil-producers) and in some important raw materials, and gaps in skilled labour, technical services and management. If all these resources and factors of production could be imported from abroad, the problem would be to a large extent reduced to the foreign trade gap and to the availability of the required amount of foreign financing.

But, we must still have in mind 'real' limiting factors, which may create unbridgeable barriers to economic development, even if a sufficient amount of foreign financing could be supplied.

According to Seton's growth model and growth scenario, there is a possibility of increasing the average rate of growth of GNP in the 'average' LDC from the present 5.5 per cent p.a. up to 6.7 per cent p.a., within the acceleration period of 7 years, by increasing the volume of investment by approximately 9 per cent a year.

If, after that period, GNP growth were kept steady (at 6.7 per cent per annum) through another 51 years, the average LDC could attain the present level of income and standard of living of an average developed market economy country within a period of 58 years. The scenario adopted and the assumed rate of GNP growth in an 'average' LDC look moderate and not excessive in the light of the actual achievements of many countries in the past 30 years.

* Director, Institute for International Economic Relations and International Law, Central School of Planning and Statistics, Warsaw

Nevertheless, one may ask whether it will be feasible to achieve such a steady rate of growth through such a long period as 58 years. Experience shows, rather, a tendency for growth rates to fall, once a higher stage of development, and a higher level of income per capita, has been achieved.

It might seem, therefore, more realistic to adopt an assumption similar to that in the UN study (led by Wassily Leontief) on *The Future of the World Economy* (1), where the projected average rate of growth for a group of countries is reduced by 1 per cent when the average income of the group falls within a higher income range. (For example a 4 per cent rate was adopted for regions with $ 3.000 – 4.000 per capita, 3 per cent for $ 4.000 – 5.000); On such an assumption, however, the initial acceleration of the rate of growth, and the required increase in the volume of investment during the 'acceleration period', would have to be considerably greater so as to allow for progressive declines in the rate of growth with a growing income per capita, and yet still assure the calculated average rate of growth of GNP of 6.7 per cent a year over the whole period of 58 years.

One may doubt whether such an acceleration could be achieved in the present complicated political, social and economic environment – at least within the first half of the 1980s.

(b) *Objectives and priorities*

The main objective of Seton's scenario, as I understand it, is not the elimination of the income gap between LDCs and developed countries, but achievement by the 'average' LDC of the *present* real income and standard of living of developed market economies. There would still be – even in 2030 – a substantial income gap between the two groups.

One may then ask whether it is really advisable for the LDCs to replicate the way and pattern of economic development of market economy countries and their standard of living. It seems that there are other, more important, objectives and priorities which might and could be attained by LDCs, and in a shorter time. I would refer, in particular, to what has been described as the 'Physical Quality of Life' (PQL), measured by such indicators as infant mortality, life expectancy and illiteracy; it is this that ought to be adopted as a main objective and measure of progress in the LDCs.

I would like to remind the reader of the extremely interesting statistical study prepared by John W. Senell and the Staff of the Overseas Development Council, published in *World Development Agenda 1977* (New York, 1977, Annex A); comparative statistics are compiled for practically all countries of the world, including socialist countries. We find from this study that by the mid 1970s the East European socialist countries were able to achieve – during a period of about 30 years – a Physical Quality of Life index similar to that of highly developed capitalist countries, despite a level of income per capita still 2 – 3 times less. For instance, the PQL index is 94 in Poland, Hungary and Bulgaria, 95 in Czechoslovakia and 96 in the Democractic Republic of Germany, while it is 94 in Italy, 95 in the Federal Republic of Germany, 96 in USA, 97 in United Kingdom and France.

It seems to me that LDCs ought to formulate their own objectives and development priorities and that their main task is not so much to achieve the present standard of living of developed market economies as their first priority, but to set priorities such as those measured (for instance) by the Physical Quality of Life Index.

(c) *Methods of Financing*

On the financial aspects, the question is whether it would be possible to assure sufficient foreign financing to achieve the required acceleration of the rate of growth of LDCs. Seton calculates a need for about $ 12 billion of net foreign financing per year for an 'average' LDC during an initial period of 17 years (including all forms of public and private investment).

Seton gives special attention to the idea of 'taxation' of higher income countries (over $ 500 a head), in some proportion to their per capita income. The idea may appeal to some, especially to less developed countries, but it does not seem realistic enough, or likely to be acceptable to most donor countries.

In this context, I would refer to Chapter 11, where *Bogomolov* commends a more realistic proposal, submitted to the United Nations by socialist countries and calling for agreed reductions in the military expenditures of the permanent members of the UN Security Council, and for the use of an agreed part of those reductions for the increased aid to LDCs. Again *Streeten* (Chapter 10) calculates that 3 per cent of present world military expenditure ($ 450 billions a year) would double the present official development assistance to LDCs from the OECD countries. Unfortunately, Western members of the Security Council have not responded to that proposal. It is doubtful whether they would be willing to respond positively to more ambitious schemes. I do not believe that the tax proposed would stand a chance in my country. Most people would be against the transfer of part of our national income to other countries in the form of an obligatory tax. The idea of taxing countries with an income per capita of over $ 500 would put a substantial burden on many middle-income countries which were able by their own efforts to break 'the vicious circle' of poverty and to achieve their present level of income. Those countries still look at the present income gap between themselves and most developed countries as excessive.

Consequently Poland stands for extensive aid programmes for LDCs, including financial help (but not obligatory taxation). In our judgement the Development Aid Facilities cannot be limited, only or mainly, to financial help. There are other and – in our opinion – more important and effective forms of aid. There is 'aid through trade' and other equitable forms of overall international economic cooperation, including long-term trade agreements, stabilisation of export markets and assurances of an easy access to them, technical assistance programmes, technology transfers, different forms of industrial cooperation and specialisation agreements, as well as different forms of assistance in education, medical services and so on.

External financing of economic development may also be a helpful method of speeding up the process of economic growth, with a higher level of consumption than otherwise would be possible. It may be especially important and effective if provided in the forms of long-term governmental credits or credits of international organisations, at low interest rates. Foreign credits of commercial banks, including multinational banks which are the main source of this type of financing, are also important sources for financing imports of capital equipment and technology, as well as food and essential raw materials. One cannot forget, however, that commercial bank credits are available only at a relatively high interest rate. The developing countries ought to be careful not to get involved too rapidly in excessive borrowings exceeding rates of growth of export earnings and debt service ability.

Growing indebtedness represents growing accumulation of claims against the resources of the LDCs; after a not very long period (10 – 12 years) net transfers to creditor countries may create very heavy pressures on the balances of payments of LDCs. In many cases, as is known from experience, export earnings of a number of LDCs are insufficient to keep pace with the growing claims of foreign creditors and with the growing import requirements. The excessive indebtedness may then lead to the so-called 'indebtedness trap', which in turn may not only slow down the rate of growth, but may even stop it entirely for a time.

In direct private investment, the situation is rather more complicated, since foreign capital is willing to go to LDCs only when investors are assured of a high rate of return. After a period of accelerated growth, the profit transfers to the developed countries may create far greater pressures on LDCs' balances of payments and exportable resources than debt repayments to creditors.

Besides, LDCs have to take into account other adverse aspects of foreign direct private investment, such as foreign control over the most valuable natural resources of the country, foreign influences on investment decisions and on the pattern of economic development. Foreign companies make their decisions not from the point of view of the national interests of the host country but from that of their own long-term strategies.

To generalise, one may say that a heavy reliance on foreign sources for financing economic development represents a substantial risk, from the point of view of the national interest of LDCs.

Finally, I would like to express full agreement with the opinion expressed in the UN study on *The Future of the World Economy,* where the stress is laid on internal factors, and especially on indispensable social and institutional changes, as measures leading to greater effectiveness of public policies for accelerating economic development. 'Investment resources coming from abroad would be important but are secondary as compared to internal sources' (2).

References

(1) United Nations, *The Future of the World Economy,* New York, 1976.

(2) Ibid: (preliminary version) page 50.

Philipp Rieger*

In his review of balance of payments developments, *Bhaduri* (Chapter 5) is misled by a set of questionable and obsolete statistics. It is simply not true that 'almost the entire deficit in international payments' is held by the non-oil LDC's or that 'the current account surplus is almost exclusively shared by industrialised OECD and OPEC'. The bunching together of all industrial countries into one group gives a highly misleading impression. It is important to differentiate between the seven major industrial countries and the group of smaller OECD countries which like the non-oil LDCs are hardest hit by the oil-price increases. This group had to grapple with severe current account deficits in all years since 1973 and most probably they will have to bear the brunt also in future. They are also strongly affected by the oil-price induced stagflation in the major industrial countries. Even the remaining strong industrial nations like Germany and Japan appear to be running into deficit now.

* Director, Austrian National Bank, Vienna

In referring to the rising indebtedness of LDCs, Bhaduri contests 'the widely held impression that the dominance of private creditors in the external debts of developing countries is extremely or even primarily due to the rise in oil prices since 1973'. He sees no 'dramatic break' around 1973/74 in an almost inherent tendency operating since 1967. It is quite true that the rise of the Euromarkets anteceded their new role of recycling a major part of the OPEC surpluses – both to non-oil LDCs and to industrial countries running current account deficits. Until 1973 (and in 1978) industrial countries lent their earned surpluses. After 1973, Eurobanks started to act mainly as *intermediaries.* I maintain that the 'special event' of 1973, i.e. the fourfold increase in the price of oil, gave an entirely new dimension to the international financial markets and provided them with a new role.

It amounted to a 'dialectical leap' (in Hegelian or Marxian terminology) – a substantial quantitative increase producing a new quality. Before 1973, and parallel with the rise of transnational corporations a process of multinationalisation of banking had taken place. The transnational banks were willing and prepared to accept the huge surplus funds of OPEC and also to accept the risks of transforming funds placed for relatively short periods into medium and long-term credits. And the OPEC obviously preferred the intermediation of the transnational banks to the far more risky direct lending to LDC's for longer periods. The somewhat cumbersome Bretton Woods institutions were neither ready, nor did they then have sufficient funds, to shoulder the task of oil-price induced deficit financing. Moreover, the LDCs preferred, and many of the more creditworthy still prefer, recourse to the private financial markets to accepting conditions attached to certain IMF credits. Many observers maintain that the easy access to private financial markets actually hampered and delayed the necessary adjustment process of deficit countries. In the discussions on the creation of a substitution account, I noted with some surprise the reluctance of the LDCs to see the dangerous growth of the Euromarkets in any way controlled.

While I greatly regret the overwhelmingly poor performance of the industrial North (including the developed socialist countries) in giving aid to the LDCs, Bhaduri's contention that 'low ODA assistance has almost been a conscious policy to facilitate transnational banking operations in the South' appears to me to suggest a rather far-fetched 'Machiavellian Plot'.

If we wish to remain within the realms of objective facts, it is a fact that ODA has *overcompensated* the cumulative trade-deficit of LDCs with OECD in the 4 years 1974-1977 ($ 54 : $ 41 billion), while total official flows from OPEC have only partly offset the mainly oil-price induced trade deficit of the non-oil LDCs in the same period ($ 30 : $ 77 billion). Their concessional assistance amounted to only $ 21 billion.

Adolf Nussbaumer

Financial relations between North and South reflect a good part of the problems developing countries have to face, and we should be grateful to *Bhaduri* for the very interesting information and the personal comments he has made. There are, however, some problems which merit further discussion.

Is it really true that the low ODA assistance has almost been a conscious policy to facilitate transnational banking operations in the South, as Bhaduri suggests? Or is it rather because of budgetary restraints in developed countries and an insufficient awareness of development needs by large sections of the population that governments find it difficult to expand ODA? If so, then the banking system has come just in time to facilitate an increase of capital flows to developing nations. That this notion cannot be rejected out of hand might be supported by the fact that recently even governments which so far have been very anxious to keep trade and aid separate have welcomed mixed credits to middle income developing countries and newly industrialised countries as an appropriate means to increase trade. Is our real worry now the dominance of private banking in the recycling of international finance, or rather that the capacity for recycling of the private banking system might not suffice to solve future problems, should OPEC surpluses continue to rise?

Furthermore, the danger of financial imbalance on a world scale seems much more important to me than to the author. Certainly, *Table 5.3* suggests that the OPEC surplus continues to fall, and OECD has been bold enough to extrapolate this tendency even into 1979. But now, in the first half of 1980 we must be aware of the fact that a second wave of oil price increases is striking the industrialised countries, and not only them, and that this will create new difficulties for all of our countries. At the same time the Eurobanking system shows a decreasing ability to attract and absorb OPEC funds (*Table 5.4*) leaving more of the burden to recycle these funds to OECD countries as well as to the Socialist bloc and to the developing countries themselves.

Moreover, more recent developments make us fear that Bhaduri might be mistaken in some of his conclusions. Contrary to his final remark there was no definite tendency towards a lower rate of annual OPEC surplus at least for 1979 and 1980, and due to the international banking system's limited capability for recycling, a larger share of the burden will have to be shouldered by the developing countries themselves; so that a relatively sharp increase in the price of oil might once again have a destabilising influence on the world economy. Even so, we should not permit ourselves to disregard all other reasons for instability in the developing world; on the contrary, developed industrial countries, in cooperation with OPEC countries, should face their responsibilities towards the poor nations and increase their efforts to help them to solve their immediate as well as their long-range development problems.

Marian Paszyński

I would subscribe to the criticisms expressed by *Calcagno* and *Kñakal* (Chapter 6) about the negative aspects of the operation of transnational companies (TNCs) in the Third World. There is, however, another side of the story, which they neglect: why do developing nations accept TNCs' investments in their economies? There must be some rationale behind developing countries' policies in this respect. It seems that they cannot do without TNCs as providers of capital, technology, managerial skills and marketing experience and facilities – all factors lacking in a developing economy.

If developing countries cannot get along without investment by TNCs and if, at the same time, the operations of these corporations bring several negative consequences, what could be a reasonable strategy towards the transnationals?

There exist two basic possibilities for dealing with TNCs in developing countries, with two options in each case. First, developing nations may try to edge out TNCs. They could do it by nationalisation. But several problems arise, difficult to resolve. (i) A country can nationalise assets, but can hardly nationalise managerial skills or marketing experience. Therefore, nationalisation could very often be followed by contractual agreements with nationalised companies for the management of nationalised enterprises and for marketing their products. Such agreements are often no less profitable to the TNCs than direct productive operations; this seems to be corroborated by *Table 6.8*, which shows that in the Middle East, where there was disinvestment in 1970 – 1977, (due to nationalisation of foreign companies' assets), the outflow of investment income was greater than in any other developing region. (ii) The question arises whether developing countries nationalise with or (a rare case) without compensation. If they do it without compensation, they cut themselves off from the inflow of new capital from abroad, whether from private or – frequently – from public sources, and the final balance might be disadvantageous to the nationalising country. If they nationalise with compensation (generally in foreign exchange), one may wonder whether, taking account of the scarcity of foreign exchange, nationalisation is the best way of dealing with TNCs. Sometimes it may prove counterproductive.

The other option for an edging-out policy is that of expanding public sector operations. President Julius K. Nyerere came out several years ago against using scarce foreign exchange resources as compensation to nationalised foreign companies (except for companies occupying the 'commanding heights' of the economy) instead of using these resources to finance the foreign exchange component of public sector investments. He pointed out that in this way not only can the economy expand faster but a countervailing power can be established to enable a developing country to bargain more successfully with TNCs.

However, the edging-out policy cannot eliminate TNCs from the economy of developing countries. If these countries are bound to live with the TNCs, the priority for their strategy would be to devise effective instruments of control of the TNCs or, rather, ways of subordinating their operations to the interests of the overall economic development of the host country. We may consider the extension of control over TNC operations on the national and on the international level. An individual country is in a weak position to control TNCs, not only because its economic potential is no match to that of a global corporation, but also because, by their very nature, the operations of TNCs transcend national boundaries. The TNCs can switch operations from one country to another whenever they feel their interests endangered.

A multilateral approach towards controlling TNCs therefore seems much more likely to be effective. This does not amount to support for the international codes of conduct now being debated in various international fora. Any international code – if any agreement should emerge among developing and developed countries on such a code in the foreseeable future (especially agreement in respect of its obligatory nature) – would be effective only if translated into national legislation in both host and mother countries, which is rather doubtful.

On the other hand, internationally coordinated national actions by host countries may prove more successful. It might resemble the collective bargaining recently undertaken by international trade unions with TNCs; the unions recognise that a national approach to collective bargaining (even a strike on the national level) is not effective, precisely because of the ability of the TNCs to manipulate operations over a transnational area. If concerted action (e.g. laying down conditions for entry and operations of a TNC, for which an internationally agreed code of conduct might provide guidelines) could be agreed upon by a sufficiently large number of potential host countries, especially develping ones, effective control over TNCs could be brought nearer to reality. This, however, would require a greater degree of unity of minds among developing countries, not on the level of generalised demands but on the more concrete objectives for pragmatic negotiations, than has yet, unfortunately, materialised. So far, what we see is, rather, growing competition for the inflow of foreign capital, reflected in the increasingly liberal codes for attracting overseas investment.

Göran Ohlin*

(a) It seems a serious weakness of the kind of calculations made by *Seton* that countries whose economic policies result in a low marginal propensity to save would lay claim to extremely large amounts of support over a very long period of time, regardless of whether they are very poor or not, as shown in his tables. On the other hand good performance in economic policy would be penalised. Chiefly for this reason I would not wish Seton's scheme to be a model for international development assistance.

(b) Fears have been expressed over the burden of international indebtedness. But it makes little sense to add up the total debts of South or East or West. To these debts correspond equal claims, and it is in nobody's interest to have them repaid very fast. Individual debts are continually being rolled over, and the question is whether the situation is dangerously unstable. It would be desirable to have much of the international debt on longer maturities than at present, but compared with other threats to the world economy today the international debts do not seem frightening; and if the world economy is to function adequately in the years ahead we have to look forward to a good deal more debt rather than less.

* University of Uppsala

PART III – THE TRANSFER OF TECHNOLOGY

Chapter 8

APPROPRIATE TECHNOLOGY AND THE NATIONAL ECONOMY OF DEVELOPING COUNTRIES

Heinz-Dieter Haustein*
Harry Maier+

Economic modernisation is a central concern of most developing countries. The critical situation in most of these countries – hunger, illiteracy, disintegration of traditional cultural and social structures – leaves no alternative but social, economic and technological modernisation. Of course technological modernisation will not automatically solve the problems faced by these countries; indeed inappropriate technological strategies may create more problems than they solve. The question is: what kind of technology is needed to cope with the present situation in these countries?

Technological modernisation is an important precondition for the improvement and evaluation of national economies which should be able to supply the population with food, homes, employment, education possibilities, health care, and fields of cultural activity. This is an important precondition for participation in the international division of labour and in the cultural and scientific technological progress of mankind.

To propose that these countries should hold their technology, economy, society and culture at their present stage, or initiate a technology to serve traditional values, is an

* Economic University 'Bruno Leuschner', Berlin, GDR; also with the International Institute for Applied Systems Analysis (IIASA), Laxenburg, Austria.

+ Task Leader, Management and Technology Area, IIASA, Laxenburg, Austria.

irresponsible underestimation of their real problems. Preservation of the status quo is out of the question, and attempting to preserve the status quo will incur great human suffering. The need for technological, organisational and social innovation, both in the developed and in the developing countries, is too great.

8.1 The innovation process

Social, organisational and technical innovations are different parts of a joint system (*Figure 8.1*). Without technological change it is impossible to alter the organisational and social system. On the other hand, technological innovations without organisational and social innovations will not improve the living conditions of the population or secure the development of an independent national economy.

Figure 8.1

The innovation process in a hierarchical context

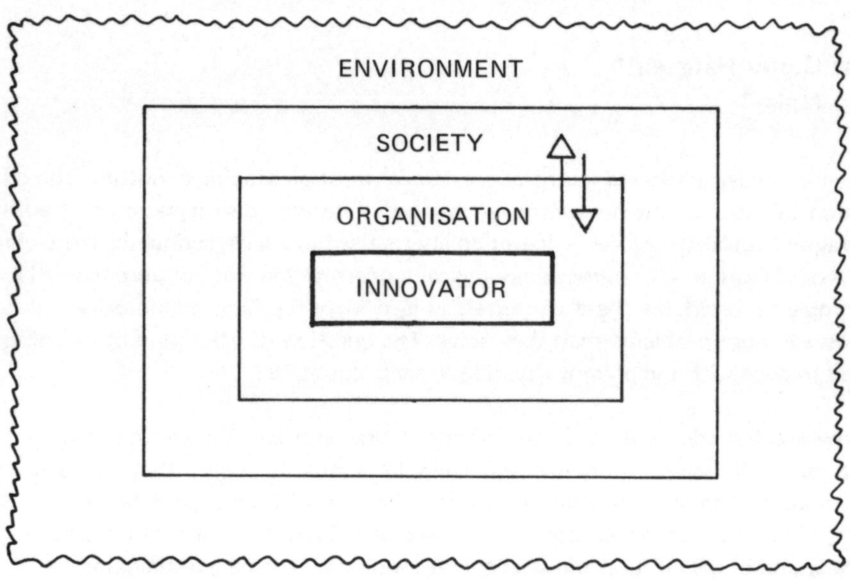

The need to consider both the social and technical sides of the innovation process has important consequences for the approach we use to identify appropriate technologies for the developing countries. Two kinds of approach are possible. On the one hand, we can start from a single technological change and look at its social consequences and implications or at the governmental measures needed to ensure its efficiency. This is, for example, the main aim of technology assessment (TA). On the other hand, we can go out from social needs and goals, from existing and forthcoming leaks or bottlenecks in resource processing systems, and then look at the given field of technological possibilities for a technological fix. We could call this latter approach socio-economic opportunity analysis (SOA) (*Figure 8.2*).

Figure 8.2

The role of TA (Technological assessment) and SOA (Socio-economic opportunity analysis)

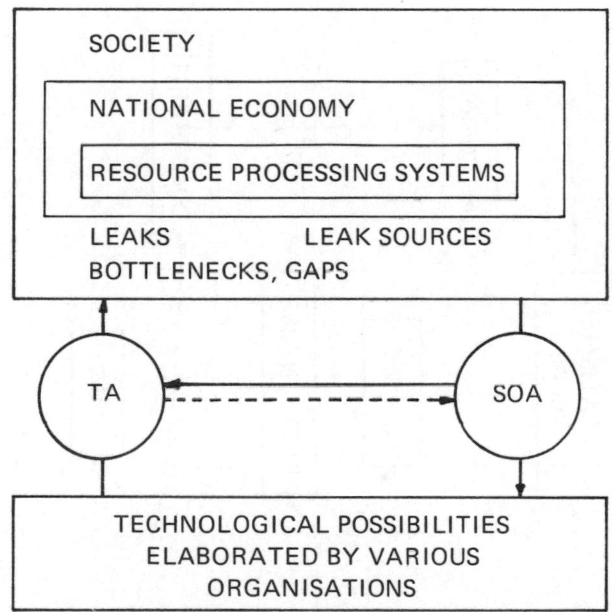

Both approaches are important for developing countries. Ideally the two will be used in a complementary fashion in formulating policy for improving the technical basis in the developing countries. SOA is especially important in orienting the national technology policy (*Figure 8.3*).

The importance of the second approach (SOA) can be appreciated by looking at the nature of the innovation process. Innovations are the units of technological change. A technical innovation is a complex activity which proceeds from the conception of a new idea to a solution of the problem and then to the actual utilisation of the new item of economic or social value. The pace of technological change has made innovation a key concept in today's world. Social, economic and technological innovations are essential for survival in a world with resource shortages, hunger, illiteracy, wastage of human capabilities and great imbalances between the different parts of the world.

Figure 8.3

SOA (Socio-economic opportunity analysis) in the context of national problems

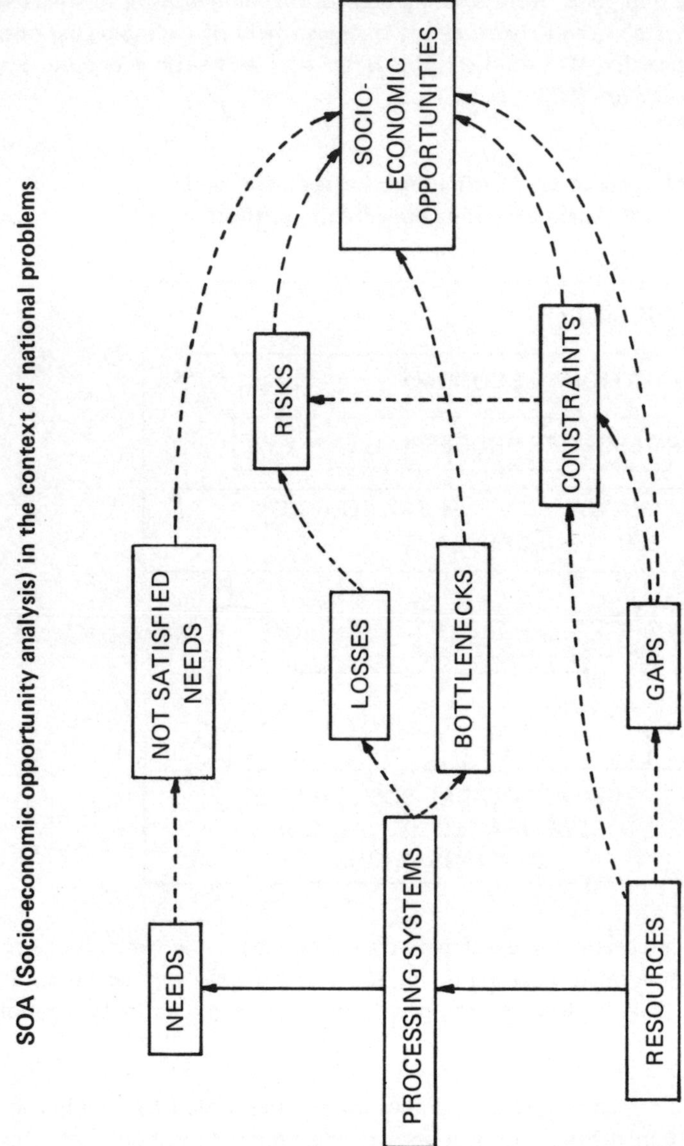

Generally speaking, innovation comes about through the fusion of a recognized demand and a recognized technical feasibility into a design concept. This is truly a creative act in which the association of both elements is essential. If a technical advance alone is considered, it may or may not result in a solution for which there will be a demand. Similarly, search for a response to a recognized demand may or may not result in a solution, depending on the technical feasibility in the current state of technical knowledge (*Figure 8.4*). One of the clearest and most common findings from different case studies on innovation is the domination of demand factors. For example, in the study by S. Myers and D.G. Marquis, it was found that technical factors accounted for only 21 per cent of the innovations studied, and demand factors, market and production factors accounted for 75 per cent of the innovations (1).

The conclusion of this story is: technical appropriateness is insufficient. In planning for socially adaptive technical change one must also recognize, and respond to, current and future national demands; one must strive to develop from the body of international technical knowledge a national technical potential capable of responding to demand.

Currently, most developing countries are unable to do either. They generally lack the ability to articulate their real demands from the point of view of gaining national goals. Their internal market is dominated by external forces and goals. Moreover they are unable to create an indigenous basis for technological development and improvement, because currently the forces which work against this are too strong. We will mention here only the brain drain and patent policy.

The gap in the capability of the developing countries to articulate their indigenous demand for innovations and the lack of technological knowledge results in a difficult situation.

We know that energy consumption per capita is an important indicator not only of living standards, but also of the technological level. The distribution of energy use is presently very unequal; region I (United States and Canada) with 6 per cent of the world population consumes 32.2 per cent of the world energy production. Region V with 38 per cent of the world population consumes only 4.1 per cent of world energy production. Therefore the per capita energy consumption is 52 times higher in region I than in region V. For other indicators of the relative place of different groups of economies in the world see *Table 8.1*.

All this indicates that the raising of the technological level in the developing countries is a global problem and is crucial for the future of mankind. This is the great challenge of our time, and to coming generations.

At present, developing country technologies are characterised not only by their low average levels but also by great disproportionalities in internal technological development.

Figure 8.4

Scheme of introduction of new technologies

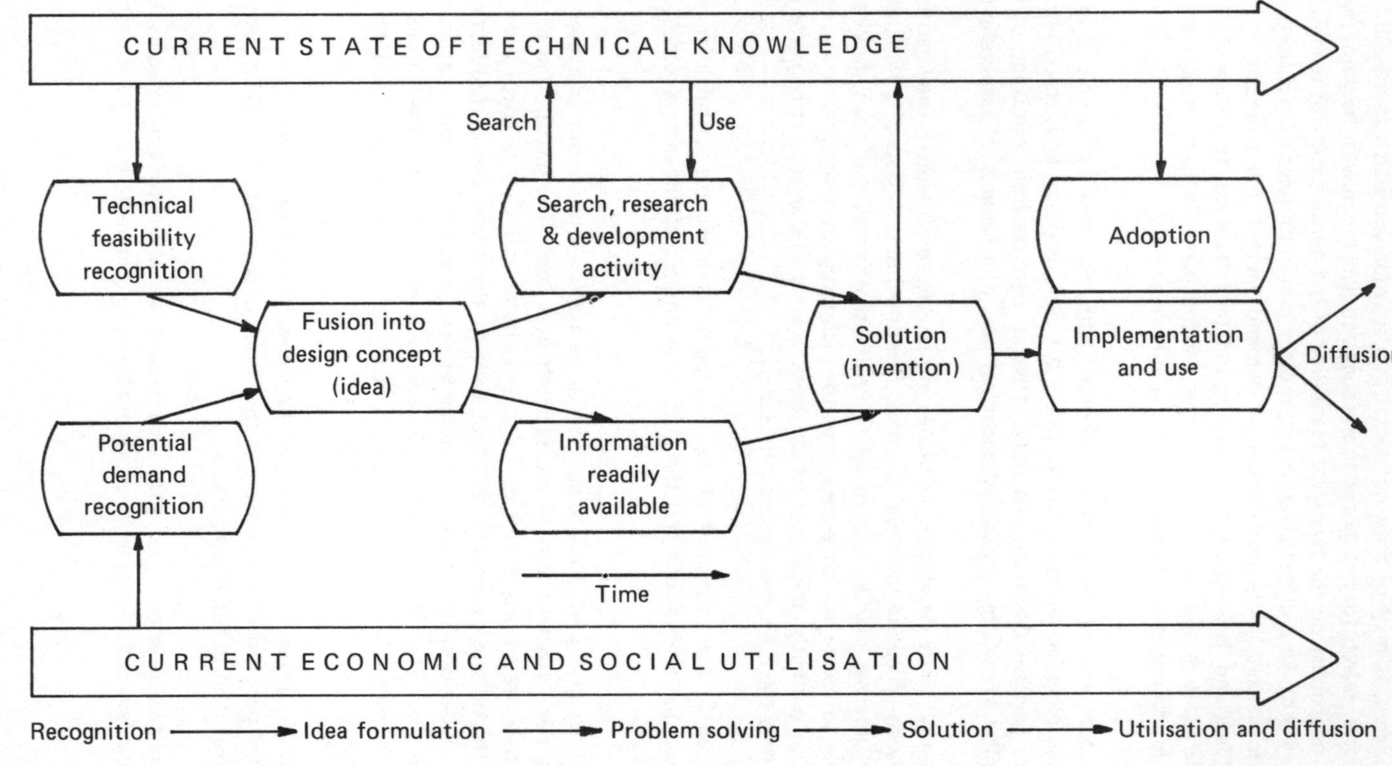

Source: J. Myers and D.G. Marquis, *Successful Industrial Innovation,* National Science Foundation, NSF-69-77. J. 32.

Table 8.1

Percentage shares of different socio-economic systems in world totals

	Surface	Population	Raw material output	Industrial production	Scientists & engineers	Patent notifi-cation	Patent notifi-cation abroad
	1977a)	1977a)	1970b)	1975c)	1970-73d)	1974	1974
Socialist countries	26	33	28	40	49	30	3.5
Comecon countries	18	9	.	35	.	.	.
Developing countries	49	48	27	10	6	2	0.5
Developed market economies	25	20	45	50	45	68	96

a) *Statistisches Jahrbuch der DDR 1978,* p. 29. — b) W. Sprote, G. Thole: *Internationale Wirtschaftsbeziehungen und Entwicklungsländer,* Staatsverlag Berlin 1978, p. 24. — c) J. Kuczynski: *Die Krise der kapitalistischen Weltwirtschaft,* Dietz Verlag, Berlin 1976, p. 10. — d) EEC, *East-West Technological Co-operation,* Brussels 1976, p. 207.

Sophisticated firms and producers, often foreign owned, are islands in an ocean of pre-industrial production. These sophisticated parts of the national economy are not integrated into the national division of labour, but are isolated groups, more closely linked to foreign than national control. The production of the modern sectors in developing countries tends to be oriented towards the demands and needs of the developed countries populations and the affluent minority in the developing economies. Standing apart as they do, the sophisticated sectors of developing economies often play a disruptive role in the national economy. They not only fail to accelerate economic development, they also often tend to destroy the traditional technological basis without creating a new technological basis able to meet national needs in the medium and long-term perspective. The concept of 'dual economy' is a reflection of — and to some extent an apology for — this situation, but it is not able to show the way for the establishment of an integrated national technical basis, with a productive relationship between the different technological levels.

8.2 The levels of technology

Table 8.2 shows the different technological levels which exist in each country. In all countries, lower level systems a to c exist side by side. But in the industrialised countries the production volume of a and b technology is very low and the different technological levels function as parts of an integrated national economy. The concept of intermediate technology is largely oriented towards furthering semi-mechanised technologies (level b), but this cannot help us meet the objectives of the developing countries to increase their standards of living. It is also not possible to jump from technology level b to d. In most cases the developing countries have not enough investment, skilled workers, and infra-

Table 8.2

Levels of technology

	Content	Example
Level a	Manual drive, task execution, control and logical functions	1. Drop spindle 2. Spinning wheel 3. Improved spinning wheel
Level b	Substitution of mechanical for human energy (power tools)	Spinning wheels with external drive power
Level c	Substitution of the mechanical for human energy and task execution	1. Selfactor 2. Ring machine 3. Open-end spinning
Level d	Complete substitution of mechanical-technical for human operation, including control and logical functions	1. First generation automated equipment 2. Second generation automated equipment

structure to use the d technology. This technology is also not appropriate for creating a national technical basis capable of producing enough goods for the population and for securing employment. The developing countries are faced with the problem of allocating their limited resources and investment between the different levels of technology in a way that optimises their utilisation of domestic, natural and human resources for producing the stream of goods and services needed to meet the demands of their populations. Therefore one cannot say what is the appropriate technology from the standpoint of a single company, branch, or territory – one must look at the economy as a whole, its resource situation and accumulation potential. This is why the prevailing approach, in which one looks only to the features of a single technology, or to technologies of a specific technological level, is inadequate. The developing countries need an efficient mixture between the different types and levels of a technology. True, there currently seems to be a deficiency of technologies which utilise natural and human resources of the developing countries – often referred to as 'soft', small-scale and low capital technologies, which make extensive use of local labour and raw materials. These kinds of technology are important in the present stage of development and it is necessary to pay greater attention to developing such kinds of technology. But this could be only a part of the technical basis of a country.

The small-scale sugar plants developed in India, which now account for more than 20 per cent of the country's production, are a good case in point (2). The average investment per ton of output is two and a half times smaller than in the large modern plants, and the investment per worker nine times less. Differences in production costs however are much smaller (less than 20 per cent), and the present balance in favour of the small-scale technology could easily be tilted. This in fact is what happened with a rather similar type of technology in Ghana. Analyses made in 1969 showed that the small-scale, low-cost sugar technology was more attractive from an economic point of view, but four years later, with the rise in wages and the improvements in modern large-scale plants, the situation was completely reversed. Economics can, of course, also operate in favour of the small-scale, low-cost technology. In India, for instance, the sudden rise in the price of imported oil has helped to make cow dung much more attractive as a fuel. However important such kinds of technology might be, we must not foster the illusion that it is possible to use only this kind of technology to solve the problems of the developing countries. 'Appropriate technology' is not a synonym for soft technology. The problem is to integrate such technologies into the national technological basis. Both extreme approaches – 'small is beautiful' and 'big is wonderful' – are inappropriate. The technical basis must include hard and soft, large and small, high and low technologies in appropriate proportions in order to improve the economic efficiency of the countries and help them use the benefits of the international division of labour.

Unless integrated into a mixture of different types and levels of technology in the development of a national technology basis, low-cost labour-intensive technologies would only be another term for low labour productivity and low standards of living. This would mean recommending underdeveloped technologies to underdeveloped countries.

Table 8.3 shows the impacts of different technological levels on the satisfaction of national needs in the developing countries. The results of our evaluation are:

(a) Governmental technology policies should aim at finding the right mixture between technologies a, b, c, and d.

(b) Technologies b1, c1, and c2 must have a dominating role. This results from the balance of benefits and expenditure criteria.

(c) We see also that it is necessary to strengthen the capabilities of developing countries to move from technology a and b to c3 and d1, and to develop technology from levels c and d which are particularly important for the developing countries.

A good example of this is the solar pump developed by a European firm in cooperation with the University of Dakar, and currently being introduced on a large scale in Mexico. It uses a widely available source of energy – the sun – to provide villagers with a scarce but vitally important resource – water. Although it is technically very sophisticated, it requires virtually no maintenance and seems to have, potentially, a very long life.

Table 8.3

Impact of different technology levels on the national economy of developing countries

Criteria	a1	a2	a3	b1	c1	c2	c3	d1	d2
	Levels of Technology								
Effects on growth of production	0	1	2	2	2	3	3	3	3
Better satisfaction of basic income needs	0	0	1	1	2	3	3	4	4
Employment effect, capital growth, savings	3	3	3	3	3	2	1	0	0
Effect on labour skills	0	0	0	1	2	2	3	4	4
Impact on national division of labour	0	0	0	1	3	3	4	4	4
Use of national resources	4	4	4	3	3	3	2	1	1
Integration in national market	4	4	4	4	3	3	2	1	1
Accomodation to national conditions	4	4	4	4	2	2	1	0	0
Linkage to international developments	0	0	0	0	1	2	3	4	4
Sum of benefits	15	16	17	19	21	23	22	21	21

Expenditure criteria	a1	a2	a3	b1	c1	c2	c3	d1	d2
	Levels of Technology								
R & D intensity	0	0	1	1	2	2	3	4	4
Demand on the infrastructure	0	0	0	1	2	2	3	4	4
Optimum production scale	0	0	0	0	1	2	3	4	4
Import share	0	0	0	1	2	3	4	4	4
Sum of expenditure criteria	0	0	1	3	7	9	13	16	16

Evaluation:
0 without importance
1 little importance
2 medium importance
3 high importance
4 very high importance

8.3 Requirements for a technological policy

Successful establishment of an integrated national technical basis in the developing countries requires that governmental technology policy should play a key role. Governments' main goals should be the following:

(a) creation of domestic complexes focusing on national basic industry, mechanical engineering, consumer goods and export industry;

(b) development of domestic agriculture to form the resource foundation for the accumulation of means and manpower for domestic industry. This makes the success of technical innovation depend very strongly upon social innovation, including real agricultural reform and the development of agricultural cooperation. We must also bear in mind that in the developing countries, agriculture will be the basis for development of industry for a long period – not only from the standpoint of food and raw material supply, but also from the standpoint of manpower and financial sources for investment. Only on an advanced level will it be possible to change this situation; agriculture can then be developed on the basis of industry. Also in the present stage it will be necessary to make a serious commitment to use industrial processes to improve agricultural efficiency;

(c) to make maximum efforts to use the domestic natural and human resources;

(d) to develop self-reliance in the mechanical engineering industry and equipment production;

(e) to extend and improve the domestic division of labour;

(f) to maintain a mutually reinforcing relationship between traditional sectors which will benefit from modernisation and modern sectors which will need to draw labour and other inputs from traditional sectors;

(g) to establish and maintain a close relationship between social innovation and technical innovations;

(h) to lay a solid national scientific-technical foundation capable both of serving national needs and of holding trained manpower, i.e., stopping the brain drain;

(i) to facilitate selective transfer of technology from the developed countries in a way that will help to improve the national capability to use international know-how without sacrifices of national independence;

(j) to secure a high level of technological unification and standardisation;

(k) to establish a national system of management and planning of science and technology.

In searching for appropriate technology, one must always keep in mind the problems of employment and resources. In the next twenty years the developing countries will need more than 300 million additional jobs. Assuming that each working place costs 10,000 dollars (in the US 20,000 dollars), then 150 billion (10^9) dollars per year will be required to secure enough working places in the developing countries. 150 billion dollars is a lot of money, but then again, it is only one-third of annual world expenditure for armaments (450 billion dollars).

Many of us have the impression that only the developed countries have resource problems. This is false: the resource situation in the developing countries is much worse than that in the developed countries. Many of the former not only lack natural resources, but they also lack the technological means to utilise efficiently the resources which they do have. Moreover they are also unable to substitute new artificial resources for scarce natural resources. This situation is exemplified by one of the most constraining resources, energy.

One of the important findings of the Energy Project at IIASA conducted by Prof. Wolf Häfele (3) is that in 1975 world average primary energy consumption was about 2.1 kilowatt years per capita, per year, but 70 per cent of the world population lives at less than average consumption levels, and a depressingly large proportion at only 0.2 kwy/cap. This corresponds with the great differences in per capita GDP. Any improvement in this situation needs the better use and extension of energy production. But traditional resources – oil, coal, and gas – will be unable to satisfy more than 65 per cent of energy demand in 2030. The remaining 35 per cent will have to come from new resources like nuclear power, soft and hard solar energy, coal liquefication, etc. The great danger for the developing countries is that they will be able neither to pay the higher prices for traditional energy resources such as oil, gas and coal, nor to substitute new synthetic energy resources for the traditional scarce resources.

It poses a great challenge to the developing countries to develop their own scientific and technical basis and to take part in world-wide scientific-technological progress. The developing countries can avoid deterioration of their present condition only by establishing their own national systems of division of labour, organised to help them to use their own resources to gain equal rights in the international division of labour.

The main concern at present of government technology policy must be the stimulation of the flow of labour from a and b technologies (small scale production on a manual basis), to the c and d technologies (large scale production on a technologically advanced basis). The a and b technologies must be strongly coupled to the c and d technologies.

Conservation of the "dual economy" in the developing countries will not help them to solve their problems. Means of attaining integrated development include the following:

(a) for domestic industry (on the c and d technology level), to develop and produce appropriate technology and equipment for a and b sectors of national economy;

(b) social innovations for new organisational forms of small-scale production and productive cooperation between small-scale production units and large-scale factories;

(c) development of education systems and elimination of illiteracy. Generally educational systems need to be made more production-oriented. Such educational innovation is crucial, because the old educational systems, whose main aim was conservation of the traditional social structures, are to a large extent consumption-oriented and incapable of preparing the new generation to cope with the problems resulting from the process of industrialisation and from global development;

(d) to support the small-scale, labour-intensive, export-oriented sectors and to stimulate selective export lines based on large-scale production;

(e) to establish technological consulting points and service feasibilities (especially for agriculture and handicrafts);

(f) to step up the R & D expenditure for the technological development of small-scale industry;

(g) to promote stimulation measures for the technical development of large-scale industry through brokerages, credit, guaranteed markets, etc.

These measures aim to integrate small scale production into the national socio-economic and technological basis. Only through the integrated development can the natural and human resources of the nation be effectively employed to attain the economic growth needed to meet the needs of the population.

Developing country planners must seek a combination of different technological levels which will lead to well-proportioned development of the technical basis. This combination could have the following features:

(a) use of surplus manpower for the production of labour-intensive means of production;

(b) concentration on the import of advanced technology (levels c and d) on key operations of the core processes. The other processes should be based on labour-intensive technologies;

(c) use of the limited stock of advanced equipment for demonstration and education;

(d) transfer of old means of production to small-scale firms;

(e) promotion of a strategy of high standards of quality in means of production;

(f) establishment of a closed technological cycle from raw materials to final products on the basis of the national division of labour;

(g) avoidance of non-integrated investments and technological conservatism.

Table 8.4 shows an example of the possible combination of different technologies. This indicates the necessary direction of technology transfer which could help the developing countries cope with their problems. This technology transfer includes:

- hardware supply (equipment),
- installation and operation of new technology (software),
- organisation for efficient management of technology ('orgware').

The transfer of hardware is much easier than the transfer of software, or of orgware which is socially and culturally specific and often cannot be transferred without social, economic and cultural changes. The extent of change in the system of cultural and social values depends on the strength of the social forces which affect it. The developing countries at present pay dearly for technology transfer (more than 15 per cent of the net proceeds from exports), but the results of this transfer have not helped to solve the serious problems of these countries. Reasons vary: the most important are the social forms by which this transfer takes place, the inappropriate character of the transferred technology, and social conditions in some of the developing countries which make them unable to absorb new technologies. Two key measures for the better use of technology transfer for national needs are:

(a) assurance that the transferred technology can be integrated into the national system of division of labour;

(b) creation of a scientific-technical basis which can effectively absorb the transferred technology.

Table 8.5 provides a rough approximation of the magnitude of the effects of different forms of technology transfer. Note that the contribution of the forms of division of labour increases geometrically as one moves from left to right (from non-integrated use of raw materials to full integration into the national economy and export sectors) while the influence of appropriateness of technology increases linearly from top to bottom

Table 8.4

Variants of technological basis of a production process with high acceleration effect and high employment effect

Level	Example	Technology level of core of the main process	Technology level of the auxiliary and side process of pre- and incremental operations of the main process	Supply of equipment produced with technologies on the level —			
				a	b	c	d
I	Synthetic production	c, d	b		x	x	x
II	Synthetic yarn manufacture	c	a	x	x		
III	Weaving of synthetic cloth	c	a	x	x		
IV	Weaving of improved synthetic cloth	c	a	x	x		
V	Sewing	a	a	x			

Table 8.5

Stages of technology transfer and its evaluation

(Numbers designate approximate magnitude of the effects of various forms of technology transfer)

Degree of suitability	Impact on the national division of labour	Without integration of national system of division of labour, using only raw material	Without integration of national system of division of labour, using only manpower	Part integration in the national system of division of labour	Integration in the national division of labour including export
		1. (1)	2. (2)	3. (4)	4. (8)
1.	Transfer of conventional technology (0)	1	2	4	8
2.	Transfer of partially appropriate technology (1)	2	3	5	9
3.	Transfer of highly appropriate technology (2)	3	4	6	10

as one progresses from conventional to highly appropriate technologies. The matrix entries are the sum of the row and the column values.

To illustrate the table's meaning, a foreign-owned and -operated mining enterprise using foreign labour would fall in the upper left hand corner of the matrix and would have an influence of 1 on a scale from 1 to 10. A domestically-owned enterprise, using domestic labour and inputs from other domestically operated enterprises, selling its products both on domestic and export markets, and using technologies well adapted to local circumstances would fall in the lower right category and have an impact value of 10.

There are different modes of technological development in the developing countries. In *Table 8.6* we try to evaluate them with respect to developing country objectives. We need the right mixture between these different modes of technological change. The most favoured mode (capital export through multinational companies) cannot solve the problems of these countries because it does not help to develop their technical capabilities. The other modes are more difficult, but they can help to develop technological self-reliance. In this connection the governmental technology policy has to play a great role in:

- national planning
- resource allocation
- evaluation
- financial support
- sales promotion
- export promotion
- subvention.

8.4 Conclusions

Development is a complex social process which rests in large part upon the internal innovative capabilities of a society. It is critical that the developing countries should gain effective control over the three primary factors influencing the initiation and successful implementation of technical innovation: the market, production, and technical factors. Demand factors are critical for the success or failure of new technologies. Therefore the developing countries must think about how to create and identify demand from the point of view of national needs, as well as how to connect demand with technological feasibilities. This requires a concept of the development of the national technological basis.

Innovation is not a single action but a total process of interrelated sub-processes. It is not just the conception of new ideas, not the invention of a new device, nor the development of a new market. Innovative capability of society can only be improved if government policy tries to stimulate all stages of the innovative process: the invention

Table 8.6

Different modes of technological innovation and its preconditions in developing countries

Sources of technological innovations

Necessary preconditions	1.	2.	3.	4.	5.	6.	7.
(1) Qualification of labour force	0	2	2	3	4	4	4
(2) National R & D potential	0	1	1	3	4	4	4
(3) National management	0	2	2	3	4	4	4
(4) National market	1	3	3	4	4	4	4
(5) National information system	0	2	2	3	4	4	4
(6) National experimental basis	0	2	2	3	4	4	4
(7) · National mechanical engineering	0	0	1	3	4	4	4
(8) Mental motivation	1	3	3	4	4	4	4
(9) Material interest	3	3	3	4	4	4	4
(10) Infra-structure	1	2	2	3	3	3	4
(11) Integration in the national division of labour	0	2	2	3	3	4	4
(12) Integration in international division of labour	4	2	3	3	2	3	4
(13) Sum	10	24	26	39	44	46	48

1. Foreign investments — 2. Input of foreign technology for national private firms — 3. Import of appropriate technology for national private firms — 4. Import of technology for nationalised firms and governmental development programmes — 5. National technology development in firms — 6. National technology development in the framework of national programmes — 7. National technology development in the framework of international and national programmes.

Evaluation: 0 without importance; 1 little importance; 2 medium importance; 3 high importance; 4 very high importance stage, the technical realisation stage and the commercialisation stage. It is not possible to have appropriate technology without mastering the interlinkages between these different stages.

The question 'What is appropriate technology?' cannot be answered from the standpoint of a single technology. The same technology may or may not be appropriate, depending on how it is integrated into the national technological basis and what is its influence on national development. A well-integrated national technology must include a mutually reinforcing development of different types and levels of technologies: labour-intensive, capital intensive, small-scale, large-scale, low-cost, traditional and sophisticated. The problem is to combine these different technologies in a way that efficiently meets national needs. Currently, we find that the developed countries typically produce and export technologies oriented towards filling their own needs and goals. A 'gap' exists for technologies which are not only highly efficient in concrete processes and which can effectively use human and national resources in the developing countries, but which can also be easily adapted to the specific conditions of developing countries. Helping the developing countries to create such technologies and to fuse them with advanced technologies should be a high priority concern in international cooperation and in international technology transfer.

References

(1) J. Myers and D.G. Marquis, *Successful Industrial Innovation,* National Science Foundation, USA, 1969.

(2) M.K. Garg, "The scaling down of modern technology, the crystal sugar manufacturing in India", *Appropriate Technology,* 1976.

(3) W. Häfele, "Global Perspectives and Options for Long-Range Energy Strategies". Keynote address at the "Conference on Energy Alternatives", East-West Center, Hawaii, 9-12 January 1979.

See also: C. Norman, "Massenproduktion oder Produktion durch die Massen", *Europa Archiv* 17. J.539, 1978.

Chapter 9

ADAPTING R & D PROGRAMMES TO THE NEEDS OF LESS DEVELOPED COUNTRIES

Arne Haselbach*

9.1 Some assumptions

The following paper is based on a number of assumptions which should be stated as clearly as possible in summary fashion to facilitate discussion.

The first basic assumption of this paper is that situations are different and that, therefore, models and mechanisms used for solving problems need to be adapted.

A second assumption is that the scientific and technological potential of the Northern industrialised countries will continue to be very important and that their vested interests should lead them to make a major contribution by assisting in the development of technology appropriate to the solution of the problems of the less developed parts of the globe.

A third assumption is that local people know many things, especially concerning the socio-cultural environment, better than foreigners.

A fourth assumption is that the people of any given country should have the decisive say concerning the direction of their country's development.

A fifth assumption is that cooperation in adapting R & D to the needs of less developed countries will produce results acceptable to both (or all) sides only if those concerned come to the conclusion that – on balance – cooperation in the specific undertaking is something which will further their respective interests.

The consequence of these assumptions is that it is impossible to design, or – better – that it is unreasonable to propose, a global masterplan for the development of science and technology or for the adaptation of R & D to the needs of less developed countries (or for any other category of countries for that matter).

If it does not seem possible or reasonable to draw up such a masterplan for the adaptation of R & D to the needs of less developed countries, another approach to the

* Director, Vienna Institute for Development.

problem has to be found which consists in designing a process of adaptation rather than in making suggestions as to what should be adapted and how.

Following this approach it seems necessary to ask, and to try to answer, some questions and to discuss a number of principles and mechanisms which together would allow the design of a process of adaptation – based on clarifying the interests involved and taking time and environment into account – which might be acceptable to all parties concerned.

Among the many questions which ought to be asked in considering how to adapt science and technology to the needs of less developed countries, I intend to deal with the following:

– is adaptation necessary?
– what would be the interests involved?
– what is to be adapted and why?
– what should adaptation concentrate on?
– how should cooperation be designed?

9.2 On the necessity to adapt

> 'No technology developed for use under one set of conditions can be used under another set of conditions without some degree of adaptation'.
>
> G. Ranis

There is a wide variety of technical, socio-cultural and economic reasons for adaptation of technology to the situation in less developed countries. Clearly, not all of these reasons apply in each individual case; but it is difficult to imagine any single case where the reasons that do apply would not call strongly for some adaptation to be carried out.

(a) Technical aspects:

The number of technical reasons being very large, the following list is merely indicative.

(i) *Physical environment:*

Temperature (higher temperatures necessitate larger dimensions of cooling systems or higher resistance of materials; big changes in temperatures must be calculated in view of heat expansion e.g. rails, buildings, cables).

Moisture (needs to be considered in packaging and storage; prevention of mould, bacteria and corrosion; transport problems in rainy season).

Dryness (scarcity of water: changes in cooling systems may be necessary which in turn lead to important changes in construction and operation; forest fire may have to be reckoned with; fire precautions in buildings and stores; dust-control measures in factory and transport; air-conditioning).

Radiation (corroding effects on plastics, rubber, etc.).

Wind (intensity; may sometimes carry sand or salt).

(ii) *Inputs:*

Raw Materials (different kind or different composition).

Intermediate Products (may not be available according to specifications used in planning of production process).

Energy (supply variations; different specifications of electric current; etc.).

(iii) *Norms and standards:*

Technical norms (measurements, right-hand or left-hand screw thread; etc.);

Industry standards;

Environmental legislation.

(b) **Socio-cultural aspects**

(i) *Techniques are historical products*

Creations of techniques are historical processes in which the moment in time, and the social, cultural and economic circumstances in which such techniques are being developed, largely determine the characteristics of the technique as well as the characteristics of the results or products they produce:

— Scientific and technological knowledge is different at different times and at different places.

— Even if knowledge on how one could solve a particular problem is available such a solution will only be transformed into a technique if those who have the knowledge have reasons to assume that there will be enough clients likely to use it, or — in other words — that it will be profitable to develop it.

— The level of income at the time and place of developing the technology decisively influences the characteristics of the techniques developed:

- the health of workers, as well as the degree of education and training in specific skills, depend on the level of income;
- the capital available for investment per worker depends on the level of income;
- the minimum productivity necessary to compete depends on the wage level and therefore on the level of income.

— The level of income influences not only the characteristics of the techniques but also the kinds and characteristics of the products : it is well known that not only the volume of consumption goes up with rising incomes but that the composition of the products consumed and used by individuals also changes (potatoes — bread — meat; radio and film — black and white television — colour television, etc.).

— Any technique depends on the availability in the society of the products needed as inputs for production of the capital equipment and for production of the final product.

— Any technique must produce goods or services which can either be used as intermediary products in other processes of production or which will fit into the existing patterns of consumption.

(ii) *Values and socio-economic structures*

Any technique which is to be introduced must not only fit into a larger web of techniques and products but also into a given society with its socio-economic structures and socio-cultural traits. The kind of organisation of the productive apparatus in particular, and of society in general, have an important influence: a technique is likely to be very different if it is to be used in a family size enterprise or in a subsidiary of a transnational corporation with a high degree of division of labour both within the subsidiary and on a global level. The scale of production, the kind of inputs, the degree of specialisation, the methods of organisation of production and management techniques applied will have to be adapted accordingly.

Among the socio-cultural aspects, I would like to mention in addition to the differences in value systems only family structures (with their influence on consumption patterns and work behaviour) and local tastes and preferences which have major influences on what is accepted or rejected.

(c) **Economic aspects**

For economists I would like only to list some of the obvious economic aspects which work in favour of adaptation:

— differences in factor endowment;
— qualifications of the work force;
— different relative prices of raw materials and auxiliary inputs;
— market size;
— availability of infrastructure;
— availability of foreign exchange;
— impact of government policies on transborder transactions;
— other governments incentives and disincentives (e.g. taxes and subsidies).

8.3 Why should the North assist in adaptation?

> 'The present world economic and technological systems are neither meeting the basic needs of millions of people nor adequately serving the interests of rich and poor countries'.
>
> Report of the Jamaica Symposium

Assisting the less developed countries to satisfy the basic needs of their populations by efforts to adapt science and technology, and working for the establishment of a just and equitable international order in science and technology, are self-evident tasks given the ideologies of East and West – whether one refers to international solidarity or to Christian or other religious ethics. In addition, there are at least four groups of arguments why all Northern countries should actively promote, support and invest in the adaptation of R & D to the needs of the less developed countries, all of which seem to be tangible in terms of their real interests. Such adaptation, and the results achieved through such R & D, would help to

a) contribute towards world peace and security;
b) serve the economic interest of the North;
c) solve problems with which the North is also directly faced;
d) contribute towards finding solutions to long-term structural problems of the North.

As regards the contribution to world peace and security, the literature on development abounds in statements, which need not be repeated here. Such adaptation, however, could get a major push from disarmament agreements – for which it would be useful since it could help in the conversion of military R & D – the world's largest reservoir of scientific and technological know-how – to socially useful purposes.

The direct economic interest of the North will be served since it can, inter alia, be safely assumed that

– higher productivity and wider distribution of benefits resulting from a major stimulus to appropriate technology will increase purchasing power in the less developed countries – part of which will, no doubt, be used to finance imports and increase employment in Northern countries;

– higher agricultural production resulting from higher investment in agricultural research in less developed countries, for example, would reduce the inflationary impact of rising agricultural production costs in industrialized countries.

Among the problems directly facing the North are the problems of energy and raw material supplies and prices. A better use of local renewable raw materials and energy sources in the wake of important R & D efforts is likely to reduce the pressure on supplies, to increase the probability of continued supply, and to keep prices down in comparison with what would otherwise happen.

A major push to diversify technological development would most likely contribute to bringing about a major change in the orientation of technological development, in societal priorities, in the feasibility of achieving sustainable and environmentally sound long-term development and would most certainly lead to a serious questioning of technologies hitherto considered as 'proven'. Given the loss of the wide societal consensus about the appropriateness of the trend of developments in industrial societies, such a discussion, based on gaining concrete experience, might de-emotionalise current controversies and might in the longer term help to overcome a series of other problems resulting from alienation in the North.

9.4 Research and technological capacities in less developed countries as a precondition of adaptation

A process of adaptation in which both (or all) partners have a say presupposes clarity of objective and the ability to act according to those objectives by both (all) sides involved. Ability to act according to one's objectives in this field depends on the capacity to generate the technologies needed, or – if that capacity is not available – on capacity to monitor and evaluate available technologies, to choose among them, to adapt those which are selected to the socio-cultural environment and to the objectives adopted, to utilise, diffuse and assimilate them effectively, as well as to acquire suitable technologies from the developed countries on equitable terms.

Since most less developed countries have no significant scientific and technological infrastructure of their own (in the Northern sense of those terms) as well as suffering a serious lack of trained and experienced manpower, they have generally been unable to generate the technologies which they need (and which can compete with Northern technologies). For the same reason, they have great difficulties in assessing, selecting, and adapting these technologies in accordance with their objectives. A process of adaptation which will serve the interests of the less developed countries presupposes, therefore, as the first and individually most important measure, the building and/or strengthening of an autonomous capability for problem solving, decision-making and implementation in all matters relating to the application of technological knowledge, experience and skills to productive processes. This capability is the essence of technological self-reliance.

For analytical reaons it may be useful to distinguish between research capacity and technological capacity.

Research capacity, as defined by SAREC (Swedish Agency for Research Cooperation with Developing Countries) involves:

– ability to identify independently, and to define, research tasks and their relation to the development problems and the development work;

- ability to plan and carry out important research; or to commission and direct important research which cannot be successfully tackled with domestic technological, financial and human resources;
- ability to assess, choose and adapt research results for domestic application;
- ability to offer the country's own research workers an environment that is sufficiently stimulating to counteract migration to technologically advanced countries;
- ability to disseminate and apply research results;
- ability (in finance and staff) to utilise the opportunities offered by international research cooperation and to take an active part in such cooperation.

Technological capacity is a much wider concept. It refers to the capability to use technology and to participate in the innovative process. It should not be equated with research capability since technology is not developed only in high level R & D institutions. Technological innovation is a 'bottom-up' as well as a 'top-down' process. Innovation comes from the users of technology as well as from scientists and engineers. Government, local governments, farmer cooperatives, indigenous enterprises and other local non-governmental organisations and individuals are domestic technological innovators.

The technological capacity which needs to be developed should include, inter alia,
- the mastery of the technology to the point of being able to replicate it with minimum external assistance;
- the ability to carry out local adaptations;
- the ability to up-grade traditional technologies;
- the ability to develop new tools and new techniques;
- the ability to assist producers to up-grade their skills.

Institutions with research and technological capacities are needed at several levels in both central locations and in sub-regional centres. Such institutions cover not only specialised research institutes and sophisticated laboratories, staffed with persons of the highest possible professional training, but also consulting and engineering firms, R & D units in enterprises, and field R & D centres for small farmers and small and rural non-farm entrepreneurs.

Building the requisite research and technological capacity is necessarily a complex, time-consuming process that has to take place at all levels of a society and must be supported by basic changes in the educational system. Research and technological capacity building necessitates also giving attention to supportive mechanisms, such as documentation and information, and introducing specific measures to improve availability of information with easy access of potential users at all levels and in all locations. Policies designed to improve technological capabilities must also include specific measures to popularise science and technology, including the training of individuals capable of identifying information needs for interaction with potential users, so that the mass of the population can participate and benefit from their use.

9.5 On the need for selection, adaptation and design of products and processes

(a) Products

The major decisions which have to be taken prior to decisions on adapting R & D in less developed countries concern the choice of products.

Insofar as decisions on the choice of products are taken by governments, they are taken not so much with a view to establishing a coherent national science and technology policy but are – and have to be – based on a wide variety of considerations, including the availability of investment funds, export strategy, industrialisation policy and many other aspects of economic and social policies. In this context, one has to remember that many decisions on products are not in the hands of governments at all.

In considering the appropriateness of products it is useful to conceive of a product as an aggregate of characteristics. The combination of different characteristics in a given product is the result of perceived needs, and effective demand, in the socio-economic situation at the time and place of its origin (or further development) as well as of techniques available then and there. Any of the individual characteristics embodied in a product may or may not serve a particular function related to the needs and priorities of the society where the product is to be used. It is therefore important to disaggregate analytically the different characteristics of products.

In this way it is possible to determine whether all of these characteristics are needed, whether some characteristics needed are missing and whether some of the functions can be fulfilled in a different form. Such analyses may come to the conclusion that the product should be produced as it is, or that it ought to be modified, or that an alternative product would serve better. In taking the decision one should always remember that the choice of characteristics and the resultant products is the crucial point for the realisation of development strategies, since the decision on what kinds of products are to be produced includes the decision about who will be able to use them – or in other words whose needs are being catered for.

(b) Processes

Any change in the characteristics of products may necessitate substantial changes in the production processes. Similarly, most of the technical, and many of the economic and socio-cultural, aspects discussed above in the context of the necessity to adapt will result in changes in the production processes. It is, however, essential to mention also that choices of processes are in most cases made implicitly in decisions on buying equipment. Such decisions are, again, influenced by many considerations which have little to do with general decisions on a national science and technology policy. Needless to say, the choice of processes in the different stages of the production of any product embodies decisions on the number of jobs to be created, on the use of local raw materials or imported intermediate goods; thereby, the choice has a major influence on the distribution of income within the country and vis-à-vis the rest of the world.

9.6 Some considerations on needs and orientation

(a) Central problems of development strategy

There are two central objectives for any world-wide development strategy:

(i) the eradication of poverty and improvement in the quality of life;
(ii) the correction of the major imbalances in wealth, power and technology.

(b) Different groups have different needs

It is important to differentiate between technology required to meet overall production objectives set by the state, and the requirements of large and small private entrepreneurs in different lines of production, the resource-poor farmers, the landless and the urban unemployed. Adequate research policies ought to include discussions on who will benefit from research and whether the results of such research can be easily adopted by any given target group in their actual environment. A policy on adapting R & D should offer alternatives which would allow decision-makers to make their choices.

More specifically the following two questions ought to be discussed, the answers having important implications for R & D policy:

(i) *Are there any purely technical problems?*

Development is about the satisfaction of needs. To that end, both growth and equity are needed. Today there is growing agreement among development experts that most immediate obstacles to development are institutional, social and political.

On this basis, the answer to the question can only be that, in the context of development, no technical problem can remain a purely technical issue since the fact whether, and especially how, a technical problem is solved has many non-technical implications (e.g. present research favours technical solutions that require capital-intensive inputs which have to be imported by Third World countries). In discussing R & D for less developed countries it is, therefore, important to distinguish between purely technical research, i.e. research aiming at finding technical solutions taking only technical dimensions into account, and development-oriented research, which aims at finding solutions which will contribute to overall development.

In the past, support by Northern countries was mostly directed to purely technical research. Such research is certainly needed and will help to solve constraints imposed by the environment, inadequate technology and scarce resources. For such research to contribute to development, the decision-making must take other than merely technical dimensions of the problems into account and must be directed towards overall development objectives.

(ii) *Are research and technology scale-neutral?*

It is often said that most agricultural research, in particular, produces scale-neutral technology, thus being equally relevant to rich farmers and to farmers with no, or limited, access to productive resources.

Whatever the power structures in the society, research and technology are not likely to be scale-neutral in their effect. If it were scale-neutral, why should there be such a lack of technology suitable to the needs of resource-poor farmers?

Among the questions that must, therefore, be asked are the following:

- Whose problem is it that one is trying to solve?
- Will the results of the research be potentially usable by both large and small farmers?
- Whom is it likely to benefit most?

If one looks at the impact of the major technological breakthroughs in new grain seeds and pesticides, it has turned out that they have benefitted first and foremost the already advantaged. Will it be different with the current research on nitrogen-fixing grains and plant photosynthesis, the result of which might be potentially usable by rich and poor alike? Or can research be primarily directed towards the poor majority, as would be the case with research on schistosomiasis, almost entirely a disease of the poor? Most research in recent years has been of the first category. Clearly the need is to give greater priority to the latter two, including social science research on how to extend the benefits of research to the poor.

(c) **Focus on the small and resource-poor**

> 'The developing world is overwhelmingly a world of smallness.'
>
> Report of the Jamaica Symposium

(i) *A world of smallness*

Four-fifths of the farms in less developed countries are five hectares or less in size. Nearly half are just a single hectare. Most business and industrial establishments are equally small family firms or enterprises that employ only a handful of people.

The focus of research ought to be the largest problem. If it is true that most of the population of the less developed countries lives in this world of smallness, it is there that the focus of an R & D policy should lie.

(ii) *Small can be highly efficient*

There exists a strong and widespread bias against smallness. The usual justification, that small sized units and small-scale technology are necessarily inefficient and backward, is supported neither by experience nor by economic analysis.

– Productivity

In countries that have developed high-productivity agriculture on farms that average just a single hectare in size, there are 175 – 225 productively employed farmers per 100 cultivated hectares. Their incomes are rising. We know that output per hectare and per unit of capital are higher on small farms. Hence investing in small farms will maximise output, maximise employment, and minimise the capital cost of agricultural advance. The characteristics of small businesses and industrial enterprises parallel those of small farms in many respects. Here, too, the output per unit of capital is often higher than in many larger, capital-intensive industries.

– Technology

We know from the history of a few countries and from experience with the many community programmes all over the world, that tools and machines can be designed for micro-enterprises that are more productive than traditional technologies, and that are low-cost and job-creating rather than labour-displacing. Such technology is neither second-rate nor second-hand, but the 'latest and best' for its purpose and frequently based on sophisticated scientific research.

– Economic importance

Experience shows that even on the micro-economic level there are not only economies of scale but also economies stemming from a high degree of motivation, of flexibility and of adaptability – characteristics in which small-scale units excel. What is more important is that a small increase in productivity across a large part of the population has a big influence on the macro-economic level. We now know that in labour-abundant economies there is an enormous and mostly untapped potential for increasing production, and for creating jobs in very small-scale enterprises, and that this can be done without compromising efficiency.

(iii) *What needs to be done*

To provide technologies for small producers in order to maximise job creation, capital accumulation, growth and investment, there is need for a systematic effort similar to other major scientific attacks on problems considered extremely important; two approaches ought to be followed in parallel.

– A systematic effort and more resources

Very little of the world's research budget is at present spent on the needs of the poor majority of the world – whether on research useful to small farmers or on health. Yet small farmers, and those who depend on them, make up perhaps one half of humanity. In health, over one hundred times more research funds are devoted to the diseases of the rich, such as cancer and heart ailments, than to schistosomiasis, river blindness, diarrhea and other afflictions that affect literally hundreds of millions of the poor. Progress in assisting the small and resource-poor to meet their needs, by improving technologies and skills, will require greatly increased relevant research in the social and natural sciences and in technological R & D. Only a systematic effort, of a kind similar to other major scientific attacks on world problems, will be able to produce the results needed.

– Scaling down large-scale production processes

Large-scale production processes can be scaled down in many more cases than is normally considered feasible. That this is possible has been satisfactorily demonstrated for several processes, including bricks and cement, paper, textiles, packaging, sugar and a wide variety of agricultural equipment. The approach to be used is the common procedure in management when new processes are to be developed.

– Up-grading existing local technologies and skills

The procedure to be followed would entail systematically surveying needs to establish the characteristics that products should have, followed by systematically surveying the technologies actually used and by the same token the technological skills available, locating the knowledge needed to up-grade the technologies used and the available skills, getting the necessary adaptation and/or design work carried out, assisting in getting the field-testing done. From here on the process is different since it also needs the designing and institutionalising of dissemination mechanisms, which have to reach an enormous number of villages. This procedure is only an adapted version of that widely used for large-scale investments. It needs to be used for small activities as well.

(d) A more appropriate mix of technologies

The proposed focus on the small and resource-poor is not a suggestion to do away with large-scale, capital-intensive technologies for which small-scale technologies cannot be a replacement. Clearly, the two technologies are complementary.

By combining support of vast numbers of small-scale units, whether micro-enterprises or farms, with investment in large-scale industry, it might be possible to achieve rapid growth and come closer to creating the employment needed. The proposed focus seems necessary, however, to counterbalance the trend towards putting all resources into large-scale centralised technology, a trend which has dominated in past years and still continues, and which is not likely to solve the problems of any but a small minority of the world's inhabitants whether in the rich or in the poor countries.

9.7 Towards balanced and mutually beneficial cooperation in R & D

> 'Any collaboration between unequal partners inevitably leads to domination by the better equipped, better financed and better trained partners, These difficulties are, however, not insuperable provided priority is given to their systematic correction with the clear objective of establishing genuine partnership'.
>
> New forms of collaboration in developing research and training

(a) Correcting present imbalances

The present position is one of extreme imbalance between North and South. This leads to the necessity of:

– ensuring that the balance of advantage from collaboration in R & D, between industrialised-country institutions and Third World countries, accrues to the less developed countries;

– strengthening those forms of collaboration which are mutually beneficial and of abandoning those in which the current relationships are extremely unequal;

– overcoming the existing ingrained behaviour patterns which arose from many years of enormously imbalanced relationships and of bringing about a new 'culture' of cooperation.

– recognizing the changing role of scientists and engineers in developed countries in development policy of less developed countries; and

– taking the fundamental interests of the 'weaker' partners into consideration, since effective collaboration on equal terms will never be possible without substantial strengthening of the weaker partner in such cooperation.

Making full use of the comparative advantages of institutions in the developed and less developed countries – the greater financial and technical resources and access to scientific and technological information in the developed countries and the more immediate grasp of the problems of development and the greater access to local policymakers in the Third World countries – will add to the mutual benefits flowing from cooperation.

Another major imbalance lies in the fact that most cooperative links exist between Northern and Southern institutions while there are very few cooperative links between less developed countries. To include measures which would help building links across the South would be both necessary and useful in any cooperative venture.

(b) **Joint decision-making and control**

> 'Good intentions are not sufficient — meticulous attention to a whole range of details is needed for success'.
>
> New forms of collaboration in development research and training

Joint decisions will have to be taken in advance on who sets the priorities, designs the project, allocates the finances and manages the project. Agreement on definition of priorities is a precondition for effective collaboration. Yet past experience shows that only in a minority of cases have research priorities been discussed and defined in advance with all partners. Often financial agencies have taken the lead in defining priorities with the research institution of the rich country, followed with little significant participation by the Third World research institutions. Unless this ordering is reversed, collaborative development research will only rarely match the interests and perspectives of the Third World.

The national development priorities in the given problem area must, then, be the starting-point in setting the research orientation and research priorities. Care must be taken to specify their relation to existing international research priorities; more specifically, the differences (in objectives, etc.) from these international research priorities have to be worked out meticulously so that hypotheses and methodologies will be chosen to fit the circumstances and not necessarily the international research fashions.

A number of classical problems will also have to be dealt with jointly which may include, inter alia,

- low degree of specificity of the overall national research policy
- lack of research coordination
- gaps in research management
- lack of adequate resources for research
- facilities for research training to increase the number of research workers in general and the availability of specific expertise in particular; and last but not least
- gaps between research and production units.

There must also be agreement in advance on how the results of the project will be shared, who will have the right to patent the resulting technology, if any, where data from research will be stored and how access to them will be organised and under what conditions.

In larger projects the fact that scarce financial and human resources of the poor country will be involved in the envisaged research cooperation often implies that a de-facto reorientation of research priorities within the overall national research policy is likely to take place — a reorientation which might become even more marked due to the continuing financial commitments needed on the national level to make full use of project results and to provide support on a regular basis for the capacities established. Longer term commitments, including core and general financial support, ought to be the consequence.

(c) Division of labour in R & D

Since it is one of the most important objectives of such cooperation to contribute towards the building of R & D capacity in the less developed countries, most of the research should be carried out in their own institutions.

There are however certain research problems that can be tackled only at an international level or in industrial country institutions. By and large, these problems will involve sophisticated analysis and equipment which may not be available in the less developed countries' institutions. It is, however, important to keep in mind that the utilisation of results will still require a viable national research system.

References

I am greatly indebted to the authors of the following publications on which I have freely drawn in writing the foregoing article. The respsonsibility is, of course, my own.

United Nations Conference on Science and Technology for Development, *The Vienna Plan of Action on Science and Technology for Development,* United Nations, New York 1979.

Independent Commission on International Development Issues (Brandt Report). *North-South: A Programme for Survival,* Pan Books, London 1980.

Frances Stewart, *Technology and Underdevelopment,* Macmillan, London 1977.

Francisco Sagasti and Alberto Araoz, *Science and Technology Policy Implementation in Less-Developed Countries: Methodological Guidelines for the STPI Project,* International Development Research Centre, Ottawa 1976.

UNIDO, *Conceptual and Policy Framework for Appropriate Industrial Technology,* Monographs on Appropriate Industrial Technology, No. 1, United Nations, New York 1979.

"Mobilizing Technology for World Development — Report of the Jamaica Symposium", in: Jairam Ramesh and Charles Weiss, Jr. (Editors) *Mobilizing Technology for World Development,* Praeger Publishers, New York 1979.

Yelavarti Nayudamma, *Endogenous Development: Science and Technology,* Occasional Paper 78/3, Vienna Institute for Development, Vienna 1978.

Tanzania National Scientific Research Council, *Science and Technology for Development: African Goals and Aspirations in the United Nations Conference,* Report of a Symposium held in Arusha, Dar es Salaam 1978.

Hans A. Havemann and Hussein M. Rady, "Technologiehilfe für die Dritte Welt: Die Evolution der Entwicklungstechnik", *Aachener Studien zur internationalen technisch-wirtschaftlichen Zusammenarbeit,* No. 20, Nomos Verlagsgesellschaft, Baden-Baden 1979.

Gordon C. Winston, "The Appeal of Inappropriate Technologies: Self-Inflicted Wages, Ethnic Pride and Corruption", in *World Development,* Vol. 7, pp. 835-845., Pergamon Press Ltd. 1979.

Bo Bengtsson, "Strengthening National Agricultural Research", Part II: Summary and Conclusions, Report from a SAREC Workshop, *SAREC Report* R 2 : 1980, Swedish Agency for Research Cooperation with Developing Countries, Stockholm 1980.

James P. Grant, "An International Challenge: Science and Technology for Managing the World Food Problem" in: Jairam Ramesh and Charles Weiss, Jr. (Editors) *Mobilizing Technology for World Development,* Praeger Publishers, New York 1979.

G. Ranis, "Appropriate Technology in the Context of Redirecting Industrial Development Strategy: Concepts and Policies" in: UNIDO, "Conceptual and Policy Framework for Appropriate Industrial Technology", *Monographs on Appropriate Industrial Technology, No. 1,* United Nations, New York 1979.

Ibrahim H. Abdel-Rahman, "Operational and Policy Choices for Technology and Industrialization in Developing Countries" in: UNIDO, *Conceptual and Policy Framework for Appropriate Industrial Technology,* Monographs on Appropriate Industrial Technology, No. 1, United Nations, New York 1979.

James Pickett, "The Role of Science and Technology in Development" in: Jacques De Bandt, Péter Mándi and Dudley Seers (Editors) *European Studies in Development,* Macmillan (in association with the European Association of Development Research and Training Institutes), London 1980.

"Pugwash Guidelines for International Scientific Cooperation for Development" *Pugwash Conferences on Science and World Affairs,* Geneva 1979.

"New Forms of Collaboration in Development Research and Training" in: *International Social Science Journal,* Vol. XXVII, No. 4, 1975, UNESCO, Paris 1975.

Arne Haselbach, *Die Konsequenzen der Konferenz der Vereinten Nationen über Wissenschaft und Technik im Dienste der Entwicklung für Österreich,* Vienna Institute for Development, Vienna 1980.

COMMENTS ON PART III – THE TRANSFER OF TECHNOLOGY

Aleksander Lukaszewicz*

Haustein and *Maier* (Chapter 8) and *Haselbach* (Chapter 9) both dwell upon essential links in contemporary thinking on development promotion. It is a commonplace that without technological advancement, the LDCs will not be able to overcome backwardness and the resulting social calamities. The ways and means of securing this advancement, and their application at the right time in the right place, are much less recognised. I regard both chapters as very competent contributions precisely to these last questions. This is not because the authors were the first to shed light on the problems, nor the first to recognise and cope with them. Their main merit is (i) their very clear codification of existing knowledge; (ii) their complementary approach in proposals for solving them (going, rightly, well beyond purely economic considerations); and (iii) their grasp of the issues in a historical perspective. These three areas, however, provoke me to expand the arguments since there remain gaps in the reasoning that it is worth trying to close.

When referring to gaps in reasoning, I do not intend to take issue with the logic only but with the logic of activities which seem to be highly recommendable. The literature of the subject abounds with recommendations, usually emphasising priorities. In the chapters under discussion the emphasis is rather on complementarity of actions, and their time sequence. While fully approving this approach, I cannot but notice some gaps therein, from which my comments stem.

Several authors in this book have devoted much effort and argument to the adaptation of modern technologies to conditions in the LDCs and to the modernisation of the technologies already there. I would like to put this problem in a somewhat different perspective.

(a) The adaptation issue cannot be properly treated as a basis for action, if it is not linked with the absorption issue. The two are neither identical nor substitutes. Adaptation of a given unit to new conditions always brings about absorption of certain patterns – in technology, in organisation, in the institutional set-ups, in consumption, in behaviour or – more generally speaking – in the 'ethos'.

The adaptive processes signify, above all, a mutual structural adaptation of interacting units; while absorptive processes signify the transmission of characteristics and properties of socio-economic processes from the units or organisms which had attained

* Department of Economics, University of Warsaw

them earlier to those which have matured later. This also applies to institutions that specialise in creating, introducing and disseminating innovations.

The difference should also be noted between active and passive adaptation and absorption, since the difference affects the time in which the desired changes can materialise. If we take, for example, two systems, one mature and active, the other immature and passive, the latter's absorptive capacities are limited, which means that its contacts with the active system are also limited in scope and in time. The creative impulses from the active system meet the absorptive barrier in the passive system, leading to the disappearance of positive feedbacks. By contrast, if the initially passive system has the will to embark on ventures in adaptation, the positive feed-back, and the absorptive capacities, will grow, until an active absorptive capability is achieved. No one imaginable socio-economic system (including a national economy) is able to survive and develop without a certain absorptive capacity, since it exists as part and parcel of the social and international division of labour. The place of a system within a given environment is largely determined by the prevalence of active or passive absorptive capacities.

(b) Adaptive and absorptive capacities remain dependent on natural conditions, natural endowment, population size and density, particularly in relation to the economic structure determined by these conditions. In this respect, different sectors generally display differences in adaptive and absorptive flexibility and in the speed at which the new patterns (technological, organisational, etc.) are transmitted from outside. These differences cannot be escaped when the priorities of a development strategy are being set; they help in identifying soft spots and bottlenecks. Thus both existing and projected structures should be studied from the point of view of adaptive and absorptive capacities.

The structural approach must also be studied from another angle. While adaptive processes belong mainly to the 'real' sphere (round-about ways of production and distribution), the absorptive processes concern rather the 'information' sphere, broadly understood (from information flows within elementary socio-economic units, through educational and scientific establishments, up to the mass media).

The informational sphere thus comprises both elements which are taken as social values *per se* (education, science, culture) and also elements which have strong developmental value. In the decision-making process and resulting allocation of resources, neither should be omitted or neglected. For the developing economy, the strengthening of absorptive capacities is among the top priorities.

(c) The *spatial* approach to the development process must also be considered. Much to the detriment of understanding, and even more to the detriment of practical development strategy (natural environment protection in particular), the spatial dimensions of socio-economic phenomena have too often been stubbornly and conspicuously neglected by economists. This is unfortunately the case in the chapters under discussion.

The emphasis on adaptation in the initial development stages (e.g. initial industrialisation) may be to a certain extent justified by acute scarcity of resources and by consequent vigorous attempts to make maximum use of economies of scale and external economies.

The often polarised spatial structures of the developing economies, and inadequate understanding of the role that 'development poles' play in socio-economic advancement, may seriously hamper the adaptational process and the broadening and strengthening of the absorptive capacities of the economy as a whole and of its regions. Local bottlenecks in the economic and social infrastructure may paralyse even existing absorptive capacities; so may erroneous planning of human settlements and local gaps in the informational structure. Such weaknesses lead to degenerated types of development (enclaves, monocultures etc.).

(d) There are some specific features of adaptation and absorption phenomena in the developing economies. These economies, seeking more advantageous places in the system of the international division of labour, face the extremely difficult and uphill process of adaptation to the world economy. This is also a precondition for their economic and political independence.

Wherever in the world economy the adaptation processes occur, transfers of technology and of organisational, consumption and behavioural patterns changes go together. These transfers, being more often than not imposed from outside, may not be fully absorbed and may induce delayed reactions. Even if the transfers are controlled by the developing country they may not be rational from a long-run point of view.

During the very long and not very rapid development of the present developed countries, efficient and ramified absorptive mechanisms were established. Their informational structures are well adjusted to allow these countries to pursue passive and active absorption.

This is not the case for the developing economies of today, which will long remain in a position of passive absorption. I share the authors' views about possible remedies but would like to pose somewhat differently the desirable paths for development strategies:

— broaden the entry channels into the economies concerned, while strengthening their powers for selecting among options;
— increase absorptive capacity through gradual extension and perfection of the informational structure;

— embark on vigorous research aiming at a strategic vision of the transition to the stage of active absorption, wherever feasible;
— assume a rather long period of passive absorption, taking special care of agriculture where a particularly careful selection of inward transfers is highly desirable;
— monitor the structural aspects of socio-economic policies, since selective regulation of structural changes exerts an important impact on the absorptive process; while the regulation of absorptive processes gives a strong impetus to structural changes: this demonstrates the compatibility in development of the real and informational spheres.

In this framework, the undisputable priority belongs nowadays to the proper organisation for passive absorption. Otherwise, the stage of active absorption — still remote — cannot ever be reached.

(e) The very obvious question arises of how to fit this reasoning to the triangle-type interactions (East-West-South) which are the main topic of this book. I can touch only some of the problems.

(i) *Paszyński* (in Chapter 2), following Michał Kalecki's argument, rightly stated that socialist economies and developing economies are supply-led economies. No less important is the fact that socialist economies have successfully overcome economic and social backwardeness, thus being the pathbrakers in the specific historical conditions of the 20th century. It should be added, moreover, that the overcoming of backwardness has been possible not only because of the strong will for development in these societies and their enormous mobilisation of economic, social and political potential but also because the development effort has been centrally organised effort in a planned way. These factors together contributed substantially to a relatively quick transition to the stage of active absorption. Needless to say, not all these economies are equally advanced in this respect, and much must still be done to remove or weaken the barriers to adaptation and absorption. The conclusion is rather obvious: a pattern is available for the developing economies, although — as historical experience has always, and often painfully, taught us — mere emulation does not guarantee success. Besides there is not one pattern but rather a whole gamut of patterns.

(ii) At several points in this book, East-West cooperation in technology transfer to the developing economies has been discussed. I will not elaborate on this point, simply agreeing with the view that opportunities in this field are far from exhausted and are continuously increasing.

In the combined efforts supported by the whole UN system, more emphasis should be put on increasing absorptive capacities and to improving the compatibility between productive and absorptive capacities. This requires, however, more harmonious overall development which may get a substantial impetus from socio-economic planning, as comprehensive as possible (of course, avoiding mechanical emulation of any particular pattern). In stressing the role of development planning, one must clearly stress the role of the public sector as a leading force, let alone as the dominant instrument for creating and strenghtening absorptive capacities. There is no substitute for this in the developing economies. The filtering and selection of available patterns, the impact on investment projects and on the techniques of production, the impact on motivational factors, the defence and promotion of national cultural identity — all these are duties and obligations of the State. Unfortunately, the State is often 'soft' (in Gunnar Myrdal's sense): this 'softness' tends to preserve the vicious circle of poverty and backwardness.

(iii) The content of the absorption process is rich and ramified. But recognition of it seems still rather limited and its existence often neglected. This negligence and ignorance go hand in hand with high and hard barriers to absorption and adaptation. It seems hardly possible to expect that persuasion will work wonders, unless supported by in-depth research on the main factors and forces behind the absorption and adaptation processes. Again, the research assistance provided by the developed countries, coming from various schools of thought or from unbiased teams, (necessarily interdisciplinary) may substantially contribute to the diagnosis. And the lack of diagnosis has broken the neck of too many ambitious and radical development programmes.

Tamás Szentes*

In the international literature of development economics there has been much discussion of technology transfers and the choice of 'appropriate technologies'. Unfortunately, there are often many ambiguities in both the arguments and the terminology. Many scholars argue for the application of 'labour-intensive technology' in the developing countries because of the abundance of unskilled labour, and criticise the transfer of modern technologies, or even industrialisation as such, because they have failed to reduce unemployment. Others refer to the need for developing countries to 'catch up' the advanced countries technologically, to increase productivity and export competitiveness; these scholars therefore recommend 'capital-intensive' technologies.

Labour intensity, however, does not exclude the application of modern technology or of highly sophisticated capital equipment within a given factory, industrial workshop or production process. The labour-intensive character of a certain project, from the point of view of the given national economy as a whole (i.e. its intensive overall employment effect), is even less synonymous with the application of poor, low-level technology.

While labour intensity is often valued at the enterprise (i.e. micro-) level, unemployment is a social (i.e. macro-) problem which requires the employment effect to be assessed

* Karl Marx University of Economic Sciences, Budapest

accordingly. The total number (and quality) of jobs created by a new project, however, does not depend only or primarily on the type of technology applied in it. What is decisive from a macro point of view is the linkages (through both input and output) with other projects and branches of the economy. It is perfectly possible that an industrial project employing many workers (and therefore considered to be 'labour-intensive') will create fewer jobs in the national economy as a whole than another project using highly mechanised, even automatised, technology and requiring only a few workers, but creating employment in other sectors supplying its inputs or using its output.

The debate on the choice of technology is meaningless if the problem of appropriate technology is isolated from the *choice of industries, of products and of consumers;* if the effects of the internal pattern of linkages – the potential for upward and downward linkages – are left out of consideration; and if the basic question: *'what product for whom?'* is not answered.

In fact the reason for the failure of a certain type of 'industrialisation' cannot simply be attributed to its 'labour-saving' or 'capital-intensive' technolgy. The reason, rather, is the 'enclave' character of the industries, their isolation from the rest of the economy, especially from agriculture, and the type of products (and consumers) chosen (e.g. import-substituting industries producing luxury items for a narrow local élite).

It follows that the choice of technology, from the point of view of the national economy as a whole, is not a choice between 'capital-intensive' and 'labour-intensive' technologies (or something in-between). The real issue is *where* (and when), and for *whose interests* (to produce what for whom), to apply one or another type of technology.

Christopher Saunders

I would support the need for a clearer link between the principles proposed by the contributors and their application in practice to economic structures and development strategies. One advantage of both chapters is that they concentrate upon processes rather than upon products. The distinction is important, because categories or hierarchies of technical processes, from the simple to the sophisticated, are applicable to most products. This implies that specialisation between economies should be in terms of types of process, rather than in terms of our favourite categories of labour-intensive and capital-intensive products or industries. Thus structural change can consist not just in 'switching resources' between one industry and another, but rather of 'up-grading' a wide range of industries; and this can apply to both developed and developing economies.

Friedrich Levcik*

There is general agreement that the scientific and technological potential of the industrialised countries, whether market or socialist economies, should be put at the disposal of the LDCs to overcome their technological and economic backwardness. However there are limits and constraints, on both sides, to transferring technologies in ways which would benefit the LDCs. First comes the question of the 'appropriateness' of the technologies to be introduced into the LDCs. The prevailing opinion seems to be that a policy of 'walking on two legs' should be pursued; this implies that labour-intensive, capital-intensive, small-scale, large-scale, low-cost traditional and sophisticated types and levels of technology should be introduced in accordance with the concrete conditions in each case.

Some consider as essential a development model starting with the construction of large-scale basic industries. In this connection, some take the view that the LDCs can select from ready-made patterns of technology, the public sector playing a leading role. But this concept is by no means generally accepted. It is pointed out that while national programmes and plans for technological development of the kind applied by the CMEA countries may have the merit of giving a general orientation to technological development, yet at the same time the proper incentives to absorb new technologies at the enterprise level are often missing. The adaptation of technology to the requirements of LDCs is also stressed. It is pointed out, however, that transfer of technology cannot be a substitute for necessary institutional reforms, as the recent experience of some CMEA countries has shown. There seems, rather, to be a complementarity between transfer of technology and changes in economic institutions, each reinforcing the impact of the other on efficiency and productivity.

The view is held by some contributors that a change in the distribution of the gains from transferred technologies is crucial for fruitful cooperation between LDCs and industrialised countries. This raises the question of the role of the transnationals. It seems to be generally agreed that the power of the transnationals to manipulate the distribution of gains in their own favour is a permanent danger, not only to LDCs but to the industrial nations as well. From this stem the current efforts by international organisations to find ways of taming the power of the transnationals by appropriate codes of conduct applicable not only to technology transfers but also to other activities.

The CMEA countries have developed instruments which effectively hold at bay the adverse impacts of the transnationals, with which CMEA countries frequently deal. It is debatable whether these experiences can be put to use by the LDCs; they may lack the institutional conditions and instruments needed to get the benefits of doing business with the transnationals while at the same time minimising the adverse effects.

* Director, Vienna Institute for Comparative Economic Studies

PART IV – IMPROVING THE INTERNATIONAL DIVISION OF LABOUR

Chapter 10

THE NEW INTERNATIONAL ECONOMIC ORDER: DEVELOPMENT STRATEGY OPTIONS

Paul P. Streeten*

10.1 The lag of institutions behind technology

The international dissemination of cultural influences has enormously increased. Its ultimate cause is the advance of technologies in transport and electronic communications and growing urbanisation. Popular songs, styles in dress and hair styles, attitudes to divorce, abortion, homosexuality, drugs, even crimes, are spreading rapidly across the globe. While in previous ages the common culture was confined to a thin layer of the upper class, today it has reached the mass culture in many countries. In the huge underdeveloped regions of the South, however, the masses of people live in extreme poverty and cultural isolation, though a small upper class has become part of the international culture. Even among the élite, there are now moves to assert indigenous cultural values and to establish national and ethnic identities. It is partly a reaction against the rapid spread of the mass culture of the West.

International relations have grown not only in the cultural but also in the economic sphere. This growth is usually measured by the rapid growth of world trade in the last two or three decades, a growth that was substantially faster than the growth of GNP, so that the ratio of exports to GNP has also grown. World trade has increased from over $ 100 billion in 1960 to over $ 1 trillion in 1977, and the ratio of exports to GNP has risen from 13.7 per cent in 1960 to 21.8 per cent in 1976.

* Director, Center for Asian Development Studies, Boston University.

Taking a longer historical perspective, the ratio of trade to GNP for the main industrial countries is not much higher now than it was in 1913 (1). But there has been a large increase in the trade share of the private sector. The aggregate ratio conceals this because of the large increase in the public sector and the relative rise in prices of those services that are not internationally traded.

It is useful to draw a distinction between integration and interdependence (2). International integration was probably greater in the nineteenth century, when national governments adhered to the gold standard, fixed exchange rates, and balanced budgets, than today, when domestic policy has set up targets for employment, growth, price stability, income distribution, and regional policy, among other objectives, while at the same time rejecting the constraints which integrated the world internationally (3). Greater economic interdependence consists in greater international mobility and substitutability of goods, services, and capital, and greater mobility across frontiers of management and technology.

But in trade, as in culture, the poorest countries did not share in this expansion. The share of the low-income countries, excluding the petroleum-exporting countries, fell from 3.6 percent in 1960 to 2.2 percent in 1970, and to 1.5 percent in 1977. Of the total exports of the industrial countries 17.3 percent went to the non-oil-exporting developing countries in 1970, but only 15.8 percent in 1977 (4). The notion that we have become one interdependent world has, therefore, to be qualified.

While cultural dissemination and economic interdependence between countries have grown, international cooperation between governments has lagged and in some cases grossly failed. The gap of our times is not so much, as is often said, that between science and morality, as that between our soaring technological imagination and our inert institutional imagination. While our scientific and technological imagination has leaped ahead, putting man on the moon, deciphering the genetic code, discovering new subatomic worlds, and probing the recesses of inner space and the farthest reaches of outer space, our institutional and social imagination has lagged inertly behind. The most flagrant failure of international cooperation is the arms race and the $ 450 billion annually devoted to military expenditure, which has increased violence in the world.

International cooperation for meeting the impending energy crisis has also failed. There is need for a global energy programme for conservation and exploration of alternative sources of energy.

National policies to fight the evils of pollution have been successfully designed, but the solution of problems of gobal pollution (like that of the oceans or air across national boundaries) have been much less effective. The same is true of policies to prevent excessive depletion of non-renewable resources.

There has been almost no international cooperation in fighting the world-wide crisis of unemployment, accompanied by inflation and sagging growth. National policies are being pursued in isolation, the balance of payments surpluses of a few countries are kicked around from country to country, Japan and West Germany are exporting their unemployment, and what each country does often increases the difficulties of others. There is no exchange of information on investment plans, hence we lurch from excess capacity to shortages in steel, fertilisers and shipbuilding.

International cooperation for development — our main concern here — has also lagged behind the challenge to eradicate world poverty. Insufficient attention has been paid by analysts to this discordance between the (partial) success of interdependence and our failure to cooperate and use it for our joint benefits.

The failure in cooperation has been accompanied by a growth of intergovernmental organisations, fora and conferences charged with tackling these issues. The call for the exercise of our institutional imagination must not be confused with its opposite: the growth of a bureaucracy that opposes new ideas and spawns additional obstructionist bureaucrats. Even though practical solutions are proposed, the resistance, often on some minor point, by one or two governments, prevents joint action. This resistance to global action on the part of governments is in stark contrast to the successful coordination of international action by big business — by the transnational corporations and by the banks in the Eurocurrency market. We have the framework for inter-governmental action, but it is largely unused.

There are two opposite forces at work. National integration has contributed to international disintegration. The rejection of the gold standard, of fixed exchange rates and of balanced budgets has liberated national policy to pursue a growing range of national objectives, but has contributed to international disintegration. The rejection of irrational constraints by each state has produced world-wide irrationality. At the same time, the integration of the upper classes of developing countries into the international system has contributed to national dualism, national division and national disintegration in some developing countries. Hence the call for 'delinking' and the assertion of a national identity, based on indigenous values.

There are, however, some instances of successful inter-governmental cooperation, usually in specialised, technical fields: The Universal Postal Union (more than one hundred years old), the International Telecommunications Union, the International Civil Aviation Organisation and the World Meteorological Organisation are examples of outstanding successes in international cooperation. The World Health Organisation and UNICEF have also been successful. Stressing the technical, non-political aspects of co-operation helps to remove issues from becoming politicised. Functional solutions at the global level work. I shall return to this theme and the lessons to be learned at the end of the paper.

10.2 Origins of the call for a NIEO

The developing countries' call for a New International Economic Order has many diverse sources, some going far back in history. At the root of this call lies the dissatisfaction with the old order which, it is felt, contains systematic biases perpetuating inequalities in power, wealth and incomes and impeding the development efforts of the developing countries. Three phenomena can be singled out that gave the demand for a New International Economic Order special impetus: the disappointment with aid, the disappointment with political independence, and the success of OPEC.

Development aid, on which so many hopes had been pinned in the 1950s and early 1960s, after a vigorous beginning, partly inspired by the Cold War, was regarded as inadequate in amount and poor in quality. A target for official development assistance to the developing countries of 0.7 percent of the gross national product of the developed countries had been set up. But the net official development assistance given by the DAC members fell from 0.42 in 1964 – 66 to 0.30 in 1976. Intergovernmental aid negotiations led to pressures, frictions, and acrimony. Although it was correctly seen that for aid contributions to be effective a country's whole development programme had to be scrutinised, developing countries found it intolerable that donors who contributed only one to two percent of the national income of the recipients should meddle in their economic and political affairs. Performance criteria and political, as well as economic, strings produced tensions and recriminations, which led to a plea for a 'quiet style in aid'. By this was meant a transfer of resources that would be automatic or semi-automatic, hidden, or at least unconditional. The inefficiencies and inequities (as a result of the capricious impact) of commodity agreements, trade preferences, debt relief, SDR links, etc., were regarded as a price worth paying for a hoped-for larger volume of transfers and a defusing of diplomatic tensions.

The second source of the call for the automatic, concealed, unconditional transfers of the NIEO is the disappointment with political independence that has not produced the hoped-for economic independence. True, most Latin American countries have been independent for a long time, but it is precisely from there that the doctrine of *dependencia* has emerged. It explains the demand for 'sovereignty over resources' and the hostility to some features of the transnational corporations and, more generally, to the international rules of the game as they had evolved after the war.

The third cause is the success of OPEC (and a few other mineral exporters), which appeared to offer an alternative to the appeal to the conscience of the rich. This success was accompanied by a change to a sellers' market and to world shortages of food and raw materials. These events encouraged developing countries to explore the scope for similar actions on other fronts, to emphasise joint bargaining, the use of 'commodity power', and the exercise of power in other areas, such as the treatment of transnationals.

Interpretations of the NIEO

The NIEO means different things to different people. Under its banner, a great variety of interpretations have been gathered. Three distinctions are useful in clarifying some of the ambiguities.

Some have interpreted the NIEO as a demand for exemptions from established rules. Non-reciprocal preferences for manufactured exports, debt relief, more concessionary aid fall under this heading. Others have interpreted the NIEO as a radical change in the rules.

A second distinction is between those who seek a few more concessions from the developed countries, more aid, more trade preferences, contributions to commodity agreements, better access to capital markets, cheaper technology transfer, debt relief, etc., and those who want fundamental structural change, in the form of new institutions and a shift in power relations.

A third distinction is that between those who interpret the NIEO as being essentially about rules and restraints, like those laid down at Bretton Woods and the GATT, whether the demand is for exemptions from old rules or for new rules, and those who interpret the restructuring to refer to the totality of economic, political and even cultural relations. This second interpretation sees in the post-colonial power structure the continuation of domination and dependence, caused not only by rules, procedures and institutions designed by the powerful, rich countries, but also by numerous other factors, such as the thrust of science and technology, the priorities in Research and Development, the cumulative nature of gains, the structure of markets, the influence emanating from the mass media, the educational systems and the values they impart, etc.

The discussion about appropriate rules for international economic relations has suffered from a long-standing confusion. It is the confusion between *uniform* (sometimes also called *general*) principles or rules (the opposite of specific ones, and therefore necessarily simple) and *universal* principles or rules (which may be highly specific and complicated, provided that they contain no uneliminable reference to individual cases). Further confusion is caused if a third characteristic of rules is added: *inflexibility* over time, and confused with either uniformity or universality. A rule is capable of being *altered,* though it remains either uniform, i.e. simple, or universal, i.e. may have a lot of 'exceptions' written into it. The 'equal' treatment of unequals is not a principle of justice, and a general rule commanding it is an unjust rule. In order to prevent partiality and partisanship, rules have to be universal, i.e. not contain references to individual cases. They may not, indeed should not, be uniform. They should pay attention to the varying characteristics and circumstances of different countries.

Those who charge the developing countries with asking for exemptions from rules are guilty of this confusion between *uniform* and *universal* rules. Thus a differentiated system of multi-tier preferences, according to the level of development of the exporting countries, may be best and most just for a group of trading countries at different stages of development. A fair system of rules also points to the differentiation in responsibilities and rights according to circumstances. Middle income countries would not have the responsibility to give aid, but neither would they receive it. They would not have to give trade preferences, but neither would they receive them. Even finer differentiation would be possible. A country like Saudi Arabia might be asked to contribute to loans because of its foreign exchange earnings, and to aid because of its income per head, but might receive trade preferences because of its low level of industrialisation. The 0.7 % aid target would be replaced by a system in which those below a certain income per head are exempted, and the percentage target rises with income per head.

There is, of course, a practical and tactical case for *simple* rules, which might overrule the case in fairness for universal (though complex) rules: they are less open to abuse and easier to police. And there may be a tactical case for uniform rules; they may be easier to negotiate. It is for such pragmatic reasons rather than on theoretical grounds that one may advocate that rules should not be too complex, and should not be changed too often. (5)

Any specific proposals, like non-reciprocity in trade concessions, or trade preferences, would, of course, have to be examined on their merits. But the distinction between 'exemption from rules' and 'drawing up new rules' is logically untenable, to the extent to which the call for exemption is really a call for a set of *universal* rules that pays attention to the different characteristics and circumstances of different countries, just as income tax allowances for dependants or lower rates on earned than on unearned income, are not 'exceptions' but reflect our notions of fairness.

Those who are concerned with changing the rules of international relations are aiming partly at removing biases in the present rules, partly at the exercise of countervailing power where at present the distribution of power is felt to be unequal, and partly at counteracting biases that arise not from rules but from the nature of economic processes, such as the cumulative nature of gains accruing to those who already have more resources, and the cumulative damage inflicted on those who have initially relatively little (polarisation or backwash effects).

Insofar as the NIEO is about strictly economic relations, there is scope for positive sum games. But insofar as it is about national power relations between sovereign states with different aims, power is by its very nature a *relative* concept, and what is at stake are zero sum games. The demand for greater participation in the councils of the world and for corrections in the biases of the international power distribution are bound to diminish the power of the industrialised countries.

It is part of the weakness of the poor countries and of the syndrome of underdevelopment that they have not succeeded in articulating these pleas altogether convincingly. An unsympathetic approach can always find faults and criticise specific proposals and the manner in which they are presented. A more imaginative approach would attempt to understand the underlying grievances, even though often badly expressed and poorly translated into concrete proposals. An entirely adequate approach would require a well staffed, highly qualified secretariat of the Third World, which would muster the evidence, prepare the case for international negotiations, and propose feasible reforms, worked out in detail.

10.3 Heterogeneity or homogeneity of the Third World?

The NIEO has been acclaimed by *all* developing countries, but the diversity of their interests is reflected in the long list of the UNCTAD Agenda, by the strains caused by specific proposals, such as debt relief, by the inconsistency of some of the targets, and by the OPEC oil price rise. Concern with reforming the international system has, at least in the rhetoric, been closely linked with concern for the world's poor. But the poor are largely in what is sometimes called the Fourth World: South India, sub-Saharan Africa and a few islands. Their need is mainly for additional financial and technical assistance. The more advanced countries of the Third World need better access to capital markets, to markets for their manufactured exports and to modern technology.

The cohesion between these two groups of countries has been maintained largely because OPEC has used its petropower to press for other reforms on the agenda, such as the inclusion of non-energy issues in the Paris Conference on International Economic Cooperation (CIEC) discussions, initially intended to be devoted solely to energy. It has succeeded in the liberalisation of IMF credits, and the liberalisation of the compensatory finance facility. OPEC has also given substantial aid.

The cohesion of the Third World may also be threatened by the formation of North-South blocs, Europe forging special ties with Africa through Lomé, Japan (and Australia and New Zealand) with East Asia through ASEAN, and some non-oil Arab countries with the Arab members of OPEC. It would not be surprising if, in default of global progress, developing countries were to attempt to strike bargains with specific developed countries, or groups of them. Some of the weaker and poorer countries are bound to suffer, inequalities to be increased, and the cry of neocolonialism to be raised again. Such fragmentation of the world into regional blocs is not in the interest of development or of the developed countries.

In spite of heterogeneity and diversity of interests, there are strong common interests in the Third World, which can provide a basis for collective action. These countries are, by and large, poorer than the developed countries (the existence of borderline cases with small populations does not destroy the distinction), many have been colonies and they benefit and suffer from the impulses propagated by the advanced, industrial countries in similar ways. (6)

In answering the question whether homogeneity or heterogeneity is stronger among the countries of the so-called Third World, we would have to begin by listing criteria for a typology of countries, relevant to the dimensions of what might constitute the 'Third World'. These might include income per head, growth rates, inflation rates, indicators of economic structure (such as proportion of the labour force in agriculture, trade ratios), human and social indicators (life expectancy, infant mortality, literacy), water supply, indicators of inequality, population growth, indicators of dependence such as concentration of exports by commodities and by destination, statistics of brain drain, political indicators, etc. If we find that on the whole the same countries cluster round each end of these scales, the division will be found to make sense. If, on the other hand, groupings cut across the conventional North-South division, we may have to revise our typology and the notion of a homogeneous 'Third World'.

But it may be both tactically wiser and in the service of truth to acknowledge that many problems of the developing countries are not just the problems of a block, but are common to us all: there are rich and poor among the OECD countries, there are relations of dominance and dependence between developed countries, and even between regions within one country, there are biases and imperfections in the system of international relations that discriminate against members of the First World and there are important interest alignments that cut across national frontiers. On the other hand, many of the objectionable features of the relations between the industrial and the developing countries are replicated in those among the stronger and weaker developing countries. If 'delinking' of the Third World were to become a reality, much the same problems would arise in the relations between, say, Brazil and Bolivia as now arise in the relations between the USA and Latin America as a whole.

Moreover, there is another danger for the fate of the poor within what has been called the 'trade union of the Third World'. This danger is that, as in the original trade union movement, the benefits from joint action may be reaped by the stronger members, who wield the power, and the weakest and poorest get left out.

For reasons such as these, emphasis on the homogeneity of the Third World may be both mistaken and misguided, and an appeal to universal principles and globally shared problems may be wiser.

10.4 Criticisms of the NIEO

There has been no shortage of criticisms of the proposals under the NIEO. Very often these have taken the form of evaluations by professional economists, in the light of the objectives of efficiency and equity commonly accepted in the profession. Yet, a proper evaluation ought to start from the objectives of the developing countries themselves (or specified groups within them), and distinguish between criticisms of the objectives and criticisms of the proposed means of achieving these objectives. There is also the danger that we may impute objectives to the developing countries that they do not share with us. One difficulty is that in the discussions ends and means have been confused, so that greater self-reliance, larger shares in income, wealth, or power, larger shares in industrial production, or trade, earnings stabilisation, price stabilisation of particular commodities and price stabilisation of all exported commodities, have been debated at the same level. An appraisal of the NIEO is likely to come to different conclusions according to whose objectives are chosen, according to the degree of generality at which the instruments for these objectives are discussed, and according to whether we are discussing ends or the appropriateness of instruments.

Another source of confusion is the fact that criticisms often compare the proposals with some 'ideal' solution, when in fact they should be compared with the most likely alternative. Thus, transfers through commodity agreements may, by some criteria, be thought to be worse than direct transfers through unconditional, untied, grants, which can be related to the needs of the recipients and the capacity to pay of the donors. SDR creation should be guided by the world's liquidity requirements and should, ideally, be separated from increases in development aid, not fused together in a 'link', etc. But the NIEO proposals have to be seen in the context of a world which is not 'ideal' but very imperfect. The alternative to doing things badly is often not doing them at all.

Another question is whether NIEO proposals should be assessed individually or collectively. It is possible to raise criticisms against each individual item on the Agenda, some at least of which would be answered by accepting certain packages. The Common Fund has been criticized for its inequitable impact on distribution between countries; debt relief, on the other hand, which benefits the poorest countries, has been criticised for its impact on capital markets, of concern mainly to middle income countries. A package of the Common Fund, debt relief to the poorest and soft ODA might meet the needs of both middle and low income countries.

Criticisms have also been directed at the objectives and motivations of the NIEO. It has been easy to disprove the argument that reparations are due for the exploitation in the colonial era. But the disproval is irrelevant, because the case for progressive redistribution of income and wealth and for international contributions to poverty eradication does not depend on the infliction of past damage. Few believe that colonial rule was necessarily harmful, though it would be difficult to prove that it was necessarily beneficial. It should be plain that international measures are crucial for both growth and equity, but that the international environment can facilitate or impede domestic advance.

A more fundamental criticism of the NIEO has been along the following lines. Moral imperatives apply only to individuals, not to governments. If international transfers are to be justified on moral grounds, donors must ensure that the moral objectives are attained. This implies highly conditional, targeted transfers for basic human needs, poverty alleviation, reduction of unemployment, etc. The proposals of the NIEO do not meet this condition, since the distribution of benefits between countries and within countries is capricious. Only strict control and monitoring by donor countries can insure that the target groups are reached.

The first point to be made in reply to this criticism is that in a complex, interdependent world institutions have to be used as vehicles for achieving moral objectives, even if it were agreed that only individuals are the appropriate ultimate targets of moral action. Up to a point, these institutions have to be trusted to concern themselves with the intended beneficiaries. The risk of some leakage has to be accepted. Family allowances intended to benefit children are paid to mothers and fathers who might spend them on gambling and drink. Local governments receive grants, intended for their citizens, from central governments, or states and provinces in a federation from the federal governments. It is therefore perfectly legitimate to apply moral rules to states, which are the necessary conduits for channelling funds to individuals in the world order as it exists. (That this principle is accepted even by the advocates of the view that only individuals are appropriate moral targets can be seen when these same advocates demand debt service from countries whose governments have changed since the debts were incurred, or when they demand that multinational companies should be treated as 'moral persons'.) Of course, funds accruing to governments through commodity agreements and debt relief can be spent on the wrong purposes and may benefit the rich in poor countries, but so may aid funds. The best method to make it probable that donor objectives of poverty alleviation are achieved is not to rule out institutional intermediaries, nor to attach strict performance criteria to all transfers and monitor meticulously expenditure, but to select governments committed to anti-poverty policies and support them. Such selection is, to some extent, consistent with the proposals of the NIEO.

But a dilemma remains. Developing countries insist on national sovereignty in the use of resources, while the supporters of larger transfers in the developed countries through overseas development assistance, the Special Drawing Rights link, debt relief, the integrated commodity programme or any other vehicle, stress the need for monitoring performance and internal reforms to benefit the poor. The resolution of this dilemma can be found in moves towards the 'global compact', or the 'planetary bargain' which Mr. McNamara, the Aspen Institute, Mahbub ul Haq and others have advocated. But as the positions of the North and South are at present defined, we are still some way from such a global compact. The North is not prepared to transfer the additional resources, the South is not prepared to give the necessary undertakings.

A final criticism of the call for a NIEO is that it is sterile, because relations between states and institutions needed to support them are constantly changing. But this is not a valid objection to constructive responses, because an order can incorporate rules and procedures for orderly change and adaptation to new circumstances.

It is unfortunate that the developing countries have chosen a set of ill-designed measures to translate worthy objectives into reality. Generalised debt relief (now dropped), and commodity schemes insofar as they are concerned with more than price stabilisation, are regarded by many professional economists as inefficient and inadequate ways of achieving the objective of significant transfers of income, wealth and power, and of achieving a radical restructuring of the international system. In addition, the conflict over the demand by the developing countries for sovereignty over the use of resources, and by the developed countries for careful targeting and internal reforms, adds a serious obstacle in the way of reaching agreement. On the other hand, it is at least equally unfortunate that the developed countries have not responded more constructively and imaginatively to the pleas of the developing countries.

10.5 Alternative responses by the Third World to the current impasse

The responses of the Third World to the current impasse in the dialogue can be discussed under the following headings:

(a) self-reliance, in the sense of doing desirable things for themselves and for each other, whether on the basis of an individual country, a group of countries or the Third World as a whole;

(b) exercise of joint bargaining power to counter biased income, wealth and power distributions;

(c) exploration of areas of common and mutual interest between the South and North;

(d) evolution of rules, procedures and institutions to avoid mutually damaging confrontations and conflict.

(a) *Self-Reliance: What can the developing countries do by and for themselves?*

This area overlaps with the subsequent two. Greater self-reliance will increase bargaining power and make it more likely that adjustments in imperfections and inequalities will be brought about. If self-reliance raises incomes and purchasing power, it will give rise to new common interests. But self-reliance is not in need of these secondary justifications. In the longer term, most of the things developing countries need, they can produce for themselves, and most of the things they can produce, they themselves need.

Reduced dualism and a more poverty-oriented approach will tend to create greater intra-Third World trade opportunities. Various forms of joint multinational enterprises will give rise to opportunities of investment coordination. Monetary cooperation can encourage trade expansion, and growing trade, e.g. through Third World preferences, can be financed by intra-Third World financial cooperation, such as clearing or payments unions. Mutual aid and technical assistance in rural development, family planning, technology, are often more effective between countries that are not at too dissimilar levels of development than when inappropriate methods are transferred from highly advanced countries. Joint activities could be developed in professional associations, in research, in the exchange of information, in education and training, in transport and communications, in food and energy policy. In these ways, the developing countries could make themselves less dependent on concessions from the rich countries and, at the same time, evolve their own styles of development.

Such a strategy calls for new types of institutions. A strong Third World secretariat, with a first-class staff and Third World loyalties has been proposed. Institutions in other fields, like a bank capable of creating monetary assets for Third World trade, or a board coordinating investment decisions, or a community of developing country governments monitoring each other's basic needs policies, (7) are possibilities.

(b) *Exercise of joint bargaining power*

In addition to such actions of self-reliance, the developing countries could use joint action in certain spheres to strengthen their power in bargaining with the developed countries. The debate over the course of the terms of trade has been shunted on to the wrong track, by disputing the question as to whether they had deteriorated historically. The relevant question is not the terms of trade now compared with what they were, but what are they now compared with what they should and could be. Producers' associations in some instances might take the place of commodity agreements on which consuming countries are represented. The fact that current price rises might speed up the process of inventing substitutes is not necessarily an argument against them, for the greater short-term receipts could be used for diversification funds. The question is complicated not only by the difficulty of estimating short-term and long-term elasticities of demand and their interdependence, but also by the possibility of the developed countries retaliating by raising their export prices. But it might be easier to get agreement of purchasing countries on non-retaliation than on commodity agreements.

Joint action vis-à-vis multinational corporations could replace or reinforce a generally agreed upon code. Developing countries could agree not to erode each other's tax base by giving competitive tax concessions and to apply similar rules and guidelines. Bargaining power can be used also in other spheres, such as overflying rights for airlines, narcotics control, patent law, etc. The main obstacle is that some differences among developing countries are as great as those between them and the developed countries, and joint action is difficult to achieve without a much stronger system of incentives to form and adhere to these agreements. Producers' associations are notorious for their instability, for the more successful the agreement is in raising the price, the stronger the incentive for individual members to defect. And the fear that others may operate outside the agreement, or that all may have to operate without the agreement, is itself a powerful destabilising force. More thought should be devoted to mechanisms to create incentives to penalise outsiders and defectors, and to reward adherents, as well as to strengthen solidarity, in order to increase the stability of joint action.

Successful cooperation among developing countries may not be possible in all areas but may be feasible in some, e.g. in improving the terms of technology transfer, in bargaining with multinationals, in controlling migration of professionals, in reaching joint action on taxation of foreign investment.

Topics (c) and *(d)*

Much has been written recently on the importance of exploring mutual interests. Clearly, this is a promising area because it provides a firmer basis for action than unilateral, unrequited concessions. Since reform in this area is in the interest of both the developing and developed countries, it will be discussed in the next section that deals with the response of the developed countries.

10.6 A constructive response by the developed countries

Although some of the proposals of the developing countries for a NIEO have not been well designed, the response of the developed countries has not been constructive or imaginative. If the package proposed at present were to be the only one on which developing countries could agree, this would be an argument for supporting it, in spite of its deficiencies. It is, however, worth considering modifications of this package (it has already been modified by the abandonment of the demand for general debt relief and the scaling down of the Common Fund) and alternative packages. It would require a separate paper to map out such alternatives but it is possible to lay down certain principles on the basis of which progress may be made.

There are three areas in which more thought should be devoted to the design of appropriate policies.

a) First, there is the area where developed and developing countries have common or mutual interests. (The two, though often confused, are clearly not the same. The former refers to objectives pursued by cooperation, the latter by exchange.) This covers the exploration of positive-sum games.

b) Secondly, there is the area of the avoidance of negative-sum games. Other countries can be not only sources of positive benefits, but also of threats that we must try to avert. Coexistence in an interdependent world can give rise to the production of goods; but it can also give rise to the production of 'bads', which have to be combatted by 'anti-bads'. The exploration of areas of joint action for 'anti-bads' may be even more important than the search for goods.

c) Thirdly, there are areas where existing biases, discriminations and imperfections in the international economic order work against the interests of the developing countries and where we have to explore joint methods of correcting them. This looks like an area of zero-sum games, although long-term benefits to all may accrue. Under this heading would also fall more 'voice' for the developing countries and concessional, gratuitous transfers.

Clearly, the three areas overlap, and each overlaps with self-reliance on the part of the developing countries. Where there is common interest and harmony, so that reforms yield joint gains, there remains the division of these gains between rich and poor countries which can give rise to conflict. Self-reliance by the poor may be in the short-term and long-term interest of the rich countries. They may prefer Korea to sell its shoes in Lahore, and Taiwan its textiles in Indonesia, to having their own markets swamped. And the correction may impose short-term losses on rich countries but benefit them in the long run.

Following on from the work in these areas is the question of the links between restructuring the international system as it affects relations between governments, and the consequential domestic measures required in both developing and developed countries to ensure that the benefits accrue to the poor, and that the costs are borne fairly.

Trade liberalisation involves both restructuring in developed countries, so that the whole burden is not borne by the dismissed workers in depressed areas; and in developing countries, so that the gains from liberalisation do not wholly accrue to big exporting firms, possibly even multinationals. In reaching commodity agreements, there should be some safeguards that the higher prices do not fall exclusively on poor consumers in rich countries, and that the restrictions that quota schemes involve are not largely borne by small farmers in poor countries, so that the big plantations benefit from both higher prices and unrestricted sales. And when we agree on debt relief, we want to be sure that it is more than relief for bankers in rich countries, whose loans are serviced out of aid funds. Such consequential domestic measures are necessary both inside developed and inside developing countries, if the ultimate impact of the reforms of the New International Economic Order is to be on improving the lot of the poor.

Common and mutual interests

Until 1973, issues of economic interdependence and development belonged to largely separate areas. Development was dealt with by development assistance and trade preferences of varying generosity. Interdependence was dealt with in the OECD. It was a matter for the rich.

The validity of this dichotomy has been questioned in the last six years. The developing countries' shares in world population, in world trade and in world production have increased. Some developing countries have now large international reserves, others large international debts (8). They supply raw materials, especially metals, on which the developed countries increasingly depend. The one-way dependence of the South on the North has now become a two-way interdependence.

International inter*dependence* should be distinguished from international *relations.* The test of the difference is this: if relations were cut off, ready substitutes could be found so that not much damage would be done. Inter*dependence* means that if relations were cut off, substantial damage would result. To illustrate: much trade between industrial countries is conducted in similar finished consumer goods and caters for slight differentiation in tastes. A smaller volume of trade (and a less rapidly growing one) with the developing countries consists of vital food and raw materials. In technical language, it is consumers' (and producers') surpluses that count, not trade volumes (values) and their growth.

Trade is not an end in itself, but a means to a more efficient allocation of resources and to greater consumers' satisfaction. The long-term importance of trade is, therefore, measured not by its total value or its rate of growth, but by (a) the difficulty in *production* of substituting domestic goods for imports by shifting resources employed in exports, and (b) the sacrifice in *consumption* of shifting from imports to domestic import substitutes, if the products are not identical, or of doing without them altogether. A vast and ever-growing exchange of Volkswagens for Morris Minors reflects small importance, a small exchange of coffee or copper (not to speak of oil) for engineering goods reflects vital dependence (or interdependence). Americans would not suffer much hardship if they had to drive Fairmonts instead of Volvos, but might if they had to drink Almadén instead of Château Margaux, and certainly would if they had to do entirely without manganese, tin or chromium imports. Total trade figures are, of course, relevant to other issues, such as change in the balance of payments, which in turn may affect consumption and welfare. But these sequences would have to be spelt out.

The most generally accepted area of mutual interest is trade liberalisation and liberalisation of the flow of the factors of production capital and labour. On trade, it could be argued that already fairly rich developed countries should weigh the costs of adjustment, probably repeated and painful adjustments, against the gains from further additions to income. Affluent countries, or at any rate their governments, might decide that it is in their national interest to forgo at the margin further income rises for the sake of a quieter life, and greater industrial peace.

The difficulty with this position is that the security of employment is not necessarily guaranteed by protection, for jobs in export trades are endangered, and that the costs of such a form of a quiet life can be very high indeed, particularly for a country dependent on foreign trade. Moreover, if several countries adopted such a position, the mutual impoverishment could be substantial.

Not only may the costs of adjustment be high, but the benefits from additional trade may be low. Sir Arthur Lewis invited us to imagine the consequences of either the rich countries of the North or the poor countries of the South sinking under the sea upon the remaining group of countries. His argument is that, after a period of adjustment, the losses would be negligible. If this were so, the large and, until 1973 rapidly growing, trade volumes are no indication of genuine inter*dependence*.

There are also mutual gains from the flow of capital. Here, special attention should be paid to measures which, without being identified with aid, could have a leverage effect on aid, such as guarantees, co-financing, improved access to capital markets and markets for manufactured exports, etc. Freer movement of goods and of capital and labour would not only register all the mutual benefits expounded by the theory of comparative advantage, but would also accelerate growth, reduce inflation, generate employment, expand choice and support the international system of trade and debt service.

The most powerful argument for international trade is not one based on the doctrine of comparative advantage, which assumes constant costs (Ricardo) or increasing costs (Heckscher-Ohlin), but one based on economies of scale, increasing returns, learning-by-doing, and decreasing unit costs, as elaborated by Allyn Young. Adam Smith had already pointed out that 'the division of labour is limited by the extent of the market'. He thought mainly of the geographical extent. Allyn Young added the reverse proposition, that the extent of the market, not only in the geographic sense, but also in the sense of the size of the income, depended on the division of labour. Production, productivity and incomes rise as specialisation proceeds. It is on the interaction between these two – the division of labour and the extent of the market – that economic progress depends. To widen the market, to raise incomes in the South, makes greater international specialisation possible, which in turn contributes to raising productivity and incomes. It has, of course, been questioned whether this style of development, relying on large-scale production and increasing specialisation, is consistent with the desire for diversity, human dignity, self-reliance, and respect for the environment.

Two specific issues under the heading of international trade are worth exploring. The first is the reform of tariff structures which now tend to cascade with successive stages of processing. Such de-escalation would improve the international location of industries and would permit developing countries to benefit from the external economies of learning effects from a primary product-based form of industrialisation. They might also be able to make better use of waste products, now discarded by the richer countries.

The second area is that of stabilisation of commodity prices. The large fluctuations that occur now benefit neither producers, who are discouraged from investing, nor consumers, who find it difficult to plan production.

On present evidence and theoretical considerations, there is not much in the argument that *general* flows of ODA to developing countries – what is sometimes called a Marshall

Plan for the Third World – can regenerate growth in the developed countries. For the Third World to be an 'engine of growth' for the industrialised countries, the quantities are too small (though they can make a contribution), and domestic measures (tax reductions and public expenditure increases) can do the same with higher political and economic returns, if the national interest were the only guide and if fuller employment were really desired. Some of the demand created in the North is from arms sales. If these were to be reduced, another source would have to replace them. Moreover, the greatest need for ODA is in the poorest countries, the trade share of which is small and only slowly growing, whereas the best 'investment' of such aid would be in the middle income developing countries, which are already earning much foreign exchange through their exports.

The argument that *specific* exports can be supplied from underutilised capacity at low, zero, or negative costs, and that *specific* imports can contribute to bottleneck-busting, and hence to the resumption of orderly growth without premature inflation, deserves closer examination.

Aid from surplus capacity has certain drawbacks. If, in the long run, the surplus capacity should be scrapped and the workers retrained, this process is delayed and an inefficient production structure is perpetuated. This can be particularly damaging if the surplus capacity competes with imports from the developing countries. If the production could have been used at home, or could have been exported at a commercial value, the costs of the aid are correspondingly higher. Nor is it always the case that recipients need or want the surplus production, when it is available, although the rapid growth of exports in the past has left certain industries, such as steel, chemicals and building materials, underutilised more than the average.

There remain, however, sectors and industries, especially those where indivisibilities are important, in which the temporary (cyclical) emergence of surplus capacity could be harnessed to the aid effort. Steel plant manufacturing capacity, shipbuilding capacity, or other heavy capital goods sectors are for technical reasons subject to fluctuations in utilisation, and periods of underutilised capacity might be used for aid-financed exports to developing countries in need of steel plants, ships, or other capital goods. Even where the case is strongest, aid from surplus capacity reduces the costs for the donor; it does not add to his gains.

As far as *imports* are concerned, developed countries wishing to resume growth are liable to run into *bottlenecks* before employment for the economy as a whole is achieved. Imports from developing countries can help to break these bottlenecks and thereby enable developed countries to resume higher levels of activity with less inflation.

The removal of certain world-wide scarcities, which now prevent countries from resuming non-inflationary, full-employment growth, may be against the interests of small groups benefiting from these scarcities, but is clearly in the interest of all countries and humanity at large. Normally, resources devoted to one sector deprive other sectors of resources. But bottleneck-busting investment in the bottleneck sector *increases* the utilisation of resources in other sectors and provides a stimulus for further investment. There is a multiplier effect. More specifically, food, energy and certain minerals fall into this category. Investment that raises the world supply of food and of energy is bound to benefit all people in the long run.

These bottlenecks can be either of a short-term nature, or they can represent long-term scarcities. In the latter case, investment by the North in the South, in order to overcome these global scarcities, can make a contribution to the resumption of long-term orderly growth without inflation. But in the long-term, interdependence is likely to be less than in the short term, because substitutes for, and economies in the use of, the scarce materials are possible. With technological advance, it is doubtful whether, in the long run, any country or group of countries can be said to be wholly dependent on some other countries. This is true both for the North and for the South. It greatly reduces the alleged significance of global interdependence.

Institutional innovation in the field of minerals and energy requires resolution of the present conflicts between companies and governments. Exploration is a risky business in which one lucky strike has to pay for numerous unlucky strikes. This type of risk is borne more efficiently by an intergovernmental organisation, which would also add to available information and reduce friction in negotiating contracts. A new institution could also supply finance for host country equity in new developments and for processing facilities in developing countries.

An area of positive-sum games is policies towards transnational corporations and direct private foreign investment. In the past, fears of expropriation, restrictions on repatriation or remittances, price controls and other policies reducing profitability or leading to losses have caused uncertainty and have raised the required rate of return on foreign investment. This high rate of return has, however, often led to the very measures that the investor feared, for host governments felt that companies were taking out of the country more than they were putting in.

There is a specific dilemma for developing countries. If the rate of reinvestment of foreign profits is lower than the rate of return on the capital invested, remission of profits presents a drain on foreign exchange. If, on the other hand, the rate of reinvestment of foreign profits exceeds the rate of return, on plausible assumptions about the rate of growth of national income and the capital-output ratio, a growing proportion of the stock of capital is going to be owned by foreigners. This dilemma between foreign exchange losses and alienation of assets has led some countries to expropriate foreign enterprises. A reduction in the uncertainty about such measures would reduce both the rates of return required by the companies and incentives to host governments to take measures that raise risks for companies. Well designed measures to reduce uncertainty can increase the flow of foreign investment, induce companies to take a longer-term view, alleviate fears of host governments, and thus benefit both firms and host countries.

Among such measures would be investment guarantees, agreements on arbitration procedures, sell-out and buy-out options after agreed periods at prices to be determined by agreed procedures, model contracts, investment codes, joint ventures, and new public-private hybrid institutions, combining the virtues of private initiative and enterprise with those of a commitment to development.

Another area of mutual interest for policies toward multinational firms is the application of anti-trust action to the international behaviour of these companies. It is just as much in any industrial country's interest that its companies should not act like cartels or monopolies internationally, as it is that foreign companies should not monopolise its domestic market. There is now an asymmetry in that anti-trust action and restrictive practices tend to be outlawed for domestic activity but permitted (or even encouraged) for international ones.

The conclusion to which these considerations lead is the need for a new international institution which would comprise some of the areas now covered by GATT, some of those covered by UNCTAD, and some not covered at all. Such a new International Trade and Production Organisation (as Miriam Camps (10) has called it) would be concerned with laying down rules and principles not only for tariff and non-tariff barriers to trade, but also for intra-firm trade (which now escapes these rules), for state trading, increasingly important also in mixed economies, for restrictive business practices, agricultural products and raw materials (now under UNCTAD), for services and for investment. The multilateral trade negotiations have not solved the problems of structural adjustments that a new, changing international division of labour calls for, nor have they touched on the investment wars that have tended to arise from the attempts of national governments to capture for themselves taxes and other benefits from private investment, thereby eroding the potential gains from investment. (Institutional arrangements to prevent these wars fall under the next heading, 'avoiding negative-sum games'.) It may be argued that it is better to build on existing institutions and procedures, but as Gerald Helleiner has reminded us, Clausewitz said 'A small jump is easier than a large one, but no one wishing to cross a large ditch would cross half of it first'.

Common interests can also be established in cooperation in the management of the global commons: ocean fisheries, air and sea pollution, radio frequencies, civil air and merchant shipping routes and world monetary conditions. The already mentioned success of some international institutions devoted to technical aspects of international cooperation, like the International Postal Union or the International Telecommunication Union or the World Meteorological Organisation bear witness to the possibility of successful international cooperation if strictly defined technical areas are at stake. As a by-product of this global management, revenues might be raised from some of these activities, like ocean fisheries or international travel.

Avoiding negative-sum games

The essence of interdependence is that members of the world community are able, by unilateral action, to inflict harm on others. The fear that others may take such action can be a sufficient condition for defensive, detrimental action of this kind.

The prime example in this field is the arms race which absorbs scarce resources and, beyond a certain critical point, which we have long ago exceeded, breeds violence. Between 1946 and 1976 120 wars were fought, 114 of them in the Third World. The number of people killed is somewhere between those killed in the First and Second World Wars. It has often been noted that economic growth has not abolished poverty. It is less often noticed that large defence expenditure has actually bred violence. The Laffer curve, whatever may be true for taxation, seems to apply to expenditure on arms. Three percent of the total annual expenditure of $ 450 billion now devoted to armaments would be doubling the annual resources devoted to official development assistance given by the OECD countries. But such arguments do not cut any ice until it can be established that the expenditure at present levels is counterproductive and that we would get better security from a reduced volume of expenditure.

In the economic area protectionism and deflation to protect the balance of payments are instances of negative-sum games. In the area of private foreign investment, actions by both parent and host governments to tilt the advantages from private foreign investment in their direction have similarly destructive effects. Large incentives are offered to bid for these investments in 'investment wars', like the trade wars of the Thirties. Overfishing, the pollution of the sea and the global atmosphere and the excessive exhaustion of non-renewable resources are other examples. Coordination of policies and international institutions for cooperation are needed to avoid such mutually destructive actions.

The institutional responses might be illustrated by internationally coordinated action. In order to avoid the self-defeating and mutually destructive actions arising from attempts to correct balance of payments deficits imposed by a few persistent surplus countries, an international central bank, with power to create liquid assets, is necessary. It has been argued that the system of flexible exchange rates has restored full autonomy for national monetary policies. But this is by no means as obvious as is often thought. Hardly any government would permit completely 'clean' floating; and 'dirty' floating may well require larger rather than smaller reserves to counter speculative attacks. For the creation of these an international central bank is necessary.

A second institutional reform would be a mechanism for some form of coordination of investment decisions, so as to avoid the swings between overcapacity and shortages of capacity from which we have suffered in the past. Opponents of such coordination fear this encourages the entry of market-sharing agreements and cartels, but in many national plans coordination of investment decisions has proved entirely compatible with maintaining competition.

Other illustrations would be agreements to refrain from trade and investment wars and the already mentioned establishment of international firms that would combine the virtues of private enterprise and freedom from bureaucratic controls with the objective of promoting development. Another area would be taxes on activities where independent national actions now lead to the deterioration of the world environment: a tax on overfishing, on polluting the sea and atmosphere, or on mining non-renewable natural resources.

Zero-sum games

Exploration of areas of zero-sum games, that is to say actions where a sacrifice is required on the part of the developed countries in order to benefit the developing countries, comprises three fields. First, the correction of imperfections and biases in the existing world order which work against the developing countries. Second, transfers of resources from the rich to the poor. And third, more 'voice' for them in the councils of the world.

10.7 Existing biases, imperfections and discriminations in the international system and how to correct them (11)

An international economic order that discriminates systematically against one group of countries can give rise to confrontations and conflicts and to negative-sum games in which all lose. But the appeal to correcting inequities need not be wholly an appeal to national self-interest. There is an independent moral case for a just world order.

Countries should be willing to cooperate in correcting biases in market structures and government policies that are damaging to the developing countries. Such corrections would contribute to a more equitable and therefore acceptable world order and, by reducing frictions and conflicts, can be seen to be also in the long-term interest of the developed countries.

A response along such lines would meet the demands of both efficiency and distributive justice. Not only are the specific proposals more in line with the canons of economic efficiency, but, by accommodating the developing countries' call for a fairer international order, they would prevent the recriminations and conflicts that are bound to cause international disorder, one of the greatest sources of inefficiency.

At the national level, governments attempt to provide macroeconomic stability through monetary and fiscal policies, to redistribute income through progressive taxes and social services, to guarantee farmers an adequate income, to correct for the worst features of free competitive markets, and to cushion victims against the damage of change. All these government actions are in the nature of public goods. There is no international government to do any of these things on a global scale. In the 19th century Great Britain, and for about 25 years after 1945, the USA, provided a power centre that fulfilled some of the functions of an international government, such as providing compensating capital movements, financial institutions, and being a lender of last resort. Since about 1970 such a centre has been lacking. The international organisations have been too weak to fulfill the required functions. International institutions are needed to provide internationally the 'public goods' of stability and equity that civilised national governments provide as a matter of course for their citizens. The implementation of such reforms would be a contribution to the foundation of a stable, equitable and prosperous world order.

Whatever our motivation for correcting imperfections or biases in the present international economic order, such biases occur in various fields. The division of the gains from trade may be very unequal because a few large buying companies from rich countries confront many weak sellers from developing countries, and the demand for the final product is fairly inelastic. Or the bulk of the processing of raw materials from developing countries may be done in the developed countries, who reap the large value added, not because they enjoy a comparative advantage but because of market power and policies, such as cascading tariffs, or discrimination in shipping or credit. Or the distribution of the gains from productivity growth between exporters and importers may be uneven, so that improving commodity terms of trade are consistent with deteriorating double factoral terms of trade.

In this context, thought should be given to what reforms are needed, by creating new or changing old institutions, rules, policies and by other measures to change the location of economic activities and to improve the developing countries' bargaining power, so as to reduce the bias in the distribution of gains from trade.

There are imperfections in the export markets of developing countries. There are also imperfections in the supply of imports. Developing countries are often faced with import prices that are higher than those charged to industrial countries and often suffer from price discrimination, restrictive trade practices, export cartels, inter-firm arrangements for the allocation of markets, etc. There exists evidence that small countries pay higher prices for imported machinery, chemicals, iron and steel than large countries. The USA prohibits cartels internally, but specifically exempts export cartels. Should there not be an anti-trust law internationally, just as there is one to protect US citizens?

There are imperfections in access to market information. The ability to buy cheap and sell dear depends upon full market information. The large transnational firms possess this but firms in poor developing countries do not. The disadvantage is cumulative:

ignorance about how to acquire information about production processes reinforces the absence of information about these products or processes themselves. There are imperfections in access to knowledge and technology. Several measures have been proposed to correct this bias. They involve reforms of the patent law, in the market for technology and in the thrust of Research and Development expenditure. There is a bias in the developing countries' access to capital markets. There may be no shortage of finance in Eurocurrency markets, suppliers' credits or through the World Bank, but there may be a bias in the markets for new bonds and capital issues. Much needs to be done in order to reduce imperfections and other obstacles in the way of access to the world's capital markets.

Imperfections in labour markets are reflected in the present bias in the admission and encouragement of certain types of professional manpower, often trained by the developing countries (Brain Drain), and the considerably less free movement of unskilled labour. The world's division into nation states, each monopolising the physical and technical assets within its boundaries for its own benefit, is not consistent with a rational or moral or acceptable world order.

Does the international monetary system discriminate against developing countries? Monetary restrictions have an important impact on unemployment. The SDR-aid link is probably dormant for a while, but there should be a gold-aid link. As Central Banks sell gold to the IMF for SDRs, the IMF can sell the gold and use the receipts for contributions to IDA.

Transnational corporations also introduce imperfections. How can we strengthen the bargaining position of developing countries in drawing up contracts with TNCs? How enlarge the scope for 'unbundling' the package of capital, management, know-how and marketing? What is the role of public sector enterprises in negotiating with private TNCs?

An analysis of the distribution of gains arising from much-touted 'outward-looking' foreign investment, where the quasi-rents and monopoly profits accruing to capital, management and know-how go to the rich countries, while the near-subsistence wages for semi-skilled labour go to the developing countries, would be useful. The world in which we live corresponds to neither of two popular models: it is neither a truly 'liberal' world in which all factors are completely mobile across frontiers, so that they can seek their highest rewards; nor is it the world of the textbooks in which all factors are completely immobile internationally and trade is a substitute for factor movements. Some factors of production, such as capital, management and know-how, are fairly mobile internationally, though in abundant supply domestically, and earn high rewards, whereas unskilled and semi-skilled labour are immobile internationally and earn low rewards. This has important implications for the distribution of gains from trade, technology and investment, and for the attitudes towards multinational firms.

There are biases in political news coverage. Are the media biased in the scope and content of their news coverage? Is there a need for additional press agencies representing the point of view of developing countries?

Should reforms in all these areas take the form of restoring genuine competition, to reduce market power concentrations in rich countries? Or should they take the form of mobilising countervailing power, like organising numerous poor producers (as the trade unions did in the nineteenth century)? Or should they take the form of changes in rules, institutions or legislation? Should there be reforms in the accumulation, selection and dissemination of information and knowledge? Many current recommendations are based on the false premise that existing markets are competitive and efficient, and spread the benefits of economic progress speedily and widely. This assumption is quite unrealistic for the world as a whole.

Resource transfer

A new international economic order calls for a substantial increase in the amount of resources to be transferred to the developing countries, with the primary objective of eliminating the worst aspects of poverty within the lifetime of a generation. The specific forms this transfer takes is a secondary question. It has been proposed that developed countries should commit themselves to a total, but that each country should be free to decide in what form it wishes to make its stipulated contribution, whether through commodity agreements, preferences, debt relief, additional ODA, etc. Such an approach would prevent differences among developed countries over specific instruments blocking the achievement of an agreed objective.

The rational way would be an international, progressive income tax, with a lower exemption limit and a rising aid/GNP ratio as income per head rises. Other tax proposals have been made, such as a tax on over-fishing, on global pollution, on seabed resources, on international travel, on armaments, etc. But an international income tax would be the most rational way towards automaticity in contributions and fair sharing.

Monitoring of the objective – poverty eradication – can be done in a way that would avoid the intrusion of donor-country performance criteria, with all the suspicions to which this would give rise, and without the abuse of funds received by developing countries. Harlan Cleveland has proposed a system like that under the Marshall Plan, in which the developing countries themselves would examine and monitor each other's performance in reducing poverty. Accepted extra-national secretariats are another possibility.

'Voice'

The demand of the developing countries for greater participation in the international decision-making process calls for a reform in the membership and voting system of international institutions. More 'voice' for the developing countries is likely to remove some of the frustrations that spring from the perception of powerlessness. But greater participation by the developing countries would be pointless if it were accompanied by reduced contributions from the industrial countries.

The demand for 'more voice' is, of course, ultimately a demand for a different power distribution. Power to achieve common objectives can be a positive-sum game, in the sense that joining others can strengthen this power. But where objectives conflict, power is a zero-sum game. If there were a harmony of interests, more voice would not be needed. The demand for 'more voice' implies that certain objectives of the claimants have not been met. What is ultimately at stake is a restructuring of power relations.

10.8 The relation between narrow and 'higher' national self-interest

We can build on areas of common national interests, emphasising mutual benefits to be derived from, e.g. resumption of orderly and equitable growth in the world economy, forswearing self-defeating protectionism, exploring ways of increasing the resources in globally scarce supply, etc. But while there is considerable scope for positive-sum games in exploring areas of common and mutual interests, and of avoiding self-defeating, mutually destructive policies, there is also a 'higher' interest in a world order that both is, and is seen to be, equitable, that is acceptable and therefore accepted, and that reduces conflict and confrontation.

All societies need for their self-regulation and for social control a basis of moral principles. Individuals are ready to make sacrifices for the communities they live in. Can this principle stop at the nation state? A belief in the harmony between self-interest and altruism is deep-seated in Anglo-Saxon thought and action. One is reminded of the eighteenth century Bishop Joseph Butler: 'when we sit down in a cool hour, we can neither justify to ourselves this or any other pursuit, till we are convinced that it will be for our happiness....' The only question is why it appears to be easier to identify, or at least harmonise, individual happiness with the national interest than with that of the world community. It is odd that a moral, disinterested concern by rich countries with the development of the poor is hardly ever conceded. As hypocrisy is the tribute vice pays to virtue, so professions of national self-interest in the development of poor countries may be the tribute that virtue has to pay to vice. Let us, in the present fashion for stressing common and mutual interests, not underestimate the power of moral appeals. Holland, Sweden and Norway, which have put international cooperation squarely on a moral basis, have hit the 0.7 % aid target. It is the countries in which aid has been sold to the public on grounds of national self-interest where the effort is sadly lagging.

The common interests must also be defined in terms of different time horizons: the next year, the next five years, the next twenty years. There may be conflicts and trade-offs between these different time spans. For example, concessionary aid to the poorest may involve economic sacrifices in the near future but, by laying the foundations for a world in which all human beings born can fully develop their potential, it contributes to the long-term interest of mankind.

One difficulty is that in democracies adults have votes, but children and the unborn have no votes. The fight is not only against powerfully organised vested interests, but also against all our own short-term interests that neglect the interests of future generations.

The 'higher' interest in an acceptable world order can be defined either in moral terms or in terms of the desire to avoid negative-sum games, to avoid breakdown and chaos. Whatever the definition and justification, its aim is to transform adversary relationships into cooperation. When interests diverge or conflict, the task of statesmanship is to reconcile them. This is a task quite distinct from, and more important than, that of exploring areas of common or mutual interests. It is in this light that cooperative actions to eradicate world poverty and to restructure the international economic order have to be seen.

Towards a new institutional structure

Three principles emerge that would underly a new international institutional order. First, it should be based on common or mutual interests, whether these are lower or (preferably) higher interests (including moral interests), short-term or (preferably) long term. Second, it should go beyond talk to action. And third, it should be genuinely multilateral (though not all institutions need be global). Multilateralism was imposed in the nineteenth century by the *Pax Britannica,* and after the second World War until 1971 by the *Pax Americana.* The task is now to build a genuinely multilateral order in the place of arrangements of dominance and dependence. Such an order of interdependence is possible only among equals.

References

(1) The ratio of exports to GNP for the UK was 19.3 percent in 1913 and 20.7 percent in 1976; for the USA, 6.5 percent in 1913 and 6.8 percent in 1976; and for Germany 20.5 percent in 1913 and 22.3 percent in 1976.

(2) For another distinction, viz. that between interdependence and international relations, see p. 233.

(3) To say that the world was more integrated in the nineteenth century than it is today implies using a definition of 'integration' which does not comprise equal opportunities for all citizens. Clearly, the opportunities were very unequal. But the world resembled more a single country than it does today.

(4) In the low-income developing countries exports were 13.8 percent of GNP in 1960 and 15.7 percent in 1976. Low-income countries are those with an income per head of less than $ 300 in 1975.

(5) Of this long-standing confusion between universal and uniform, or general, rules even such a clear-headed thinker as David Hume is guilty. Hume contrasts the highly specific reactions when we are seeking our own self-interest with the 'universal and perfectly inflexible' laws of justice. He seems, like many others (including GATT), not to make a necessary distinction between general principles (the opposite of specific ones and therefore necessarily simple) and universal principles (which may be highly specific and highly complicated, provided that they contain no uneliminable reference to individual cases). Thus, Hume says, in one place 'universal and perfectly inflexible', but lower down 'general and inflexible'. And the use of the word 'inflexible' conceals a confusion between a principle being able to be altered (which has nothing to do with its universality or generality) and its having a lot of exceptions written into it (which is consistent with universality but not with generality). Hume evidently thinks that the rules of justice have to be simple, general ones. He argues that unless the rules are general, people will be partial in their application of them and 'would take into consideration the characters and circumstances of the persons, as well as the general nature of the question ... the avidity and partiality of men would quickly bring disorder into the world, if not restrained by some general and inflexible principles'. But this is fallacious. In order to prevent people from being partial, the principles have to be universal, i.e., not contain references to individuals; they may, and indeed should, not be general; surely our judgments based on them ought to 'take into consideration the characters and circumstances of the persons, as well as the general nature of the question'.

(6) For a valiant attempt to demonstrate common factors in the Third World, see Ismail-Sabri Abdalla, 'Heterogeneity and Differentiation – The End of the Third World?' *Development Dialogue,* 1978:2.

(7) See Harlan Cleveland, *The Third Try at World Order,* New York, 1976.

(8) The share in total world trade of all developing countries has increased from 21.4 % in 1960 to 24.6 % in 1976, (though excluding major oil exporters the share declined from 14.8 to 10.2); their share in international reserves has increased from 17.8 % in 1960 to 45.9 % in 1976 (excluding OPEC from 13.8 to 20.2); their share in population from 72 % in 1960 to 76 % in 1976; and their share in production from 18.2 % in 1960 to 22.6 in 1976, measured at constant 1975 dollars.

(9) Irma Adelman, in private correspondence, has suggested that the major influence of international trade on development is that it enables a country to decouple production from consumption, and thereby presents more options for development policy.

(10) Miriam Camps, *The Case for a Global Trade Organization,* Council on Foreign Relations, New York, 1980.

(11) This subject is well treated in Gerald K. Helleiner, *World Market Imperfections and the Developing Countries,* Overseas Development Council, Washington D C, Occasional Paper No. 11, 1978.

Chapter 11

THE CMEA COUNTRIES AND THE NEW INTERNATIONAL ECONOMIC ORDER

Oleg Bogomolov*

It is six years since the 6th Special Session of the UN General Assembly adopted the 'Declaration on the Establishment of the New International Economic Order' and the 'Plan of Action'. At the 29th session of the General Assembly the developing countries, supported by the socialist states, secured the adoption of the 'Charter of Economic Rights and Duties of States'. Important decisions of all the subsequent sessions of the UN General Assembly, of the 4th and 5th sessions of the UNCTAD, and of the 5th and 6th conferences of the non-aligned countries, were devoted to problems of building the New International Economic Order (NIEO). These documents have created a certain political basis for elaborating a complex of practical measures aimed at improving the position of the developing countries in the world economy and at securing for them new sources for economic, scientific and technological progress.

11.1 The need for a new order

The movement for the restructuring of the world economy has to be increasingly reckoned with in world politics, for it has been brought about by the objective needs of the present time.

The post-war decades, including the early 1970s, were characterised by high and relatively stable rates of growth of the world economy, by the development of the scientific and technological revolution and by its large-scale introduction in the production of industrial countries. However, these processes occurred in a world divided into two socio-economic systems, the bulk of industrial production, trade and scientific and technical exchanges still remaining within the framework of the world capitalist economy. Considerable growth of the scale of production activity under conditions of spontaneity, and lack of a mechanism for co-ordinating the interests of countries at different levels of development, have acutely sharpened contradictions within the non-socialist world, and have led to further polarisation of its member countries, to the deepening of inequality, and to intensified exploitation of less developed countries by the more developed.

About half of the world population – 2,000 million people – live in the developing countries, but account for only 9 per cent of the world's industrial production. As

* Director, Institute for the Socialist World Economic System, Academy of Sciences of the USSR, Moscow

many as 1,000 million people are illiterate, 800 million live in poverty and suffer from chronic malnutrition, and the number of jobless amounts to 300 million. It should be stressed that the economic gulf continues to widen: the ratio of per capita output between the two groups of countries has reached 13 : 1, compared with 10 : 1 at the beginning of the post-war period; for industrial production the ratio is 31 : 1. Even under favourable conditions, by the year 2000 per capita industrial output in the developed countries will be nine times larger than in developing states.

Obviously, one of the most dangerous contradictions in the world economy is the deepening conflict between the industrial countries of the West and the developing countries. The main benefits of modern technological progress accrue to a few industrial capitalist states, whereas the people of economically backward countries practically fail to enjoy its fruits.

For decades, artificially reduced prices for fuel and raw materials imported from the developing countries have been one of the very essential factors promoting the maintenance of high rates of growth of the Western powers, the modernisation of their fuel and raw material resources and the reduction of production costs in the entire reproduction process. Some estimates suggest that of the 200 billion dollars paid per annum in the early 1970s by consumers in industrial states for imports of fuel and raw materials, the producers and exporters – the developing countries – received a mere 30 billions.

According to estimates cited in the report of the Club of Rome, various discriminatory practices in world economic relations cause damage to the developing countries to the tune of 50 – 100 billion dollars per annum. The growing protectionist trends in developed capitalist states in the second half of this decade are causing serious damage to the foreign trade of the developing countries and to the process of establishing their national industries. The unfavourable development of prices for goods exported to the developing countries (other than members of the OPEC group) has led to a tremendous deficit in their balance of payments – rising from 24 billion dollars in 1974 to 38 billion dollars in 1978 and, according to preliminary estimates, doubling again in 1979. The foreign debts of the developing countries have reached an astronomic sum of 350 billion dollars. In a number of countries the reimbursement of foreign investors' profits, debts and interest alone amounts to 20, 30 and more per cent of their export revenue.

The ever expanding penetration of foreign capital into the economies of the developing countries has become a most important means of exploiting them (the West's direct investments alone in the developing countries have now reached about 100 billion dollars). Foreign capital controls some 40 per cent of industrial production and 50 per cent of the exports of the developing countries, the strongest positions being held by transnational corporations – above all, American ones. The scale of their activities enables them to exert tremendous influence not only upon the economies of the developing countries, but also upon their internal political life and foreign policy orientation.

The 1973 – 1974 energy crisis has shown that the established international system of energy and raw material supplies is extremely vulnerable. The industrially developed countries of the West, whose per capita consumption of natural resources is 20 times larger than that of developing countries, possess, according to the estimates of Western specialists, only 10 per cent of the world oil reserves, 2 per cent of the world reserves of natural gas, and relatively inconsiderable amounts of major kinds of mineral resources, including iron, non-ferrous metals, phosporus, asbestos, etc. Their economic growth in the long term is inconceivable without deliveries from outside of resources in short supply. However, this is impossible under the former economic conditions with the ever widening economic lag of the developing countries.

Many facts point to growing interdependence in the economic development of countries, which is also true of the countries with different social systems and levels of industrialisation. The division and cooperation of labour on a world-wide scale is the result of the colossal scale of production and rapid progress of technology in our time. The economic possibilities and prospects of individual countries depend, whether they want it or not, to a greater or lesser extent on how the world economy is functioning.

Along with national economies and different economic structures of individual countries, the existence of the world economy, and of the international economic order common to all, should be regarded as one of the realities of modern social life. Mankind cannot but worry about the state of the world economy; nor rest assured of the protection of the human environment.

The functioning of the world economy is arousing increasing alarm. Although exchange of goods and technologies between countries is expanding, international flow of capital is increasing and industrial activities are being internationalised, the symptoms of the incurable disease which is corroding the mechanism of the world economy are manifesting themselves ever more clearly. This mechanism fails to cope with such problems as liquidation of the widening gulf between industrially developed and developing states, non-equivalence of international exchange, unceasing inflation and devaluation of currencies, meeting the needs of countries in the raw materials, power resources and foods which are in short supply, and provision of equal access for all countries to the latest achievements of scientific and technological progress. The blame lies with the exploiter relations prevailing in the world economy, as well as with the irresponsible and selfish behaviour of international monopolies. The impact of world socialism on the improvement of the world economy is growing, but its relatively small share in world trade (about 12 per cent) must be taken into account.

The unfair international economic order is causing considerable damage to socialist countries, too. The growing anxiety about the existing situation in the world economy, which runs counter to the vital interests of many countries, especially developing states, has found its reflection in the proposals aimed at restructuring international economic relations.

The main content of the programme of the new international economic order advanced by the developing countries consists of two demands: firstly, the establishment of complete sovereignty over own natural resources and economic activities, and their utilisation in the interests of overcoming backwardness; secondly, the creation of an international mechanism for the redistribution of incomes from world economic exchanges in favour of economically backward states. The analysis of the proposals put forward by the developing countries shows that the movement for a new international economic order is in essence a movement of a general democratic nature and is being directed against exploiter relations in world economic links. It does not set radical goals which are beyond the framework of the social systems existing in these countries; the success of the movement can even lead to the consolidation of the pro-capitalist forces in a number of developing countries. The NIEO concept includes liquidation of the exploitation of the developing countries by foreign capital, international democratic control over prices for major commodities, the monetary system and the activities of transnational monopolies, and increased financial and technical aid to the young national states. The implementation of these demands would mean substantial progress within the system of international economic relations as compared with the present situation. However, this is linked with a long and persistent political and economic struggle in the international arena.

11.2 CMEA views on the NIEO

Naturally, the socialist countries do not keep aloof from the sharp political struggle waged on these issues. The attitude of the CMEA countries to the demands for restructuring world economic relations on fair and democratic principles was set forth in their joint statement to the 4th conference of UNCTAD in 1976, as well as in the statement of the Soviet Government 'On Restructuring International Economic Relations' of 4 October 1976. The stand of these countries is determined, above all, by the high responsibility history places on the new social system in solving the global problems of our time.

The anti-imperialist, general democratic direction of the developing countries' concepts of NIEO explains why the socialist countries support this movement in principle. The socialist countries are not interested in world economic chaos. A world economic system based on the principles of equality, justice, non-discrimination and mutual benefit would fully meet their collective and national-state interests. At the same time, it is obvious that no viable world economic system is conceivable without taking adequate account of the specific interests of the countries of the socialist community.

The restructuring of the world economy cannot be confined to the sphere of relations between industrial capitalist countries and the countries liberated from the colonial yoke. The democratisation of the world economic system also requires complete normalisation of East-West relations and elimination of such phenomena as artificial restriction of economic ties between countries with different social systems, of discrimination in trade on political and ideological grounds, and of the deformation of the international division of labour imposed by the policies of the Western powers and their economic alignments. It is with these demands that the socialist countries are seeking to supplement the NIEO concepts.

The practice of international division of labour and cooperation within the CMEA sets an example of balanced and just solution of many of the problems posed by the movement for the NIEO. This is the real experience of restructuring world economic relations on the principles of equality, respect for the interests of all the cooperating countries and friendly mutual assistance for the sake of common progress. This experience is closely watched by the progressive world public. Of special interest for the developing countries in the NIEO context are the methods of cooperation within the CMEA framework aimed at evening out development levels and bringing the economic structures of the member countries closer to one another, as well as special measures of the socialist community aimed at rendering assistance to the least developed countries to overcome their backwardness and to build a modern economy.

In support of the developing countries on the NIEO issue, the socialist states stress the necessity of effecting progressive social transformations, and mobilising the internal potential for economic growth, as the main ways of changing the position of the developing countries. The Soviet Union and many other socialist countries are resolutely opposing all kinds of Utopian projects for world redistribution of wealth, which divert the peoples of the developing countries from the urgent tasks of the struggle for their national and social liberation and for maximum use, on this basis, of internal possibilities for socio-economic progress. Excessive attention to external aspects of development, however important they are, may give rise to illusions about the possibility of overcoming backwardness and of building a modern independent economy largely as a result of implementing the NIEO demands, increasing the inflow of resources from developed states and providing freer access to their markets. The main impulses for development should be determined by the internal requirements of a country, and by mobilising all possible reserves for meeting them. Naturally, favourable conditions outside a given country can greatly facilitate and accelerate the process of overcoming backwardness and building a modern economy. It is the formation of such favourable external conditions for the development of all countries, above all the developing countries, that the socialist states regard as the main task of the movement for the establishment of the New International Economic Order.

The analysis of the main items of the developing countries' programme of changing the world economic order shows that, with few exceptions, they meet the interests of the socialist states or, in any case, do not directly contradict these interests. This refers to such items as the unrestricted right to dispose of the national resources, including nationalisation of foreign property; establishment of stable prices for the developing countries' export goods – raw materials and fuel – including the principle of 'indexing' prices (i.e. of automatically increasing prices for raw materials and fuel proportionally to the growth of prices for manufactured goods); building up buffer reserves of goods compensating fluctuations of supply and demand, and other measures aimed at stabilising the developing countries' export returns; expanded manufacture of their traditional and new industrial goods for the markets of developed countries; establishment of new channels for technology transfer and regulation of the activity of transnational corporations; a reform of the international trade and monetary-financial systems, etc. Naturally, implementation of the above demands is being opposed by the imperialist powers which so far possess sufficient economic and political power to uphold their privileges, although they have to manoeuvre and in some respects go against their own interests.

The NIEO also reveals a certain contradiction and narrow-mindedness in the developing countries' views. Thus, for instance, the discussions held at international meetings show that the socialist countries do not agree with the developing countries' attempts to lay similar claims, guided by the thesis of universal solidarity, on all industrial states irrespective of their social systems. Such an approach obliterates the fundamental difference between socialist and capitalist countries and relieves the latter of the responsibility for the colonial past and for the present state of the developing countries. This, in particular, refers to the developing countries' demand that their debts should be written off and that they should be granted a fixed share of the industrial countries' gross national product (GNP) in the form of aid.

Also, one cannot but see that the deepening differentiation of the developing countries strengthens elements of pragmatism in the policies of some of them, trends towards compromise with imperialism and attempts to exert pressure on socialist countries, above all with regard to the question of the amount of aid.

At present, the capitalist powers are pumping out from the developing countries much more resources than their entire current aid intended both for defence and development. The West's aid can and must be increased taking into account its historical responsibility and the scale of its current exploitation of the developing countries' resources. The socialist countries have never plundered the developing countries; nor do they derive today any unilateral advantages from their relations with them. Therefore, the socialist states do not, and cannot, regard it as their "moral duty" to allot a fixed share of their GNP to them in the form of aid.

It goes without saying that alliance with the national liberation movement, and every possible support of the young national states in their efforts to strengthen their economies and secure social progress, remain most important aspects of the foreign policy of the socialist community. Within the framework of this policy, the socialist countries render on favourable terms large-scale technical assistance to the young national states, transfer modern technology to them, grant credits, and assist in training national personnel and qualified workers. The socialist countries declare that they are prepared to increase aid for development purposes, especially if progress is made toward the settlement of the disarmament problem and if military budgets are reduced.

In 1973, the Soviet Union, supported by other socialist countries, proposed that the military budgets of the permanent members of the UN Security Council should be reduced without waiting for the execution of other major measures in the field of disarmament, and that part of the sums thus released should be used for economic advance of the developing countries. At the 1978 special session of the UN General Assembly on disarmament, the USSR put forward new proposals stipulating that these countries should agree on a definite amount for each country's military budget reduction, in real terms rather than in percentages, on the concrete sums to be allocated by each of the above states to increase aid for the developing countries, and on the setting up within the UN framework of a mechanism for distributing these sums among the recipients. Support of these initiatives would greatly facilitate the implementation of many items of the NIEO. Regrettably, the other permanent members of the Security Council have not responded to these proposals.

At the turn of the 1970s – 1980s, most socialist countries attach ever greater importance to comprehensive intensification of the national economy, to the increase of its effectiveness and quality and to the mastery of the achievements of the modern scientific and technological revolution. The use of the benefits and advantages of a broad international division of labour has become an important factor promoting intensification of the national economies of all the CMEA member countries. At the same time, there is an obvious need to secure further strengthening of the material prerequisites for the participation of the CMEA countries in the world dividion of labour, rationalisation of their ties with states which have different social systems, pooling of their efforts for the solution of common tasks, and neutralisation of negative trends revealed in recent years.

At present, the CMEA countries are making increasing efforts to ensure that their bilateral and multilateral cooperation, including joint construction of big production projects, specialisation and cooperation in production and scientific and technical integration, is devoted to the solution of the principal scientific and technological problems. This will make possible the raising of economic effectiveness and will also expand the scale of foreign economic relations with third countries.

The most promising fields for such cooperation between the CMEA member-states — providing also for access to markets of third countries — could be ferrous and non-ferrous metallurgy, production of mining equipment and equipment for atomic power stations, transport and agricultural machine-building, production of hydraulic and pneumatic devices, and irrigation and reclamation plants, a number of branches of machine-tool manufacture, etc.

It is self-evident that to tackle the broader and more complex tasks in the development of specialisation and production cooperation within the CMEA framework will require further improvement of the internal and international mechanism for the implementation of cooperation; in particular, it will require better stimulation of the foreign economic activity of socialist enterprises, their increased interest and responsibility, improvement of the procedures for concluding agreements on specialisation and cooperation, etc. At present, the socialist countries are working in this direction.

The vast scientific and technical potential of the CMEA countries (the Soviet Union alone accounts for some 20 per cent of the world's patent file) may become a prerequisite for the growth of business-like cooperation with many countries on a cooperative basis.

In the NIEO context the CMEA countries pay special attention to the expansion of trade and economic and scientific-technological cooperation with the developing countries. Economic ties with this group of states are growing fast on the whole, and the developing countries have turned into big trade partners of the CMEA countries (they account for over 10 per cent of the latter's foreign trade). At the same time, the use made by the partners of the enormous potential possibilities of this flow of trade is far from complete. A comparatively low reciprocal share in the trade turnover of both groups of countries hampers the use of large-scale effective forms of international co-operation for the solution of the partners' important economic problems.

11.3 Tasks ahead for the CMEA countries and the LDCs

It is reasonable that during the next 10 — 15 years the efforts of both groups of countries should concentrate on the solution of the following tasks:

(a) organisation by the CMEA countries of large-scale imports from the developing countries of fuel and power resources, above all of oil and several kinds of raw materials and tropical foods;

(b) fuller use of the CMEA countries' powerful machine building potential for expanding exports of machines and equipment to the developing countries (they account now for some 30 per cent of exports to these countries and meet a mere 4 – 5 per cent of their import requirements);

(c) growth of CMEA countries' imports of manufactured goods and semi-finished products from the developing countries, including imports on the basis of cooperation agreements and compensation deals;

(d) implementation of a manoeuvre with a view to reorienting part of the East-West trade flows to the developing countries;

(e) solution of institutional problems hampering the development of relations with the developing countries in some CMEA member-states, and their joint action;

(f) accomplishment of trilateral projects with the participation of socialist, developing and capitalist countries.

Realisation of these trends in cooperation is greatly facilitated by promoting the elaboration of national programmes for the strengthening of the developing countries' productive forces and by the participation of several socialist countries in their implementation. Such pooling of efforts and resources by two or more CMEA member-states, for implementing big economic projects in third countries, is reasonable, since in a number of cases one country cannot act alone because of the shortage of production capacities or lack of some kind of production.

What is meant, above all, is cooperation in prospecting for minerals, in increasing extraction and processing of several kinds of raw materials, in building industrial and other projects, etc. Such activity will, on the one hand, promote socio-economic progress of the developing countries, and, on the other hand, can be used by the CMEA member-states to increase the number of sources for the purchase (also on a compensation basis) of the kinds of raw materials they need, and to step up imports of labour-intensive manufactures and of new products made by these countries' national industries.

There are certain possibilities for joint development in these countries of production, as well as scientific and technical infrastructure, e.g. for joint complex construction (including deliveries of the entire equipment required on the basis of division of labour) of power transmission lines, substations, water supply systems, ports, educational establishments, medical institutions, research laboratories, a telephone system, etc.

The interest in enhancing the effectiveness of capital investments, and of meeting more fully the CMEA countries' requirements in power and raw materials resources, makes it expedient to increase CMEA imports from countries outside the region, above all, from the developing countries. This will account for a considerable growth of trade turnover between these groups in the 1980s and, obviously, in the following decade.

Large-scale imports of fuel and raw materials from countries other than the CMEA member-states can be secured if the established forms and methods of cooperation, and its financing and material and technical supplies, are supplemented by new methods. The connection between the measures for expanding imports of fuel and raw materials and those contained in the 'Fuel-raw materials' long-term programme of cooperation (perhaps, in the form of a special programme), may create a convenient organisational framework for their implementation. An important role in this field will be played by contacts and cooperation between planning bodies of socialist and developing countries, as well as by the work of existing and, perhaps, newly established international organisations of the socialist countries.

The expansion of exports of machines, equipment and know-how from the CMEA countries to the developing countries' markets can be secured by partial orientation of the newly established production capacities in machine-building towards the markets of these states.

In this connection, the point at issue is a certain change of functions and methods of economic and technical assistance rendered by the CMEA member-states to the developing countries. This assistance will serve more than before as a means of shaping a stable division of labour between these two groups of countries. Therefore attention will be paid to the promotion of construction by our partners of enterprises oriented towards the CMEA countries' markets, as well as towards the use of such new forms of cooperation as long-term industrial cooperation and compensation deals, expansion of the network of joint marketing companies, implementation of multilateral projects on the basis of cooperation between interested CMEA countries, trilateral cooperation, etc.

In implementing the Comprehensive Programme of Socialist Economic Integration the CMEA member-states are expanding their possibilities for cooperation with the countries of Asia, Africa and Latin America. Long-term mission-oriented programmes of cooperation, aimed at meeting economically well-grounded requirements of the CMEA countries for fuel, energy, raw materials, food, and major kinds of modern equipment, envisage the participation of the developing countries in the integration activities if they find it beneficial. These programmes open up prospects for establishing stable long-term business relations on the basis of division of labour and reciprocal complementarity of production structures, and of the use of more advanced forms of economic and scientific-technological interrelationships.

Recent practice testifies to the fact that effectiveness of the socialist countries' economic assistance to the developing states increases for both sides if it is rendered not so much in the form of building selected industrial, transport and other projects as in the form of multibranch regional industrial and agrarian-industrial complexes which transform the socio-economic image of the respective countries and the structure of their cooperation with the CMEA member-states. A search for, and practical tests of, various forms of mixed and joint enterprises are under way. Multilateral cooperation among the CMEA countries is being used more widely in rendering economic and technical assistance to the developing states.

Relations between the two groups of states, in which democratic principles are consistently observed and which reflect the community of interests in the struggle for restructuring the unjust system of international economic relations, will continue to develop and deepen rapidly, demonstrating in practice the transition to a new organisation of the world economy, which is already in progress.

Chapter 12

A ROUND OF GLOBAL NEGOTIATIONS ON INTERNATIONAL ECONOMIC COOPERATION: A PREVIEW

Odette Jankowitsch*

At the end of 1979, the General Assembly of the United Nations decided (1) to launch, at its special session in August 1980, 'a round of global and sustained negotiations on international economic cooperation'. The holding of a special session had already been decided in 1977 for the purpose of adopting a new international development strategy for the Third Development Decade and to assess the progress made in various fora of the UN towards the establishment of a New International Economic Order.

The third (2) special session of the General Assembly devoted to matters of economic development was thus intended to fulfill three main objectives: to evaluate progress achieved since 1974, formally to adopt a new strategy, and to agree on a framework for negotiations. The complementarity of these objectives needs no explanation: it now seems evident that no progress has been achieved, since the adoption of the Declaration on a New International Economic Order, in bringing about major changes in international economic relations and development; that a new strategy is needed for the 1980s; and that an intensive phase of negotiations may accelerate a process that, to most people, seems to have come to a standstill.

The initial agreement on the need for negotiations, reached at the end of 1979, contains, in its broad formulation, the history, the purpose and the object of the negotiation (3). Indeed, in its preambular paragraphs, resolution 34/138 takes note of the fact that it was the sixth Conference of Heads of State or Governments of Non-aligned Countries (NAC) that had suggested such global negotiations; it further emphasises the need to establish a new system of international economic relations based on the principles of equality and mutual benefit. Such a new system calls, in the terms of the resolution, for 'bold initiatives' and requires 'new, concrete, comprehensive and global solutions'. It specifies that global negotiations should take place within the UN system and within a specified time-frame and should include major issues in the areas of raw materials, energy, trade, development, money and finance; these negotiations should contribute to the implementation of the international development strategy for the Third UN Development Decade.

* Bureau of Studies and Programming, UNESCO, Paris. The views expressed do not necessarily reflect those of UNESCO, with which the author is currently affiliated.

The purpose of this paper, written before the results of the special Session are known, is only to throw some light on the various proposals put forth during preparatory work for that session, and to attempt to reflect – beyond the specific outcome of this 'round' – some characteristics of the present international development problem. A brief conclusion raises issues of the effectiveness and realism of global approaches and of the ambiguous relationship between the search for global solutions and the diversity of economic realities and interests.

The paper is based mainly on formal and informal documents issued by both developing countries (Group of 77) and developed countries (EEC and OECD sources) and reports of the pertinent UN committee meetings.

12.1 Possible content and modalities of global negotiations

There is no doubt today that most industrialised countries of the OECD have accepted the need to reopen some form of negotiations with the developing countries, or at least to react positively to Third World initiatives for a renewed North-South dialogue. Needless to say, the strongest motivation for this acceptance is to be found in the rather gloomy prospects (4) for the world economy as a whole. A background paper on the world economic situation submitted for the EEC countries by Italy to the first substantive session of the Committee of the Whole, dated April 1980, (5) concluded by stating that in the light of a strongly deteriorating economic situation, aggravated by uncertain prospects, each country might adopt an economic policy dictated by the sole concern of limiting the possible impact of the present crisis on its own activity and national income. The juxtaposition of such individual national policies could not possibly lead to an optimal situation at the world level. Adjustment policies, as required by the new energy situation, may lead to a cumulative and prolonged recession; new protectionist measures would seriously endanger the principle of free trade; budgetary problems would lead to a further reduction of development aid. Unless 'adequate concertations' take place at the world level on the basic elements of the present situation, it may lead to a 'menacing crisis'.

These basic elements for concertation include first of all the search for adequate solutions to the problems raised by *external imbalances* – recycling oil surpluses, and a collective effort to reduce both inflation and the uncertainties about energy. Furthermore, concertation should contribute to loosening the constraints due to scarcity – hampering both economic growth and the decision-making of all economic agents. This constraint applies, first of all, to *energy*, but also to *food*. Thus, in the view of the countries of the European Communities, global negotiations have to evolve around three main themes: external imbalances, energy and food.

A detailed draft agenda for the global negotiations based on these three priority themes was presented by the EEC (and its member states) to the session of the Committee of the Whole (6).

In addition to the position papers submitted to the Committee, several statements of a formal or informal nature made by other OECD countries at the UN, or discussed within the Group on North-South Economic Issues functioning at OECD since autumn 1979, point to the same concept of an agenda for the global negotiations.

The statement made by the representative of Sweden at the April 1980 session also refers to the fact that 'all countries ... are facing exceptional difficulties, although of different character and that [we must] combat tendencies to limit ourselves to national or bilateral solutions ... a truly multilateral effort is necessary'; the paper concludes that '... the agenda has to be selective if [we are] to make concrete progress'; 'food, energy and external balances should be given priority'.

The issues covered by these items would include:

a) *Food:* — Increased agricultural production in the developing countries, supported by technical and financial assistance within a framework of agricultural reform and rural development.
— Concrete elements of a system for improved world food security, including food aid.

b) *Energy:* The global round of negotiations should offer a first opportunity for a thorough exchange of views within the UN on global long-term energy problems, and on measures and policies jointly to manage the transition from oil, taking into account the importance of energy for world economic development, the energy resource situation and the needs and priorities of all groups of countries. It would be extremely useful if the conference could devote some time in an appropriate forum to analysing energy forecasts and, as a second step, to defining the problems that arise from such forecasts for different groups of countries. The analysis of forecasts and the definition of problems should be part of the agenda for the negotiations. Thereby, one could arrive at at common basis for concrete measures. Improved predictability regarding all aspects of the world's energy future is another natural agenda item as is the security of long-term energy supplies for all countries.

c) *External balances:* This new formulation regroups several issues pertaining to bilateral and multilateral economic relations and of a 'negotiable' character. The following items, linked particularly to the debt problem, would be included in the agenda:

— recycling, which will require a major effort by the appropriate institutions in the short and long run;
— the transfer of non-concessional resources;

– official development assistance (ODA): the emphasis is on the least developed countries; it also continues to be seen as a tangible expression of international solidarity;
– fight against protectionist tendencies;
– stabilisation of export income, in particular of commodity producing countries.

Position of the developing countries

The developing countries (Group of 77) expressed a definite idea of the *purpose* of negotiation in all documents: agreement by the international community is to be achieved on 'concrete ... measures designed to ensure new, comprehensive and global solutions ... on the basis of the principles guiding the establishment of the NIEO ...; to 'secure a more rapid development of developing countries', and 'the restructuring of international economic relations'. (7) The *procedure* proposed is a UN conference convened by the General Assembly at a high political level, with universal participation, to function from January 1981 to September 1981. The Conference should meet throughout at UN Headquarters – and result in a 'package agreement'. The agenda, in keeping with the wording of the initial resolution is to cover 'major issues in the fields of (a) raw materials, (b) energy, (c) trade, (d) development, (e) money and finance'.

This approach bears some resemblance to the North/South-Paris conference of 1975: indeed, it seems to combine both a lesson and a legacy from that experiment, which was an attempt to reach a package deal through short negotiating sessions within a limited time-frame. The legacy is the renewed attempt to negotiate a comprehensive agreement at high political level within a limited time-span maintaining, so it is hoped, a *momentum* that no regular UN Committee or Conference can achieve; the lesson drawn from the failure of the Paris conference, however, is that negotiations should be open to all UN Member States and not limited to a selected group of 'negotiators'. Again, issues relating to energy are an integral part of the overall development problem and are not to be treated in isolation. The Group of 77 paper quoted above provides some detailed annotations to the main five agenda items:
– Under 'raw materials', negotiations should complement ongoing work undertaken within UNCTAD, notably the Integrated Programme for Commodities and the Common Fund.
– Under 'energy', emphasis is put on its interrelationship with the other issues; the item includes the concept of transition to new and renewable sources of energy, effective conservation measures, purchasing power of the unit value of energy exports, priority measures in favour of developing countries.
– 'Trade' relates essentially to the issues of protectionism, structural adjustment policies and access by developing countries to the markets of developed countries.
– 'Development' refers to the broadest set of required measures listing food and agriculture (food aid, food security), industry, (deployment, industrial financing, adjustment policies), transport, science and technology and assistance to the least developed countries (establishment of a fund for the least developed countries).

— 'Money and finance' includes the net transfer of resources (ODA, multilateral assistance, non-concessional loans, the debt problem, balance-of-payment financing), the reform of the international monetary system (notably effective and equitable participation of developing countries in the decision-making process), and compensation to developing countries for the effect of imported inflation.

In both proposals, procedure and substance are intimately linked: successful launching and ultimate success of the negotiations seems to require a minimum agreement *ab initio* on agenda and procedure. So far, however, disagreement persists as to both.

Position of Western industrial countries

To the industrialised countries, the three clusters of subjects, as proposed (food, energy and external imbalances), respond to the criteria of priority and of urgency, and appear, at least to some extent, to be susceptible to resolution through a global negotiating process. This implies, on the 'procedural' side of the argument, that other matters contained in the Group of 77 concept ought not to be debated outside the existing institutional fora; first of all it was repeatedly stated that the subject of money and finance should only be discussed within the IMF. Matters concerning trade should not be removed from GATT — and UNCTAD. More generally, global negotiations should not duplicate current work within other UN institutions and, in fact, should consist only of an initial conference to give guidance at a political level to the continuing process, and, of a final negotiating session that would attempt to bring the whole 'package' together.

Although our analysis is necessarily limited to the present 'state of play' based on initial position papers, it sufficiently exposes the magnitude of disagreement between the industrialised countries and the developing countries. The different proposals are summarised schematically in the *Annex.*

In fact, disagreement on procedure and agenda reflects to a large extent the fundamental differences as to the aims and purposes of negotiations. For the developing countries, as has been consistently stated since the VIth Special Session of the General Assembly, it is the very structure of international economic relations that has to be changed. To the OECD countries, on the other hand, the dominant issues remain energy, and the slow growth prospects of their own economies; it is considered desirable to maintain a dialogue with the developing countries, but politically difficult to agree on anything that implies firm and quantified commitments within a specific time-frame.

12.2 Outlook — limits to global negotiations?

Any attempt at assessing the chances of success or the risks of failure of an initiative that may amount to an intensified phase of development talks during 1981 should be based on two essential sets of considerations:

First of all, international cooperation for development is a long-term process; it is a permanent component of international economic as well as political relations. Against this background, however, trends and changes can be perceived: the present situation is certainly very different from that of ten years ago. It is characterised by the persistent combination of inflation and unemployment in the industrialised countries, by shifts in the international division of labour and industrial production (states protect against each other the competing production of subsidiaries of the same transnational corporation), by the consequences of what has been described as 'the energy revolution', and, predominantly in the developed countries, by the emergence of new values and aspirations linked to the concepts of 'quality' of life and 'quality' of environment.

These changes are not only quantitative; they affect the very structure of economic realities and thus call for changes in the structure of economic relations. Indeed, all recent attempts to apply earlier solutions to achieve a *status quo ante,* e.g. for unemployment or inflation, work only temporarily or not at all. This applies to national as well as to international measures and also gives a more precise meaning to the concept of 'interdependence'.

The second consideration is that there is no central economic decision-making power; there is no single 'motor' to the world economy. Economic decision-making in industrialised countries is essentially based on three sets of factors whose inter-relationship has changed; the first and predominant one arises from the needs and pressures of the national economy — whose needs and pressures, and their effects, are most immediately perceived; the second is the relationships between industrialised countries, where a steadily growing machinery of consultation, both bilateral and multilateral, co-ordinates economic decision-making and forecasts the potential reciprocal effects of any measure adopted; the third set of factors is given by the 'rest of the world', i.e. notably the developing countries. The major change that occurred in the 1970s refers to their role. Indeed, developing countries have over the last decade increasingly emerged as actors in the international economic environment — both as a group and, for some, as individual nations, notably as competitors on world markets. Their raw materials, their markets and their labour are part of the international economic system. This means that not only do the decisions taken by industrialised countries affect the rest of the world economy, but also that decisions taken by developing countries affect industrialised countries, individually and as a group. As a result, the perception of absolute raw material dependence, and of relative supply vulnerability — notably of Europe and Japan — has become a permanent policy factor in relation to all raw material producing countries. Actors have thus become more numerous and also entered more fields of the international economy since the early 1970s.

The conclusions to be drawn from these two sets of considerations is first of all that a serious attempt has to be made to establish new workable structures for international economic relations. The second conclusion is that the participation of all actors has to be ensured at all levels.

These conclusions point to both the strength and the limits of a negotiating process to take place within the framework of the United Nations. At present, the elements of a feasible package, or the substance of possible trade-offs at a world level, cannot be very clearly determined. Energy, for example, is no doubt a subject of vital concern to all groups of countries, developed, developing, oil exporters and importers, free-market and centrally planned economies. Nonetheless, the question has to be asked whether in fact the industrialised countries, and OPEC, are ready to enter into multilateral energy negotiations with definite negotiating positions for a long-term commitment. Thus, if a bargain is to be struck between OPEC and the industrialised countries, it does not seem very clear what the latter can offer in order to obtain predictable prices and supplies of oil. Even if energy were to be the only item on the agenda, all issues of economic growth and development, of finance and industry, would necessarily have to be raised in its context.

The limits are therefore not related to the number or definition of agenda items, but to the intentions of the negotiating partners and to their own readiness to act.

References

(1) General Assembly Resolution 34/138.

(2) Both the sixth and seventh special sessions (1974 and 1975) were devoted to issues of development.

(3) The initiative to request the industrialised countries to enter again into specific negotiations on 'major issues in the field of raw materials, energy, trade, development, money and finance', 'within the UN system' and 'within a specified time-frame' had emerged at the VIth Summit of the Non-aligned Countries (NAC) in September 1979 (Economic Resolution No. 9); the proposal was accepted by the Group of 77 and reformulated into General Assembly Resolution 34/138, adpted by consensus in December 1979. It was agreed that the global round would be prepared — as regards both procedure and content — by the Committee of the Whole which was to complete its work by August 1980.

(4) To some extent, the underlying hypothesis of the Report of the Independent Commission on International Development Issues under the Chairmanship of Willy Brandt, *North-South: A Programme for survival* (Pan Books, London and Sydney, 1980) is also defined as 'Unity to avert catastrophe' ('Current trends point to a sombre future for the world economy and international relations', p. 46). Other approaches developed in the Brandt Report, however, are based on some more positive definitions of interdependence, and on the concept of solidarity. See also: 'Neue Impulse für den Nord-Süd-Dialog? Vorbereitung der Globalverhandlung in der UNO'. *Neue Zürcher Zeitung,* 17 April 1980, p. 13).

(5) (A/AC.191/I/1980/CRP.2) The Committee held two more sessions in May and June 1980.

(6) A/AC.191/I/1980/CRP.3 (April 1980)

(7) Proposals by the Group of 77 (A/AC.191/I/1980/CRP. 1. 31 March 1980)

Proposed procedures for global negotiations

Procedural topic	Group of 77 position (G-77)	EEC position	US position
I. The Global Body	Creation of Conference on Global Economic Cooperation for Development	Creation of centralised body for overall guidance of negotiations	Continuation of Committee of the Whole
A. Membership	All UN members to participate equally; Non-government bodies representing LDC interests to be inivited	All countries who wish to participate in UN specialised fora may do so; all relevant non-governmental bodies to be invited	Same as EEC
B. Mandate	(1) Negotiate resolutions leading to (2) package agreement to which all participants committed	(1) Global agreement forming the basis for (2) appropriate measures of implementation	(1) Generalised resolutions with agreed objectives (2) Summarise results in an integrated and coherent manner
C. Decision-making	Unclear (Reference to commitment on final package)	Unknown	Consensus
II. Organisation of Work			
A. Centralisation/ Decentralisation	Conference should be centralised in New York	Decentralisation and maximum use of existing specialised bodies	Same as EEC
B. Relationship to other negotiating bodies	Reinforce ongoing negotiations; ongoing negotiations should not interfere with Global Negotiations; impasses brought to Global Negotiations	May give impetus to other negotiations, facilitate conclusion of agreements.	No interference with ongoing negotiations
C. Subsidiary bodies	Creation of subcommittees under conference	Establishment of non-duplicative ad hoc groups	Use existing UN system fora
1. Energy	Conference subcommittee	Ad hoc group	Leave open for discussion
2. Universality	All UN members present with equal voting rights	Unknown	UN system fora open to all nations who wish to join
III. Time Frame	January 5 – September 11, 1981	Completed before 36th UN General Assembly (same as G-77)	Same as G-77 and EEC

Chapter 13

EAST-WEST-SOUTH PATTERNS OF TRADE

Göran Ohlin*

13.1 North-South, East-West in the World Economy?

Although there were occasional references to the rich North and the poor South of the world in earlier years, it was only during the Paris CIEC talks in 1977–78 that 'North-South' became a concept. The Paris talks were a political exercise from which the Soviet Union and her allies had been excluded. It is ironic to recall that only slightly earlier an attempt had been made to bury the notion that international politics must be seen in terms of an East-West conflict between the Soviet Union and the United States. Attention was then drawn to the multipolar nature of the situation and the new power of Europe, Japan, and China.

North-South came to refer to the polarisation of the negotiating process in the United Nations and other international organisations, where Group B and the Group of 77 remain locked in combat over issues of international economic reform, with the Soviet Union and China on the sidelines. As the years go by, even the terms North and South seem in many ways less and less meaningful. In their everyday dealings the countries of all parts of the world find new partners. The disparate interests of the industrialised countries in Group B are asserting themselves, and the oil-exporting countries and the NICs (Newly Industrialising Countries) are emerging from the Group of 77 as new elements on the map of international economic policy.

Yet it would be rash to write off the simple distinctions entirely. Economically, there is still a poverty curtain between North and South, although its boundary may be in the process of shifting. And on this view of the world, the Soviet Union and her European allies belong to the North by virtue of their economic achievements. In another sense it is equally undeniable that the economic system of those countries sets them apart from the rest of the world.

Thus, it makes some sense to speak of an East-West-South division of the world economy, and this paper will explore some – but only some – aspects of their increasingly complex interaction.

* University of Uppsala, Sweden

North-East or South-East?

The Soviet Union and her CMEA allies in Europe are certainly industrialised but the Soviet Union itself contains vast regions that might be described as underdeveloped, and some of the East European countries are only at the beginning of their industrialisation. On purely economic criteria the CMEA countries will on most scales lie close to the borderline between developed and developing countries. The per capita income of the USSR in 1977 is estimated (in terms comparable with international accounting concepts) at some $ 3000 and that of other CMEA countries as slightly lower, except for the German Democratic Republic which comes close to $ 5000.

The income bracket of $ 2500 – 3500 is precisely the twilight zone where the poor North, e.g. Greece and Spain, rub shoulders with the affluent South.

In this paper, the 'East' means Eastern Europe, including the USSR, but not the Far East and Mainland China. The 'West' is shorthand for 'the industrialised market economies', i.e. the OECD – often called the North although it includes both Japan and Australia and New Zealand. The 'South' is short for the non-oil exporting developing countries, lately termed NOPECs in contrast to the major oil-exporters who, although they are developing countries, are thought and spoken of as a distinct group here shown as OPEC in the tables.

The intermediate position, economically speaking, of the East lends an additional perspective to the essentially political statement made by the USSR at the Seventh Special Assembly of the United Nations in 1975:

> We shall never accept, neither in theory nor in practice, the notion that the world could be divided into poor and rich, into North and South, putting the Socialist countries in the same box as the capitalist ones.

13.2 The network of international trade

International trade gives rise to far more statistics than other aspects of economic life, and the result is a flow of laborious calculations of the distribution of each country's exports among other countries, of the share of crude fertiliser and other products in each country's trade, and countless other pieces of mostly dispensable information. Comparisons of one foreign-trade statistic with another may serve a descriptive purpose, but for an understanding of the role and determinants of trade such statistics are obviously not sufficient by themselves.

For one thing it is clear that in a broad view of international economic geography, resource use, and industrial location, foreign trade cannot be seen in isolation from domestic trade and production. To compare foreign trade patterns of sovereign states, without recalling that some are continental in size, count hundreds of millions of inhabitants, and contain vast varieties of natural resources, while others are city states with tiny territories and populations, is quite mindless.

In the case of Eastern trade there is the additional difficulty that the foreign trade of planned economies in the East is in important respects something quite different from foreign trade in market economies. Where government trading agencies are responsible for the bulk of foreign trade and domestic price structures are divorced from world prices, foreign trade is not swayed by the same forces as in the mixed economies in other parts of the world. In some respects, foreign trade in the East obviously serves the same function of participating in the international division of labour, but how and to what extent it serves this function are open questions, and it also serves different functions of a more political nature. In spite of all that has been written about Eastern trade, it can hardly be said that there is a clear model or paradigm for it.

In spite of the interest of many Eastern planners in 'planimetric' methods of optimising foreign trade patterns, there seems to be no decision-making arrangement or system of incentives designed to make it likely that import and export decisions result in gains from trade in the simple sense that the resource cost of exports is less than that of imports. Instead, the accounts of policies and practices of Eastern foreign trade give the impression that cost considerations play a subordinate role compared with the many other objectives pursued in foreign trade.

Not so long ago the most striking thing about Eastern trade was the relative lack of it. The autarkic orientation of the USSR was quite explicit, and even trade among the Eastern countries was modest. An attempt to assess its volume by historical standards was made in the 1960s by Rune Hellberg, then with the ECE. Looking at the prewar foreign trade of the East European countries and extrapolating them, he concluded that intra-trade between the European CMEA countries was only one-fifth of what it used to be. (1)

But ever since Stalin's death international trade has gained ground in the planning philosophy of the Soviet Union and its allies. A crude measure of the role of foreign trade is the ratio of exports or imports to GNP, and with all due qualifications for the difficulties of translating material product into GNP, and for other statistical pitfalls, it seems clear that foreign trade ratios of Eastern countries are now at least in the same league as those of other countries. The foreign trade flows of the Soviet Union seem to be only some 5 per cent of GNP, but other large countries too are small traders. In spite of recent increases the US in 1976 had an import ratio of 8 per cent; that of India was about 7 per cent. As for the other European CMEA countries, their foreign trade ratios clustered in 1976 around 20 per cent, which happened also to be the trade ratio of West Germany.

However, if the volume of overall foreign trade in Eastern countries is roughly comparable to that of other industrial countries, it is well known that much of it consists of trade among themselves. Some such tendency is to be expected, as trade with neighbouring countries looms large in the accounts of all countries. One must look a bit more closely at the pattern of trade.

In the world trade matrix in *Table 13.1* the flows of trade inside and between the major groupings of the world economy are indicated. A simple test sometimes applied is to see how closely the exports from a region correspond with the pattern of total imports by other regions. If exports flowed 'neutrally' to markets of the world in proportion to their size, the exports of all regions would show the same pattern. We might call this a 'null hypothesis'. *Table 13.1* shows that in fact the exports of West and South conform fairly closely to this hypothesis. Thus, in 1976, West accounted for 69 per cent of total world imports, and 72 per cent of the exports of West and 69 per cent of the exports of South went to West. The shares going to other regions were also fairly close to those for world exports in the bottom line of *Table 13.1*.

Table 13.1

World Trade Matrix, 1976

Billion dollars

EXPORTS	IMPORTS: West	OPEC	South	East	World
West	465 (72 %)	55 (9 %)	88 (14 %)	37 (6 %)	645 (100 %)
OPEC	105 (80 %)	0	25 (19 %)	2 (2 %)	132 (100 %)
South	83 (69 %)	6 (5 %)	23 (19 %)	8 (7 %)	120 (100 %)
East	28 (30 %)	4 (4 %)	11 (12 %)	52 (55 %)	95 (100 %)
World	681 (69 %)	65 (7 %)	147 (15 %)	99 (10 %)	992 (100 %)

Note: The figures have been derived from *Table 7* in GATT, *International Trade 1976/77*. 'North' is what is there called Industrial Market Economies plus Australia and New Zealand. 'OPEC' is Oil-exporting Developing Countries: 'South' consists of Other Developing Countries. 'East' is there called Eastern Trading Area; it includes China but this makes only a small difference.

East, on the other hand, showed a completely different pattern. Its exports to the South were comparable, proportionately speaking, to those from West and from the world as a whole. But it exported vastly less to West and correspondingly more to itself than the null hypothesis would imply. Although East accounted for only 10 percent of world imports, it took 55 per cent of its own exports.

The comparison may be pushed a step further. On the null hypothesis the pattern of trade would in 1976 have been that of *Table 13.2*. (The null hypothesis could also be said to mean that imports from other regions will be proportional to their shares in world exports. (2)) In *Table 13.3* the actual pattern is compared with that of the null hypothesis. A percentage of 100 represents complete agreement. Apart from the lack of trade inside OPEC the most striking result is the deviation of East. Other flows show percentages in a relatively narrow band around 100 but that of East is over 500.

Table 13.2

Null-Hypothesis Trade Matrix, 1976

Billion dollars

EXPORTS	IMPORTS West	OPEC	South	East	World
West	443	42	96	64	645
OPEC	91	9	20	13	132
South	82	8	18	12	120
East	65	6	14	9	95
World	681	65	147	99	992

Table 13.3

World Trade: Actual/Null Hypothesis, 1976

Percentages

EXPORTS	IMPORTS West	OPEC	South	East	World
West	105	130	92	57	100
OPEC	116	0	128	15	100
South	101	76	129	67	100
East	43	69	78	548	100
World	100	100	100	100	100

A comparison of this kind provides at least a provisional benchmark without which figures for the distribution of trade tell us very little. Indeed, they are often abused. In the North-South dialogue it is not infrequently found objectionable that 70 percent of the exports of South go to West while only some 15 percent of the exports of West go to South. It is considered a source of dependency, an indication of the lopsidedness of the world economy. In a sense it is precisely that, and the income levels underlying this pattern may well be considered objectionable, but the pattern of trade is certainly comprehensible in the light of *Table 13.1*. Similarly, the volume of South-South trade, which is of the order of 20 per cent, is sometimes found to be objectionably small in view of the interest in promoting economic cooperation among developing countries. While it may well be below its future potential, intra-South trade is actually, as *Table 13.3* shows, slightly higher than the overall pattern of world trade might make one expect.

On the other hand, one must not press this simple analysis too far. It contains a good deal of statistical sleight-of-hand. The figures of the null hypothesis are weighted averages, and the dominance of the trade of the West is such that its ratios are bound to fall close to the averages, and small percentage deviations from the null hypothesis for large flows are bound to be offset by large deviations in small flows. But even with this caveat, the comparisons do not seem to be entirely without interest.

Is the dominance of intra-bloc trade in the East primarily the result of political autarky and avoidance of dependence on outside sources of supply, or is it due to the greater ease of agreement and cooperation between countries that manage and plan their economies in the same manner? Whatever the answer, it seems reasonable to make a very sharp distinction between the intra-trade of the East, in which trade flows are incorporated in the five-year plans and a certain pattern of industrial specialisation is pursued, and the trade outside CMEA in which other considerations play a greater role and considerable instability from year to year tends to prevail. If planned targets guide intra-trade, the failure to meet plan targets often explains the recourse to outside sources in order to meet shortfalls in food or other important categories. The import of technology also plays a great role, not only in the trade with licences which is of course not shown here, but also in the trade in manufactures.

Finally, political considerations are bound to matter more than in market economies when trade itself, as in Eastern countries, is seen as a form of economic cooperation resting on bilateral mutual agreements.

All these considerations put their stamp on Eastern trade both with West and South and make it necessary to see Eastern trade as in many important ways a different phenomenon from other trade flows in the world economy.

13.3 The composition of trade

The structure of international trade, and especially the relative shares of primary commodities and manufactures, has always invited much speculation, mostly based on geopolitical premises or on some implicit notions of the nature of economic growth. To possess a wide range of primary commodities within one's boundaries is obviously a good thing, but to rely either on exports or on imports of them is regarded as less satisfactory, whereas exports of manufactures are cherished.

The composition of trade is certainly important in numerous ways — different categories of exports are more or less sensitive to demand fluctuations, and disruptions of import supplies may be more or less serious. But it is dangerous to attach much importance to crude categories like primary commodities and manufactures. Stereotyped mercantilist notions still haunt discussions of this subject. Commodity exports are often associated with low degrees of development and exports of manufactures with advanced industrialisation, but the facts are not so simple. In 1976 primary commodities made up 85 per cent of the exports from Australia and New Zealand but only 70 per cent from the non-OPEC South.

Looking at world flows between major regions (*Diagrams 13.1* and *13.2*), one is in fact struck by the prevalence of substantial flows of both manufactures and commodities in almost all directions. The major exceptions are that OPEC exports no manufactures and that exports of manufactures by the South to the East are insignificant. In order to find the pattern of trade characteristic of many developing countries — dependence on a few export commodities, and heavy imports but no exports of manufactures — one has to go much beyond the regional classification used here and look at the least developed countries in the South.

It may seem somewhat surprising that East is a net supplier of primary commodities to all other regions. It is also a major importer of some essential materials such as bauxite and alumina. In the future it may come to import other minerals such as phosphate, lead, zinc, and molybdenum. What attracts greater attention and much speculation is its future need of energy supplies. In spite of the efforts to achieve self-sufficiency in food East also remains subject to wide swings in harvests and has recently, as is only too well known, been a very big importer. Western speculations about these matters often seem to underestimate the flexibility of 'economic needs', especially in an economic region of the size of the East. That Eastern countries, or any other, choose to import food or other supplies should often not be taken to mean more than that it seems advantageous compared to other options.

It is of interest to international economic reform attempts that the East, although it exports a variety of primary commodities, has not been anxious to enter into arrangements with other commodity exporters or to align itself with the South in the demand for international measures to stabilise commodity prices. Indeed, to break into markets or increase its exports, the East has often priced its products below world market levels. The low Soviet oil prices were in fact an important factor in the creation of the OPEC

Diagram 13.1

The network of trade in manufactures, 1976
billion dollars

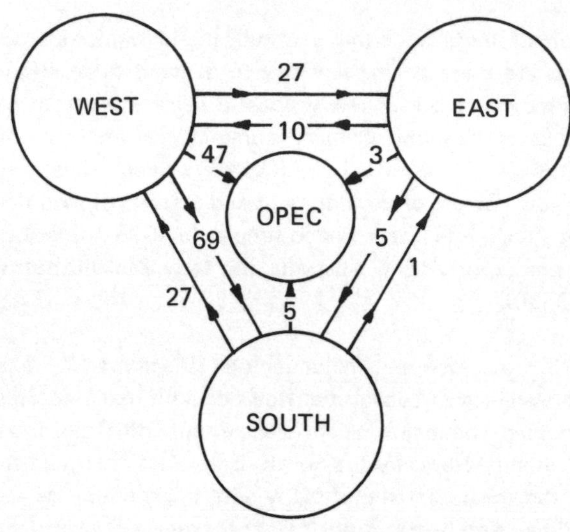

Diagram 13.2

The network of trade in primary commodities, 1976
billion dollars

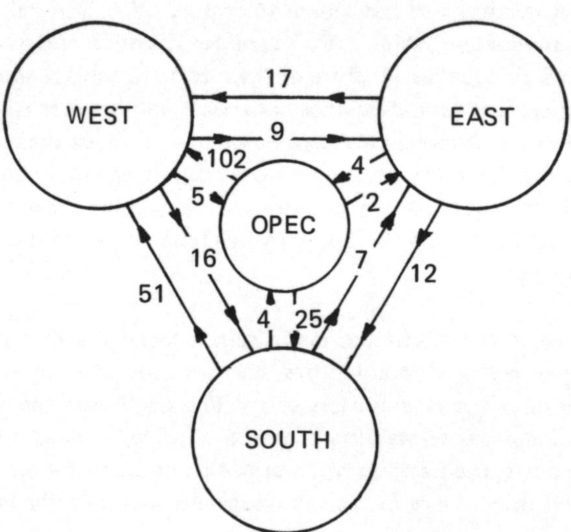

in 1960. One of the positions taken by East in these matters is to advocate, as a preferred alternative to buffer stock arrangements, more widespread use of long-term contracts, which is its own way. It is also the way of many of the transnationals in international commodity markets when they impose on those markets patterns of vertical integration that can also be found in the East.

Looking at world trade flows in primary commodities with the same technique as that already applied to total flows, the results are surprisingly similar (*Table 13.4*). Except for commodity exports from the South to OPEC which were quite small but nonetheless twice as large as expected from a null hypothesis, the major deviations were again in the trade of the East and traceable to its large intra-trade.

Table 13.4

World trade in primary commodities: Actual/Null Hypothesis, 1976

Percentages

EXPORTS	IMPORTS: West	OPEC	South	East
West	107	130	72	78
OPEC	106	0	129	20
South	92	209	108	122
East	65	110	95	441

As to manufactures, one may recall the passions evoked in the North-South confrontations by the share of manufactures in imports from the South. In the most simple-minded versions of this dispute, a low share of manufactures in imports from the South is interpreted as an indication of protectionist policies. In fact, those shares are the highest for imports from countries against which protectionist measures have indeed been invoked, and it is obvious that supply conditions are of greater importance in this context. Analysis of the world trade matrix for manufactures indeed suggests (*Table 13.5*) that exports of manufactures from the South to the West were roughly in proportion to average import market size. The intra-trade of the South was rather higher than might be expected, while this was offset by very weak South-East exports.

Table 13.6 summarises the shares of manufactures in total exports. It actually suggests that the share of manufactures in exports from the East is somewhat lower than that of the South. However, UNCTAD figures seem to differ from those of the GATT on this point, which is a salutary reminder of the arbitrariness of the concepts to which sometimes great political significance is ascribed.

Table 13.5

World trade in manufactures: Actual/Null Hypothesis, 1976

Percentages

EXPORTS \ IMPORTS	West	OPEC	South	East
West	108	105	99	49
OPEC	154	0	0	0
South	99	103	165	21
East	27	58	62	599

Table 13.6

Share of manufactures in total trade, 1976

Per cent

EXPORTS \ IMPORTS	West	OPEC	South	East	World
West	73	85	78	73	75
OPEC	1	0	0	0	1
South	33	67	43	13	35
East	36	75	45	73	29
World	56	83	57	67	59

Mechanical analyses of trade patterns, no matter how hard they are pushed, cannot reveal whether trade was beneficial or not, or how the gains from trade were divided. But in conditions of central planning one can easily imagine that they acquire a significance of their own through their influence on administrators. Thus, it can probably be considered well established that a regime entrusting trade relations to mixed commissions supervising bilateral trade will engender a strong bias in favour of bilateral balancing. This may, in the special circumstances of Eastern trade, be virtually inevitable. The permanent shortage of convertible foreign exchange in Eastern economies seems to be beyond doubt, and it must be either a deliberate or an unintentional result of the institutional arrangements. The exchange rate does not enter, and exports seem to be held back essentially by the lack of experience of buyers' markets. The East is an exporter of technology, in some areas even to the West, but in overseas marketing it is well known to run into problems of quality, finishing, reliability, service, and habits of mind. This would make little difference if import demand could be held back sufficiently, but in an essentially administrative system for the assignment of import priorities this does not seem possible. The result is permanent pressure on the balance of payments and shortage of foreign exchange. This gives rise to the well-known return to barter in the form of compensation agreements and other arrangements for payment in kind.

The technical details of such arrangements are best left to specialists, but they also raise interesting questions of general relevance. Does the East gain or lose from these ways of doing business? It undoubtedly pays a price, and one suspects a heavy one, for the marketing tasks it imposes on Western companies who are not normally in the business of selling the goods they are sometimes obliged to accept in settlement. And Western importers or even investors are not likely to be enthusiastic about the opportunity to repay in kind.

But in the South the situation is sometimes very different. The permanent shortage of foreign exchange is a widely spread syndrome for reasons that deserve more study than they have received. Eastern offers to accept repayment in the form of future deliveries of this or that are often most appealing. The other side of the coin is the acceptance of Eastern products, for the most part light manufactures. No matter how seductive such long-term contracts appear when they are first entered into, they usually generate an incessant flow of grievances. Prices and qualities will never seem right, especially in countries which have extensive access to world markets as well. In commercial markets there are time-honoured ways of settling these problems, but in Eastern trade grievances become politicial issues to be handled through political channels, as there is no other machinery for their settlement.

It is no wonder that reform of foreign-trade arrangements has long been a live issue in the East, and that some countries have gone rather far in trying to make it possible for importers and exporters to enter into direct contacts with their trading partners in other regions of the world; this at least serves to reduce some of the misunderstandings that otherwise befoul the tortuous chain of communication between buyers and sellers in trade with the East.

13.4 Complementarity and industrial cooperation

One is easily tempted to see great potential in various triangular patterns of trade between East, West, and South. Do they not all have their comparative advantages given from the outset – the West with its high technology and surplus of capital, East with intermediate technology and much cheaper labour, while South should offer the cheapest labour of all and a wealth of resources? As the preceding inspection of world trade patterns, cursory as it was, made very clear, such a pattern is not so far obvious. Nor is there much reason to expect it in the future. In the world of today international trade patterns reflect resource endowments, economic and technical development, and political conditions. Of course all international trade is based on complementarity in a broad sense, but industrial societies are so complex and the rate of technical change so rapid that it would be futile to search for patterns of this kind without an examination of each item of world trade.

However, in the last decades the Eastern countries opened a new window for external trade in the form of so-called industrial cooperation. For the most part this is the heading under which Western firms have been invited to construct a variety of plants in metallurgical, chemical, automobile, and other sectors, with compensation agreements specifying payment in the form of packages of various products. Industrial cooperation of this kind seems to have been a successful idea. It is only reasonable to consider it an Eastern variant of Western foreign investment, though by Western standards in unusually restricted forms. By Eastern standards it has opened a gate to more direct contacts between buyers and sellers. So-called tripartite industrial cooperation involves both West and South. It usually does involve precisely the elements of complementarity that seem plausible.

Tripartite projects seem usually to have originated in tenders from developing countries. They have involved the supply of technology, management, and some equipment from a Western company, more equipment and construction work from CMEA countries, and sometimes certain inputs from the developing country ordering the turnkey plant. These arrangements were institutionalised in the early 1970s and the number of projects increased very rapidly. They have played an insignificant role in trade patterns so far but are of great symptomatic interest (3).

It is true of international trade in general that companies find it advantageous to internalise the foreign trade element, i.e. the transaction across national boundaries. That crossing always gives rise to transactions costs that may easily exceed the explicit barriers raised by tariffs and quotas. In the case of Eastern trade such transactions costs are known to become very high indeed, and given the heaviness of foreign trade administration in Eastern countries one can easily see the rise of industrial cooperation in general as conforming to a general trend from trade to investment. In the case of tripartite industrial cooperation, i.e. East-West cooperation in investments in the South, one can also see the appeal to developing countries: such cooperation may offer an alternative to reliance on Western transnationals and hold out a politically balanced solution. Apart from that, there should be unbeatable combinations of Western technology and Eastern costs. The limit to this kind of cooperation does not seem to be its economic interest but rather the extent of the willingness of the East to go ahead along these lines.

13.5 Aid and trade

The pattern of world trade in the late 1970s required considerable capital movements. *Table 13.1* gives an idea of the balances to be financed. No fallacy is more dangerous in policy-making than the assumption that existing deficits reveal a state of 'need', but the second worst fallacy is probably to assume that any and all deficits can be 'adjusted' away without very painful consequences to surplus countries as well.

In the world of today, the South is in genuine deficit on two accounts. It is so much poorer than the rest of the world that there is a genuine need to transfer resources to developing countries in the interests of accelerating a levelling of world incomes. Then there is another reason for capital flows to the Third World: by all standards it is short of capital, and there should be opportunities to use more of it. These two aspects of the rich-poor problem in the world bedevil the relations between West and South. The 'aid' of the West is carefully watched to make sure that it does not contain self-seeking elements of conventional interest loans. In the meantime, commercial lending from the West to the South has multiplied.

East-South relations are simpler in this respect. Financial aid from the East to the South is very small. According to DAC it was in 1977 some 3 percent of all ODA, and an infinitesimal fraction of Soviet and East European GNP. However, it has been concentrated on a fairly small number of recipients, and it is clear that for some of them Eastern aid has been of genuine and lasting importance. But it is all tied aid, and the terms have been harder than those of DAC countries. Repayment is of course also tied; usually it is in the form of commodities or products from the aid project.

In Western eyes, CMEA development assistance is totally inadequate both in quantity and quality, and frequent admonitions to do better in sharing the burden are delivered by Western statesmen. Such statements may sometimes be addressed to the South and intended to suggest that even if Western aid falls short of the targets set for it, it is at least vastly greater than that of the East; but there is also a genuine political interest in making international development assistance a more universal and cooperative venture. It is a mistake to seek a dialogue with the East on the premise that its aid is small and inferior. In the Eastern view the aid from capitalist countries is so flawed that its volume only makes things worse. The very features that draw criticism from the West – for instance, the tying of Eastern aid – seem to Eastern donors so natural that the criticism is incomprehensible. In the aid practices, many of the differences between Western and Eastern social and economic systems are thus reflected, and the difficulty of reconciling them is sharply exposed.

Towards more and better trade?

It seems reasonable to conclude that the most striking feature of East-West-South trade is the feeble development of the Eastern links. Even when the policies of centrally planned economies favour international economic cooperation, too many features of their economic organisation make it difficult to locate and exploit the opportunities for beneficial trade. Significant improvement would thus seem to be linked to institutional change. The experience of industrial cooperation suggests that more direct contacts between firms in the East and their counterparts elsewhere would do much to reduce the costs of ignorance and uncertainty which currently hamper trade. Another essential improvement would be the development of more effective machinery for the settlement of disputes arising in trade between state-trading economies and market economies. This is a task for GATT, in which some of the European CMEA countries are already members.

References

(1) "Some notes on East-West European trade", quoted in Klaus-Heinrich Standke, *Der Handel mit dem Osten,* Baden-Baden, 1968, p. 36.

(2) If a_{ij} are the exports from region i to region j, and a_{io} and a_{oj} are total exports and imports of regions i and j, and a_{oo} is world trade, the null hypothesis for exports is $a_{ij} = (a_{oj}/a_{oo})a_{io}$, and that for imports is identically the same: $a_{ij} = (a_{io}/a_{oo})a_{oj}$.

(3) For a detailed review of Tripartite Cooperation, see Chapter 17 in this volume.

Chapter 14

STRUCTURAL POLICY ISSUES IN PRODUCTION AND TRADE: A WESTERN VIEW

Juergen B. Donges*

The purpose of this paper is to discuss major structural policy issues arising from changes in the international division of labour, technological innovations and energy scarcities. Emphasis will be put on the Western industrial countries. In view of their strength in the world economy, the ways in which they shape their structural policies for production and trade will affect directly or indirectly both the developing and the Eastern European countries.

The major dimensions of the structural problem are first discussed. Subsequently, the characteristics of structural policies in market-oriented economies are described and then the trend towards selective government interventionism. Finally, the case will be made for a positive (rather than a defensive) response to structural change.

14.1 Dimensions of the structural problem

Since the early 1970s, the world economy has been facing several major problems. First, strong inflationary pressures, high unemployment and low rates of capacity utilisation have appeared, not only (as in the past) in most developing countries but also in the highly industrialised countries of Western Europe and in the USA. Second, economic growth has slowed down and become more erratic almost everywhere, even in the East European (CMEA) countries. Third, the quest of Western societies for an improved environment, the sharp increase in oil prices by OPEC, the microelectronic revolution and the upsurge of new sources of supply of manufactured goods from the more industrialised parts of the Third World (the Newly Industrialising Countries, or NICs) have markedly affected both the international competitiveness and the growth prospects of many industries.

If these problems were mainly rooted in a lack of effective demand, as is believed in some respectable quarters, the solution would be obvious. By pursuing expansionary fiscal and monetary policies, the advanced countries (particularly the EEC, the USA and Japan) would increase imports faster than exports and thus create additional effective demand for both the developing and the CMEA countries ('locomotive theory'). This approach is bound to fail, however, if during sustained economic growth the systemic

* Kiel Institute of World Economics, Kiel, FRG

rigidities cause bottlenecks in the restructuring of production and employment. In this case, expansionary demand-management policies would presumably have inflationary effects rather than growth effects; they would retard structural changes rather than promote them; and they would inhibit the rapid integration of developing countries into international trade in manufactures rather than facilitate it. While it may still be true that the rate of growth of the world economy is determined to a large extent by the rate of economic growth of the advanced countries, a growth of potential output (not just of demand) at reasonable levels will take place in the medium and long run only if the national economies undergo growth-oriented changes in the structure of production, i.e.

– towards new lines of skill-intensive activities, including a modern service sector, in the USA, Japan and the EEC countries;

– towards upgraded consumer and investment goods in the NICs and in Eastern Europe;

– towards the diversification of agriculture and the processing of both renewable and non-renewable natural resources in those developing countries which still specialise in the production of a few commodities for export.

While changes in the structure of production and employment are nothing exceptional in a growing world economy – as a matter of fact they are even necessary for sustaining growth – the speed with which they are occurring might possibly exceed the ability and willingness of national societies to adjust to these changes. This is the crux of the problem. It can be illustrated with respect to three major sources of structural changes: technology, energy and foreign competition.

Technology has always been a major determinant of structural changes. From economic history we know, however, that in addition to more or less continuous technical progress there have been huge breakthroughs from time to time. They have led to long waves of investment and growth ('Kondratieff-Schumpeter-cycles'), with upswings and downswings lasting about 50 years. (An empirical analysis relating to the German economy is provided by Glismann (1)). Steam power, railway construction, steel production, electricity, automobiles, aircraft, and petrochemicals induced such upswings in the past. The microelectronic technology, which has recently entered the stage of application, might push world economic development into a new long-lasting upswing, with profound changes in the structure of production of goods and services and in the way in which they are distributed.

Though our knowledge about the prospective economic impact of microelectronics, once they become diffused, is still rather limited and though analysts have so far reached conflicting conclusions, it is safe to say that this new technology displays a number of distinct characteristics, which make it revolutionary in nature (2). These characteristics refer to (a) the broad range of applications not only in industry but also in the service sector; (b) the potential for substantial cost reductions, for increases of labour and capital productivity and for savings of raw material and energy input per unit of output; and (c) the great flexibility and reliability of the production and distribution processes. The structural implications of microelectronics may thus consist of (a) a greater product differentiation; (b) a regional decentralisation of production units; (c) shifts of resources towards industries and services which apply microprocessors the fastest; and (d) a revitalising of industries which had lost international competitiveness due to rapidly increasing labour costs.

Changes in the structure of production will also lead to changes in the structure of employment, inducing job displacement in some sectors and job creation in others. Whether overall employment will decrease or increase is a matter of conjecture at this stage. On the one hand, there is much concern about the negative employment effects of microelectronics in the West and the South. On the other hand, it seems not unreasonable to emphasise the possible increases in overall employment arising from new products and services based on microprocessors. Negative employment effects may predominate if output is kept constant and if the speed at which microprocessors are applied in practice is high. One must not overlook, however, that, once output based on microprocessors increases, prices might decrease; thus, demand expands and employment rises after all. The stronger the capability of technically skilled entrepreneurs to translate microelectronic-based innovations into products for mass consumption, the larger will be the net employment gains. It is likely, however, that improved employment prospects will mainly affect skilled labour, whereas the prospects are bleak for the less educated employees.

Assuming that microelectronics hold prospects of significant net benefits for the world economy as a whole, it still remains to be seen who captures these gains the fastest. Given the international distribution of top-échelon scientists, engineers and R & D capacities, one may expect a few major industrial countries (USA, United Kingdom, France, FRG, Japan) to lead the manufacturing of the basic hardware, i.e. the integrated circuits on silicon chips. But the software of this technology may also be absorbed quite easily by both the industrial countries of the East and the NICs. For developing countries in general, the microelectronic technology, as far as its software is concerned, may even be more appropriate than the conventional capital-intensive technology which they now import from the West, if only because of the greater flexibility and of the lesser need for complementary indigenous factors (capital and labour) to produce reliable goods and services at satisfactory quality levels. On the whole, however, the applications of microelectronics are so varied that it is difficult to generalise about their effects in developing countries as compared with advanced countries of the West and East.

Energy has become an urgent determinant of adjustment in all oil-importing countries as a result of OPEC's recent price and supply policies. It is generally expected that real oil prices will be rising in the years to come. Furthermore, at least some OPEC countries may slow down output expansion on the grounds that the value of their foreign-exchange surpluses suffers a continuous erosion by world inflation, or because they do not see enough acceptable investment opportunities abroad or because they want to avoid the social strains that might follow the implementation of too ambitious development programmes (Iran-effect). And significant interruptions in supply for political reasons cannot be ruled out.

The structural implications of these developments are straightforward. On the one hand, there are negative effects. To the extent that the profitability of a particular investment carried out in the past rests upon cheap oil supplies, productive capacities will lose international competitiveness and may even become obsolete. Indirectly, high oil prices affect negatively those producers who face a slackening or declining demand for their products because consumers have to spend larger amounts of their income on gasoline and fuel oil. On the other hand, there are positive effects. They will accrue to domestic oil producing industries in the first place. In addition, the beneficiaries include those firms producing goods which can replace oil or which do not require much oil input or which face a highly income-elastic demand in the wealthy OPEC countries. The major area with a potential for benefitting from the energy-induced structural changes is the production of investment goods and the manufacture of insulating building materials. As in the case of microelectronics, the main benefits will accrue to those industries which change their production structure from high to low energy-intensity fast (ahead of their competitors if possible). Industrial countries which have shown a high capacity for product and process innovation in the past (e.g. FRG) may be in a better starting position than countries in which manufacturers have been typically slow in restructuring (e.g. United Kingdom). In no case should one expect, however, that structural adjustment to the oil prices will occur very rapidly. The reason is that the most profitable investment opportunities have still to be searched for, and such a search is time-consuming.

Foreign competition induces structural changes mainly in the USA and Western Europe as a function of the industrialisation strategies which the developing countries pursue and the export policies which the CMEA countries apply. As long as the industrialisation strategy of developing countries is inward-looking. and consists of both effectively promoting import substitution and discriminating against manufactured exports, almost no competitive pressure will be put on workers, firms and regions in the advanced countries. This is the history of the 1950s and early 1960s in most parts of the Third World (3). The lack of foreign trade-induced structural changes in the advanced countries had its counterpart in the developing countries themselves. They run, at different stages, into distorted cost and price structures in the domestic factor and product markets, low degrees of capacity utilisation, excessively capital-intensive processes of production, considerable inefficiencies at the firm level and balance of payment constraints on development.

If, by contrast, the industrialisation strategy of developing countries promotes manufacturing as a whole, not discriminating between the home and the world markets, increased import competition will fall on those sectors within the USA and Western Europe producing the goods which the newcomers might export in large quantities. Export growth could, of course, involve more trade among the developing countries themselves and between the developing and the CMEA countries. But the greatest absorption capacity is still within the highly industrialised countries of the West. A number of developing countries (the NICs) have pursued such policies since the mid-1960s. By doing so, they exploit comparative advantages better, they secure the potential benefits of international specialisation more easily, they can achieve higher levels of productivity and employment and they can obtain more sustained rates of economic growth.

On top of the structural changes induced by the South, the Western industrialised countries have to adjust also to new manufactured supplies from the CMEA countries. Though long isolated from world trade, the dependence on specialised machinery, modern technology and grain from the West has led these countries (first the resource-poor smaller ones, then the Soviet Union) by the mid-1960s to enlarge their export opportunities, including those related to manufactures, to earn hard currency (4). Although the CMEA countries, on average, are relatively better endowed with physical and even human capital than the developing countries as a whole, they compete with the latter in supplying Western industrial countries with traditional labour-intensive goods (such as footwear, clothing and leather manufactures).

However, as compared with the South, the commodity composition of CMEA manufactured exports has been shifting more rapidly to standardised capital-intensive goods, such as electrical equipment, scientific instruments, metalworking machinery, glass manufactures, pulp and paper products. Weiss and Wolter have analysed these changes for trade with the FRG (5). Hence, manufactured trade between East and West has more of an intra-industry nature than West-South trade, where patterns of inter-industry specialisation as yet prevail. The implication is that by expanding their manufactured exports, the developing countries are causing a greater adjustment pressure in the USA and West Europe than do the CMEA countries.

All this means that the changes in the international division of labour, in addition to new conditions set by recent developments in the field of technology and energy, are perceived by the advanced countries as an accumulation of shocks, which create substantial uncertainties in the business community and may induce firms to cut down long-term investment. At the same time, policy-makers in a representative democracy will come under increasing pressure to provide assistance to specific branches or even firms, as shown below (6).

14.2 Structural policies in the market-oriented countries

For long, the governmental approach to structural change consisted, in principle, of interventions at the macro-level. There was a consensus that the market mechanism, in combination with effective price competition, would ensure dynamic efficiency in industry. (This principle was not applied to agriculture and large parts of the tertiary sector, however). In such a system entrepreneurs are charged with the task of responding to structural change. They have to carry the risk of their investments. Consumer acceptance or refusal of goods offered on competitive markets is the ultimate test of whether the investment is a success (yielding a profit) or a failure (leaving a loss). On the other hand, such an approach requires governments to refrain from policies that impede structural change and to shape their policies in a way that properly supports the functioning of the price mechanism, including the provision of an adequate infrastructure for industrial growth and an effective competition policy.

In reality, it has always proved difficult to get such principles applied in a pure form. Even the USA and the FRG, which are often thought to resemble the textbook model of pure market-oriented economies, are no exception. Yet, during the 1950s and 1960s structural policies were rather complementary to the market mechanism. Many of the measures could have been justified on economic grounds at the time they were implemented. However, in general (except in France) they were not based on an analysis of the long-run growth potential of the specific activity or region selected for promotion. Actions were frequently based on partial analytical views and became permanent even if announced as temporary. This means either that the policies did not bring about the expected results or that the favoured interest groups were clever enough to go on justifying any support as in the nation's interest.

In addition to a variety of government measures aiming at promoting private investment in industry, most West European governments created public industrial enterprises or nationalised selected private firms. Among the EEC countries, France, Italy and the United Kingdom went the farthest in this direction, while the FRG exhibits a relatively lower degree of state-ownership in industry (7). If one looks at the sectoral distribution of public industrial enterprises in the advanced countries, it becomes evident that they have clear-cut policy dimensions. In fact, these enterprises are highly concentrated in a few branches. This concentration reveals various political objectives such as: (a) the enlargement of employment opportunities in structurally weak, low-income regions with a large representation of the iron and steel industry, coal mining and shipbuilding; (b) avoiding private monopoly positions in the public utilities (electricity, gas, water); (c) an increased degree of self-sufficiency in goods considered of strategic importance (steel, processed aluminium, machinery, ships, energy); and (d) the acceleration of basic technological innovations (data processing, nuclear energy).

It is questionable whether these objectives have been achieved and, even if they have, whether it was done at the lowest possible cost. While those advocating an expansion of the public sector on ideological grounds will take the accomplishments for granted, the evidence is mixed at best. On average, the performance of public industrial enterprises compares unfavourably with that of private industry. This holds for the rates of return on invested capital as well as on the propensity to undertake product and process innovations. It seems that the lack of effective competition, or the possibility of 'socialising' losses by financing them from taxpayers' money, is not conductive to high economic efficiency at the firm level. In contrast, if public participation in industrial enterprises did not prevent their managements from running them as if they were private, the chances of good performance increased. The experience of the German Volkswagenwerk and the French Renault are cases in point.

14.3 Growing micro-interventions by the advanced countries

Although officially the governments of Western advanced countries still assign to the market mechanism the task of steering structural changes in industry, they have become increasingly involved in this process (8) (9). The deeper structural changes have become, and the weaker the economic outlook, the more both entrepreneurial associations and trade unions have been tempted to demand government assistance; and the harder it has been for a government to resist such demands, particularly when electoral considerations are taken into account. The major micro-interventions consist either in providing protection to domestic industries against imports from low-wage countries, or in granting direct financial assistance to domestic firms, or in a mix of both. They all have in common that they are not neutral among industries but deliberately discriminate among industrial activities and, in some cases, even among firms belonging to the same branch. This is a radical departure from the liberal principles and efficiency criteria that geared (though not perfectly) structural policies in the 1950s and 1960s, when the world economy grew at unparalleled rates (and when whatever structural problems may have been inherent in this rapid growth could be kept below the surface). Governments in the advanced countries are pushing their structural policies into directions which, for long, have been thought typical of developing countries (with the exception of Hong Kong and Singapore), let alone of Eastern Europe where government regulation is an integrated part of the political system.

The issue of protection against imports reveals quite well the significant change in the Western policy framework for industry. Although the advanced countries prospered from the liberalisation of trade in the 1950s and 1960s and owed part of their rapid industrial growth to the advantages of increasing international specialisation, manufactured imports from low-wage countries (including Japan and the Eastern European countries) are now regarded by many as a source of serious market disruption. This holds even for the FRG, which is considered a country with among the most liberal trade policies in Europe.

The system of import protection in the Western industrial countries has always encouraged the production of labour-intensive and raw material-intensive manufactures at the expense of engineering industries – the industries with the highest growth potential. This is clearly shown by the structure of effective rates of tariff protection. They tend to be substantially higher than average for labour and/or raw-material intensive goods and substantially lower for capital-intensive products. The structure is inversely related to the structure of comparative advantage of the advanced countries' industries. The m.f.n. tariff cut agreements reached in the Tokyo Round of multilateral trade policy negotiations (inaugurated in 1973 and completed in 1979) might narrow somewhat the dispersion of effective rates of protection, but only slowly since the tariff reductions, about 35 percent on average, will be distributed over eight years. Moreover, the effective tariff rates on textiles, garments, footwear, furniture and petrochemicals will remain relatively high (10).

Nowadays, however, much more important than tariff protection is non-tariff protection. And it is much more alarming that selective non-tariff protectionism has been proliferating in recent years, thereby by-passing the principles of non-discrimination and multilateralism which have been the keystone of the GATT. Instances are the implementation of new import quotas and so-called anti-dumping duties, the Multi Fibre Arrangement (of 1973, renewed in 1977 and due to be renegotiated in 1981), bilaterally negotiated 'orderly marketing' agreements and 'voluntary' export restraints on a wide number of products – let alone the encouragement by the Commission of the EEC of an international cartelisation of industries to defend market shares against foreign competition (e.g. the Davignon Plan for the steel industry, implemented in 1977) and the French proposal for 'organised free trade' (which is contradictory in itself). The Tokyo Round has not made much progress towards removing this type of import restriction. In addition, the EEC seems determined to remain discriminatory against any particular country from which imports are growing too fast (and, one should add, whose retaliation would be felt least); this amounts to penalising the world's most efficient producers of specific goods.

While it sounds tautological to state that growing imports will adversely affect particular producers, workers and regions in the advanced industrial countries, the impact is frequently exaggerated and not adequately balanced by the positive effects resulting from expanding exports. Moreover, changes in the demand pattern, and productivity increases, have caused much larger adjustment problems and, especially, much more labour displacement. Country studies have been made by UNIDO (11) and OECD (12). The Kiel Institute has undertaken numerous empirical analyses (most recently by Schatz and Wolter (13)) on the employment effects in the FRG, which is the largest single market in Europe for manufactured goods from developing countries. The results clearly show that employment effects would be small. Similar conclusions are reached by Balassa on the basis of a very detailed commodity framework, which has been applied to trade of the OECD, the EEC, the USA and Japan (14). However, the trade impact assumes a different dimension if it is disaggregated and related to the NICs. It then appears that the market-penetration ratios by suppliers from such countries in the advanced industrial countries are well above average in the consumer goods sector, that they affect mainly low-skilled workers and small firms, and that they are highly concentrated in lagging regions. Hence trade in manufactures is still mainly of an inter-industry rather than an intra-industry type. In these circumstances, the import-impacted segments of the population might regard the interfirm, interregional and inter-professional mobility requirements put upon them as an unjust hardship. Politicians who want to be re-elected are obviously tempted to correct such 'injustices'.

Government interference with the operation of the market mechanism at the micro-level has been increased by aid to domestic industries, particularly in the form of direct subsidies, tax relief, special depreciation allowances and credits at preferential terms (15). It appears that in the EEC countries these measures have come into increasing use as substitutes for the loss of national autonomy in trade policy, and to allow governments to pursue more effectively regional policy objectives and to promote research and development activities considered of paramount importance for future industrial growth.

Aids of this kind keep net costs of production below the levels which would otherwise have been incurred and thereby preserve or strenghten the international competitiveness of particular industries or firms. The real effects are hard to assess because statistical information covering the diverse forms of government aids is limited. But scattered evidence suggests that their allocation is highly concentrated in a few branches. This concentration partly reflects regional policy actions, as some of the most benefitted industries are located in lagging regions (coal mining, steel, shipbuilding, aircraft). It also reflects the distribution of assistance to Research and Development (computer equipment, energy, chemicals, machinery, electrical engineering, aircraft). Within these industries, governments have revealed a distinct preference for a few large companies. Small- and medium-sized firms have found it much more difficult to get access to government support for their own R & D efforts. Precisely because of their small size, they cannot afford to lobby for funds as effectively as big companies and they are less able to comply with the many bureaucratic requirements imposed on applicants. Many small- and medium-sized firms have, however, a high reputation as actual or would-be innovators (especially in machinery, electrical equipment and computer technology).

In Western Europe, direct government aid to industry has been officially justified in various ways. One argument stresses the need to fill a technological gap vis-à-vis the USA. Examples of this argument are the aircraft industry and the computer technologies. Sometimes the 'infant industry' case is used as a justification for governmental aid in fields considered vital for the economy as a whole. The nuclear energy industry and other technologically advanced activities have qualified on this ground. A third type of argument revolves around international trade and regards government aid as a necessary tool to correct distortions of competition, in both domestic and foreign markets, which result from production or export subsidies available to foreign suppliers. The steel industry and shipbuilding have requested, and received, assistance on these grounds in most Western countries.

The merits of these arguments are to some extent open to question. The technological gap argument may in fact disguise the political desire to develop some prestige industries. France is the best known example, but the other countries are not far behind. On economic grounds, one may argue that the assisted activities involve positive externalities for the society as a whole. But in this case one would expect a decrease in the amounts of aid received over time, whereas in fact the amounts have increased. The 'infant industry' argument would be more convincing if it rested upon solid analyses of social benefits and costs, which is not the case; they are difficult to undertake anyway for lack of adequate data and information about the future. Then it might make more sense to aid all R & D activities equally in terms of value added rather than to adhere to the principle of project-oriented assistance as practised in most West European countries. Finally, the third argument about correcting for trade distortions would be much more appealing from an economic point of view if the subsidies and other public aid granted were less subjected to policy competition among governments (thereby frequently transforming production subsidies into export subsidies) and were more oriented towards the restructuring of the affected industries.

In sum, even when governments seek in good faith to promote industrial developments considered socially desirable, it is important to recognize that selective public aid to industry may be used defensively, with a strong protectionist or nationalistic bias in practice; and that they may be guided by short-term political expediency, which would seldom bring permanent benefit to the economy. Further, it is likely that the more the state intervenes in the operations of the market the more distortions will be created (for help to one branch or firm will be a charge on the rest) and the more one measure may contradict another. Forces working for repeal of such micro-interventions are usually weak in a representative democracy.

14.4 The case for positive structural response

The slowdown of industrial (and overall economic) growth, and the appearance of persistently high rates of unemployment during the 1970s, together with the oil price explosion and the emergence of new industrial competitors on the world market, has led to public discussion in all Western industrial countries about whether a higher degree of government involvement is needed in the control and direction of industry and investment. The case for more government involvement partly rests upon doubts about the capability of the market mechanism to steer basic structural (rather than small marginal) changes efficiently. It also reflects the extent to which the national societies have become used to getting effective relief from hardships from their governments. And there are also those who are critical of capitalism in any form for ideological reasons and therefore claim omnicompetence for the state, without mentioning the presumably negative effects on individual freedom, initiative and risk-taking.

The case against more government involvement is based on the notion that the government has an information advantage over the market but only as far as its own policies and investment programmes are concerned. By feeding the private sector *ex ante* with this information, government can substantially reduce the degree of subjective uncertainty under which growth-promoting and employment-creating investments have to take place in open economies. This uncertainty results from the fact that in the real world knowledge of future expansion of domestic and foreign demand, and of future changes in comparative advantage, is far from perfect. Why then should bureaucrats, who will normally not personally have to meet capital losses resulting from wrong forecasts, do a better job than private investors, who may go bankrupt if they take unsound investment decisions and who will therefore try to examine as carefully as possible the profit prospects of a particular project? There is no empirical evidence to support faith in a government's superior wisdom. This amounts to saying that while markets frequently operate in an imperfect manner, so do bureaucrats. One cannot justify more government intervention by emphasising the market failures which have been discovered by comparing the price mechanism actually operating with an ideal system which does not exist and has never existed in history (but only in textbooks for didactic purposes).

If a new acceleration of industrial growth is desired by the societies of the advanced industrial countries (and there would seem to be little reason to assume this not to be the case), refusing protection and defensive aids, and promoting structural changes, would be the correct policy. Economic (and industrial) growth has always entailed structural changes of production and employment and will continue to do so. Given the high per-capita income levels in the USA, Western Europe and Japan, resources will be gradually shifted from the industrial to a more modern service sector. This process is taking place already in various countries. In the FRG, for instance, the share of industry in GDP decreased from 52 to 48 percent between 1970 and 1978, while the service sector increased its contribution from 44 to 50 percent. Within industry, the shift will be from low skilled, labour-intensitve goods to activities which are engaged intensively in Research and Development, which utilise human and physical capital to a large extent and which require little raw material input. In a market-oriented economy with uncertainty about the future, it is not possible to specify the branches for which prospects are best. The task of discovering the most promising activities has to be met by imaginative and risk-minded entrepreneurs who are looking for private profits in competition with each other. In view of the factor endowment in the advanced countries, the range of promising activities presumably extends from microelectronics and the miniaturisation of appliances, through energy saving and environmental conservation, to technologically sophisticated investment goods and high-performance telecommunication apparatus, including the production of technical knowledge as such. The details, however, remain unknown *ex ante.*

Industry in the advanced countries must therefore increasingly move towards innovation. This move entails the options of (a) process innovations, aiming at lowering costs and saving or recycling non-renewable resources; (b) product innovations, consisting in moves into the manufacture of new goods facing a high income elasticity of demand; (c) locational innovations, by which production is transferred to countries where environmental costs and efficiency wage levels are lower. These options interlock at some point. The more firms succeed in making process and product innovations, the less will there be a need for locational innovations. Moreover, process and product innovations could be complementary. This is the case when new products include new investment goods; these then become the basis for improving methods of production, thereby increasing labour productivity to a level compatible with the high real wages prevailing in the most advanced industrial countries well endowed with top-échelon engineers, highly skilled manpower and managerial expertise.

Ideally, adjustments to structural change (whatever their source) should be anticipatory. This reduces frictions. In practice, however, many firms may wait too long before moving towards innovation, or may just refuse to do so, hoping that the government will not allow structural changes to materialise fully (after it has created precedents in the past). In such circumstances, there is a case for active policies stimulating private long-term investments which are forward-looking rather than defensive or nationalistic in character. For instance, the shifting of resources away from production where demand is declining, or in which the NICs as well as Eastern European countries are gaining a comparative advantage, could be facilitated by appropriate adjustment assistance. This must be linked to a clear plan by the affected company to phase out obsolete capacities and restructure into new, viable ventures. Measures which induce workers to be more mobile within the country and to retrain for new jobs and professions are also required. Another line of action relates to tax policies. Policy makers could consider ways of shifting somewhat the tax burden from factor input and efficiency incomes toward consumption and leisure. Generous depreciation allowances on investment and the right for new firms to carry forward losses are appropriate tools. Furthermore, governments could stimulate the creation of new enterprises by repealing existing institutional barriers and providing loans at preferential terms. Government incentives to R & D are also important in this context, but they should extend to small- and medium-sized firms and support, especially, basic research which produces knowledge in the form of public goods. To make such government measures effective, it will be necessary to provide for a social climate with keen competitive conditions, where innovation can flourish. A deregulation of the economy seems to be indispensable in order to assure a wide application of innovations (for instance, microelectronics in telecommunication). Last but not least, state-owned companies could be urged to set a good example and take the lead in making the appropriate adjustments. Some steps in this direction have been taken already in a number of countries, and in others are under consideration. But on the whole, import protection and government aids to declining industries, mainly under the heading of regional policy, still predominate. (For a comprehensive overview of existing policies see Wolf (16).)

Again, serious consideration is being given to pursuing an energy policy towards industry and other sectors based on straight administrative regulation of oil supplies and prices. Only the FRG has so far hesitated to become too interventionist in this field; as a matter of fact, the government has even reiterated the need to permit market forces to operate. The rationale of this approach is that price increases which are passed on to consuming firms (and individuals) will effectively stimulate energy savings and encourage the development of alternative (domestic and unconventional) energy supplies, while price controls or supply rationing will not. Those who advocate government regulation take it for granted that both oil demand and the supply of oil substitutes are extremely price-inelastic in the short and medium run. If the advanced countries succeed in limiting oil consumption and in expanding the production of domestic energy resources (coal, gas, nuclear power, oil in Alaska and the North Sea), the developing countries may benefit in various ways, as Bergman and Radetzki have pointed out (17). One can think, for instance, of less sharp price increases or of an accelerated expansion of world demand for coal and other oil substitutes of which developing countries have sizeable reserves.

To the extent that the economic structures in the USA, Western Europe and Japan change, the room for suppliers from developing countries and Eastern Europe will widen. Further progress in industrialisation, improved education systems, extended on-the-job training, as well as the acquisition and assimilation of foreign technological know-how, will lead to changing comparative advantages in these regions too. The NICs might be in a position to diversify out of the simple labour-intensive items, and to include in their export assortment more and more capital-intensive goods which belong to the mature segments of the product cycle within a given industrial branch. The microelectronic technology, as soon as it is accessible to these countries, may also provide them with the opportunity to achieve significant gains in the productivity of both capital and labour and to move into greater product differentiation. All this has important implications for the adjustment problem of advanced industrial countries: their trade with the NICs will increasingly take an intra-industry form. The least industrialised countries thereby obtain room for 'trading up', without causing an unmanageable competitive pressure in raw material- and labour-intensive activities. This runs counter to the popular 'fallacy of composition' argument, as Balassa has proved empirically (18).

The integration of manufacturing industries from developing countries into the world economy could be facilitated if these countries reshape their own trade policies. On the one hand, developing countries should gradually dismantle their own import protection, reducing tariffs to moderate levels and softening import licensing schemes. Import liberalisation would also have to apply to their mutual trade. On the other hand, their governments should refrain from providing concealed export subsidies which are difficult to justify on economic grounds and which will only call for countervailing duties in the advanced countries. Export promotion should be directed to fully offsetting the increased cost of inputs and the overvaluation of exchange rates resulting from prevailing import tariffs and controls.

In addition, developing countries may want to attract foreign direct investments in support of structural changes and the opening of their economies. If so, they should adhere to clear and steady rules and provide for guarantees against the risk of expropriation without (fair) compensation. Otherwise, they will be trapped by a creditworthiness constraint at a time when huge amounts of risk capital are needed everywhere to carry out the structural adjustment of the national economies to the new conditions in the world economy. As a matter of fact, developing countries who want to attract private foreign capital have to compete for it with the Western industrial countries, the East European countries, and perhaps also with China. Risk capital may be much scarcer in the 1980s than in past decades, so that it will be more expensive and certainly carry positive real interest rates. It is difficult to predict whether developing countries will obtain the amounts of private foreign capital for which they are looking, even if the marginal efficiency of investment is high there. However, the more effective their economic policies, the stronger their attractiveness should be.

14.5 Concluding remarks

Structural policies in the Western industrial countries have been in a state of constant flux. They were rather liberal in the initial post-war years. Afterwards, when new economic, social and political forces emerged, these policies became more interventionist and defensive in a discriminatory manner. Occasionally, the policy applied to a particular industry or firm made the government a helper of last resort, thereby postponing traditional adjustment requirements or avoiding bankruptcy. The reasons are only partly economic, but essentially political. The governments have assumed more and more responsibilities, have tried to resolve particular industry problems 'on their merits' and have given their constituency the impression that non-adjustment to structural changes is compatible with industrial growth, high employment and welfare in the long run.

Non-adjustment, however, actually entails significant costs for the society. Industry becomes more vulnerable to future changes in comparative advantage as the world economy grows, industrial growth opportunities are foregone, and the process of transforming obsolete jobs into jobs which are highly competitive internationally is retarded. Moreover, an accumulation of non-adjustment is not feasible indefinitely, because public budgets impose a financial constraint and harmonious relations between nations cannot persist in conditions of growing nationalistic policy competition among governments. Forward-looking, market-oriented policies which facilitate adjustment to structural change hold, on the contrary, the prospect of serving much better the internal and external interests of the individual countries. To pursue them effectively is easier said than done, indeed. But they are imperative in an economically interdependent world with or without a New International Economic Order.

Changing structures in the advanced countries need not, of course, benefit all developing countries in the same way (neither would the NIEO). The gains may be greater for the more developed countries in the Third World. There will always be some least developed countries unable to share in a newly expanding world economy and therefore continuing to need development aid from the West and other wealthier countries – certainly a larger volume of assistance than they have been hitherto receiving. On the whole, however, it is important for the governments in developing countries to recognize that the crucial determinants of export success are on the supply side and thus within the control of domestic economic policies. As regards access to industrial markets, there is no need to sink into despair because of worldwide protectionism. The problem is serious, but if developing countries subscribe to the Tokyo Round agreements, including the Codes of Conduct (however incomplete these still may be), they have at least the chance of influencing trade policy in the future.

References

(1) H.H. Glismann et. al., "Zur Natur der Wachstumsschwäche in der Bundesrepublik Deutschland – Eine empirische Analyse langer Zyklen wirtschaftlicher Entwicklung", *Kiel Discussion Papers,* No. 55, June 1978.

(2) R. Rothwell and W. Zegveld, "Technical Change and Employment". Report prepared for the Six Countries Programme on Government Policies Towards Technological Innovation in Industry, University of Sussex, June 1979.

(3) J.B. Donges, "A Comparative Survey of Industrialization Policies in Fifteen Semi-Industrial Countries", *Weltwirtschaftliches Archiv,* Vol. 112, 1976, pp. 626-659.

(4) J. Brada, *Quantitative and Analytical Studies in East-West Economic Relations,* Bloomington/Ind.: Indiana University, 1976.

(5) F. Weiss and F. Wolter, "Die Staatshandelsländer als Anbieter auf den westdeutschen Industriewarenmärkten", *Die Weltwirtschaft,* June 1977, pp. 109-126.

(6) J.B. Donges, "Industrial Policies in an Open Advanced Economy – The Case of West Germany", *The World Economy, Vol. 3,* 1980 (forthcoming).

(7) Centre Européen de l'entreprise publique, *Die öffentliche Wirtschaft in der Europäischen Gemeinschaft,* Brussels: CEEP 1978.

(8) S.J. Warnecke (ed.), *International Trade and Industrial Policies – Government Intervention in an Open World Economy* London: Macmillan, 1978.

(9) P. Maunder (ed.), *Government Intervention in the Developed Economy,* London: Croom Helm, 1979.

(10) GATT, *The Tokyo Round of Multilateral Trade Negotiations.* Report by the Director General, Vol. 2, 1980.

(11) UNIDO, "The Impact of Trade with Developing Countries on Employment in Developed Countries", *UNIDO Working Papers on Structural Changes,* No. 3, October 1978.

(12) OECD, *The Impact of the Newly Industrialising Countries on Production and Trade in Manufactures,* Paris, 1979.

(13) K.-W. Schatz and F. Wolter, "Adjusting to North-South-Trade – The Case of the Federal Republic of Germany". A Report prepared for the ILO, Kiel 1979.

(14) B. Balassa, "The Changing International Division of Labour in Manufactured Goods", *Banca Nazionale del Lavoro Quarterly Review,* No. 130, 1978, pp. 243-285.

(15) H.B. Malmgren, "International Order for Public Subsidies", *Thames Essay,* No. 11 (London: Trade Policy Research Centre, 1977.

(16) M. Wolf, "Adjustment Policies and Problems in Developed Countries", *World Bank Staff Working Papers,* No. 349, August 1979.

(17) L. Bergman and M. Radetzki, "How Will the Third World Be Affected by OECD Energy Strategies?", *Journal of Energy and Development,* Vol. V, 1979, pp. 19-31.

(18) B. Balassa, "A 'Stages' Approach to Comparative Advantage", *World Bank Staff Working Papers,* No. 256, May 1977.

Chapter 15

CONCEPTS OF ECONOMIC DEVELOPMENT OF THE DEVELOPING NATIONS AND PROBLEMS OF TRIPARTITE COOPERATION

Leon Zevin*

The movement for a new international economic order has focussed greater attention on structural policy, on concepts of development of the developing nations, and on problems of restructuring of world industry. This increased attention to problems that were also considered important in the past stems from several causes.

The goals of economic development, and the choice of a rational strategy for overcoming backwardness and creating an up-to-date economy on a self-sustained basis, constitute the backbone of national policy in many developing countries.

In the previous development stage economic growth not infrequently took an élitist form, was not accompanied by social progress in the country, and, instead of improving the living conditions for the majority of the population, enhanced property inequality, and, still more important, failed to reduce economic dependence or the gap with the industrial countries or to consolidate the position of a country in the world economy; the consequent disappointment of the popular masses with the results of earlier development has compelled the leaderships, as well as the scientific and business communities, in the developing countries to seek new and rational ways of economic development and the organisation of international cooperation.

This need is all the more acute because the economic and monetary crises, the accelerating inflation, and other upheavals that the world capitalist economic system sustained in the 1970s brought about a further deterioration in the economic and financial position of a large group of developing nations; their foreign debts have skyrocketed and so have the annual payments for debt service. Because of increasing protectionism and other forms of restrictive business, these countries find it more difficult to trade with the developed market economies and to sell their industrial products.

15.1 New concepts of the development process

Strategies of economic growth oriented towards import substitution, as well as the strategy that replaced it – namely, one aimed at extending export-oriented industries even if this involved their forming an enclave in a country's national economy – are

* Director, Division for Relations with Developing Countries, Institute for the Socialist World Economic System, Academy of Sciences of the USSR, Moscow

both beginning gradually to yield ground to better balanced concepts based on a complex approach to development conceived as a many-sided socio-economic evolution. This approach conditions a successful realisation of an economic growth strategy based upon progressive transformations within a country (agrarian reform and reform of public education, above all), upon a rational demographic policy, upon the maximum increase in employment, and upon the selection of structures of population, machinery and technology geared to satisfying the needs of the majority of people and, at the same time, to raising the technical level of the national economy as a whole. An important role is assigned to the public sector and to planning as effective ways of mobilising resources for the accomplishment of national revival and of directing socio-economic development in the interests of society as a whole, not of separate groups or classes. Economic activities conducted by the government of a developing country strengthens its position vis-à-vis foreign capital, and facilitates control of transnational corporations. The use of planning instruments makes it possible consciously to combine the concepts of internal and foreign economic development within a single national strategy, proceeding not only from the expected market situation but also from the country's needs.

The elaboration of a complex development strategy having regard to the specific conditions in individual countries is, naturally, a formidable undertaking for many objective as well as subjective reasons. It seems likely, therefore, that this process will proceed gradually and step-by-step. In our view, this approach helps us to understand the essence of what can be called the 'conceptual boom' which we witness at the present. The most wide-spread concepts today include: national and collective self-reliance; rural development; satisfaction of basic needs; endogenous development; the concept of non-metropolitan industries; and the priority development of small and medium-size enterprises.

It is noteworthy that these new concepts do not claim to encompass the entire complex of problems involved in socio-economic development; instead, each of them aims at a goal in *one specific field*. Thus the strategy of self-reliance (national and collective) aims at using the potentials of individual developing nations, and their joint efforts, to reduce their one-sided dependence on external factors and to strengthen their bargaining positions vis-à-vis the developed countries. In other words, the attempt is being made to create a new foundation for economic development by attaching priority to the formation of a system of horizontal links and by gradually increasing the capabilities of the developing countries' economic structures for mutually complementing one another.

The concept of endogenous development focusses on the internal sources of economic growth and on social changes – which are regarded as most important – and on the need to preclude development of the élitist type. It proceeds on the assumption that the developing nations should not seek to follow the western models of socio-economic development. This concept was originally formulated by UNESCO, and later modified by UNESCO for its 3rd General Conference. According to this concept, industrial development should be geared to serve agriculture, to promote rural crafts and to establish small- and medium-scale enterprises using large amounts of direct labour with intermediary equipment and technology adapted to local conditions. Some delegations at these conferences chose not to include here fuel and raw material industries which, by their interpretations, should be oriented towards the markets of the industrial nations.

The strategy for the satisfaction of basic needs aims at increasing employment and at providing sufficient food, dwellings, clothing, and primary communal services for every family. The strategy of rural development focuses on agriculture, promotion of crafts in rural areas, and the creation of industrial infrastructure. The concept of non-metropolitan industries, and the stress on development of small- and medium-scale industries, aim at including wide strata of the population into the economic process and at developing the resources of the most backward areas.

Thus, the concept described above, and some others, constitute a response (usually a forced response) to some of the most acute problems arising from national revival in the liberated countries. Different concepts are given preference largely because the problems have not been experienced to the same degree by countries at different stages of development. What developing countries should try to avoid, however, is orientation of economic policy towards the handling of immediate problems by short steps which result in the fragmentation of policy, breaks of continuity, and loss of perspective. These new concepts often fail to define clearly the character of the proposed scientific-technical basis of development. To assign as they do priorities to small enterprises, agriculture and agricultural industry, labour-intensive technologies, and the manufacture of simple goods to satisfy basic needs, may, while accomplishing certain urgent tasks, ultimately lead to conserving technical backwardness and stagnation in the developing countries. Pursuance of such a policy for a long time may result in the 'legitimation' of the existence of two groups of countries, with sharply different economic development levels and capacities for mastering the achievements of technological progress, as well as with different methods of developing their economies (intensive and extensive).

This situation will hardly be avoided unless a consistent policy of industrialisation is pursued, with regard, of course, for the specific conditions of each country (or group of countries) and for the socio-economic taks to be coped with at a given stage. Only industrial development can ensure the integration of a national economy into an organic whole based on a modern foundation, on the elimination of archaic structures hindering social progress, and promoting the release of the creative potential of the broad masses of the working people.

To achieve these goals, a country which has adopted that one of the alternative concepts of development which best suits its conditions should *steadily raise the technical level of its economy and create prerequisites for the formation of a national scientific-technical infrastructure and a modern system of public education and personnel training.* Increasing productivity of labour, and effective use of the vast labour resources and achievements of technological progress, will not only ensure an improvement in the standard of living but will also provide a truly equal and mutually beneficial basis for the developing country's participation in the international division of labour.

The experience of the developed countries shows that industry alone can absorb large quantities of labour, including labour released from agriculture. So far, the new concepts of development referred to above have not proved capable of ensuring full employment in the long term, or of promoting the formation of a single national economy; nor have they shown that small- and medium-scale enterprises can produce enough diverse products to satisfy basic needs.

Thus the following criteria of effectiveness should be applied to these new concepts:
– capability to change the unfavourable development trends and to satisfy the most urgent needs of the population, the poorest classes above all, while necessarily improving the standard of living;
– capacity to ensure continuity with all the rational elements of the other development strategies and concepts in use;
– long-term orientation towards the use of modern technology, moving towards this goal step by step and steadily exploiting both the achievements of scientific-technological progress and also local and intermediate machinery and technology;
– strengthening economic independence by managing the process of reproduction mainly on a national basis (a collective basis in the case of an association of several developing countries) and, simultaneously, by intensifying participation in the world economy on genuinely equitable conditions;
– active and conscious participation of the broad masses in efforts to change the orientation of socio-economic development.

Only a comprehensive strategy of national development can satisfy these criteria. This is precisely why the idea of a complex approach to defining an economic development strategy has received increasing recognition in the developing countries in recent years.

Understanding the economic development process as a complex social phenomenon has brought out one weak point in the NIEO programme: the stress on the restructuring of relations in the sphere of distribution, while, as it were, relegating the restructuring of production to the background. Meanwhile it is obvious that the aims of NIEO cannot be reached merely by measures of redistribution or by a more equitable apportioning of world income. The decisive condition for achieving these aims consists in the creation of a comprehensive growth of the productive forces through the optimal combination of internal resources with the possibilities offered by international cooperation. In working towards these objectives, the developing countries face the determined opposition of transnational corporations, which use their productive, technical, and financial power to secure maximum profits, not to serve the interests of the recipient countries.

The document submitted by a group of socialist countries to the 5th UNCTAD said that 'the transnational corporations play a decisive role in deforming the industrial development of the young countries. Removed from the sphere of raw materials production, they have retained control over their transportation, processing, selling, and financing, and are imposing upon the developing countries a type of industrialisation and economic specialisation which, while leading to a certain development of their economies, does not eliminate their dependence in the system of world capitalist economic links, but consolidates it in a new form. The increasing penetration into the developing countries' economies by the transnational corporations and private capital in its new forms poses a serious threat to the sovereignty of the young states'.

In the efforts to establish a new economic order in the world, it is thus highly important to supply the developing nations with the scientific and technical knowledge which can really help them to achieve a genuine economic independence and ensure that every one of them chooses a way of development in accord with the will of its people. Among the steps leading towards this goal, mention should be made of the following above all: assistance to governments in defining aims and methods of a state scientific and technological policy that reflects the needs of a country's underdeveloped economy; a greater orientation of scientific-technical research conducted by the developed countries, and by institutions for international cooperation, towards the needs of the developing countries; gradual efforts to promote international scientific-technical cooperation of a genuinly bilateral nature making it necessary to intensify research in the developing nations and helping them to establish their own scientific and technical infrastructures, including those on a collective basis.

The process of re-orientation of economic development policies will undoubtedly continue, in the long term, to have an increasing influence on the contents, character, and forms of international cooperation involving the developing nations. The widening and deepening of cooperation between the developing countries themselves, in the spirit of collective self-reliance, will be a new trend in this field. One may suppose that, at least in the near future, a typical form of cooperation will be the expansion of bilateral ties between neighbouring developing countries, as well as cooperation among several nations within a subregion and participation in major joint projects of interest to several countries. The similarity between the developing countries' economic structures and assortments of export goods, as well as their inability at present to deal with the more complex production and scientific-technical problems, induce them to cooperate with the developed countries, including those with different social systems. Among the most worthwhile spheres of cooperation one can list the following: joint participation of organisations from socialist and capitalist countries in the construction of major hydropower stations or thermal and nuclear stations; metallurgical complexes; prospecting for, and producing, minerals; complex development of the resources of rivers flowing through several countries and of the coastal shelf; and the creation and expansion of subregional or regional infrastructures above all for transport.

Close analysis of the development policies in the developing nations shows clearly that, although many of the concepts mentioned above are current in these countries, they adhere, on the whole, to the Lima 'Declaration and Plan of Action'; this document refers to industrialisation as the motive force for socio-economic progress and for efforts to overcome backwardness. At the recent 3rd UNIDO conference in New Delhi, the Group of 77 reiterated its determination to achieve the 'Lima target' (to increase, by the years 2,000, the share of developing countries in the world industrial output up to 25 per cent) and, with this target in view, to step up industrialisation and the creation of independent industry. In external affairs, they count on progress in realising the NIEO demands; on the attraction of financial, material, and technological resources from the developed countries; on a long-term policy of redeployment of industries from the developed to the developing countries based on the principle of 'dynamic comparative advantage'; and on the creation of a system of multilateral global consultations, on a continuous basis, encompassing all important industries and aimed at restructuring the world industrial system with regard to the less developed countries' industrialisation needs.

Efforts to build national scientific-technical potentials and to train qualified personnel for all levels of work constitute an integral part of any industrialisation strategy which aims at overcoming economic and technical backwardness, at ensuring employment, and at eliminating exploitation by foreign capital of the developing countries.

The industrialisation policy seeks to create, on an up-to-date level, a rational national economic complex capable of achieving extended reproduction on its own foundation and with regard to the special conditions of each country. A complex industrialisation, and the establishment of an independent economy, also requires that developing countries should participate actively in world trade and in the international division of labour, both because of their increasing demands for imported machinery, equipment, materials, and technical knowhow, and because of the need to expand exports of their own manufactures.

15.2 The possibilities for tripartite cooperation

Cooperation with other groups of countries in the building of national economic complexes objectively promotes tripartite forms of cooperation. Private companies in the western countries, including transnational corporations, usually choose, because of their structure, to deal with separate enterprises, or with groups of enterprises connected vertically with others within their particular branch. Such cooperation often results in a hypertrophy of separate products and branches, whose growth is stimulated not by internal needs but by external demands. Thus lopsided specialisation appears and becomes consolidated in the international division of labour. The situation is quite different when the developing countries cooperate with the socialist countries. Because economic activities are carried out by its government, the socialist country can help the developing nations to solve major inter-branch problems and to establish up-to-date local production complexes (industrial and agro-industrial) by using the mechanism of long-term inter-governmental agreements on economic and scientific-technical cooperation. If it appreciates these differences, which stem from different systems of property and economic management, a developing nation can achieve, with the help of its own economic development plan, optimal results in the use of external resources. The advantages of such tripartite cooperation are firstly that it is coordinated by the developing country concerned; secondly that it makes it possible to get rid of onesided attachment to the world capitalist economy; and, thirdly, that it helps to oppose the self-seeking activities of the transnational corporations.

If, as we believe is inevitable, the developing countries seek to raise the technical level of the economies, no matter what development strategy they are pursuing ,they will have broad opportunities for tripartite cooperation in the transfer of scientific and technical information, including cooperation within international organisations.

An active search for alternative ways of development by the young nation-states is likely to be accompanied by their extending cooperation with other countries, including tripartite cooperation. One thing is of primary importance: whereas countries belonging to one social system can maintain and even extend contacts between themselves despite the worsening of the world's political climate, this is not at all so for countries belonging to different socio-economic systems. For economic relations to develop successfully in the latter case, political confidence must be strengthened, world tensions decrease, and opponents must reject confrontation and the arms race. This is true to an even greater extent of international cooperation in which countries representing the three world groups – socialist, developing and capitalist – participate.

In its initial stages, tripartite cooperation has usually involved individual transactions, or participation in separate construction projects. Gradually, however, a trend towards arranging this cooperation on a long-term basis has manifested itself with increasing clarity, which in some cases imparts to this cooperation the features of a stable division of labour. Thus there arises an objective need to set up a mechanism for tripartite cooperation that will take into account, to the utmost degree possible, differences in forms of ownership, in methods of managing economic activities, and in the specific interests of the partners. Here one must mention the link between bipartite relations and the development of tripartite cooperation. International agreements on economic cooperation more and more often include clauses providing for joint action in third countries; thus tripartite cooperation is beginning to acquire a legal basis. It is evident that in the course of time such agreements will include, among other general clauses proposing joint actions, concrete major projects as well as branches and areas where tripartite cooperation may be worth pursuing.

The mechanism of tripartite cooperation which is being set up should be geared to solving several global problems through the efforts of countries from the three groups. This will perhaps involve a number of conferences and meetings, and the establishment of working bodies to study relevant problems and, given the agreement of the partners, to manage joint ventures.

One important point will be to harmonise the mechanism of tripartite cooperation with the integration mechanisms of separate groups of countries. There can be no doubt that, in each group of countries, integration has an increasing effect on the direction, character, forms, and methods of participation in tripartite cooperation. Tripartite cooperation is likely to develop successfully if all its mechanisms take into account the specific characteristics of all integration processes. At the same time, attempts to impose on tripartite cooperation the mechanism adopted in one individual group of countries may hinder its development. Ways of coordinating the interests of partners could include a temporary consortium, set up to deal with some concrete economic task, or some kind of tripartite long-term agreement (for example, on specialisation and cooperation, on the establishment of an organisation and consultant bureau, or on compensation transactions).

On the whole, by the late 1970s economic preconditions had become favourable for the development of various forms of tripartite cooperation, including large-scale cooperation, among the participating socialist, developing, and capitalist nations. To build on these preconditions, however, will be possible only if the international tensions which arose at the end of the 1970s are overcome and if the senseless spending of tremendous funds on a new spiral of the arms race, which certain quarters are again trying to impose on mankind, are rejected.

Chapter 16

THE NEW INTERNATIONAL ECONOMIC ORDER: REDISTRIBUTION OR RESTRUCTURING?

Tamás Szentes*

It is a commonplace that we live today in a world of *'interdependencies'*. Whatever happens in one part of the world, affects the other parts directly or indirectly. Production, technology and science are becoming more and more 'international'.

Interdependence, however, means mutual dependence, a more or less symmetrical pattern. Contrary to such a pattern, the position of the developing countries is rather one of 'pure dependence'. Their asymmetric economic dependence implies subordination, and vulnerability, vis-à-vis dominant external forces. It may take several forms (1). One of the most dangerous is manifested in foreign ownership and control over important sectors of the economy, thereby restricting national sovereignty, shaping production structures and influencing decisions and their execution.

The asymmetric and disequalising relations of the world capitalist economy can be observed in all main spheres, namely
– in *international trade,* that is, in the international flows of commodities and exchange relations; in the patterns of specialisation; in the allocation of structural roles in the world division of labour;
– in the *international flows and allocation of investment capital*: in the international distribution of capital ownership; and in control over means, sectors or capacities of production;
– in the international *flows of technologies* and in the international distribution of the capacities of technological development, of R & D centres, and, last but not least,
– in the international *flows of manpower,* and in the distribution of skills and intellectual resources among countries.

These asymmetric relations and their consequences explain the imbalances of the world economy and underlie the market and monetary crises; the great uncertainties and the growing contradictions, such as the sharpening contradiction between the 'consumers' societies' squandering raw materials and energy and the limited availability of natural resources; the 'price explosion' of certain raw materials and sources of energy; the coexistence, both internationally and internally even in the so-called poor countries, of both conspicuous luxury consumption and misery; the nutrition crisis in the agrarian

* Karl Marx University of Economic Sciences, Budapest

countries; the insufficiency of national controls; and the lack of international regulation of transnational corporations which strive to achieve a planned 'global' business activity yet, at the same time, increase anarchy in national economies and in the world market.

Since the fundamental inequalities of the world capitalist economy cannot be eliminated by mere redistributive measures and palliatives, the establishment of a *really* new international economic order requires much more attention to strategic issues than has actually been given in recent international negotiations. Without going into details, I will mention some of them (2):

(a) Full national sovereignty over the economy is a precondition for devising and executing appropriate national development strategies and, also, for establishing relations of mutual dependency based on sovereign equality between nations. Therefore it would be reasonable and necessary to establish an *international economic security system* to defend from retaliatory actions all States exercising their sovereign rights. Such a system could be based on multilateral, interstate agreements which would include commitements by each State to refrain from interfering in the economic affairs of other states and to take full responsibility for the activities or their enterprises and citizens operating abroad.

(b) The international activity of the *transnational corporations* is a problem which cannot simply be reduced to a financial issue – to the problem of private capital flows as resource transfers. Effective control and regulation of the activities of these corporations can be implemented by *collective action* of the national states concerned only if each state undertakes responsibility in proportion to the registered equity participation of its nationals. This would not only serve the interests of the developing countries by strengthening their defences against domination by the giant companies but would also serve the interests of the workers in the developed countries.

Since the majority of the developing countries have a real need for foreign capital resources and for cooperation with the transnational corporations – cooperation which may infringe upon their sovereignty and economic independence – much more attention should be devoted to *alternative forms,* other than direct foreign investments, for international economic cooperation and to the possible ways of reconciling the principle of national sovereignty with the business interests of foreign firms where direct investments have already been made. Developing countries may need to cooperate with foreign companies, not only for financial reasons but primarily to acquire new technologies and/or management services, to gain easier access to foreign markets or to share with these companies the risk involved in launching and developing economic ventures and new productive branches.

The foreign companies are not charity institutions but expect profits, and do not make investments unless they can realise returns on them. To condemn the foreign firms merely for their profit motivation in effect implies the naive assumption that business considerations cease to exist and that differences between individual, group and national interests disappear.

Instead of condemnations in principle, of all foreign companies, particularly TNCs, often accompanied by a rather uncritical practice of attracting them, realistic solutions must be found on *how* to reconcile the need for cooperation with the requirement of national sovereignty. A great many *forms of cooperation* already exist, or have been recommended by scholars, and seem suitable for avoiding, or gradually eliminating, the most harmful consequences of cooperation with foreign companies. These include: (i) those types of production cooperation and market sharing, widely practised in East-West relations, which do not involve foreign ownership and control (ii) those schemes which terminate foreign ownership by contract, or programme a gradual 'fading-out' of foreign owernship by converting direct investment capital into a kind of loan capital to be repaid from the rising revenues of the established productive enterprise. In addition may be mentioned (iii) a type of joint venture which is established and operated on a truly reciprocal basis, with a symmetrical pattern of distribution of ownership, operation and incomes, and with effective control by each partner state over the activity directly related to the national economies concerned.

(c) Economic dependence, and the losses, disadvantages and vulnerability of developing economies, are closely related to their position and role in *world trade and in the international division of labour*. There can be no doubt that serious losses to developing countries from worsening terms of trade call for immediate measures of compensatory financing. The burden of these measures should obviously be borne proportionally by those countries which gain from such changes. But the uncertainties and instabilities of world market conditions and the great fluctuations in prices and supplies are longer-term problems which affect practically all participants in international trade — depending, of course, on their shares in trade and their trade structures.

The most important strategic, long-term issue is, however, the structural transformation of world trade and of the international division of labour. Instead of developing and perpetuating primary-producing and manufacturing enclaves, efforts must be made to ensure that developing countries — in consonance with their natural and human endowments — establish also those basic industries which, because of their sectoral linkages, can become engines for developing the national economy as a whole — and within it, first of all agriculture — and for creating appropriate centres of scientific and technological research and product development. Accordingly, progress should be made in developing international economic cooperation gradually but increasingly towards an *intra-industry division of labour* and towards extending it to the field of research and development.

The aim of restructuring the international division of labour, and of making it more balanced, requires an *overall integration* of all relevant policies — policies which are rather fragmented and isolated from each other, no doubt for practical reasons, in negotiations and action programmes. First of all, the issue between primary commodities and manufactures could and should be much more closely connected with programmes of international cooperation providing for countries importing primary commodities to give direct assistance to producers to build up their processing industries based on local primary production. Thus both the importers and the producers would shift the composition of their exports and imports, gradually and in a mutually planned way, towards more balanced and equal structures, i.e. towards inter- and intra-industry division of labour.

In other words, in certain areas *new cooperation schemes* could be put into practice which link, in a long-term planned programme, the import of primary products from developing countries with the support of the development of their manufacturing industries (e.g. by exporting related machinery and gradually increasing imports of new manufactured products based on the local raw material concerned). The supply of technologies for these new industries could also be linked with support aimed at making them increasingly capable not only of adopting but also of researching, developing and producing technologies locally. Such long-term cooperation schemes, *within a programmed shift* from the division of labour between primary producers and manufacturing exporters to an inter- and intra-industrial division of labour, could resolve the contradiction between the strategic aim of developing a more equal system of international division of labour and the existing complementarities of unequal production structures. Such schemes could also take the sharp edge off the debates on 'just' or 'equitable' price relations between primary commodities and manufactures. They could also mitigate the conflicts of interest between producers and consumers, at least insofar as such schemes, by restructuring trade through building adequate structural adjustments into the *national plans* of the partners, would make possible some compensation of present 'losses' or 'gains' by future 'gains' or 'losses', respectively.

If such strategic, long-term issues are left out of consideration when short-term problems are negotiated, or are mixed up with the latter (as often happens in the discussion on NIEO), the short-term measures can be regarded, wrongly, as substitutes (or equivalent alternatives) for the required long-term changes.

(d) The grave problem of the accumulated indebtedness of many developing countries certainly deserves special attention. Besides immediate measures (such as those suggested at UNCTAD) to reduce the debt burdens of the countries in the most serious situation (of which the costs should be borne primarily by those who have profited from these countries' economy through exploitation), there is a need for new loan policies, and new patterns of debtor-creditor cooperation which could improve the repayment capacity and financial self-reliance of the recipient country; this would mean adjusting the debt service, in amount and in phasing, to the gains in production and export capacity from use of the loans, and by channelling repayments – if possible – in kind, i.e. through exports from the newly created production capacities. The strategic issue is, however, the gradual liquidation of the structural inequalities which bring about the need for financial transfers.

(e) Though merely redistributive measures can hardly solve the basic problems giving rise to inequalities, the taxing of incomes earned from the exploitation of developing nations would be a correct method of automatic redistribution. We can recall the principle, stated in the Declaration on the Establishment of NIEO, of the right of the countries concerned 'to full compensation ... for the exploitation'. Such a compensation should be a primary source of *financial transfers* to developing countries. But let me also stress the need for increased international financial assistance to poor countries, based upon solidarity throughout the world.

I believe that international assistance can be substantially and directly increased if the armaments race is stopped for good and if measures are taken to curb military and other inhuman, wasteful and unproductive expenditures.

(f) The problem of international cooperation in *science and technology* is highly relevant not only to the issue of private capital flows, foreign investments and the participation of TNCs, but also to problems in foreign trade, industrialisation and finance in the world economy, in East-West relations, and to the prospects for peaceful cooperation between countries with different socio-economic systems.

The prevailing anomalies of international technology transfers cannot be conclusive arguments for an isolationist policy, for stopping international cooperation in science and technology, or even for a general condemnation of the application of modern technologies, as such, in underdeveloped countries. Rather, they point to the need to give all nations easy access to the common treasury of human knowledge, to prevent science and technology from being misused for military purposes, and call for the application of only those forms of cooperation which do not involve technological monopolies, dependence, the transfer of inappropriate technologies or the inappropriate use of transferred technologies. For all countries striving for sovereign equality and independent development, the establishment, in certain well-selected dynamic branches of the economy, of their own technological basis, and of research and development capacities, is an imperative long-term need. On the other hand, no country, not even the most advanced, can affort to develop its own R & D in all fields, thus making its technological development completely independent, isolated from results achieved elsewhere. International cooperation has become a natural need for all nations.

The task is, therefore, to reconcile national and international interests, and to defend the developing countries from technological dependence, monopolistic subordination, unfair business practices, restrictions, the brain drain and losses caused by unfair pricing or by inappropriate technologies. Long-term, and mutually planned forms of cooperation, complex but flexible, must be developed which link, wherever possible and desirable, the transfer of ready-made technologies with promotion of local production and research capacities; similarly, the use of foreign advisers and experts should be linked, wherever possible, with the training of their local successors.

Urgent measures are also needed to reduce the harmful consequences of the international *brain drain;* these could include bilateral, or preferably multilateral, machinery for compensatory payments for the losses suffered by the developing countries which are short of qualified manpower. The general principle, included in the Declaration on the Establishment of an NIEO, of the right to full compensation for the exploitation and depletion of, and damages to ... all resources, would implicitly apply also to human resources.

References

(1) For a detailed analysis of the forms of economic dependence see T. Szentes: *The political economy of underdevelopment,* Akadémiai Kiadó, Budapest, 1971, 1973, 1976.

(2) For more details see my papers 'Crisis and internal inequalities of the world capitalist economy and the Third Development Decade', *Development and Peace,* Vol. 1, Spring 1980, pp. 150-178; and 'The Development Deadlock; views of a Marxist from the industrialized socialist world'. *The Development Deadlock,* A series of public lectures, Institute of Social Studies, The Hague, 1980, pp. 78-97.

COMMENTS ON PART IV – IMPROVING THE INTERNATIONAL DIVISION OF LABOUR

Helmut Faulwetter*

According to *Streeten* (Chapter 10), the root of the developing countries' call for a New International Economic Order lies in the 'inequalities in power, wealth and incomes ...' produced by the existing order. Of course, one must agree. Colonialism has introduced into the capitalist system a specific kind of division of labour, modified by neo-colonialism but remaining in principle unchanged till today. The relationship between developed and developing countries is characterised by inequalities leading to deep-seated consequences. But is it enough to confine ourselves to this statement? I believe we need also to identify the material conditions maintaining, and even increasing, the inequalities which still hold in the developing countries after surmounting the colonial status. This means tackling the problem more thoroughly.

I believe it is these material conditions which cause exploitation of the developing countries by the industrial capitalist countries and their transnational corporations (TNCs), and which are responsible for the immense transfer of incomes out of the developing countries (1). At the root of the demands of the developing countries for a new order, lies not only the existence of inequalities but something deeper – the exploitation and the conditions which cause it. Although not all developing countries, or their leading groups, are fully conscious of the conditions, the objective reason for their concern to improve the position of their respective countries in the world economy is the urge to overcome exploitation and thus to reduce, and finally eliminate, the inequalities. This is also reflected in the 'Charter of Economic Rights and Duties of States' which is in effect a 'constitution' for the proposed new order (2). This charter includes a number of basic statements of the rights of states, such as: 'every state has the sovereign and inalienable right to choose its economic system as well as its political, social and cultural system in accordance with the will of its people' with 'full permanent sovereignty including possession, use and disposal, over all its wealth, natural resources and economic activities', 'authority over foreign investment' and accordingly 'to regulate and supervise the activities of transnational corporations'; the right 'to transfer ownership of foreign property' and in case of expropriation to settle the question of compensation 'under the domestic law of the nationalising State and by its tribunals'; the aim is the establishment of economic and political conditions in developing countries to overcome economic exploitation. The charter declares it as 'the right and duty of all States, individually and collectively, to eliminate colonialism ... and neocolonialism' and demands 'full compensation for the exploitation' to be transferred to the respective developing countries.

* Institute for the Economy of Developing Countries of the University of Economic Science, Berlin, GDR

These statements clearly express the position of the Group of 77 and of the socialist countries of 'Group D'. The position of developed market economy countries is that many of these demands are at variance with the fundamental prerequisites for the functioning of the existing capitalist system. This had led to their formal agreement only and, even then, with reservations.

At least two questions emerge: is there this difference about the root of the developing countries' call for a new international economic order? and how does this exploitation work? We begin with the second question, and ask in what forms the transfer of incomes takes place.

One channel is obviously the transfer of profit from investment in developing countries; another is the reverse flow of technology (brain drain); then there is flight of capital and smuggling. All these transfers reduce the incomes available to developing countries. Trade barriers in industrialised countries often impose a severe strain on exports from developing countries by forcing them to accept export prices for commodities below their value, while goods and services (e.g. know-how) supplied from the imperialist countries are overcharged by monopolies.

The main channel for the outflow of the national income is, no doubt, 'internal trade' of the monopolist corporations. Several institutions have made estimates showing immense annual transfers (3). Calculations of my own have shown that, by the late-1970s, more than $ 200 billion annually have been moved, in a non-compensated form, from developing countries to industrial capitalist countries.

It is remarkable that this sum exceeds the annual investment resources at the disposal of all developing countries, and is equivalent to a major part of the annual investment in all OECD countries in productive sectors of their economies. In a sense, it can be said, that a considerable part of the economic growth in highly developed capitalist countries is based on the exploitation of the economically weak developing countries. I wish to emphasise this, because it will elucidate some later remarks.

The consequences of recognising the distinction between 'inequality only' and 'exploitation', as the real root of the demand for a new order', are far-reaching. Elimination of inequality is compatible with redistribution; but overcoming exploitation, in the last analysis, can only be the end of the process of a radical transformation of relationships, i.e., a *new* order. It is on this point that opinions differ.

Streeten, in his chapter, appears to regard the direction and extent of further efforts towards changes in North-South relations as lying in more effective action *within the existing* order. This view is increasingly put forward internationally and attempts to substantiate it are made both in western countries and by economists and representatives of leading political groups in a few developing countries. It is a basic feature of the Brandt Report and also underlies the 'basic needs' concept. The aims are a smooth involvement of the TNCs in economic relations; a better functioning of the commodity markets and the monetary and financial mechanisms; financial aid and technology transfers; a smoother functioning of the overall reproduction process; involvement of OPEC financial resources for recycling, etc. These are changes, but within the existing system.

No doubt these measures would bring further changes in global relations in favour of developing countries and may even begin there. But only if exploitation is recognised as the essential issue, will development escape stagnation.

This means this struggle will continue *for a long time*. The present slow-down in the rate of change in favour of developing countries will, no doubt, again give way to acceleration from time to time. But the core of the problem will bring about increasingly more bitter struggles. The vast range of basic conditions giving rise to struggle, and the incompatibility of the interests concerned, cannot lead to solutions satisfactory to both sides, even if a relative quiet appears at certain periods. For one side or the other, there will generally be disappointment.

Because of social struggles originating in other factors – e.g., the social struggles in both developing and highly developed capitalist countries – and factors which essentially affect the basic relationship between the weak and the strong parts of the capitalist world system, contradiction will characterise the coming historical period.

This means that together with efforts of developing countries to press for structural changes, both internal and external – and the resulting demands on the developed capitalist countries involved – the demands for *compensation* for past and present uncompensated transfers will continue to be expressed from time to time, possibly in alternating areas (e.g., aid, writing off debts, tax on brain drain).

These struggles will have considerable effects on the differentiation among developing countries. Some, especially the industrially developed like South Korea, Brazil or Mexico and, of course, also some OPEC countries, will try to find a place near the capitalist developed countries and to come to arrangements with the TNCs. In international economic relations, they will also begin to assume the position of 'exploiters'. At the same time, the position of the poor countries within the capitalist international division of labour will become increasingly disadvantageous. Their accumulation capacity, inadequate already because of the exploitation, may further diminish. This can have terrible consequences (it may involve the almost complete extinction of peoples in certain territories as one can see, for example, in Africa). The social struggles will intensify. There is a growing possibility of take-overs of power by pronounced anti-imperialist and anti-capitalist leadership groups (even though many countries may be tied more firmly to the capitalist system, which may exert increased influence on individual countries and their governments) – a fact that may give impetus to heightening of tension and struggles.

The objective necessity for developing countries to make a stand against exploitation raises the question of the *mechanisms* and institutions of the capitalist world economy (the 'macro-management of the world economy'). The probable trend of conflicts is in line with the current widespread view that the mechanisms of the market will not change the relationship between the capitalist industrial countries and the developing world in favour of the latter and, what is more, cannot even find a cure for the ailments of the capitalist system itself (monetary and financial crises, mass unemployment, almost a permanent recession). The non-Marxist theoreticians who have begun to doubt the capacity of the capitalist mechanisms to function have so far been reluctant to outline the mechanisms that must necessarily take their place. Without doubt, there is evidence of the need to look for alternative and really new solutions for safeguarding world economic relations. And this is obviously what the 'Charter of Economic Rights and Duties of States' should suggest in outline. If real sovereignty of states, equality and the surmounting of exploitation in world economic relations are to be achieved, then the existence of the mechanisms dominating relations in the capitalist sphere, i.e., the mechanisms of the capitalist market, comes into question.

Certainly, statements that I have made are far-reaching. But one cannot by-pass the consequences if one interprets the 'New International Economic Order' as only an improvement of the old order – as a capitalist order with rather more equality.

References

(1) In my view the term 'exploitation' is justified because (also according to Marx) besides 'direct' exploitation (e.g. by foreign capital operating in developing countries and transferring their profits), there is the transfer of surplus value appearing as profit on this profit.

(2) Resolution No. 3281 (XXIX) of UN General Assembly, 12 December 1974.

(3) According to UNCTAD, *The Reverse Transfer of Technology,* (TD/B/C.6/7), Geneva 1975, pp. 20 and 24, there was for instance an annual outflow through brain-drain of more than $ 10 billion; J. Tinbergen in *Reshaping the International Order,* Amsterdam 1976, Chapter 2.2, estimates uncompensated transfers at $ 50 – 100 billion; V.S. Mathur, representing International Confederation of Free Trade Unions (ICFTU) at UNCTAD V in Manila, May/June 1979, attacked the Multinationals for 'siphoning off' $ 170 billion of the profits made on commodity trade. (Cf. *Sibra,* 25 May 1975, Manila, p. 8).

András Nagy*

My comments are directed to *Ohlin* (Chapter 13) and *Donges* (Chapter 14). I appreciate greatly Ohlin's analysis, which uses very similar methods to those which I have been using in my own research for studying trade intensities between regions. The idea is to separate the factors shaping trade relations between countries – factors of attraction and resistance to trade – into two categories: (i) 'volume factors' expressing the trading potential, or propensities, of each country, determining its total exports and imports, and (ii) the trade policy, or 'economic distance', factors determining bilateral trade intensities; the methods were developed in the early 1960s in the US and France and have since been improved by other analysts (1).

The analysis of trade intensities

What Ohlin (also Savage, Deutsch and Goodman) calls the 'null hypothesis' was called by Froment and Zighera the 'normal' trade flow and expresses the 'volume factors' of the regions, assuming that each bilateral trade flow is proportional to the exporter's and importer's share (Z) in total world trade: i.e. (following Ohlin's notation in reference (2) of Chapter 13) if

$$Z_{ij} = \frac{a_{ij}}{a_{oo}}, \quad Z_{io} = \frac{a_{io}}{a_{oo}} \quad \text{and} \quad Z_{oj} = \frac{a_{jo}}{a_{oo}},$$

then the share of the bilateral flow in world trade according to the 'null hypothesis' in world trade (marked by an upper bar) would be:

$$\bar{Z}_{ij} = Z_{io} Z_{oj}.$$

The effect of all the other factors can be expressed as a residual, being the ratio between the share of the actual trade flow and the share according to the 'null hypothesis' or 'normal' flow; this gives Ohlin's trade intensity index or the 'delta coefficient' introduced by Froment and Zighera (used also in ECE studies) (2):

$$\delta_{ij} = \frac{Z_{ij}}{\bar{Z}_{ij}}$$

This index, or coefficient, expresses the ratio of the actual bilateral trade to what one could expect by taking into account only the volume factors, and represents the trade intensity between regions. These intensities reflect all the effects of 'economic distance' such as trade policy, including integration, colonial, or ex-colonial ties, discrimination, protectionism, preferences, traditional links – or the lack of them. These trade intensity

* Institute of Economics, Hungarian Academy of Sciences, Budapest

ratios have proved useful tools both for analysis and for projection, but they also have severe limitations.

(a) My first problem with Ohlin's analysis is that he uses these trade intensity indices in a way in which they cannot be used and he does not use them as I think they should be used. One of the major limitations of these indices is that they cannot be directly compared, especially if the shares of total exports and total imports derived from the flows to be compared are very different, as in the case of West and East. One cannot say, e.g., that an index of 500 for the intra-trade of the East is a sign of higher or lower trade intensity than an index of 200 for the intra-trade of the EEC. The problem can be illustrated by a somewhat simplified version of the data in Ohlin's paper (*Table 13.1*).

Table 1

World trade shares and trade intensity indices (percentages)
an illustrative example

a = normal
b = actual
c = maximal

		WEST			SOUTH			EAST			WORLD
		a	b	c	a	b	c	a	b	c	
WEST	Share (Z)	49	51	70							70
	Intensity index	100	104	143							
SOUTH	Share (Z)				4	4	20				20
	Intensity index				100	100	500				
EAST	Share (Z)							1	5	10	10
	Intensity index							100	500	1000	
WORLD	Share (Z)		70			20			10		100

Here we have only three regions instead of Ohlin's four; the trade flows are the shares in total world trade; and we filled in only the diagonals, i.e. the intra-trade of each region. The last column is Z_{io}, the share of total exports of each region in total world trade; the last row is Z_{oj}, the share of total imports of each region in total world trade. The upper row in each cell of the diagonal shows the share of the regional intra-trade in total world trade according to three assumptions: (i) 'normal' flow as defined above, (ii) 'actual' flow, from Ohlin's data for 1976 and (iii) 'maximal' intra-trade assuming that the region is completely isolationist, i.e. all its trade is intra-trade. The lower row in each cell contains the trade intensity index (δ x 100), i.e. the percentage of each share to its 'normal' share.

As can be seen from the example, the 'maximal' values of the trade intensity indices are very divergent: 143 for the West, 500 for the South and 1000 for the East, inversely proportional to their shares in world trade. (Similar great differences can be found in the intensity indices by filling out the whole trade flow matrix.) It seems evident that the indices of 'actual' trade intensities cannot be directly compared when their 'maximal' values are so divergent: if the developed industrial countries were to stop trading with both the developing and the socialist countries, their intra-trade would be only 43 per cent greater than on Ohlin's 'null hypothesis'; it could certainly not be five times greater as is the 'actual' intra-trade of East. To make these intensity indices comparable for static cross-country analysis, some normalisation procedure has to be introduced, as suggested by *Fink* (3).

While, in my opinion, the δ indexes cannot be directly used for static analysis, they are extremely useful tools both for studying time trends – for the historical analysis of structural change in international trade and for projection of future trade patterns. It is to be regretted that Ohlin does not present his findings in a historical context. I fully agree with *Seton* (Chapter 7) that our main concern is the direction in which the world is moving, but I believe that we can answer this question only if we have understood from what direction we came. I can illustrate this with a matrix of intensity indexes computed from UNCTAD trade statistics for the years 1955, 1965, 1977, for developed countries, developing market economies and socialist countries, with a breakdown into primary products and manufactures (*Table 2*).

It is well known that the trade intensity of intra-trade among the socialist countries is very high (4), but it decreased significantly between 1955 and 1977. Even stronger was the decrease in 1955 – 1965, followed by a slight increase thereafter. It is remarkable that the trade intensity was throughout higher in manufactures and declined less than in primary products.

By contrast with the intra-trade of the socialist countries, the intensity of both East-West and East-South trade increased very fast in the 22 years observed. In the case of East-West trade the export intensity of the West increased more than its imports in both commodity categories and was especially strong in manufactures. The socialist countries could not increase their export intensity in manufactures to the West between 1955 and 1965 and even with the increase of the next twelve years it remained very low (27). It should be noted also that the export intensity for manufactures from the West to the East was throughout lower than that for their exports of primary products.

Table 2

Matrix of trade intensity indexes for three regions and two commodity groups

Exports \ Imports		Total			Primary products			Manufactures		
		East	West	South	East	West	South	East	West	South
East	1955	792	28	27	743	33	32	860	19	24
	1960	619	29	37	569	39	39	667	16	35
	1965	568	32	68	495	45	68	634	19	68
	1972	622	34	68	526	52	70	677	22	66
	1977	604	43	62	508	60	63	675	27	62
West	1955	23	107	112	30	111	95	18	111	106
	1960	30	109	112	40	110	102	23	113	107
	1965	34	110	105	43	111	97	29	113	101
	1972	40	109	101	53	109	92	34	111	101
	1977	51	106	105	66	107	93	44	109	102
South	1955	26	111	99	26	104	124	25	81	153
	1960	38	113	99	41	106	117	22	91	152
	1965	58	106	105	60	103	117	46	86	163
	1972	51	104	117	55	102	123	42	94	154
	1977	44	108	104	50	103	115	24	100	131

Notation: 'East' = Socialist countries (including Asian Socialist countries)
'West' = Developed market economies
'South' = Developing market economies

Source: UNCTAD, *Handbook of International Trade and Development Statistics,* UN, New York 1979

In East-South trade, the increase in export intensity of the socialist countries was much stronger than that of the South. Trade intensities in both directions, and in both commodity groups, increased strongly in the 1955 – 1965 decade and then declined slightly. It is very unfavourable that the export intensity of manufactures from South to East, after a strong increase between 1955 and 1965 (from 25 to 46), dropped to an even lower level in 1977 than in 1955 (to 24)! This means that the export of manufactures from the South to the East increased less than either the total exports of manufactures from the South or the total imports of manufactures by the East.

This is, I think, enough to show that the time trends of the intensity indices can tell us a lot, even apart from cross-country comparisons. These indices can tell us much more if they are more disaggregated. In our project we have 12 regions and 7 commodity groups, but I can not go here into more detail.

(b) My second comment on Ohlin's analysis is a question: is the trade of the socialist countries really so different as he states?

He writes that 'in spite of all that has been written about Eastern trade, it can hardly be said that there is a clear model or paradigm for it'. Very true; I think this would be generally agreed. But is it not true also of the trade of the capitalist countries, both developed and developing? The more one reads of the ('pure', or not so pure) theory of international trade and studies the actual facts, the more it becomes obvious how far they diverge from each other, and how little the theory can be regarded as a model of what really happens in economic life.

I think Ohlin is right in saying that cost considerations play a smaller, and political considerations a bigger, role in socialist than in market economies: the problem is the difficulty of measuring and comparing the importance of these factors. The vast literature in the socialist countries about increasing the efficiency of foreign trade and on the incentives to be introduced for reducing costs and increasing prices (of exports) can be taken as an indirect indication of the neglect of costs – or rather of profits – in the actual decision-making. But when I tried, for example, to determine by regression analysis in a gravitational model whether the parameters of the socialist countries are really very different from those of other countries, I could not find any significant difference (5). If one considers trade patterns – not only of the colonial past, but even of today – one cannot avoid the conclusion that political considerations play a very important role in many trade relations and not only in the socialist countries. Is West European integration purely economic? How can the extremely high trade intensities of the ex-colonies with their ex-colonisers be explained if not by political motives? What about US-Latin American trade? And if East-West, and especially US-USSR, trade is very low, as indeed it is, whose political considerations keep it at such a low level?

I cannot deny Ohlin's criticism that: 'to break into markets or increase its exports, the East has often priced its products below world market levels'. But I think it would be difficult to verify that this is peculiar to the socialist economies, or that there is something particularly socialistic about this practice. It is well known that it developed, long before the socialist economies, as a widespread form of monopolistic competition. It was, and still is, frequently used by transnationals to overcome and dominate markets; it would be difficult to find any example of a socialist country or enterprise dominating and monopolising a Western market by price-cutting. What is more true, I think, is that because of discrimination, of the lack of competitiveness and of balance of payments difficulties, socialist economies were in certain cases 'forced' to underprice their products to keep or expand their export markets. The real danger, in this respect, is that a country can get into a whirlpool: because of discrimination it has to undercut prices, there is retaliation by more discrimination, followed by more price reduction etc.

I think these examples are enough to show why I feel that Ohlin overstates the special features of socialist countries' trade. When I read *Donges'* account (Chapter 14) of all the difficulties of structural change and adjustment in the developed industrial countries, I feel how similar are our actual problems. We are struggling, in the socialist countries, with the same problems of structural change and adjustment to world market forces, and we meet very similar resistance. We also have our problems of economic integration, as do the West European countries, the same difficulties, and yet necessity, of trade liberalisation, internal price adjustments to world market price changes etc. Even our authorities are committing very similar errors in the so called defence of national interests. Let me give you only one example.

After the explosion of world market prices in 1973 – 1974, the Hungarian price authorities proudly declared that they would do everything to defend the stability of domestic prices and that they would not let Hungarian producers and consumers suffer from the external price increases and their consequences. And indeed, they succeeded: prices of imported raw materials were subsidised, domestic prices did not change much and there was no need to adjust the structure of production and consumption. But Hungary has certainly suffered more from the long-term consequences of this stability than it would have suffered from a short-term adjustment. Terms of trade deteriorated more, and improved much more slowly, than in most other countries; the trade deficit increased fast, reaching a level which alarmed economic policy makers, and led them to introduce drastic measures: general price rises, freezing — and for some categories reducing real wages, cutting investments and — after long delay — giving serious consideration to the structural adjustment of production.

Ohlin is absolutely right in criticising the export performance of the East for its problems of 'marketing, quality, finishing, reliability, service' etc. Most Hungarian economists see only one way of overcoming these shortcomings: a happy marriage between market forces and central planning. Such marriages are difficult, especially if the partners come from separate and distant origins. Much of the economic thinking and practice which has developed on these lines in Hungary was pioneered by Yugoslav economists and politicians, and we are grateful to them. It is now generally agreed in my country that the adaptability of the economy has to be increased and that a more balanced and faster growth can be achieved only by more independence for the enterprises, by a bigger interest in their profitability, by a better alignment of domestic to world market prices and by liberalising the market forces. Only by freeing the central authorities from the tasks of detailed short-run regulation, can central planning be concentrated on medium- and long-term macro-problems of structural change, taking into account the consistency requirements of the national economy and the global problems of integration in the world economy. I can say that the criticisms of our economic performance, especially in foreign trade, in our professional papers and even in the mass-media, are generally much sharper than those of Ohlin. Let us hope it will finally help. And I ask myself, how will we be taken to task when we have successfully overcome these shortcomings and when our products and marketing become really competitive on Western markets?

The need for restructuring

I fully agree with *Donges* (Chapter 14) that the 'crux of the problem' facing the world economy today is the ability and willingness of national societies to adjust to growth-oriented structural change. And this is equally true for capitalist and socialist, developed and developing, economies. His description of the forces working for and against such adjustment in the advanced market economies tempts me to describe how similar forces operate in the Eastern European economies. All the problems of misallocation of resources – the difficulties of cost accounting and cost comparisons, the extremely complicated systems of subsidies, discriminatory taxes and tax-exemptions, lobbying for special treatment for particular industries, the conflict between cost-plus pricing and world market prices and so on – all spring from reluctance to face international competition both in the domestic and in the world market.

Restructuring national economies is always a painful operation, whether done by the government or by market forces. It demands a high price in job displacements and in capital utilisation and reallocation. What is not sufficiently understood is that although restructuring is painful and costly in the short-run, it is much less painful and much less costly in the long run than rigidity and failure to adapt.

Liberalisation of trade, opening-up of national economies, breaking down colonial links and trade patterns – all seem to be an irresistible long-run tendency of world development since the second World War. No country can avoid adaptation, but can only resist and postpone it – which means that the economies as a whole lose more in the long-run than a few groups or regions gain in the short-run. The present difficulties of the world economy can be regarded as temporary shocks in the adjustment process and the backlash of protectionism as a transitory absorption of the shock: but it seems unlikely that the great structural change in world production and trade can be stopped or even long postponed. Nothing can stop the industrialisation of both South and East, the modernisation of agriculture, or the vigorous urge of the vast majority of the world's population for a better living. This will certainly create and intensify conflicts, competition and political and economic pressures on both the local and the international level; but the outcome can only be a more integrated, interrelated world economy with a new and superior international division of labour.

One main consequence of the industrialisation and modernisation process, in both the socialist and the developing countries, is the expansion of their internal markets. It is very one-sided to look at it from the point of view of the so-called 'market disruption' of developed countries' markets. East and South are not going to compete only on Western markets, but all three groups of economies will compete in all markets and especially in the fast-growing markets of the East and the South. One should not forget that even though international trade was greatly liberalised in the past two or three decades, the great bulk of production is still within national boundaries, that the tariff and non-tariff barriers are still very high and that the development of international specialisation and division of labour is still at an elementary stage. Donges' statement that the effective tariff protection is 'inversely related to the structure of comparative advantage of the advanced countries' industries' is very significant: it shows how much is to be done and how much change is to come.

How governments or central authorities could and should promote structural change is an open question, not only in the advanced market economies, but also in the socialist economies. There is much to be learnt from the results of false assumptions about the omniscience and omnipotence of the socialist state. We can all share Donges' dislike of bureaucratic decision-making and his view that market failures in themselves are not sufficient arguments for centralisation. Whether more, or less, government-involvement is desirable can depend upon the validity of his statement that 'the government has an information advantage over the market only as far as its own policies and investment programmes are concerned'. If so, not much advantage can be expected from more centralised decision-making. But this is not necessarily so — a government may have more information advantage: a more comprehensive view of the growth of the national economy and a consistent view of the world economy, including the growth objectives of main trading partners. If this is the case, the central authorities can certainly play a more positive role in foreseeing and promoting structural change in the right direction.

They may become able to do this, but will they do it? Many examples show that they won't even if they can. The reason is that local, partial and short-run considerations dominate many central decisions. The more the central authorities are able to express general, global and long-term interests, the more positive is the role they can play in the necessary restructuring of national economies.

The choice is certainly not between an omnipotent state and no state involvement at all; the issue is what kind of decisions should be centralised and what should remain decentralised and left to the market. Past experience certainly tells us not to believe that all central decisions are good, or better than decentralised ones. But experience does not exclude the possibility that central organs can do better than in the past, and that they can find ways of directing structural change in a more forward-looking, efficient and consistent way than independent and — in a sense — isolated private investors and managers.

References

(1) I.R. Savage and K.W. Deutsch, 'A Statistical Model of the Gross Analysis of Transactions Flows', *Econometrica,* No. 3, 1960; L.A. Goodman, 'Statistical Methods for the Preliminary Transactions Flows', *Econometrica,* No. 1-2, 1963, pp. 197-208; R. Froment and J. Zighera, 'La structure du commerce mondial', *Conférence de la Société d'Econométrie, 1964;* H. Theil, *Information and Economic Theory,* North-Holland Publishing Company, Amsterdam 1967.

(2) The only difference is that Ohlin's index is equal to the 'delta coefficient' multiplied by 100.

(3) See: G. Fink: 'Measuring Integration: a Diagnostic Scale Applied to EEC, CMEA, and East-West Trade 1938-1975', *Forschungsberichte No. 42,* Wiener Institut für Internationale Wirtschaftsvergleiche, 1977. Fink suggests the introduction of an index measuring integration, called 'dsi', with the following properties:

a) if $\bar{z}_{ij} > y_{ij} \Rightarrow dsi = \delta\text{-}1$

b) if $\bar{z}_{ij} < y_{ij} \Rightarrow dsi = \dfrac{\delta - 1}{\delta_{max} - 1}$,

where: $y_{ij} = \dfrac{a_{ij}}{a_{io}}$ and δ_{max}: means the maximal value of δ as explained above. There are however several other possible ways to normalise the trade intensity indices taking into account their maximal values.

(4) High trade intensities are not rare if measured in a more disaggregated form: EEC intra-trade is around 200, trade between North and Latin America 200 – 275 and Japanese export intensity with the Asian developing countries 313 in 1977. Similarly we can find a great number of low trade intensities; for example, Japanese export intensity with the EEC increased between 1955 and 1977 from 23 to 31.

(5) See: A. Nagy, *Methods of Structural Analysis and Projection of International Trade,* Hungarian Academy of Sciences, Institute of Economics Studies, No. 13, Budapest, 1979, pp. 52-60.

Stojan Shalamanov*
Wassil Sivov*

The 1970s led to increasing disproportions in the world economy. Some reached critical parameters. The global problems — the risk of draining non-recoverable natural resources, raw material and energy; overpopulation and the impossibility of feeding the population of certain areas; accumulation of industrial waste; the spread of chemical, bacteriological and nuclear weapons — rank first. The threatening changes in the Third World made a specially dramatic impact.

The chain reactions in the rise of world prices, set off by the oil crisis at the end of 1973, accelerated the differentiation between the developed and the developing countries and between the different developing countries, and aggravated the financial situation of many of them. Their loans from the industrially developed countries increased,

* Institute for International Relations and Socialist Integration, Sofia

and the hopes of rising well-being as a result of the higher prices for raw materials were disappointed. The example of OPEC was not followed on other raw material markets. This reconfirmed the rule that new international relations are not established through organisations holding a monopoly of certain products. In fact, if the ratio of income per capita in the Third World to the advanced countries was 1 : 30 before the 'price revolution', it is today 1 : 50 (even excluding the Persian Gulf Emirates). This undermines the confidence of poor countries in the future and increases social pressure in these regions.

The trends towards autocentrism in the Third World, generated by aggravation of the economic and political situation, and determining their relations with socialist countries and developed capitalist countries, can be explained by another factor also. Between the 1950s and the 1960s, as a result of the rapid decolonisation, development of modern technologies and equipment was considered the only way of reducing the gap between newly liberated and developed countries. Much was expected from the so-called 'demonstration effect' – taking over important technological developments, and complete projects of industrial development, from industrialised countries. However, technology alone cannot solve the regional and local problems of non-industrialised countries, which depend on labour skills and on the institutional forms for application of scientific and technical methods to the existing and undeveloped production structures. There were, and still are, a number of objective conditions, such as surplus labour, lack of industrial and production traditions, and inadequate levels of education, which hinder the effective mastering of modern technologies. Furthermore, without proper criteria for selection the import of equipment in the developing countries is almost never complete. This is due both to the limited resources, and to the policy of the ex-colonial countries and private firms trying to avoid development of complete industries in those countries. In some newly liberated countries there is no long-term programme of development strictly conforming to the aims of the national economy and bearing no imprint of prestige factors. That is why the new capital investments were often dictated by certain political groupings, and not by purely economic motives. Thus introducing new technologies into the developing countries from industrialised countries does not fully justify the hopes placed upon it.

The autarkic trends in the Third World seem to result from the difficulties of re-constructing the old socio-economic structures and from the unsatisfactory results of the economic development of the liberated countries. These trends were expressed, and continue to be expressed, either as a rejection of the use of equipment from the developed countries, which does not correspond to the needs of the developing countries, or in concepts of 'Collective independence' as expressed in 1976 at the First Congress of the developing countries' economists in Algiers and at the Fifth Conference of the non-aligned countries in Colombo. Such concepts support the establishing of regional economic relations among the developing countries and the limitation of relations with the developed world.

The tendency towards regional autarky in developing areas should be regarded as a result of the existing disproportions in the world economy. It incorporates no mechanism for automatically restoring the broken balance, for certain economic reasons. In fact, the possibility of building such a mechanism is reduced by the increase of social antagonisms. The efforts of the developing countries to achieve independent regional integrations deserve attention. However, as a sub-system in the world economy, the Third World could hardly solve the problems of removing its internal disproportions without the help of the developed countries on an intergovernmental level — not on a private enterprise level.

Reinforcing the dynamics of development when disproportions exist in the world economy means in fact pushing to the periphery those developing countries which lack internal forces strong enough to follow the law of stable and balanced growth. Formally, they remain within the world economy, but develope in conditions of permanent social and economic decline. The increasing number of developing countries pushed out to the periphery leads to the increase of social and political pressures on a global scale. This strengthens the trends towards 'collective independence' of the developing countries, which means in essence self-isolation with a worsening of the political climate.

The reverse of this concept is the limited, one-sided interpretation of the new international economic order, of which the main ideas were expressed in two basic documents of the UN General Assembly: The Declaration on the Establishment of a New International Economic Order, accepted at the Special Session, and the Charter of Economic Rights and Duties of States, accepted at the 29th session. Their essence comprises three major principles: building an effective system of national control of natural resources, until their nationalisation; creating mechanisms of exchange and international cooperation which may offset price changes unfavourable to the developing countries; help in obtaining equipment suitable for up-dating the old economic and technical structures; guaranteeing an effective flow of part of the national income from the developed to the developing countries for reducing and removing the excessive disproportions in levels of income per capita.

In principle, the socialist countries support the reconstruction of economic relations on such principles. However, declaring the new international economic order in a general form is sometimes interpreted in a rather peculiar way by some representatives of the developing countries. Two points of dispute may be mentioned. In making their categorical claims against the developed 'rich' countries, these representatives make no distinction between capitalist and socialist countries. They do not take account of the fact that the countries who became rich through their former colonial dominion stress their colonial traditions in their present relations with the Third World. Socialist countries cannot be blamed for colonial plunder and are not responsible for the present disproportion in the economic levels of the developing and the developed countries. Thus social and historical criteria are unreasonably replaced by a generalised classification of 'rich' and 'poor' countries.

It should be borne in mind that most of the socialist countries have been subject in the past to economic pressure from the developed capitalist countries. This was the case for Bulgaria. It is sufficient to mention that after the liberation of the country from the Turkish yoke over the period 1889 – 1938, Bulgaria obtained loans from the developed capitalist countries amounting to a total of 40 billion Leva, while the interest paid on those loans amounted to 170 billion Leva i.e. over 4 times the loan itself. In that period, Bulgaria had one of the lowest national incomes per capita in Europe.

The other major point of dispute is the stress laid by most developing countries on that part of the new international economic order which involves the drawing of financial resources from the industrialised countries. Although a necessary condition, it does not comprise the essence of a world programme of development since the flow of financial resources as an end in itself may serve to enrich the ruling élite in an undeveloped economic structure. There is no reason for limiting the new international order to one of its peripheral aspects – that of the re-allocation of financial resources. To achieve the new order requires international reconstruction of the developing countries to overcome their old structures. This takes different forms in the varying social conditions, and specific orientations of development, for each country. It is impossible to recommend a universal strategy of development for all developing countries. But it is possible to formulate a complex of universal recommendations without which no strategy of development can be carried out.

Economic restructuring of the developing countries should be expressed by stimulating those sections of the national economy which have the highest economic yield. This can be achieved by removing the barriers imposed from outside on social and economic development, and by the gradual transformation of the traditional sector, especially agriculture. Achieving the many different tasks connected with this need should be based on an exact analysis of the dynamic social forces, and by relying on their potential.

Normal functioning of the developing economies depends on the effective operation of a state system, centralising control over incomes on the one hand, and satisfying the requirements of social justice on the other through a more equal distribution of national income. In the specific conditions of the Third World, only a strong State, able to stand up to the private monopolists, can unify the national interests and maintain social balance, especially in crisis periods.

The process of stabilisation, once started, can be maintained only by securing a 'social discipline of development', which requires a unified model of economic policy for the society. The preconditions for a basic strategy of development are reduced differences in income between the different social strata, and nation-wide access to education. The formation of a complex of general aims of development for the nation creates the unifying force for transition to accelerated economic growth.

The common aim underlying each national strategy has its economic expression in the maximising of national income. Its realisation over time should be divided into a series of stages related to the specific features of each developing economy. Typical for the strategy of overcoming economic backwardness is the observation of certain priorities, in accordance with the specific stage of development and the available material and financial resources.

A generally valid target for all developing countries, although achieved in different phases of their development, is the creation of a basic industrial complex guaranteeing stable and relatively fast rates of growth. Its size depends on the size of the territory and its population.

The second, generally valid, target for all developing countries is modernisation and accelerating the growth of agriculture. The advantages of such a national strategy of development, combining industrialisation with parallel growth of agriculture, consist in assuring a long-term supply of resources and reducing the risk of disproportions in economic growth.

The third stage target, equally applying to all developing countries, is the building of the productive and non-productive infra-structures. The determinant role of the infrastructure underlies Rosenstein-Rodan's theory of 'the great push'. In his view, it is the infra-structure that creates the conditions for activating productive factors previously limited by territorial barriers, thus making possible the realisation of a unified national social-economic policy. The distribution of labour leads to its unification in the progressive branches, and results in the formation of a unified system of values necessary for carrying out state policy.

However, production of a large surplus product alone is not sufficient. It is necessary to achieve it in a material form corresponding to public needs. Such a material form is possible only through relations with the world economy, and for most of the developing countries foreign credits and help are needed. This is how the initial 'great push' is given, without which it is impossible to have accelerated development.

In this connection, it is necessary to stress the manysided advantages offered by cooperation with socialist countries in solving the problems of accelerated economic growth in the Third World. First of all, this cooperation consists of relations between state bodies and institutions interested in the development and consolidation of the state sector in the developing countries. Furthermore, scientific and technical cooperation, involving loans for developing natural resources and for building industrial complexes, are regulated within short-, medium- and long-term governmental agreements which offer mutual advantages to the parties concerned such as firm export and import prices for raw materials and energy sources, and reliable parameters for the ecological and general economic programmes. The production units and installations built become the property of the developing countries. For stabilisation of economic growth, an important role is played by a complex of measures for restricting the spontaneous process of urbanisation, for the improvement of regional and urban planning, and for centralised town-building, for which use is made of the experience and cooperation of the USSR and other socialist countries. With the help of the USSR new town centres have been, or are being, built in India (Bakilai and Bokaro) and Syria (Tabka on the Euphrates). Thus the rational distribution of the productive forces, and the progressive social and economic transformations in the Third World, are directly conditioned by cooperation with socialist countries.

It is obvious that the decisions, declarations, programmes and appeals of the United Nations alone cannot solve the internal social and economic problems of the Third World, however precisely they are formulated. Urgent and effective actions based on equal rights and mutual advantage are needed. Mobilisation of enormous material and labour resources for realising major projects of industrialisation of the developing countries is possible only by the joint efforts of countries with different social systems, aiming at stabilisation of economic growth, and at increasing material well-being, in this lagging sector of the world economy.

Marian Paszyński

On the problems of a New International Economic Order and the global negotiations, I would like to address four issues. (a) The first is the content of the NIEO debate. We may, of course, restrict ourselves to a purely academic discussion, where NIEO objectives will be perceived in an abstract fashion as an improvement of the lot of the people in developing countries, especially of their everyday conditions of life, based upon a concept of a 'new or endogenous development' implying changing patterns of economic growth and consumption in the developing world. On the other hand, we may keep closer to reality and consider the NIEO programme, as reflected in the decisions taken in international organisations (particularly in the VIth Special Session of the UN General Assembly), as a programme of the LDC governments and not of the broad masses of population in the Third World. If we take the latter, more realistic approach to the NIEO debate, we shall have to acknowledge that the basic premise underlying developing countries' stance in the NIEO debate is the idea of 'closing the gap', which implies emulating the consumption and development patterns of the now developed countries.

(b) If the 'closing-the-gap' concept constitutes a fundamental premise of the NIEO programme of developing countries (i.e. of the LDC governments), the main import of this programme boils down to the change in power relations in the world through which 'closing the gap' could be achieved. Change in the power relations is perceived by the LDCs in both short- and long-term perspectives. In the long-run, it could be effected through changes in the rules governing international economic relations (securing preferential treatment in favour of the LDCs and discrimination against all other countries); LDCs in fact demand substitution of unequal for equal (non-discriminatory) rules so as to correct the inequalities in economic power and in the institutional systems that enact these rules and supervise their implementation (a majority voting power for LDCs). In fact they are looking for a new Havana Charter for developing countries. Being convinced that changing the balance of power in this way is, indeed, a remote possibility, developing countries seek to alter the power relationships in a shorter period by redistribution of world income through massive resource transfers. The change sought in power relations, and especially the call by LDC governments for massive resource transfers, immediately invokes the question: *change, or transfer for whose benefit?* Hitherto, as we have seen, the benefits of growth of national product have not trickled down to the lower strata of the population in developing countries. If, therefore, we are called upon to support the NIEO programme as presented, discussed and accepted in the international organisations (i.e. the NIEO professed by governments and not an abstract concept of theoreticians), we must point out that any new order on the international level must be accompanied by a new order on the national level: its implementation must not benefit exclusively the ruling élites, possessing classes or other already privileged strata of the LDC societies, or even the TNC's operating in developing countries.

(c) If I understand correctly the semantics of *Streeten* (Chapter 10), what developing countries want is new rules of the game which will be simple, uniform (not differentiated) and inflexible over time. It is becoming less and less rational to accept such a set of new rules, because: (i) developing countries constitute an increasingly heterogeneous group; hence the tendency to differentiate between the groups and not within them (the attitude towards the least developed among developing countries (1) and the trend for the establishment of more and more newly privileged subgroups that would ultimately wipe out any vestiges of differential treatment). (ii) there is a constant shift over time within the LDC group in both the level of income (e.g. OPEC countries) and the structure of the economy (e.g. Newly Industrialising Countries). It is, therefore, hardly commendable to establish new, undifferentiated and inflexible rules, to last for a long time (if not for ever), in favour of a highly differentiated and unstable group of nations. Moreover, the LDCs' demand for a new set of rules to govern international economic relations does not take into account the fact that the socialist countries, not being parties to the establishment of the old economic order, look for a restructuring of international economic cooperation that satisfies their legitimate interests too. One may wonder *whether an NIEO could be* brought into being in the interests of one group of countries only, even if we agree that this group found the least accommodation under the old rules of the game.

(d) On the issue of the 'global negotations', two aspects (apart from the doubts expressed as to their final outcome) are of particular interest. First of all, the global negotiations are somehow linked to the discussion of a new International Development Strategy for the Third UN Development Decade. Some see them as conflicting objectives but I am inclined to consider the two as complementary. I perceive global negotiations as an instrument for the implementation of the strategy and as a reflection of the growing importance that developing countries attach to negotiations leading to contractual obligations, and not simply as general political debates and their outcome in resolutions that carry no material (as distinct from moral) obligations even for the countries voting for them.

However, movement towards concrete negotiations and contractual obligations makes the position of developing countries much more difficult for at least three main reasons. One is connected with the need for unity and for a common negotiating platform as a way of exerting political pressures on parties to the negotiations, such pressures being the only effective instrument in the LDCs' hands. The second, following from the first, is that the negotiating platform of the group reflects a precarious balance of interests and compromises making it highly inflexible and unmanoeuvrable. This is, by the way, the consequence of the system of group negotiations adopted in the international organisations. In view of the different interests of various countries, a concession on one point, even a small one but affecting the interest of one subgroup within the LDCs (sometimes even the interests of a single country), requires internal renegotiation of the whole platform to restore its balance. Thirdly, because unity constitutes a prerequisite for success, LDCs – to preserve such a unity – tend to embrace within their negotiating position the particular demands of all countries of the group, thus making the platform inconsistent, unwieldy and, sometimes, even incoherent. On the other hand, the desire to avoid internal splits results in eliminating from the platform all the issues that cannot be accepted by all the countries, which makes it very general and vague.

Unless this controversy is resolved, developing countries would not be able to move very far in the global negotiating process, since they would tend to avoid negotiations on specific issues of interest to particular country groups or countries. They might, in all probability, entrench themselves again within a general and vague negotiating position that cannot lead to contractual agreements, but only to general resolutions like all the declarations and action programmes so far adopted in the framework of the NIEO debate.

References

(1) Developing countries that support verbally the principle of differential treatment in practice oppose any concrete manifestation of real preferences for the least developed countries by not accepting a simple truth that preferential treatment of one subgroup is tantamount to discrimination against the others. Their insistence upon the rule that any differential treatment should not bring harm to other developing countries nullifies the essence of the differential treatment principle.

Marie Lavigne

(a) *Bogomolov* (Chapter 11) writes that in future large-scale imports of fuel and raw materials from developing countries into the CMEA countries will be secured through coordination with the CMEA long-term programme for fuel and raw materials, implying cooperation between planning bodies of the two groups of countries, and also through existing and, perhaps, newly established international organisations. The 'fuel and raw materials long-term programme' of the CMEA is in fact a cooperation of the socialist countries of Eastern Europe directed towards the USSR (and in a much weaker degree, towards Mongolia and Cuba), helping the Soviet Union to extract more fuel and raw materials, with supplies of high-technology equipment bought in significant proportion from the West with convertible currencies (either by the International Investment Bank, or provided by the small East European countries themselves). The USSR repays in gas, asbestos, pulp, etc. Would this pattern be extended to relations between CMEA and the developing countries? If so, it would be a heavy drain on the investment resources of the smaller socialist countries. Or would it simply mean the export of Soviet and East European machinery of less advanced technology, as in the traditional cooperation schemes, on a long-term credit basis with compensation in products? Which international economic organisations would be concerned? Among the existing bodies what would be the role of the International Investment Bank, about which not much has been said for quite a long time in the area of East-South cooperation? What type of *new* international organisations might emerge?

(b) The problem of East-West-South trade in manufactures must be seen from two points of view.

(i) How can Eastern imports of manufactures from the South be increased? In total East-South trade, the share of manufactures is actually declining (as is shown by Dobozi (Chapter 3). Socialist countries regularly assert that this share is bound to increase, which seems to be in contradiction with the expansion of raw materials and energy imports, especially in view of their increasing prices compared with the prices of manufactures. Or would such imports of manufactures simply be used to wipe out the accumulated debt of the South towards the East?

(ii) To my mind, however, competition between the South and the East on Western markets is a more serious problem for the near future. I quote the example of the EEC market, where exports from both groups developed very quickly between 1970 and 1977. Here are some data for 1977:

– in that year, the East exported slightly more chemicals than the South, and this is a sphere where competition will grow, partly because of the intensity of East-West cooperation (for instance, in the building of turnkey plants for semi-finished chemical products, fertilisers, and so on; most of these investments are to be paid for by supplies of chemicals on the Western market under buy-back agreements);

– in class 6 of the SITC (metals, textiles, wood and paper products etc.), and especially in textiles, both groups progressed very quickly; still the South retained a substantial advantage, exporting three times as much as the East;

– EEC imports of machinery from the South are twice as much as from the East. The East has an advantage in cars, which may be jeopardized by the advance of some newly industrialised countries but may also be consolidated by the industrial cooperation agreements in the automobile sector between West European firms and Eastern countries;

– in consumer manufactures, the South exported four times as much as the East, the latter having an advantage only in furniture. But from 1970 Eastern exports of clothing, shoes and toys have increased very fast.

These are the facts. Is a regulation of the competition conceivable between the two groups? Hardly so, if one remembers that the main exporters in the South are precisely the countries with which the socialist countries have weak – or even bad – relations: Taiwan, Hong Kong, South Korea, Singapore ... So must we expect that the outcome will depend on the unequal degree of Western protectionism towards imports from both East and South? That would be the worst solution.

George Macesich*

Opposition to the price system and markets is certainly not in the interest of Third World countries. They, and the world, can ill afford bureaucratic tampering with the delicate market mechanism, if we are to judge from the results produced by vast bureaucratic networks of controls and regulations. The issue and principal problem is control of world inflation, and greater reliance on the market mechanism would indeed constitute a 'new international economic order'. This by no means makes light of the problem of poverty in the Third World. On the contrary, the problem is far too important to be left to decisions of politicians and international bureaucrats, however well intentioned they may be.

Policy makers in many Third World countries apparently view material sovereignty and international redistribution as the major policy goals. These goals are to be achieved through the increase of power and prestige of the UN General Assembly and particularly of UNCTAD. The more radical perception of the international economy sets the tone and language for much of the dialogue between the Third World countries and the rest of the world.

Ideas underpinning these arguments are derived from the theory of dependency (1). The theory argues that even though political independence has been gained by Third World countries, the international economic system is a hierarchical power structure in which capitalist countries constitute a centre, or metropole, that dominates the developing countries comprising the periphery. The principal element in the theory is that underdevelopment is caused by the international economic system. Moreover, a new form of dependency is being thrust upon the Third World countries by transnational corportations operating from the centre.

There is reason to believe that demands for a 'new international economic order' by at least some of its advocates is really and understandably a call for a change in the 'rules of the game' so as to facilitate entrance into world markets by those Third World countries that have acquired growing industrial power and capacity to absorb technology and capital. These countries do not envisage wrecking the international economic system; indeed, they plan to benefit from it once they have entered the market and gained a greater share. The theory of oligopoly is better able to rationalise such behaviour than a competitive model. These new oligopolists in the Third World may already have set out to establish their own transnational firms with a view to sharing oligopoly profits and rents and participating in 'managing' the international economic system.

* Professor of Economics and Director, Center for Yugoslav-American Studies, Research and Exchanges, Florida State University Tallahassee, Florida

In fact, transnationals from the Third World now rank among the fastest growing enterprises anywhere (2). Thirty-four of the 500 largest international companies are joint ventures with companies in developed countries. Countries such as South Korea, Singapore, Taiwan, Brazil, Mexico, Philippines and Yugoslavia lead the drive into transnational enterprises.

There are good reasons for taking the demand for the NIEO more seriously than hitherto. The process of integrating the world's developing nations into the world economy is not smooth. There is much suspicion and distrust of intentions and goals and indeed doubt whether the developed and developing countries are playing the game fairly. In the mid-1970s, the United States initiated the Conference on International Economic Cooperation held in Paris, which failed thanks primarily to the temper of the times. In 1981 the UN and its 152 members will discuss everything: the international monetary system, commodity prices, aid, barriers to trade and the supply and price of oil. (For a useful summary see *Odette Jankowitsch,* Chapter 12 in this volume).

Unlike the Paris conference, the Third World countries and particularly the Group of 77 (or really 119) insist on explicitly discussing energy and specifically oil prices. Since 1973 they have had serious problems with the ever-increasing price of oil. Industrial countries see in this concern, for the first time perhaps, a possibility of stabilising the volatile oil market. OPEC countries have managed for the moment to soothe the concerns of developing countries with a new aid programme.

If OPEC has at least conceded that oil prices are to be on the UN agenda, the developed countries have also moved from the rigid Paris position to one of flexibility on such issues as the indexing of oil prices to the cost of other goods and services, as sought by the OPEC countries. The United States, for its part, is promoting a 'substitution account' at the IMF whereby dollar holders are to be protected from currency fluctuations. It could well mean stability in prices and output for OPEC producers in exchange for assurance by industrial countries of the purchasing power of oil producers' earnings.

If moderates in developing countries, in pressing their case for the NIEO, fail to obtain concessions from the industrial world, the more radical voices are likely to take over, with harsh words and harsh policies as developed and developing countries retreat inward, and, perhaps, together disrupt the international economy beyond early repair.

References

(1) See, for example, T. Dog Santos, 'The Structure of Dependence', *The American Economic Review,* Papers and Proceedings (May 1, 1970), pp. 231-236; and *Latin America's Political Economy* (Garden City: Anchor Press Books, 1972).

(2) See C.H. Farnsworth 'Third World Companies Achieving Global Reach', *New York Times,* February 3, 1980.

Gunther Kohlmey*

Contradictions between political tension and détente characterise our time and influence international economic interactions. I fully agree with the recommendations for a further widening and deepening of economic relations between East and West, South and East, South and West. I would like to call attention to the need to find and establish more just and equitable forms and institutions in the international economy. This also involves rational and just changes in national and international economic structures, and in the national and international allocation of production factors. As a rule, the allocational (or structural) benefits of better integration of a national economy in the international division of labour are greater and more stable than possible gains by changes in the terms of trade. That is well known, though not always considered in economic policies.

Ricardo demonstrated in his simple two-country, two-commodity, model the comparative advantages of structural changes caused by foreign trade. But Ricardo did not analyse some elements which have since become more and more important in determining comparative advantage: decreasing costs from large-scale production and also the higher quality of R & D and of products due to international specialisation and cooperation.

In developed economies, those advantages result less from changes in macro-structures (Ricardo's wine and cloth) than from changes in micro-structures (in the production of machine-tools, synthetics, special implements, etc). Other things being equal, it should be of interest to a developed economy to foster industrialisation in underdeveloped countries, because of the gains from higher degrees of specialisation and concentration.

My table demonstrates the remarkable growth of international specialisation in GDR production of metal-cutting machine-tools, made possible (i) by the industrialisation of formerly less developed CMEA economies and (ii) by long-term agreements on international specialisation among CMEA partners.

Generally speaking, considerable comparative advantages can be gained (i) by national economic development, (ii) by levelling out the differences in the development of national economies, and (iii) by rational forms of international economic relations.

In the international capitalist economy, comparative advantages resulting from the international division of labour were, and are, evidently more lucrative for the developed than for the developing countries and on average, the social and economic gap between

* Central Institute for Economics, Academy of Sciences of the German Democratic Republic, Berlin

GDR: Production, exports and imports of metal-cutting machine-tools, 1960 – 1978
(million Marks)

	1960	1970	1975	1978	1978/1960
Production (a)	396	784	1255	1706	4.3
Exports (X) (b)	242	579	1020	1555	6.4
Imports (M) (b)	30	233	439	503	16.8
Sales on the domestic market (c)	184	438	674	654	3.6
Share of X in production per cent (d)	*61,1*	*73,9*	*81,3*	*91,1*	
Share of M in domestic market per cent (d)	*16,3*	*53,2*	*65,1*	*76,9*	
X to Bulgaria (b)	5	15	22	87	17
M from Bulgaria (b)	–	7	10	17	
X to Czechoslovakia (b)	32	41	102	152	5
M from Czechoslovakia (b)	15	48	112	106	7
X to Hungary (b)	17	19	25	33	2
M from Hungary (b)	2	14	19	21	10
X to Poland (b)	12	75	83	131	11
M from Poland (b)	2	37	56	22	11
X to Romania (b)	18	51	89	215	12
M from Romania (b)	–	3	29	63	
X to Soviet Union (b)	82	178	536	696	8.5
M from Soviet Union (b)	0,4	71	111	142	355

(a) Million GDR Marks. – (b) Million 'Valutamark'. – (c) (P + M) – X. – (d) Mark and Valutamark' are not the same; prices in marks are higher; hence the shares of X and M shown are less than they would be in terms of quantities. But we are interested in demonstrating the trend.

Source: Statistisches Jahrbuch der DDR, Berlin 1979.

the two groups has not been reduced. Linder was not alone in making this point (1). He wrote that the structural effects of foreign trade are much greater on developed than on developing countries. The reason is simple: with slow, or no, industrialisation, monocultures, dual economies etc., the spectrum of economic structures is poor. That makes it impossible to shift production factors from one activity to another even in favourable international economic conditions. Developed countries are free from that lack of flexibility. Linder concludes that 'the theory of international trade and economic structure' is a unity and one of the 'distinguishable but interrelated parts' of the theory of international trade (2).

In discussing the problems of adaptable technology transfers to LDCs, of tripartite industrial cooperation and other forms of North-South economic interactions, we should always bear in mind the aim of broadening the spectrum of macro- as well as micro-structures in LDCs. There is no future in mono-culture and dual economy, and the capitalist market mechanism cannot solve the problem of an equitable spreading of social and economic development.

Although the share of CMEA countries in the foreign trade turnover of LDCs is on average small, the activities of the CMEA region in the development of agriculture, industry and of productive as well as non-productive infrastructures in interested LDCs is greater. To mention only one simple example: workers and specialists from the GDR and Algeria are building factories in Algeria, while unskilled Algerian workers are trained in the GDR for their work in the new factories in Algeria.

Generalising, one can say that the socialist countries are interested in widening the economic structures of developing countries. Raw materials should be semi-processed or completely processed in the energy and raw material producing and exporting LDCs. In this way, the socialist countries could reduce their industrial micro-structures by improved international specialisation. Joint ventures are one possible method. Another is tripartite industrial cooperation – East-West-South cooperation as well as East-West-South interactions.

A statement was made by CMEA states at UNCTAD IV (Nairobi, 1976) about the interlinking of economic structures of LDCs and socialist countries: 'Implementation of the national economic plans of the socialist countries ... will contribute to increases in the CMEA countries' volume of trade with the developing States, to improvements in the structure of that trade, to the introduction of various forms of industrial cooperation, and to a growth in scientific and technical links. The formation of complementary economic structures on the basis of mutual advantage will be accelerated' (3). Such interlocking of economic structures is certainly a long process, but it has been started already by selective activities.

To sum up, the deepening of international economic interdependencies includes the development of economic structures in LDCs, and changes in interactions between national and international economic structures, in favour of a world-wide social and economic development. New structures in the international division of labour are necessary and possible; to bring about such new structures is the aim of East-West-South relations.

References

(1) S. B. Linder, *An Essay on Trade and Transformation,* John Wiley & Sons, New York, 1961.

(2) ibid., p. 11

(3) *Proceedings of the Fourth UNCTAD,* Nairobi, UN, New York, 1977, Vol. 1, p. 158

Göran Ohlin

I do not, as some commentators on my Chapter 13 seem to think, believe that Western trade is a model of perfection while Eastern trade is shot through with imperfections. It is clear enough that there is, as the UN euphemism has it, 'considerable scope for improvement' throughout the international economic system. What I wanted to do was not to discuss imperfections but rather the systemic difference between administered trade and market-based trade, and some of the issues that arise in trade on the interface between different systems. *Paszyński* refers to Kornai's suggestion that Eastern economies are supply-constrained and Western economies demand-constrained, and that this could well be used to explain the persistent pressure on Eastern balances of payments. *Nagy's* demonstration of the trends in trade intensity among Eastern economies and between them and the rest of the world is very interesting, and one wonders why the trend towards more intra-bloc trade before 1965 halted thereafter.

On another issue, *Streeten* (Chapter 10) seems to consider ease of negotiating international rules to be a secondary matter, but international arrangements in the economic sphere can only be understood in terms of negotiation. This is why there is no need to discuss the importance of mutual interests. Unless there are mutual interests in reaching an agreement, negotiations among nation states will not succeed.

Some contributors put much stress on the need to change power relations in a New International Economic Order. However, I do not see how power relations can be changed through negotiation. Power is not a commodity that can be handed over to another country. There is of course much to be said for restraint in the use of power by those who have it, and I also think it is possible to argue that international arrangements today do not adequately reflect changes in international power relations that have already taken place, and that the international order should not serve as a check on future changes in power relations as developing countries become more important partners. But surely one cannot redistribute power in the world by negotiation.

PART V – NEW FORMS OF EAST-WEST-SOUTH COOPERATION

Chapter 17

TRIPARTITE INDUSTRIAL COOPERATION AND THIRD COUNTRIES

Patrick Gutman*

Far from being an ephemeral phenomenon, Tripartite Industrial Cooperation (TIC) – the joint construction by Eastern Europe (1) and the West of industrial complexes in a great variety of Third World countries – constitutes a practice which is tending to become generalised.

A growing number of TIC operations has been registered – 88 projects were in progress or completed between 1976 and 1979 against 138 during the years 1965 – 1975. There has also been a significant increase in the number of Protocol agreements for cooperation in third countries between Western – in particular West European – engineering firms and Socialist Foreign Trade Organisations (FTOs): 82 in 1976 – 1979 against only 38 in 1965 – 1975. According to studies made by UNCTAD (2), TIC represented the equivalent of slightly more than one-eighth of total imports of investment goods by the developing countries in 1964 – 1973 (3). This method now represents about 8 to 10 per cent of East-West agreements for industrial cooperation signed up to the present time (4).

It is a particularly original practice for capitalism to seek in Eastern Europe the necessary support to win contracts in international bidding on invitations from the developing countries. The inclusion of services and/or equipment tendered by FTOs in western bids, or vice-versa, brings about a reduction in the global cost of projects which Third World countries wish to carry out. These tactics for international industrial marketing are particularly efficacious at a time of ever keener inter-capitalist competition, for TIC

* Institut d'Etude du Développement Economique et Social (IEDES), Université de Paris-I.

demonstrates at the same time the will of the East European countries to play an enhanced role in the international division of labour (5).

It is relatively easy to define the motives which lead the partners of West, East and South to develop TIC operations, but an assessment of the impact of TIC on the development of Third World countries is a far more delicate matter. Although the declared aim of the Western and Eastern partners is to give the South the benefit of the dynamics of East-West relations, TIC in practice may not entirely fulfil the hopes placed on it. In other words, in view of the experience of TIC over the past fifteen years, can the practice really be qualified as 'tripartite', or is it not merely straight East-West cooperation in third countries?

It is precisely on this last point that TIC can give rise to controversy and requires all the more careful analysis. The contribution which the relations between developed countries of the East and West could make to a solution of the problems of the Third World would be the best justification for these links. The temptation is therefore great to demonstrate that East and West are really helping the South through TIC, and to present the practice as more natural and easier than it is in reality, because it is a way of 'retrieving' East-West cooperation for the benefit of North-South relations (6).

We have tried to avoid this temptation by keeping our approach as factual as possible, basing it on a statistical analysis of TIC during the past fifteen years.

17.1 TIC and third countries: practice and recent evolution

Western engineering firms and socialist FTOs, assisted to a greater or lesser degree by local industries, carried out joint ventures for building industrial complexes in forty countries of the Third World during the period 1965 – 1975, and their activities were extended to sixteen other third countries in the period 1976 – 1979. During the fifteen years they completed 230 TIC projects in 56 countries of the Maghreb and Middle-East, Africa, Asia, Latin America and the Mediterranean (7) (*Table 17.1*). The practice of TIC is thus seen to have become widespread and is not limited to a few specific countries which merely for political reasons want to use this method of cooperation.

It is noticeable that no great changes took place from one period to the other in the relative shares of the five above regions. This is the first lesson to be drawn from a comparative analysis of recourse to TIC in third country regions. The only changes are small: a drop in the share of Asia, compensated by a rise in Africa, and a drop in Latin America compensated by a rise in the Mediterranean region.

The greatest number of TIC cases is found in the oil-producing countries: Iraq, Iran, Algeria, Libya and Kuweit are among the countries which practised TIC most, reaching a total of between 8 and 30 operations each for the whole period 1965 – 1979. Thus the region Maghreb and Middle East topped the list with more than half the operations. This, of course, reflects the policy of the oil-rich countries to use their oil profits to carry out intensive industrialisation (8). The large number of East-West links in OPEC countries equally reflects the interest shown in them by the industrialised partners. The increased shares of Iraq and Iran and the reduced shares of Egypt and Morocco may be partly explained by modifications of foreign policy.

It is noticeable that at a time when Africa became the main area of East-West competition, it registered an increase in its share from one period to the next from 14.5 to 18.2 per cent. These shares are still small, considering Africa's potential resources of energy and minerals. Only Nigeria and Guinea used TIC to any extent in the 1965 – 1975 period. Sudan joined them in 1976 – 1979. The remaining cases are dispersed all over the African continent without any particular concentration in any one country.

In Asia, the largest relative share in TIC is taken by India with nearly 9 per cent of the world total in 1965 – 1975 but with a considerable reduction in 1976 – 1979. This decline is noticeable for the Asian continent as a whole.

In Latin America, the most characteristic feature of TIC operations is the considerable financial stakes involved and the gigantic size of the projects themselves, necessitating the participation of numerous multinational consortia. This is particularly the case for hydro-electric power dams (Itaïpu and Yacereta). The small number of cases, however, demonstrates that US firms generally regard Latin America as their own preserve and continue to retain the lion's share of work on capital projects for themselves without recourse to TIC. It must also be borne in mind that Latin America consists chiefly of semi-industrialised economies, which is reflected in a greater share of local industries in capital projects than in other regions. The fact that industrialisation has spread more or less evenly throughout Latin America is reflected in the even spread of TIC operations over most of the countries in the region.

It thus appears that TIC, which in the early years (1965 – 1970) was the outcome of fortuitous arrangements to improve chances in international bidding, has now become a permanent factor in the strategy of Western firms and socialist FTOs. In addition to East-West joint bidding, facilitated by protocol agreements for cooperation in third countries, joint East-West companies have now been formed especially to erect industrial complexes in third countries:

– In 1973, the joint company PROTINAS (Hungary 50 per cent – FRG 50 per cent) was established to deliver turnkey farm and agricultural equipment particularly to Arab countries. It has completed projects in Lebanon, Iraq and more recently in Syria. (9)

– In 1975, the joint company POLIBUR Engineering Ltd., (with headquarters in Manchester) was founded by POLIMEX-CEKOP (Poland) and BURMAH Engineering, of the BURMAH OIL Company Ltd. (GB), to export turnkey industrial plants for the

Table 17.1

Involvement of third world countries in tripartite industrial cooperation by region, 1965 – 1975 and 1976 – 1979

	1965 – 1975			1976 – 1979		
	Number	% (a)	% (b)	Number	% (a)	% (b)
Algeria	9	6.5	12.3	6	6.8	12.8
Egypt	6	4.3	8.2	0	–	–
Iran	9	6.5	12.3	8	9.1	17.0
Iraq	14	10.1	19.2	16	18.2	34.0
Jordan	1	0.7	1.4	1	1.1	2.1
Kuwait	5	3.6	6.8	3	3.4	6.4
Lebanon	4	2.9	5.5	0	–	–
Libya	8	5.8	11.0	6	6.8	12.8
Morocco	9	6.5	12.3	0	–	–
Syria	6	4.3	8.2	2	2.3	4.3
Tunisia	0	–	–	4	4.5	8.5
United Arab Emirates	1	0.7	1.4	1	1.1	2.1
Yemen	1	0.7	1.4	0	–	–
Total Maghreb and Middle-East	73	52.9	100	47	53.4	100
Cameroon	2	1.4	10	2	2.3	12.5
Congo	2	1.4	10	0	–	–
Dahomey	1	0.7	5	0	–	–
Ethiopia	0	–	–	1	1.1	6.3
Gabon	1	0.7	5	1	1.1	6.3
Guinea	3	2.2	15	1	1.1	6.3
Madagascar, Rep. of	0	–	–	1	1.1	6.3
Mauritania	1	0.7	5	0	–	–
Niger	0	–	–	2	2.3	12.5
Nigeria	5	3.6	25	4	4.5	25.0
Senegal	1	0.7	5	0	–	–
Somalia	0	–	–	1	1.1	6.3
Sudan	0	–	–	3	3.4	18.8
Tanzania	1	0.7	5	0	–	–
Togo	1	0.7	5	0	–	–
Zambia	1	0.7	5	0	–	–
Total Africa	20(c)	14.5	100	16	18.2	100
Afghanistan	0	–	–	1	1.1	12.5
Australia	0	–	–	1	1.1	12.5
Bangladesh	0	–	–	1	1.1	12.5
India	12	8.7	60	1	1.1	12.5
Indonesia	0	–	–	2	2.3	25
Korea, Rep. of	1	0.7	5	0	–	–
Malaysia	2	1.4	10	0	–	–
Pakistan	2	1.4	10	0	–	–
Philippines	0	–	–	1	1.1	12.5
Singapore	2	1.4	10	0	–	–
Sri-Lanka	1	1.4	5	0	–	–
Thailand	0	–	–	1	1.1	12.5
Total Asia	20	14.5	100	8	9.1	100

(Table 17.1 continued)

	1965 – 1975			1976 – 1979		
	Number	% (a)	% (b)	Number	% (a)	% (b)
Argentina	2	1.4	14.3	0	–	–
Bolivia	0	–	–	1	1.1	16.5
Brazil	4	2.9	28.6	0	–	–
Chile	1	0.7	7.1	0	–	–
Colombia	1	0.7	7.1	1	1.1	16.5
Cuba	1	0.7	7.1	0	–	–
Ecuador	0	–	–	1	1.1	16.5
Guyana	0	–	–	1	1.1	16.5
Paraguay	2	1.4	14.3	0	–	–
Peru	1	0.7	7.1	1	1.1	16.5
Uruguay	1	0.7	7.1	1	1.1	16.5
Venezuela	1	0.7	7.1	0	–	–
Total Latin America	14	10.1	100	5	5.7	100
Cyprus	0	–	–	1	1.1	8.3
Greece	3	2.2	27.3	3	3.4	25
Turkey	8	5.8	72.7	8	9.1	66.7
Total Mediterranean	11	8.0	100	12	13.6	100
Total	138	100		88	100	

(a) % of world total. – (b) % of the region. – (c) of which one unspecified North African case. In some cases, more than one developing country is involved in a project.

production of chemicals, building material, paper and cellulose, refrigeration, agricultural and food products, etc. (10).

– Founded in 1976, the joint company TECHNIPEX (headquarters in Paris) is the result of a fusion of bank and industrial capital: France is represented by TECHNIP with 40 per cent and the Banque Nationale de Paris with 10 per cent, while Poland is represented by POLIMEX-CEKOP with 45 per cent and POLSKA KASSA OPIECKI with 5 per cent. Its main purpose is the delivery of turnkey plants in the Middle East, Africa and Asia (11).

– In 1977, TECHNICON SPA was established in Genoa as a joint Soviet-Italian company for constructing steel and tinplate plants in third countries. This company, comprising ITALPIAMTI, a subsidiary of IRI, the state engineering group (with 50 per cent), and LICENSINTORG, the Soviet FTO (with 50 per cent), is believed to be the first joint venture set up by the USSR with a foreign firm (12).

This development is a new departure from the usual procedure of protocol agreements. The association of East-West engineering undertakings and banks for work in the developing countries is a more permanent form of cooperation than mere East-West protocol agreements for third markets. These specially created joint companies institutionalise the practice of TIC on a wider basis, amounting in fact to an enlargement of East-West industrial cooperation. In a typology of forms of cooperation, the joint companies must be placed on the highest level, on a par with co-production, if not higher.

17.2 The division of work between the partners

The specific character of TIC, and its relation to the distribution of work, need to be examined to see whether it is the result of complementarity or, on the contrary, the outcome of competition between the partners.

A detailed study of forty cases of TIC between France, the East and Third countries shows that the main cost advantages for the developing countries in joint East-West bids are the very low prices quoted for furnishing certain Eastern equipment and assembly work, coupled with unbeatable credit and financing terms. *Table 17.2* enables us to make the following assessment of the all-round strategy:

– *The West* needs to integrate materials manufactured and assembled by the Eastern countries so as to take advantage of their highly competitive prices. By doing so through TIC, Western engineering firms:
a) improve their chances of winning contracts in international bidding;
b) gain a political advantage in the Third World of working in partnership with Eastern FTOs;
c) avert cut-throat competition from East European countries.

– *The East.* Thanks to their price and credit approach, Eastern FTOs have been able to force the export, through TIC, of their plants and equipment, either:

(i) by winning difficult contracts in stiff bidding, as main contractors with the inclusion of Western technology, or
(ii) by being included as sub-contractors in capitalist projects.

– *The South,* at least theoretically, gets the best out of the commercial and financial competition between East and West in international bidding. Third countries, by taking the most favourable credit terms offered by both East and West through TIC can considerably reduce the burden of financing the plants which they want to build. Moreover, the existence of a clearing system between the East and third countries can be a supplementary advantage for the latter inasmuch as it reduces their foreign currency requirements for payment. Settlements are made through buy-back or counter-trade arrangements (13), which improve the balance of payments of the developing countries and at the same time give them foreign market outlets.

TIC brings down the *immediate* cost of a project for the South, but the analysis of the division of work between the partners shows that the industrial share of third countries, nearly always limited to civil engineering and/or assembly work, is small or negligible. Thus the third countries are the less active partners in building their own industrial complexes; the socialist FTOs, since they are specialised in assembly work themselves (14), entice the third country, by favourable commercial and financial terms, to renounce the use of its own local labour even though it is often technically qualified for the work.

Table 17.2

TIC 'France-East-South' (1965 – 1975), partners' contributions by type of work (a)

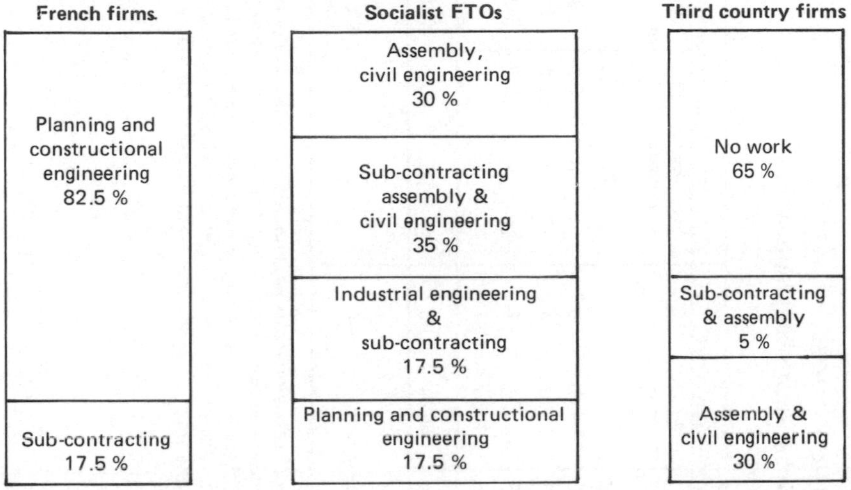

French firms	Socialist FTOs	Third country firms
Planning and constructional engineering 82.5 %	Assembly, civil engineering 30 %	No work 65 %
	Sub-contracting assembly & civil engineering 35 %	
	Industrial engineering & sub-contracting 17.5 %	Sub-contracting & assembly 5 %
Sub-contracting 17.5 %	Planning and constructional engineering 17.5 %	Assembly & civil engineering 30 %

(a) The percentages are arrived at by taking the average of partners' contributions to 40 projects.

The resultant imbalance in the cooperation of the three East-West-South partners is seen in *Tables 17.2* and *17.3.*

Table 17.2, setting out the relative share in the work, by type of contribution, of the partners in 40 projects, shows that TIC, at any rate for the time being, is a dual process with marked complementarity between East and West, and, at the same time, with manifest competition between East and South. It also shows the minor part of the third countries in the work on the projects. *Table 17.3,* setting out in detail the relative value of each partner's share in the work in 34 East-West-South projects – the West being France – shows the South to have an even smaller share in monetary value than when set out by type of contribution in *Table 17.2.* The average share of the South in the work is less than 10 per cent of the global value of the projects. Study of the figures in detail reveals the great extent of East-West complementarity. The figures for France and the East, studied side by side in the '1 – 20 per cent' and the '76 – 100 per cent' brackets, show such complementarity that the residual share of the southern third countries is negligible. That is why the Secretariat of the Economic Commission for Europe (ECE) includes in its study (15) only projects in which southern firms participate directly under the terms of the contract. Even by this method of approach, the contribution of the South is a minor one. According to six socialist FTOs interviewed by the ECE, the southern share in monetary value varies between 15 and 40 per cent, being usually much nearer the lower figure.

Table 17.3

TIC 'France-East-South' (1965 – 1975)
relative share in monetary value of each partner's contribution
(in millions of Francs)

Percentage of cost of each project	France's share				Eastern countries' share				Third countries' share			
	Number of projects	%	Value mn. Francs	%	Number of projects	%	Value mn. Francs	%	Number of projects	%	Value mn. Francs	%
0 – 1	–	–	–	–	–	–	–	–	21	61.8	–	–
1 – 20	10	29.4	438	15.9	22	64.7	491	8.7	8	23.5	90.3	8.8
21 – 50	6	17.6	257	9.4	6	17.6	270	4.8	4	11.8	234.7	22.9
51 – 75	7	20.6	616	22.5	2	5.9	254	4.5	1	2.9	700	68.3
76 – 100	11	32.3	1431	52.2	4	11.8	4605	81.9	–	–	–	–
Total	34	100	2742	100	34	100	5620	100	34	100	1025	100
Percentage of total cost of the 34 TIC projects (a)	25.7 %				52.7 % (b)				9.6 %			

(a) The total amount does not come to 100 % because a few Western non-French sub-contractors have not been included in the table; the 12 % roughly corresponds to the purchase of foreign technological processes by French main contractors. – (b) The high figures are explained by the fact that the USSR obtained three exceptionally big contracts; consequently there is a considerable discrepancy between the relative share of certain socialist countries in terms of number of projects and in terms of the value of these same projects. The USSR itself, which represents only 18 % of the total Eastern commitments, however accounts for 85 % of the total value obtained by all Eastern countries in the TIC exercise (cf. P. Gutman and F. Arkwright (1976), in Select Bibliography).

TIC in its present stage is thus seen to be East-West cooperation *in* third countries rather than tripartite cooperation in the real sense of the words. The very mechanism of invitations for international bidding makes for competition rather than cooperation.

However, the relationship of today might hopefully evolve from one of 'East-West seller – South buyer' to that of a partnership. This would imply a radical change of perspective. The present practice of cooperating simply in the erection of plants would develop into a permanent relationship, in which the partners took part in *tripartite mixed companies* for co-production and commercialisation of its fruits. Moreover, if the three partners were to contribute capital on an equal basis, this would necessarily lead to a continuing process of transferring to the South technology for improving production, as the partnership would involve the distribution of profits.

Certain multilateral co-production ventures exist already:
– the MIFERGUI NIMBA joint co-production venture in Guinea, for mining iron ore (16); partners are to receive part of the return on their investments in the form of iron ore; extracted ore not purchased by the partners will be jointly marketed abroad.
– in Nigeria, IMARSEL CHEMICAL Ltd. has been functioning for several years as an example of a tripartite mixed company. It was jointly established by MEDIMPEX (Hungary), which has a 40 per cent equity share, and MEDIMPEX's affiliate, PHARMA LABATEC S.A. (Switzerland), 20 per cent equity. Initially the company engaged only in commercial activity, marketing Hungarian pharmaceuticals. Its activities have expanded to local manufacture on the basis of components imported largely from Hungary. Sales in 1977 amounted to 5.6 million dollars. (17)

17.3 Sectoral analysis of TIC and development

It should be said at once that we shall not attempt to deduce from this specific analysis the *general* trend of development in third countries. TIC has too small a part of total investments in capital goods to warrant any such attempt (18). Our aim is simply to examine the sectoral characteristics of the projects carried out through TIC. The question at issue is whether TIC, through the type of development to which it gives rise, constitutes an original method, or, on the contrary, simply follows the stereotype pattern, with all its consequences for the developing countries.

This study is necessarily only a preliminary and general approach (19). A more complete examination of the impact of TIC on development in third countries would have to include an extensive inquiry on the spot so as to assess, inter alia:
– the insertion of industrial complexes in the national economy and, in particular, how they fit into the already existing industrial pattern;
– the nature of the transfer of technology which takes place and to what extent it is suitable for the local economy (employment, redistribution of income, etc.);
– to what extent it dovetails with the world economy, and its consequences for the international division of labour.

Hitherto, all studies of TIC, to my knowledge, including the very rare assessments based on concrete cases, have met these difficult questions.

On the basis of our sample of 226 TIC operations, completed or in progress (principally operations in 1976 – 1979), and of an additional 199 Protocol agreements (20), we can assess the sectoral nature of development to which TIC has given rise, as shown by experience in 1965 – 1979 (with a break at 1975 to illustrate changes during the period). The sectoral breakdown of operations in the Third World, made on the basis of the final production sector, is shown in *Table 17.4*.

The largest share is taken by projects for increasing the *energy* capacity of third countries. These represent 40 per cent of the TIC cases, with noteworthy stability from one period to the next. A sub-division of the energy category shows that:

– 68 per cent of the projects are for the production of electric power,
– 24 per cent are for oil refining,
– the rest are for the production of coal and natural gas.

Two third of the electric production projects are for thermal power plants and one third for hydro-electric power. The large proportion of thermal plants is explained by the water shortage in a number of third countries (21). The construction of thermal power plants is sometimes accompanied by sea water desalination plant.

The second largest share is taken by *intermediate goods industries,* which represent nearly 30 per cent of TIC cases both in the years 1965 – 1975 and in 1976 – 1979. The sub-division shows:

– 40.3 per cent of the projects for basic chemicals (of which mineral chemicals – particularly fertilisers – account for 81.5 per cent and organic chemicals for 18.5 per cent);
– 17.9 per cent are for iron and primary steel;
– 16.4 per cent for building materials and glass;
– 13.4 per cent for paper and cardboard;
– 10.4 per cent for non-ferrous metallurgy;
– 1.5 per cent for foundry and metal work and transformation of plastics.

The third share is taken by *consumer goods industries,* which represent nearly 15 per cent of TIC cases for the whole period 1965 – 1979. The sub-division shows:

– 54.5 per cent of the projects are for the agricultural and food industries;
– 36.4 per cent for textiles and clothing.

There are practically no projects for para-chemicals and pharmacy or for the 'Leather-footwear-wood-furniture' group.

Table 17.4

Sectoral analysis of tripartite industrial cooperation, 1965 – 1975 and 1976 – 1979

	TIC concrete cases						Protocol agreements					
	1965 – 75		1976 – 79		1965 – 79		1965 – 75		1976 – 79		1965 – 79	
	No.	%	No.	%	No.	%	No.	%	No.	%	No.	%
1 Agriculture	1	0.7	1	1.1	2	0.9	0	–	0	–	0	–
2 Energy – Production – Distribution	55	39.9	36	40.9	91	40.3	2	5.4	10	12.2	12	10.1
3 Mining	6	4.3	2	2.3	8	3.5	1	2.7	3	3.7	4	3.4
4 Intermediate goods industries	41	29.7	26	29.5	67	29.6	7	18.9	17	20.7	24	20.2
5 Equipment goods industries	8	5.8	4	4.5	12	5.3	5	13.5	10	12.2	15	12.6
6 Consumer goods industries	23	16.7	10	11.4	33	14.6	8	21.6	8	9.8	16	13.4
7 Building & public works	0	–	4	4.5	4	1.8	0	–	2	2.4	2	1.7
8 Commerce, services	2	1.4	0	–	2	0.9	1	2.7	2	2.4	3	2.5
9 Transport	2	1.4	2	2.3	4	1.8	1	2.7	2	2.4	3	2.5
10 Other	0	–	3	3.4	3	1.3	7	18.9	5	6.1	12	10.1
11 Multi-sector	0	–	0	–	0	–	5	13.5	23	28	28	23.5
12 Total	138	100	88	100	226	100	37	100	82	100	119	100

See *Annex I* for further details of the breakdown by sectors

See *Annex II* for an analysis by country of participants, and *Annex III* for a list of Western and Eastern enterprises involved.

The fourth share is taken by *equipment goods industries,* which account for only 5.3 per cent of TIC cases. The sub-division shows:

- 66.6 per cent of the projects are for land transport equipment;
- 16.7 per cent for mechanical equipment;
- 16.7 per cent for electrical and/or electronic equipment.

The other branches account for less than 10 per cent of the projects between them, as follows: *Mining* 3.5 per cent; *Building and public works* 1.8 per cent; *Transportation* 1.8 per cent; *Commerce, Services* and *Telecommunications* 0.9 per cent; *Agriculture* 0.9 per cent.

The sectoral distribution of Protocol agreements is somewhat different from that of the completed projects. Three points have some significance:

– *Energy* takes a considerably smaller relative share (10.1 per cent against 40.3 per cent), although there is a marked increase in 1976 – 1979 over 1965 – 1975;
– *Intermediate goods industries* take a smaller relative share (20.2 per cent against 29.6 per cent);
– *Equipment goods industries,* on the contrary, take a higher relative share (12.6 per cent against 5.3 per cent).

Do these sectoral variations in the numbers of protocol agreements and those of completed projects indicate an evolution in the practice of TIC?

Is there a tendency to set up more diversified sectoral structures for the productive systems in the developing countries? In particular, does the tendency to lay greater emphasis on the development of the equipment goods industries herald a fundamental change in the character of operations? As has been shown (*Tables 17.5* and *17.6*), the completed projects have been limited chiefly to energy and to a few intermediate and consumer goods industries, that is to say to the basic infrastructure of third countries. But it has yet to be ascertained whether TIC favours a more inward-looking focus, creating inter-sectoral links, which is an indispensable condition for real development. Without such inter-sectoral integration, TIC would merely help to raise the level of development without changing the outward-looking focus of the economies of third countries.

It is certainly premature to jump to conclusions from the slender indications gleaned from statistics of the protocol agreements. Even if the signs are considered encouraging, they must be interpreted with prudence for three reasons;

– Protocol agreements, from their very nature, have only an indicative value.
– The existence of a high proportion of multi-sectoral protocol agreements is liable to reduce the difference between the figures for protocol agreements and implemented

projects ((in particular for intermediate goods industries, whose share might thus be higher).

— Finally, and above all, the potential changes which are discernible from the protocol agreements cannot necessarily be imputed to TIC as such.

They may simply reflect a general evolution in the demands of the third countries engaged in progressively adapting their productive systems. If so, then TIC would simply be following the general economic trend of the developing countries rather than determining it. The data in the TIC sectoral tables, examined side by side with statistics for foreign contracts implemented on a traditional non-tripartite basis, tend to indicate a significant correlation between the types of TIC projects and the general structure of imports of capital goods in developing countries. If these indications are borne out, TIC would be shown to have no specific character in determining the type of development brought about.

17.4 Concluding remarks

The future of TIC as a way of promoting development in third countries will depend on the will and ability of the Eastern and Western partners to increase their association with the South so that it also becomes a real partner. For the time being, one cannot help noticing a discrepancy between the tenor of most of the discourse on TIC and the facts themselves as they appear from the analysis of the partners' respective contributions to the projects or from a sectoral analysis.

It seems necessary to distinguish between the merits of TIC as a particularly appropriate means of international industrial marketing for the Eastern and Western partners and its real value for the development of third countries. In this respect, current studies of TIC generally tend to treat it as an autonomous phenomenon, arising solely from decisions of third countries as a sequel to their invitations for international bidding. It should, on the contrary, be borne in mind that TIC is at the same time a manifestation of the dynamics of the systems — both East and West — and consequently one factor in the interplay of their competition and perpetuation.

TIC offers the two systems, East and West, the possibility of avoiding a clear-cut choice between simply giving up, or maintaining, an ill-accepted position; it allows each of them to seek what might be called a 'political-moral surety' in the opponent's southern sphere of influence. The surety does not even have to be advertised, for it is implicit in the execution of joint projects (22). TIC thus provides East and West with the possibility of limited but effective cooperation in the South.

Sectoral structure of TIC in third countries, by region

Sectors / Regions 1965 – 1975 = A 1976 – 1979 = B		Agriculture No.	Agriculture %	Energy No.	Energy %	Mining No.	Mining %	Intermediate goods No.	Intermediate goods %	Equipment goods No.	Equipment goods %
Maghreb &	A	1	1.4	27	37	2	2.7	18	24.7	4	5.5
Middle-East	B	0	–	16	34	1	2.1	16	34	2	4.3
Africa	A	0	–	5	25	3	15	6	30	2	10
	B	1	6.3	7	43.7	1	6.3	2	12.5	1	6.3
Asia	A	–	–	9	45	1	5	9	45	–	–
	B	–	–	2	25	0	–	4	50	–	–
Latin America	A	–	–	6	42.9	–	–	6	42.9	2	14.3
	B	–	–	3	60	–	–	1	20	0	–
Mediterranean	A		–	8	72.7	–	–	2	18.2	0	
	B	–	–	8	66.7		–	3	25	1	8.3
All regions	A	1	0.7	55	39.9	6	4.3	41	29.7	8	5.8
	B	1	1.1	36	40.9	2	2.3	26	29.5	4	4.5
Of which in	A	1	1.9	15	28.8	2	3.8	12	23.1	4	7.7
OPEC	B	0	–	20	41.7	2	4.2	16	33.3	0	–

Table 17.5

1965 – 1975 and 1976 – 1979

Consumer goods		Building & public works		Commerce, services		Transport		Other		All Sectors	
No.	%	No.	%	No.	%	No.	%	No.	%	No.	%
19	26	0	–	–	–	2	2.7	0	–	73	100
6	12.8	2	4.3	–	–	2	4.3	2	4.3	47	100
2	10	0	–	2	10	–	–	–	–	20	100
3	18.7	1	6.3	0	–	–	–	–	–	16	100
1	5	–	–	–	–	–	–	0	–	20	100
1	12.5	–	–	–	–	–	–	1	12.5	8	100
–	–	0	–	–	–	–	–	–	–	14	100
–	–	1	20	–	–	–	–	–	–	5	100
1	9.1	–	–	–	–	–	–	–	–	11	100
0	–	–	–	–	–	–	–	–	–	12	100
23	16.7	0	–	2	1.4	2	1.4	0	–	138	100
10	11.4	4	4.5	0	–	2	2.3	3	3.4	88	100
16	30.8	0	–	1	1.9	1	1.9	0	–	52	100
5	10.4	2	4.2	0	–	1	2.1	2	4.2	48	100

Relative share of each region in TIC, by sector

Sectors / Regions 1965 – 1975 = A 1976 – 1979 = B		Agriculture No.	Agriculture %	Energy No.	Energy %	Mining No.	Mining %	Intermediate goods No.	Intermediate goods %	Equipment goods No.	Equipment goods %
Maghreb &	A	1	100	27	49.1	2	33.3	18	43.9	4	50
Middle-East	B	0	–	16	44.4	1	50	16	61.5	2	50
Africa	A	0	–	5	9.1	3	50	6	14.6	2	25
	B	1	100	7	19.4	1	50	2	3.8	1	25
Asia	A	–	–	9	16.4	1	16.7	9	22	–	–
	B	–	–	2	5.6	0	–	4	15.4	–	–
Latin America	A	–	–	6	10,9	–	–	6	14.6	2	25
	B	–	–	3	8.3	–	–	1	3.8	0	–
Mediterranean	A	–	–	8	14.5	–	–	2	4.9	0	–
	B	–	–	8	22.2	–	–	3	11.5	1	25
All regions	A	1	100	55	100	6	100	41	100	8	100
	B	1	100	36	100	2	100	26	100	4	100
Of which in	A	1	100	15	27.3	2	33.3	12	29.3	4	50
OPEC	B	0	–	20	55.6	2	100	16	61.5	0	–

Table 17.6

1965 – 1975 and 1976 – 1979

Consumer goods		Building & public works		Commerce, services		Transport		Other		All Sectors	
No.	%	No.	%	No.	%	No.	%	No.	%	No.	%
19	82.6	0	–	–	–	2	100	0	–	73	52.9
6	60	2	50	–	–	2	100	2	66.7	47	53.4
2	8.7	0	–	2	100	–	–	–	–	20	14.5
3	30	1	25	0	–	–	–	–	–	16	18,2
1	4.3	–	–	–	–	–	–	0	–	20	14.5
1	10	–	–	–	–	–	–	1	33.3	8	9.1
–	–	0	–	–	–	–	–	–	–	14	10.1
–	–	1	25	–	–	–	–	–	–	5	5.7
1	4.3	–	–	–	–	–	–	–	–	11	8
0	–	–	–	–	–	–	–	–	–	12	13.6
23	100	0	–	2	100	2	100	0	–	138	100
10	100	4	100	0	–	2	100	3	100	88	100
16	69.6	0	–	1	50	1	50	0	–	52	37.7
5	50	2	50	0	–	1	50	2	66.7	48	54.5

References

(1) Eastern Europe refers to Bulgaria, Czechoslovakia, GDR, Hungary, Poland, Romania, USSR and Yugoslavia. These countries will also be referred to as the East or Eastern countries.

(2) 'Tripartite Industrial Cooperation', Study by the UNCTAD Secretariat, for Seminar on industrial specialisation through various forms of multilateral cooperation, Geneva, December 1975, (TAD/SEM. 1/2 November 25, 1975).

(3) Imports by developing countries from the world of goods in SITC, section 7, excluding estimated imports of passenger road vehicles and their parts. (cf. TAD/SEM. 1/2, p. 14, footnote 3).

(4) The percentage varies from one study to another, depending on the criteria adopted to define TIC and the number of TIC cases considered. In 1977, Klaus Bolz put the number of third country East-West projects at about 6 per cent to 7 per cent of all East-West deals (*East-West Markets,* 22 August 1977, p. 11). In 1979, the ECE Secretariat put the number of joint projects (F1 + F2 + H1) at 9.5 per cent of its sample of East-West Industrial Cooperation contracts. (TRADE/R. 392, 9 October 1979, p. 7).

(5) An interesting study has recently been published on this subject by Elizabeth Kridl Valkenier, 'The USSR, the Third World and the Global Economy', which clearly shows recent changes in the assessment of the concepts of 'international division of labour' and of 'world economy' in the Soviet Union. See *Problems of Communism,* July-August 1979, pp. 17-33. See also the study of William Diebold, 'The Soviet Union in the World Economy' in *Soviet Economy in a Time of Change*, Volume 1, pp. 51-70, Joint Economic Committee, Congress of the US, 96th Congress, 1st Session, Washington, 1979.

(6) Guy de Lacharrière, 'The Role of East-West cooperation for the development of Tripartite Cooperation', UNCTAD Seminar, December 1975, Geneva, (TAD/SEM. 1/16), p. 2.

(7) To facilitate the analysis, five regions have been chosen which group third countries as homogenously as possible.

(8) The increased oil prices do not, of course, explain the nature of TIC itself — East-West-South operations. At best, the large oil profits explain the emergence of triangular 'West — Rich South (OPEC) — Poor South (Third World)' operations. See T. Scharf, *Trilateral Cooperation,* OECD, Development Center, Paris, October 1978.

(9) *Le Courrier des Pays de l'Est,* October 1975, p. 16 and *Marketing in Hungary,* No. 2/1979, p. 5.

(10) *Revue de l'Economie Polonaise,* No. 4 (409), 16-28/2/1979, p. 5.

(11) *East-West Markets,* 17/5/1976, p. 3.

(12) *Moscow Narodny Bank Press Bulletin,* 21/9/1977, p. 12.

(13) For further details, see P. Gutman and F. Arkwright (1976) in Select Bibliography.

(14) This is a policy which China seems to want to adopt as well, and she may very soon take part in tripartite operations. The first skeleton agreements which she signed in August and November 1979 with Western firms are indicative of this policy. They provide for the Chinese National Public Works Company to furnish labour to ITALSAT, an Italian engineering subsidiary of the state-owned IRI, and to the French Building Federation, for public works in the civil engineering branch outside China — in particular, in the Third World. This development was made possible by the adoption at the end of June 1979 of the law on foreign investments in China which applies also to the creation of joint companies abroad using Chinese labour. Cf. *Le Monde,* 8/8/1979, p. 19 and *Les Echos,* 7/8/1979, p. 3 and 28/11/1979, p. 11.

(15) ECE Secretariat, Joint CTC/ECE Unit, 'Promotion of trade through industrial cooperation, Tripartite Industrial Cooperation: Results of an inquiry', Note by the Secretariat (*TRADE/ R. 373/Add. 1*), 12 October 1978, p. 13.

(16) With the following capital distribution: Guinean Government (50 per cent) and nine other partners: Nigerian Government (13.5 per cent), Libyan Government (10 per cent), Algerian Government (7 per cent), NICHIMEN (Japan) (7 per cent), INI-SIERRA-MINERAI-COFEI (Spain) (5.75 per cent), MINERAL IMPORT-EXPORT (Romania) (2.5 per cent), SOLMER (France) (2 per cent), USINOR (France) (2 per cent), Liberian Government (0.25 per cent). See *Le Moniteur du Commerce International,* No. 229, 19/6/1978, p. 16.

(17) See Carl McMillan, 'The political economy of tripartite industrial cooperation', Appendix, p. 37, V.b., *Institute of Soviet and East European Studies,* Carleton University, Ottawa, Research Report No. 12, 1980.

(18) The figure, according to estimates made by the UNCTAD Secretariat in 1975, represented slightly more than 12.5 per cent of the total imports of capital goods by the developing countries during the period 1964-1973. See 'Tripartite Industrial Cooperation', Study by the UNCTAD Secretariat, *TAD/SEM. 1/2,* November 1975, p. 14.

(19) At least on the level of a global sample, for studies on national applications of TIC – in particular Austrian and French – include sectoral elements; Cf. F. Levcik and J. Stankovsky (1978), P. Gutman and F. Arkwright (1975 and 1976) in Select Bibliography.

(20) Even though protocol agreements have only a relative value, since they do not refer to specific individual projects, they nevertheless reflect the sectoral choices of the East and West undertakings with regard to the types of projects which they are designed to realise in third countries.

(21) Except in Latin America (Itaipu, Yacereta) and in certain cases in Africa (Kaufe) where the flow of water is sufficient for gigantic dams to be built.

(22) A more detailed treatment of this question will be found in P. Gutman, 'Tripartite Industrial Cooperation and East European', in *East European Economic Assessment,* for the Joint Economic Committee, United States Congress, forthcoming.

Select bibliography

L. Akar, "Cooperation between Hungarian and FRG Companies on Third Markets", *Marketing in Hungary,* No. 2/1979, pp. 5-9.

K. Bolz, "Tripartite Industrial Cooperation – A Western view", in C.T. Saunders, ed., *East-West Cooperation in Business: Inter-Firm Studies,* Vienna-New York, Springer Verlag, 1977, pp. 79-89.

M. Davydov, "UNCTAD and Tripartite Industrial Cooperation" in C.T. Saunders, *op.cit.,* pp. 97-104. (This article has also been published in N. Watts, ed., *Economic Relations between East and West,* London, Macmillan, 1978, pp. 231-238.)

H. Faulwetter and G. Scharschmidt, "Some Aspects of Tripartite Cooperation", in C.T. Saunders, *op.cit.,* pp. 89-95.

I. Gazda, "Marketing of capital goods in cooperation on third markets", *Marketing in Hungary,* No. 1/1975, pp. 27-31.

P. Gutman, "Tripartite Industrial Cooperation and East Europe", in *East European Economic Assessment: A Compendium of Papers,* Joint Economic Committee, Congress of the United States, Washington D.C., forthcoming.

P. Gutman and J.C. Romer, "Coopération Industrielle Tripartite Est-Ouest-Sud et Dynamique des Systèmes" in *L'Annuaire de l'URSS et des Pays Socialistes Européens édition 1978,* Strasbourg, Librairie Istra, 1979, pp. 587-627.

P. Gutman, "Etat Présent et Perspectives de la Coopération Industrielle Tripartite Est-Ouest-Sud", unpublished working paper presented at the GERPI Seminar on *The Future of North-South-East Economic Relations*, January 20-21, 1978, Paris.

P. Gutman and F. Arkwright, "Coopération Industrielle Tripartite Est-Ouest-Sud; Evaluation financière et analyse des modalités de paiement et de financement", *Politique Entrangère*, No. 6/1976, pp. 615-641.

P. Gutman and F. Arkwright, "La Coopération Industrielle Tripartite entre pays à systèmes économiques et sociaux différents de l'Ouest, de l'Est et du Sud", *Politique Etrangère,* No. 6/1975, pp. 621-655.

I. Ivanov, "Tripartite Industrial Cooperation: Recent Situation, Problems and Prospects", Discussion Paper, *UNCTAD Seminar, Geneva, 2-5 December 1975,* (TAD/SEM. 1/7).

E. Kemenes, "Tripartite Cooperations: Possibilities for Expanding Business Relations", *Marketing in Hungary,* No. 4/1978, pp. 3-8.

E. Kemenes, "Phénomènes Nouveaux de la Compétition Internationale Contemporaine", in *Compétition Internationale et Redéploiement Géographique,* Editions Masson, 1978, pp. 33-55.

L. Kiss, "Experience on Development of Electric Equipment Joint Ventures on Third Markets", *Marketing in Hungary,* No. 2/1979, pp. 27-30.

G. de Lacharrière, "Le Rôle de la Coopération Est-Ouest pour le Développement de la Coopération Tripartite", Discussion Paper, *UNCTAD Seminar, Geneva, 2-5 December 1975,* (TAD/SEM. 1/16).

F. Levcik and J. Stankovsky, "Recent Trends in Tripartite Industrial Cooperation: Austria's Experience", Report submitted to UNCTAD, December 1978.

C.H. McMillan, "The Political Economy of Tripartite (East-West-South) Industrial Cooperation", Research Report No. 12, January 1980, East-West Commercial Relations Series, *Institute of Soviet and East European Studies,* Carleton University, Ottawa, Canada.

K. Pavela, I. Kiss, L. Horvath, I. Nagy, "Cooperation on Third Markets, Four Statements by four Directors General", *Marketing in Hungary,* No. 2/1975, pp. 19-24.

U.N. Economic Commission for Europe, "Promotion of Trade through Industrial Cooperation: Tripartite Industrial Cooperation Contracts, Results of an Inquiry", Note by the Secretariat, (TRADE/R. 373/Add. 1), October 12, 1978.

U.N. Conference on Trade and Development, "Tripartite industrial cooperation and cooperation in third countries", Study by the UNCTAD Secretariat, UNCTAD V., Manila, May 1979, Item 17 — Supporting Paper (TD/243/Supp. 5), April 20, 1979.

U.N. Conference on Trade and Development, "Tripartite Industrial Cooperation", Study by the UNCTAD Secretariat, *Seminar on industrial specialization through various forms of multilateral cooperation, Geneva, 2-5 December 1975,* (TAD/SEM. 1/2), November 25, 1975.

Vienna Institute for Comparative Economic Studies, "Recent Trends in Tripartite Industrial Cooperation: Austria's experience", Vienna, *Mitgliederinformation,* 1979/8.

E. Zagorski, "Trójstronna kooperacja przemysłowa Wschód-Zachód-Południe", (East-West-South Tripartite Industrial Cooperation), *Handel Zagraniczny,* No. 9/1976.

L. Zurawicki, "Perspektywy współopracy trójstronnej Wschód-Zachód-Południe", (The Prospects for Tripartite Cooperation), *Sprawy Miedzynarodowe,* No. 5/1978, pp. 80-89. (A similar article by the author, "The Prospects for Tripartite Cooperation" was published in *Intereconomics* (FRG), No. 7-8/1978, pp. 184-187 and in *The ACES Bulletin,* XX, 2, Summer 1978, pp. 57-66.)

Annexes to Chapter 17

Annex I

Sectoral breakdown of TIC operations
(on the basis of final production sectors)

1. Agriculture
2. Energy
    - 2.1 Coal
    - 2.2 Electricity
        - 2.2.1 Production (thermal – hydro-electric)
        - 2.2.2 Distribution
    - 2.3 Natural gas
    - 2.4 Oil
        - 2.4.1 Extraction
        - 2.4.2 Refining
        - 2.4.3 Distribution
    - 2.5 Water
3. Mining
    - 3.1 Non-ferrous
    - 3.2 Iron ore
    - 3.3 Non metallic ores
4. Intermediate goods industries
    - 4.1 Iron works and primary steel transformation
    - 4.2 Non-ferrous metallurgy
    - 4.3 Building material and glass
    - 4.4 Basic chemicals
    - 4.5 Paper and cardboard
    - 4.6 Rubber and transformation of plastics
    - 4.7 Foundry and metal works
5. Equipment goods industries
    - 5.1 Mechanical construction
    - 5.2 Electric and electronic construction
    - 5.3 Land transport material
    - 5.4 Ship construction, aeronautics and armaments
6. Consumer goods industries
    - 6.1 Agricultural and foods products
    - 6.2 Parachemicals/pharmacy
    - 6.3 Textiles – clothing
    - 6.4 Others (leather – footwear – wood – furniture, etc. ...)

7. Building & public works
   7.1 Building
   7.2 Public works
8. Trade, services & telecommunications
   8.1 Hotels
   8.2 Telecommunications
   8.3 Others (banks, engineering, etc. ...)
9. Transportation and communications
   9.1 Land (road – rail)
   9.2 Maritime
   9.3 Aviation

A. Western involvement in TIC, 1965 – 1975 and 1976 – 1979

Western Participations (a)	TIC concrete cases (b) 1965 – 1975: 138		1976 – 1979: 88		Protocol agreements 1965 – 1975: 37		1976 – 1979: 82	
	Number	%	Number	%	Number	%	Number	%
Austria	19	11.0	13	13.1	6	16.2	6	7.3
Belgium	9	5.2	3	3	1	2.7	7	8.5
Canada	1	0.6	0	–	0	–	2	2.4
Denmark	1	0.6	0	–	0	–	1	1.2
Finland	1	0.6	4	4	0	–	9	11.0
France	46	26.7	15	15.2	9	24.3	9	11.0
FRG	36	20.9	24	24.2	11	29.7	21	25.6
Ireland	1	0.6	0	–	0	–	0	–
Italy	22	12.8	8	8.1	2	5.4	9	11.0
Japan	4	2.3	6	6.1	1	2.7	3	3.7
Netherlands	1	0.6	2	2	2	5.4	2	2.4
Spain	5	2.9	0	–	0	–	0	–
Sweden	4	2.3	1	1	1	2.7	5	6.1
Switzerland	8	4.7	8	8.1	0	–	3	3.7
Unted Kingdom	10	5.8	10	10.1	1	2.7	3	3.7
United States	4	2.3	5	5.1	3	8.1	2	2.4
EEC	126	73.3	62	62.6	26	70.3	52	63.4
Total West	172(a)	100	99(a)	100	37	100	82	100

(a) The totals of participations (172 and 99) differ from the total of cases (respectively 138 and 88) because of the involvement of more than one Western country in certain projects. – (b) Projects implemented or under way (planned or under negotiation excluded).

B. Eastern involvement in TIC, 1965 – 1975 and 1976 – 1979

Eastern Participations (a)	TIC concrete cases (b)				Protocol agreements			
	1965 – 1975: 138		1976 – 1979: 88		1965 – 1975: 37		1976 – 1979: 82	
	Number	%	Number	%	Number	%	Number	%
Bulgaria	7	4.8	0	–	6	16.2	10	12.2
Czechoslovakia	19	13.0	6	6.7	1	2.7	1	1.2
GDR	5	3.4	10	11.1	0	–	4	4.9
Hungary	40	27.4	18	20.0	14	37.8	24	29.3
Poland	27	18.5	25	27.8	11	29.7	20	24.4
Romania	16	11.0	5	5.6	3	8.1	5	6.1
USSR	17	11.6	10	11.1	1	2.7	15	18.3
Yugoslavia	15	10.3	16	17.8	1	2.7	3	3.7
CMEA	131	89.7	74	82.2	36	97.3	79	96.3
Total East	146(a)	100	90(a)	100	37	100	82	100

(a) The totals of participations (146 and 90) differ from the total of cases (respectively 138 and 88) because of the involvement of more than one Eastern country in certain projects. – (b) Projects implemented or under way (planned or under negotiation excluded).

East-West protocol agreements for cooperation in third countries, 1976 – 1979

Western firm	Eastern FTO	Types of projects
ALFA-LAVAL (Sweden)	KOMPLEX (Hungary)	Cheese making
ATLAS COPCO (Sweden)	Bulgarian FTO	Roadbuilding & mining equipment
ALSTHOM ALTANTIQUE (France)	Consortium of Bulgarian FTOs	Shipbuilding, nuclear power generation, electrical equipment
ARMERAD BETONG AB (Sweden)	Consortium of GDR FTOs	Construction
BALLAST NEDAM (Netherlands)	ENERGOPOL (Poland)	Power transmission equipment
BASF (FRG)	Bulgarian FTO	Chemicals & petrochemicals
BROWN-BOVERI (Switzerland)	POLIMEX-CEKOP (Poland)	Electromachines & metallurgical equipment
BROWN-BOVERI (Switzerland) & SIEMENS (FRG)	TRANSELEKTRO (Hungary)	Electrical equipment
BURMAH ENGINEERING (UK)	POLIMEX-CEKOP (Poland)	Turnkey plants through the joint venture POLIBUR Engineering Ltd (Chemical, agricultural machinery, wood & paper, refrigeration industries)
BURMEISTER & WAIN (Denmark)	Consortium of GDR FTOs	Heavy machinery
CIFAL (France)	TECHNOIMPORT (Bulgaria) & MACHINOEXPORT	Equipment and turnkey plants for the foodstuffs, furniture & wood processing industries
CIT-ALCATEL (France)	ELEKTRIM (Poland)	Telecommunications systems
C. ITOH & Co Ltd. (Japan)	State Committee for Foreign Economic Relations & Ministry of Foreign Trade (USSR)	Asbestos industry
CREUSOT-LOIRE (France)	POLIMEX-CEKOP (Poland)	Chemical plants
DATASAAB (Sweden)	ISKRA (Yugoslavia)	Electronic equipment for air-traffic control
DEUTSCHE BABCOCK AG (FRG)	MINERGOMASCH (USSR)	Power stations, heavy mechanical engineering
DUNLOP (UK) & PIRELLI (Italy)	CHEMOLIMPEX & TAURUS (Hungary)	Rubber tires, conveyor belts, gaskets
ELBA-WERKE (FRG)	EGPEP (Hungary)	Heavy duty equipment & concrete production
ELBA-WERKE (FRG)	NIKEX (Hungary)	Construction equipment
ELI-UNION AG (Austria)	MASHINOEXPORT (USSR)	Mine lifts
ENERGIE & VERFAHRENS-TECHNIK (EVT) (FRG)	TRANSELEKTRO (Hungary)	Grinding & Firing equipment
ENI (Italy)	HUNGARIAN FOREIGN TRADE BANK (Hungary)	Petroleum & gas
ENI (Italy)	INA (Yugoslavia)	Oil exploration
FATA (Italy)	TECHMATRANS (Poland)	Handling equipment, warehouses
FERROSTAAL (FRG)	LICENSINTORG (USSR)	Iron & steel works

Western firm	Eastern FTO	Types of projects
FIAT (Italy)	Bulgarian FTOs	Transport, construction, chemicals, tourism
FIAT (Italy)	HUNGARIAN FOREIGN TRADE BANK (Hungary)	Automotive industry
FIAT (Italy)	VEB CARL ZEISS JENA (GDR)	Joint construction of planetariums, observatories and solar research centers
FREYSSINET INTERNATIONAL (France)	KOMPLEX (Hungary)	Construction
FRIEDRICH KRUPP GmbH (FRG)	POLIMEX-CEKOP (Poland)	Mechanical industry & raw materials
GI e GI SAS (Italy)	Consortium of Soviet FTOs	Cattle feeding complexes
GLASS (FRG)	KOMPLEX (Hungary)	Agricultural machinery
GUTEHOFFNUNGSHÜTTE (FRG)	Bulgarian FTO	Metallurgy, heavy machinery, chemical & petrochemical industries, materials handling
HERA (FRG)	GANZ (Hungary)	Electrical & electrotechnical equipment
HITACHI (Japan)	ENERGOMASHOEXPORT (USSR)	Power stations
IMPERIAL CHEMICAL INDUSTRIES (UK)	INTERCOOPERATION (Hungary)	Chemicals & petrochemicals
ITALPIANTI (Italy)	LICENSINTORG (USSR)	Tin & steel mills through the joint venture TECNICON SPA
KAGERER GmbH (Austria)	CSEPEL (Hungary)	Tube-drawing machinery & equipment
KAISER RESOURCES Ltd. (Canada)	MINERALIMPORT EXPORT (Romania)	Metallurgical coal, mining projects
KONE OY (Finland)	Soviet FTO	Materials-handling & woodworking equipment and plants
KONTRAM (Finland)	TECHNOPROMEXPORT (USSR)	Power plants
LOGABAX (UK)	Soviet FTO	Computer equipment for nuclear power stations
LE FOUR INDUSTRIEL (Belgium)	METALEXPORT (Poland)	Equipment & turnkey plants for the thermal treatment of metals
MANNESMANN (FRG)	KOMPLEX (Hungary)	Food processing machinery and turnkey plants
MAYEKAWA (Japan)	KOMPLEX (Hungary)	Refrigeration plants
METALLGESELLSCHAFT (FRG)	MAT HUNGARIAN ALUMINIUM (Hungary)	Joint exploitation of raw materials
OCCIDENTAL PETROLEUM (US)	Romanian FTO	Offshore oil drilling, exploitation of bituminous shale, chemicals
OTTO DUERR (FRG)	METALEXPORT (Poland)	Linings
OUTOKUMPU (Finland)	TRANSELEKTRO (Hungary)	Electrical equipment for power stations
OUTOKUMPU (Finland)	TSVETMETPROMEXPORT (USSR)	Nonferrous mining & metallurgical
OUTOKUMPU (Finland)	GEOMIN (Romania)	Exploration, exploitation & processing of non ferrous ores
PROTINAS (FRG)	BABOLNA AGRICULTURAL COMBINATE (Hungary)	Turnkey farms & agricultural equipment

Western firm	Eastern FTO	Types of projects
RAUMA-REPOLA (Finland)	Romanian FTO	Oil drilling rigs, joint built rigs, mining, ore dressing operations
RAUTARUUKKI OY (Finland)	Soviet FTO	Steel works
ROBERT BOSCH (FRG)	Bulgarian FTO	Pneumatics & hydraulics, electric truck engines
SALZGITTER (FRG) MASCHINENFABRIK AG	POLIMEX-CEKOP (Poland)	Sugar factories
SERSEG (France)	HUNGARIAN ROAD-BUILDING TRUST (Hungary)	Bitumen emulsifying plants
SIEMENS (FRG)	MEDICOR WORKS (Hungary)	Medical equipment & installations
SIEMENS (FRG)	POLIMEX-CEKOP (Poland)	Plastic & petrochemical works, cold-storage warehouses, freezing plants
SIMMERING-GRAZ-PAUKER (Austria)	Soviet FTO	Machinery for activating & enriching sundry substances
SIMMONS Ltd. (Canada)	CENTROZAP (Poland)	Steel structures for pulp & paper factories
SOBERI (Belgium)	CENTROZAP (Poland)	Siderurgy, metallurgy, mining
SPAN DECK Inc. (US)	INTERCOOPERATION & NIKEX (Hungary)	Long-span, light roof structures
STRÖMBERG (Finland)	TRANSELEKTRO & METEX (Hungary)	Power generating equipment
SYBETRA SA (Belgium)	Consortium of Bulgarian FTOs	Heavy industry, cement, food-stuffs and engineering
SYBETRA SA (Belgium)	POLIMEX-CEKOP (Poland)	Chemical plants
TECHNIP (France)	TECHNOKOMPLEKT (Bulgaria)	Construction machinery, food processing equipment for chemical & petrochemical industries
TECHNIP & BANQUE NATIONALE DE PARIS (France)	POLIMEX-CEKOP & POLSKA KASSA OPIECKI (Poland)	Engineering for turnkey plants
TIEFBOHR-GmbH & CO-BETRIEBS-KG (FRG)	STROJEXPORT (Czechoslovakia)	Water prospecting works
UNIVERSAL ENGINEERING Corp. (Switzerland)	KOPEX (Poland)	Coal energy complexes
VALMET OY (Finland)	Ministry of the Pulp & Paper Industry (USSR)	Paper-making machinery & equipment
VEREINIGTE EDELSTAHL-WERKE (Austria)	CHEMOKOMPLEX & OKGT (Hungary)	Turnkey plants through the joint venture IGA
VMF-STORK (Netherlands)	Bulgarian FTO	Materials handling & transport equipment
VOEST-ALPINE (Austria)	CENTROZAP (Poland)	Steel & rolling mills
VOEST-ALPINE (Austria)	INVEST-EXPORT & MASCHINENEXPORT (GDR)	Oil refinery
VOEST-ALPINE (Austria)	KOPEX (Poland)	Mining & metallurgy
VOLVO (Sweden)	MOGURT & CSEPEL (Hungary)	Automotive industry, through the joint venture VOLCOM
WECO WEHMEYER & Co (FRG)	G.K.N.T. (USSR)	Lenses for glasses
WARTSILA (Finland)	Romanian FTO	Oil drilling rigs, joint built rigs, mining, ore dressing operations

Source: Various press reports

COMMENTS ON PART V – NEW FORMS OF EAST-WEST-SOUTH COOPERATION

Carl H. McMillan*

The vision often raised of East and West setting aside their traditional rivalry to cooperate in the industrialisation of the Third World is certainly an attractive one. But to what extent is it grounded in reality? Many of the published references to tripartite industrial cooperation (TIC) are assertions about its rationale and significance backed by very little factual information.

We can be grateful for *Gutman's* efforts (Chapter 17) to provide an empirical basis for more meaningful discussion of the tripartite phenomenon. Empirical work on this subject is especially difficult because of the absence of official, national statistics to draw upon. The researcher must create his own data base, extracting information directly from participating firms. This is not only laborious but frustrating, as firms are often reluctant to provide details of business arrangements conducted in a commercially and politically sensitive area. Thanks to the work of Gutman and others who have supplemented and extended the pioneering UNCTAD survey, conducted in 1974 - 75, the broad outlines of the nature and scope of TIC have been established. We know roughly how many TIC projects have been undertaken and when, what Eastern and Western countries have been involved, where in the South the projects have been located and in what industrial sectors. As a result, we have an essential, preliminary basis for understanding. We must recognise, however, that this is merely a first step, and that it must be followed up by efforts to obtain answers to more searching questions, if we are to determine a) whether TIC is *in practice* beneficial to all parties concerned and b) if so, how it may be encouraged.

The present form of TIC

Gutman rightly stresses that TIC must at the present juncture be regarded as East-West industrial cooperation in the South. The broad outlines with which we are furnished nevertheless leave important gaps in our basic knowledge even of the East-West dimensions of such cooperation.

The sweeping definition employed in empirical studies of TIC encompasses all Third World projects in which there are *any* inputs by both Western firms and Eastern enterprises. These projects accordingly fall into two broad categories:

* Professor of Economics; Director, Institute of Soviet and East European Studies, Carleton University, Ottawa

a) Projects in which a Western firm or Eastern enterprise participates only as the supplier of some equipment or technology.
b) Projects in which an Eastern enterprise and a Western firm bid jointly on a project in the Third World.

In the first case, East-West cooperation is minimal. What is involved is merely international sourcing of some elements of a capital project, which extends beyond the traditional bounds of Eastern or Western regional sourcing. While the lessor of the subcontract is more typically an engineering-construction firm, the subcontracting firm will usually be a producer of machinery or equipment.

In the second case, a more significant East-West collaboration occurs. The Eastern and Western partners jointly engage in the planning, bidding and construction phases of the project, and in some cases establish an on-going institutional relationship through which they can jointly search out further opportunities for collaboration. The partners to such arrangements are typically engineering-construction firms and enterprises, or the engineering affiliates of capital goods producers.

We do not know what proportions of the reported TIC cases fall into these two categories. We know too little about the nature, motives and roles of the Eastern and Western parties to such deals. As a result, important questions about the dynamics of TIC at the micro-level remain unanswered. The data nevertheless suggest that at its present stage of development most TIC remains a relatively primitive form of East-West industrial cooperation. The majority of cases involve *ad hoc,* temporary associations, where one party plays a distinctly secondary role as supplier under a sub-contract. There are cases where the partnership is not only more balanced, but is also institutionalised, in the form of consortia, and even joint venture companies, formed to carry out capital projects in third countries. While still rare, these are the more interesting and promising objects for closer study.

The current dimensions of TIC

I believe that the current economic importance of TIC can easily be exaggerated. TIC remains, in my view, a distinctly marginal phenomenon, in terms of East-West, East-South relations. Gutman quotes an UNCTAD source to the effect that TIC represented the equivalent of an eighth of the imports of investment goods undertaken by the developing countries in 1964 – 73. It should be stressed that this does not mean that an eighth of such imports were carried out under TIC agreements; merely that UNCTAD's estimate of the total cost of TIC projects in the period (presumably including construction costs) amounted to the equivalent of an eighth of total relevant imports for which a breakdown by commodity classes was available. In any case it is hard to imagine that the little more than 200 concrete cases of TIC which Gutman reports over the entire 1964 – 80 period could account for even an eighth of Third World imports of capital goods.

Gutman's survey shows an average of some 16 TIC deals concluded annually over the entire fifteen-year period, with the annual rate apparently rising to 22 in the past four years. This is not very impressive when we consider that the enterprises and firms of 8 Eastern, 15 Western and at least 56 Southern countries are potential partners to such deals.

In sum, I think we should be asking why TIC has not been more widespread. What are the principal obstacles to its development? To answer such questions, more in-depth case studies are required. The aggregate data have served their purpose; we now need to try to discern what lies beneath them.

The broader significance of TIC

Given the passive role played by the Southern 'partner' in most TIC agreements, Gutman justifiably questions the benefits accruing from TIC to the South. Certainly there is a need for much more research on the impact of TIC on the developing economies before any conclusions can be drawn about the relative merits of joint East-West, as against unilateral Eastern or Western, projects in the Third World.

Gutman nevertheless assumes that important cost advantages accrue to the developing countries from East-West collaboration. This may be true, but it is an empirical question which cannot be resolved in the absence of comprehensive analysis of project financing. *A priori,* one can as easily speculate that East-West consortia serve to restrict the competitive nature of bids on capital projects in the Third World, and thereby limit the cost advantages from collaboration which are passed on to the developing country. The politicised context in which many TIC agreements are concluded, and the prominent role of state agencies in decision-making, must surely be taken into account before any conclusions based on competitive assumptions can be drawn. Others, however, are better qualified than I to comment on the impact of TIC from the perspective of Third World development goals. I should like instead to turn to some brief comments on the East-West implications of TIC.

I believe that the impetus for TIC has come primarily from the Eastern side. This is clearly so at the governmental level; in bilateral meetings and in multilateral fora, Eastern representatives have consistently sought to promote joint projects in third countries. It is probably also the case at the enterprise level, although here I must admit the lack of conclusive evidence one way or the other.

One striking piece of evidence demonstrating the Eastern initiative at the micro-level is provided by the joint venture companies to which Gutman briefly alludes. In my own research I have identified eight mixed equity companies established (by enterprises in Hungary, Poland and the USSR, with partners in Austria, Belgium, Finland, France, FRG, UK and USA) to undertake capital projects in third countries.

We must ask what lies behind these Eastern initiatives. I believe that they are rooted in the increasing concern of the Eastern countries (especially the smaller East European countries, less well endowed than the USSR in natural resources) to expand and deepen their relations with the Third World. These countries have sought in particular to develop Third World capacities to produce raw materials, and semi-finished products of an energy- and raw-material-intensive nature, to meet their own growing needs. In this regard, it is interesting to note Gutman's finding that the most active TIC partners have been the Eastern and Western European countries, with the USSR and USA less involved than other members of their groupings. (There have been no reported instances of direct US-USSR cooperation in the Third World.)

TIC is only one instrument, of a secondary order of importance, through which these Eastern policy objectives in the Third World are pursued. The Eastern countries have also engaged individually or jointly in capital projects in the developing countries, often on a compensation (buy-back) basis. They have increasingly undertaken direct investments in the developing economies. When Eastern enterprises find themselves unable to meet all project requirements, or otherwise to win a bid on their own, they turn to Western firms for assistance. The Western role is to provide special technology not otherwise available and/or to facilitate Eastern access to certain Third World markets. The technology factor appears to be especially important. Thus if East-West industrial cooperation serves in general as an important channel for the transfer of Western technology in order to increase the competitiveness of Eastern industries on world markets, TIC is a form of East-West industrial cooperation which enhances the ability of Eastern capital goods and related industries to carry out projects on Third World markets.

Some Western firms have found it profitable to respond to these Eastern initiatives. Occasionally, they have developed partner-like relations with Eastern enterprises to bid jointly on a continuing basis. Such partnerships may prove to be the forerunners of an important trend in East-West relations, but it is too early to draw firm conclusions in this regard.

Western governments have also been willing to respond to Eastern initiatives by including the desirability of TIC in the agreed texts of East-West cooperation agreements and by otherwise encouraging national firms to engage in joint projects with Eastern enterprises. They have apparently done so in the hope of (at least marginally) increasing their capital goods exports to both Eastern and Southern markets. Careful analysis of the record of TIC projects to date, and of their impact on North-South as well as East-West relations, will provide the basis for more sophisticated Western policy responses.

Göran Ohlin

Fears that tripartite industrial cooperation would put an end to competition seem quite exaggerated. Many East-West ventures seem to have been successful precisely in competitive bidding in Third World countries, and there is certainly a strong *prima facie* case to expect considerable cost advantages in many instances.

Aroon K. Basak*

I would first like to congratulate *Gutman* (Chapter 17) on his paper which provides an astute and clear analysis of growth trends of Tripartite Industrial Cooperation (TIC). One sees from his data that TIC has grown from a coverage of 40 to 56 countries, involving a substantially greater number of projects. I have three questions to ask.

(i) Is TIC truly a new form of international industrial cooperation in which the South is a real partner?

Gutman has shown that while there is evident complementarity between enterprises from the East and West, there is a low residual value for enterprises from the South. He has also demonstrated that tripartite mixed companies and multilateral co-production ventures seem to thrive. On the first point, I wonder whether the present share of the South might only represent local currency expenditure, e.g. civil construction for setting up industrial plants. On the second point, I would ask whether tripartite mixed companies and multilateral co-production ventures are possibly not just reflections of the classical model of direct foreign investment with a wider foreign participation. Have Eastern companies moderated the attitudes of Western companies through such cooperation? In any event, it would appear to me that East-West cooperation has the seeds of a real foundation of partnership (perhaps following the old maxim 'if you cannot beat them, join them'). On the whole I would suggest that TIC is a particular form of East-West consortium set up for coordinated and effective marketing in developing countries. I feel this is conceded in Gutman's last sentence: 'TIC thus provides East and West with the possibility of limited but effective cooperation in the South'.

(ii) What is the impact of TIC on developing countries?

Because East and West would jointly contribute inputs in line with least costs, is it possible to ensure that global costs to developing countries would necessarily and correspondingly be reduced? I have three concerns:

* Deputy Director, World Bank; UNIDO Cooperative Programme, UNIDO

(a) I wonder if the sum of the lowest factor prices under competition would represent the selling price of the total product when competition is removed; or putting it another way, whether the selling price of the total product would in fact not be higher? I would greatly appreciate statistics and analyses penetrating this question.

(b) The best results of international competitive bidding are obtained through unpackaged bidding. Would TIC militate against this advantage?

(c) The apparent attraction of supplier credits often turns out to be an illusion when the bid offer is evaluated as a whole.

(iii) What changes in the present TIC concept might make it more meaningful to the South?

The earlier discussion on the New International Economic Order (NIEO) highlighted the fact that:

– the present international power structure is underpinned by the command of the North over technology and industry;
– the NIEO perpetuates a one-sided dependence of the South on the North for its engine of growth, its flow of technology and its supply of finance;
– certain new developments have appeared in the South through the emergence of a few capital surplus countries on the one hand, and countries capable of supplying technology on the other.

In the above context, true global cooperation should entail Southern capital and technology cooperating with Northern capital and technology, within new modalities of *industrial enterprise cooperation.* The concept 'industrial enterprise cooperation' would mean a long-term and complex industrial interaction between a DC (1) and a foreign enterprise with mutual performance obligations, with some institutionalising of a community of interest in a specific project and with the existence of a lasting interest in cooperation. The advantage of using the notion of 'industrial enterprise cooperation' is that it can also encompass the forms of industrial interaction employed in East/West and East/South relations, where DFI (2) through completely-owned subsidiaries is mostly absent but where a functionally comparable long-term industrial cooperation through delivery of industrial plants with payment in resultant products seems to constitute a form of quasi-investment.

Furthermore, 'industrial enterprise cooperation' allows another important development in the organisational structure of industrial interaction. Not only in the field of investment, but also in other commercial transactions between the North and the South an

(1) DC – Developing Country. – (2) DFI – Direct Foreign Investment

increasing complexity can be observed e.g. through a packaging of services and equipment resulting in some convergence of those transactions with various forms of investment. The sale of industrial equipment and technology has extended to technical assistance, design of industrial complexes, civil engineering, and the organisation of long-term interaction. This has been particularly the case in East/West relations where forms of industrial cooperation (e.g. supply of technology and complete plants in exchange for production) have been designed to fulfil cooperative functions otherwise inherent in equity investment. Another example is contracts which have been extended to include post-operational assistance and some measure of payment through production, with respective performance guarantees taking the place of the investor's risk in traditional foreign investment. Industrial enterprise cooperation seems at present the concept best suited to emphasize the shift away from DFI and from simple commercial transactions towards a new mode of interaction with more cooperation and mutually undertaken coordination.

In order to ensure that industrial enterprise cooperation is an exercise in *development* and not merely that of *setting up means of production,* one could visualise either an unpackaging of the resource inputs or packaging them through such forms as – terminating joint ventures – buy-back arrangements – industrial leasing – produit-en-main.

Perhaps these new concepts of enterprise cooperation could be married to that of TIC.

LIST OF PARTICIPANTS
in workshop held in Dubrovnik, May 1980

Prof. Ljubiša Adamović	– Faculty of Political Sciences, Belgrade
Dr. Ede Bakó	– Chief Economic Adviser, National Bank of Hungary, Budapest
Mr. Aroon K. Basak	– Deputy Director, World Bank – UNIDO Cooperative Programme, UNIDO, Vienna
M. Yves Berthelot	– Head of Research, OECD Development Centre, Paris
Prof. Amit Bhaduri	– Centre for Economic Studies and Planning, School of Social Sciences, Jawaharlal Nehru University, New Delhi
Mr. Alfredo Eric Calcagno	– Director, International Commerce and Development Division, UN Economic Commission for Latin America, Santiago, Chile
M. Bernard Cazes	– Head of Division, Commissariat Général du Plan d'Equipement et de la Productivité, Paris
Dr. István Dobozi	– Associate Professor, Institute for World Economics of the Hungarian Academy of Sciences, Budapest
Prof. Dr. Juergen B. Donges	– Kiel Institute of World Economics, Kiel, FRG

Prof. Dr. Ivo Fabinc	– Ekonomska faculteta Borisa Kidriča, Ljubljana, Yugoslavia
Prof. Dr. Helmut Faulwetter	– Institute for the Economy of Developing Countries of the University of Economic Science, Berlin, GDR
Dr. Ingrid Gazzari	– The Vienna Institute for Comparative Economic Studies, Vienna
Prof. Patrick Gutman	– Institut d'Etude du Développement Economique et Social (IEDES), Université de Paris-I
Mr. John P. Hardt	– Associate Director, Senior Specialist Office, Congressional Research Service, The Library of Congress, Washington, DC
Dr. Arne Haselbach	– Director, Vienna Institute for Development, Vienna
Dr. Odette Jankowitsch	– Bureau of Studies and Programming, Executive Office of the Director-General, UNESCO, Paris
Dr. Victor C. Johnson	– Staff Associate, Subcommittee on International Economic Policy and Trade, Committee on Foreign Affairs, US House of Representatives, Washington, DC
Prof. Dr. Norbert Kloten	– President, National Bank of Baden-Württemberg, Stuttgart
Prof. Dr. Gunther Kohlmey	– Central Institute for Economics, Academy of Sciences of the GDR, Berlin
Prof. Dr. Rikard Lang	– University Zagreb and Ekonomski Institut, Zagreb
Prof. Dr. Kazimierz Laski	– Johannes Kepler University, Linz, Austria and The Vienna Institute for Comparative Economic Studies, Vienna

Prof. Marie Lavigne — Director, Centre d'économie internationale des pays socialistes, University of Paris-I Panthéon-Sorbonne, Paris

Prof. DDr. Friedrich Levcik — Director, The Vienna Institute for Comparative Economic Studies, Vienna

Prof. Dr. Aleksander Lukaszewicz — Department of Economics, Warsaw University, Warsaw

Prof. Dr. George Macesich — Director, Center for Yugoslav-American Studies, Florida State University, Tallahassee, Florida

Prof. Dr. Harry Maier — Task Leader, Management & Technology Area, International Institute for Applied Systems Analysis, Laxenburg, Austria

Prof. Carl H. McMillan — Director, the Institute of Soviet and East European Studies, Carleton University, Ottawa, Canada

Dr. András Nagy — Institute of Economics, Hungarian Academy of Sciences, Budapest

Dr. Deepak Nayyar — School of African and Asian Studies, University of Sussex, Brighton, England; Professor of Economics, Indian Institute of Management, Calcutta

Prof. DDr. Adolf Nussbaumer — Secretary of State in the Federal Chancellery of Austria, Vienna

Dr. Alexandre P. Ognev — Principal Scientific Secretary, Institute of World Economy and International Relations, Moscow

Prof. Göran Ohlin — University of Uppsala, Uppsala

Dr. Marian Paszyński — Foreign Trade Research Institute, Warsaw

Dr. Philipp Rieger — Director, Austrian National Bank, Vienna; Chairman of the Workshop

Prof. Christopher T. Saunders	– Sussex European Research Centre, University of Sussex, Brighton, England
Prof. Norman Scott	– Director, Trade and Technology Division, UN Economic Commission for Europe, Geneva
Prof. Dr. Francis Seton	– Nuffield College, Oxford
Prof. Dr. S. Shalamanov	– Director, Institute for International Relations and Socialist Integration, Sofia
Mr. Vassil Sivov	– Institute for International Relations and Socialist Integration, Sofia
Prof. Eugene B. Skolnikoff	– Director, Centre for International Studies, Massachusetts Institute of Technology, Cambridge, Mass.
Prof. Dr. Józef Soldaczuk	– Director, Institute for International Economic Relations and International Law, Central School of Planning and Statistics, Warsaw
Prof. Paul P. Streeten	– Overseas Development Council, Washington, DC
Prof. Dr. Tamás Szentes	– Karl-Marx University of Economic Sciences, Budapest
Prof. Dr. Leon Zevin	– Director, Division for Relations with Developing Countries, Institute for the Socialist World Economic System of the Academy of Sciences of the USSR, Moscow

Observers:

Dr. Rudolf Dirisamer	– Zentralsparkasse und Kommerzialbank·Wien, Vienna
Mr. Peter Ruof	– The Ford Foundation, New York

INDEX*

* Compiled by *Audrey Bamber*